Contents

LEGEND FOR PLANS

▬▬▬	Covered seating
▬▬▬	Covered standing
	Uncovered seating
▬▬▬	Uncovered standing
♿	Disabled Facilities, wheelchairs access and viewing areas
▽	Main entrances
▼	Main exits

D0227610

A VERY WARM WELCOME

Once again, it gives me great pleasure to welcome all football fans to the 1995/96 edition of The Tartan Special Scottish Football League Review.

This is the fifth occasion that I have had the privilege to write the introduction to Scottish football's premier reference book and I would take this opportunity to thank Scottish Brewers for their continued and welcome sponsorship of this very prestigious publication.

Although the launch of this season's Review has been delayed slightly and we have now witnessed the first few weeks of football action on the domestic front as well as on the European and International arena, it has given me the perfect opportunity to not only reflect on the events of the past season, but, has also provided me with the chance to look forward with optimism and anticipation to the season ahead.

First of all, if we look back at the events on the park last season, we saw many dramatic and pulsating moments of action. Despite its critics, the new four division set-up provided excitement, drama and uncertainty, with Championship, Promotion, Relegation, European and Play-Off issues not being decided until the final few weeks of the season, and indeed, it was not until 4.40 p.m. on the very last Saturday that several important issues were ultimately settled. The interest generated by this extremely meaningful and competitive set-up can be witnessed by the encouraging increase in average attendances at many clubs in all four divisions and I am confident that this positive trend will continue in the season ahead.

On the domestic front, Rangers won the Bell's Premier Division quite comfortably, however, both the chase for a European place and the fight to avoid both the one automatic relegation spot and Play-Off place provided fans with plenty to talk about, creating high spectator and media interest throughout the final few weeks of the season. In the Bell's First Division, Raith Rovers held on to win the Championship and put the seal on the most remarkable season in their history, whilst their Fife rivals, Dunfermline Athletic, had to contend with being involved in the first ever Play-Off matches against, to everyone's surprise, Aberdeen, with the Pittodrie outfit finally proving too strong for the East End Park club. In the Bell's Second Division, Greenock Morton won the Championship by playing exciting and entertaining football while Dumbarton, after a "winner takes all" match against Stirling Albion in the final match of the season, secured the second promotion spot. In the Bell's Third Division, Forfar Athletic captured the title in impressive and convincing style with Montrose just pipping one of the new clubs, Ross County, to gain the other promotion spot.

However, if the Bell's League Championship provided many memorable moments, The Coca-Cola Cup Competition was no less dramatic and on a day in November, 1994 that the whole town of Kirkcaldy will never forget, the aforementioned Raith Rovers defeated Celtic in a dramatic penalty shoot-out decider to not only lift the trophy but also take the club into Europe for the first time in their history. Celtic, to their credit, overcame this disappointment and ended six seasons without a major domestic trophy by winning the Tennents Scottish Cup at Hampden Park six months later, by defeating another First Division club, Airdrieonians. However, the Diamonds enjoyed a tremendous season in all cup competitions and apart from narrowly losing out to Raith Rovers in a penalty shoot-out decider at the Semi-Final stage of The Coca-Cola Cup, they took some consolation by winning The B & Q Cup, defeating Dundee in another exciting Final at McDiarmid Park, Perth.

If that was the events which shaped last season on the domestic front, our International team also put themselves into a promising position to qualify for the European Championship Finals in England next June with some spirited performances. As I write these notes, they have just defeated Greece and Finland in a three week spell at the start of this season and hopefully, they have now done enough to qualify for these final stages and we can all look forward with optimism in the months ahead as players perform to an even higher level in order to impress Craig Brown with a view to gaining selection to the Scotland squad for these Finals. Additionally, Rangers should be congratulated on having reached the Champions League stage and together with Celtic in the Cup Winners' Cup and Raith Rovers in the U.E.F.A. Cup, I am certain that we can look forward with eager anticipation to some great European nights in the next few months.

Scottish Football League Management Committee, Season 1995/96

J. Y. Craig, J.P., C.A. (President), G. J. Fulston (Vice-President), G. S. Brown (Treasurer), I. R. Donald, R. Fleeting, R. C. Ogilvie, D. W. M. Cromb, J. Oliver, G. W. Peat, C.A., J. W. Baxter, J. L. Smith, J. McGoogan, LL.B.

Three years ago, I mentioned in this very column that we must look very closely at a number of important areas and in particular, the skill factor, by providing the proper platform to encourage youngsters to develop their technique and skill level comparable with that displayed in other countries throughout the world. In that very season, we introduced the Under 18 Youth Division and in the three seasons since then, some very promising players have begun to emerge and play at first team level. These have included for example, Stephen Glass, Charlie Miller and Jim Hamilton, who apart from having become established at first team level, are now playing regularly for the Scotland Under 21 team, which also looks to have qualified for the knock-out stages of the European Championships, by playing some tremendous football. We have now taken it a stage further by introducing an Under 16 and Under 15 Youth Development Initiative, which will not be competitive, points do not make prizes and the emphasis will be on developing the skill element as well as educating young players on the many other aspects of the game. Hopefully, our game will benefit shortly from this new structure which is now in place.

As you will see from the content and quality contained within this publication, the preparation of this book requires a tremendous amount of time and effort and I would take this opportunity in extending my sincere thanks to the following:-

David C. Thomson (Editor); all other staff at The Scottish Football League; our 40 Member Clubs; Alan Elliott and Jim Jeffrey; our contributors; the many sectors of the Scottish media for their assistance; our sponsors, Scottish Brewers; Creative Services and in particular Nick and Dave Kelly; Programme Publications, especially Bill Cotton and Linda Austin.

I do hope that whatever club you support, you enjoy an exciting and incident packed season with meaningful, competitive and I trust, exciting matches being provided throughout the season.

ENJOY THE SEASON.

YULE CRAIG
President,
The Scottish Football League.

A WORD FROM OUR SPONSORS

For over 30 years, ale drinkers throughout the UK have been enjoying Younger's Tartan Special.

Since 1749, when William Younger first started brewing in Leith, near Edinburgh, the range of Younger's ales have spread worldwide and today are easily identified by the "Father William" trademark.

As Tartan grew to become Scotland's favourite ale, so did its commitment to supporting sport at all levels across the country. For many years, Tartan Special Football Awards were bestowed monthly upon players and managers as recognition of their contribution to Scottish football.

Other popular sports such as golf, boxing and bowling have also benefited from sponsorship by Tartan Special. In 1994, the Tartan Special Indoor Bowling Classic attracted top bowlers from all over Scotland. The St. Andrew's Sporting Club in Glasgow, under the banner of Tartan Special, brought quality boxing to thousands of enthusiasts. In more recent years, Younger's Tartan Special teamed up with the Scottish Professional Golf Championship to attract a field of top golfers to compete in a four day tournament at Dalmahoy Golf, Hotel and Country Club.

Continuing to support Scotland's national game, Tartan Special is delighted to sponsor the 1995/96 Scottish Football League Review, an essential reference book for all football enthusiasts.

TONY McGRATH
Managing Director,
Scottish Brewers

Celtic Park's new North Stand

Grounds for Celebration

The Scottish football supporter sometimes gets the uncanny impression that he has wandered into the wrong country by mistake. To those besotted by the game, all the roads, motorways and miles of scenery only really exist to fill in the gaps between one club and the next. It is the grounds that matter. Now, however, those destinations often take you by surprise.

Scottish football may be in the midst of the greatest revolution since professionalism arrived in 1893. Stadiums which looked as if they belonged in the last century are being bulldozed everywhere. The effect on the economy must be dramatic. One wonders where else the construction industry could find so many projects on such a scale. Inevitably, it is the major undertakings that attract the headlines.

Celtic, of course, have spent £17m on a 27,000-seater stand whose sweep and majesty make it one of the spectacular sights in British football. Rangers continue to find ways of improving Ibrox, even though it is already lavish, and are now inserting seats at the corners. Hampden Park, the National Stadium, will shortly embark on the most ambitious phase of its redevelopment when the construction of a new main stand begins.

Marvels are perhaps taken for granted in such places, however. The real surprise lies in the renewal which is also underway at less likely locations. The renewal of the very fabric of

Scottish football continues apace beneath the Premier and even the First Division. In the Second Division, for example, a third stand is underway at Broadwood as Clyde's ground moves toward completion.

Queen's Park, as owners of Hampden, are something of a special case but even if no other member of the Third Division is involved in a venture on quite that scale there is still some dramatic activity. The merger that formed Caledonian Thistle, who were admitted to The Scottish Football League last season, also created a number of problems. The progress of their plans to build a new stadium, though, testifies to a growing stability.

Ross County, who joined the League at the same time, already had a modern stand holding 319 people at Victoria Park. Now another one, that is four times bigger, has been erected at a cost

of £585,000. Amenities such as an artificial pitch, a bar and a club shop are also in place. The Ross County officials take a justified pride in their achievements.

"We are delighted with the progress we have made," said the Commercial Manager, Brian Campbell. "Apart from Hampden, we have one of the best grounds in the Third Division. In fact, give us a few years and we'll outstrip them as well!" The enthusiasm, of course, is not confined within the club. Ross County have tapped the faith of people in Dingwall and the surrounding area with some innovative offers. For a modest £1000 you can buy a 50-year season ticket. For those who are slightly more fickle, a short-term 25 year version is available.

"At £1 a game it is a great bargain which will quite quickly pay for itself," pointed out Campbell.

The East Stand - Ross County

Ross County's innovative 50 year ticket

So far, 61 people have bought the 25-year ticket. Half a dozen have set their sights on season 2046 and taken up the 50-year option. A hotelier has actually bought two of them, although he is a 51-year old. "We might have to make special arrangements for him to attend in 2046," joked Campbell. "Seriously, though, he and the others are just showing their desire to help the club."

It is easy to be overawed by the visions of cantilevered roofs and swish facilities. Your jaw also drops at the sums of money being raised by the football clubs in partnership with the game's great benefactor, The Football Trust. Who for instance, would have expected, even a few years ago, to hear that Falkirk were about to embark on a new £5.5 million stadium?

Despite the dazzling appearances of these places, though, we ought to reflect on the emotions which make all these achievements possible. The enduring passion for Scottish football makes the difference. Any other business would have regarded a massive investment programme as impracticable or downright insane.

People respond to rebuilt grounds. The phenomenon has been repeated again and again, ever since the construction of McDiarmid Park coincided with St. Johnstone's ascent to the Premier Division and move to full-time status. This does not happen merely because fans happen to enjoy clean toilets, appetising food stalls and decent seats.

A much deeper reaction is involved. Supporters see the redevelopment of stadia they have known all their lives as a sign of hope. It renews their trust in a club and their belief in its future. Celtic perhaps provide the most spectacular

recent case. Their current figure of around 25,000 season tickets almost quadruples the total sold at the old ground two seasons ago.

The clamour for tickets is not confined to the Old Firm. In Edinburgh, Hibernian, with two new stands in place at a cost of £4 million, now have 5,000 season ticket-holders, a record for the club's entire history. There has been a similar encouraging trend for Heart of Midlothian, who built a second new stand this summer.

Hibs and Hearts, in common with a vast number of other clubs, have temporarily had to cut expenditure in the transfer market while resources are devoted to the rebuilding. Fans have not been deterred and show a greater tolerance and understanding than they are often given credit for. The devotion to Scottish football is seriously underestimated.

Businessmen, the most realistic people of all, do recognise its scale, however. The three sponsors of our

Gordon Dalziel, Scott Thomson and Stevie Crawford celebrate Raith Rovers' Coca-Cola Cup victory.

major competitions – Bell's, Coca-Cola, and Tennents – are the most powerful companies ever to back the game in this country. We should all be grateful for their millions, but it does no harm to remember that they also find Scottish football a good investment.

The Bell's Scottish League is surely more glamourous than ever. Not so long ago, it would have been impossible to envisage Paul Gascoigne playing in this country unless he had to come to Scotland for some sort of pre-season friendly. Now he joins another

Paul Gascoigne

of international football's greatest players, Brian Laudrup, and holder of the World Cup scoring record (with five goals against Cameroon), Oleg Salenko, in an Ibrox pool on which £10 million has been spent this summer.

Celtic too have paid a club record fee of £2.2 million for the German forward Andreas Thom, another of those names that is instantly recognised in every country. Yet despite the economic dominance of the Old Firm, football in Scotland has proved delightfully unpredictable in recent years. Rangers, of course, are attempting to win the Premier Division title for the eighth season in succession, but in other respects, results have been volatile.

Dundee United may be infuriated at their demotion to the First Division, but their mishap at least proves that no club, whatever its previous record, can ever be sure of its safety. A healthy sport will always carry that element of

Ally McCoist celebrates the crucial goal against Greece

risk. Our Cup competitions have contained the greatest surprises of all.

Raith Rovers' astounding victory over Celtic on penalty kicks to claim The Coca-Cola Cup last season was among the most astonishing results in the whole history of Scottish football. The surprises of the tournament, however, involved far more than the afternoon of 27th November. Earlier in the tournament, to take the exploits of just one club, First Division Airdrieonians had eliminated both Motherwell and Hibernian.

Later Alex MacDonald's team would reach the Tennents Scottish Cup Final for the second time in three years, losing to Celtic on this occasion. The range of winners in our two major domestic Cup competitions since 1990 proves that our game is far more closely contested than we tend to believe. Aside from Rangers and Celtic, Hibernian, Raith Rovers, Aberdeen, Motherwell and Dundee

United have all lifted trophies. It is a fairly wide dispersal of honours.

In Scotland we are, of course, subject to endless debate over the quality of our football. This can be healthy, since there is no cause for complacency. At the same time, though, incomplete comparisons are often made. The performances of our clubs in Europe has been bitterly disappointing in recent years and people naturally yearn for the standards reached in, say 1967.

Not only did Celtic win the European Cup and Rangers reach the Cup Winners' Final that year, but Kilmarnock were also in the Semi-Finals of the Fairs Cities Cup (the competition which later became the UEFA Cup). If we are going to wallow in the 1960s, though, we are also under an obligation to remember it as the decade in which Scotland made absolutely no impression on international football.

In those days, the World Cup Finals

were for other nations. The 1990s are perhaps a mirror image of that period. While our clubs have had a lean time, the national team has performed with extraordinary consistency and dedication. The discipline and pride they showed in March to take a valuable European Championship point from Russia in Moscow were outstanding.

There was even an element of bravado in Craig Brown's planning. Instead of being used merely to contain Andrei Kanchelskis, Tom Boyd was asked to carry the play forward in the early stages. The Russians were clearly bewildered and the Celtic full-back even had chances to score. The 0-0 result helped place Scotland in a promising position in Group Eight and this was followed by wins against Greece and Finland to put the national team in pole position to qualify for the final stages. The thought of a place in the matches in England next summer ought to be a spur to excellence for players throughout the Premier Division.

We do not, of course, have any reason to loll around feeling pleased with ourselves. There are legitimate reasons for anxiety. On too many occasions, we watch our club sides in Europe attempt to compensate for technical deficiencies through willpower and organisation. It can be an embarrassing sight.

An Independent Review Commission, whose members include the great Dutch coach, Rinus Michels, has now been set up to examine the problems of Scottish football. Even before it was created, however, far reaching initiatives were already in place to enrich the grassroots of the game.

Manager, Craig Brown and Scotland squad members

Kevin Harper (Hibernian)

With no fuss or fanfare, The Scottish Football League, for instance, has now set up a structure for club football at under-18, under-16 and under-15 levels. The under-18 set-up has been running for three years and it is quietly booming, with the number of competing clubs having increased from 9 to 15.

Even in so brief a period, there have been distinguished graduates. Stephen Glass not only played last season but made a vital and precocious contribution to Aberdeen's survival in the Premier Division. Charlie Miller of Rangers is already being talked of by Craig Brown as a Scotland international player of the very near future. At Dundee, Jim Hamilton has also become an important player, and Kevin Harper of Hibernian scored a hat-trick for the Under 21 team against Finland in September. Brian McLaughlin of Celtic is another youngster who looks set for a great future in the game.

The new under-15 and under-16 levels will, in this country's experience at least, be revolutionary. The emphasis on raw competition will be removed in the Youth Development Initiative so that stress can be placed on learning about the game and its skills. A typical operation involving, for example, Rangers and Aberdeen, will feature much more than 90 minutes of worthless frenzy.

The teams can expect to meet at 11am and jointly be given an hour's coaching from club and SFA coaches. Then the players will mix over a sandwich and cup of tea before listening to an invited speaker who will broaden their understanding of football at large. Possible topics might include refereeing, contracts, media relations, nutrition, investment planning, and the work of the Players' Union.

After that comes a game with a difference. With no referee involved, the teenagers will be forced to respect one another and agree decisions among themselves. By applying the Laws of the Game, the teenagers should come to grasp them and the difficulties officials face. There is no League and therefore no points at stake. The game must be played purely for its own sake.

Scottish football has entered a period of quiet but profound change. Too few people, however, have been prepared to acknowledge that our national sport already shows many signs of vigorous health as it faces the challenges of the future.

KEVIN McCARRA
(Scotland on Sunday)

Brian McLaughlin (Celtic)

Charlie Miller (Rangers)

Season of Success

The obvious conclusion to take from the 1994/95 Bell's Premier Division programme, was indeed that Rangers were in "seventh heaven" after they captured Championship number seven in a row.

But that would only tell part of the story, of a campaign which saw others improve their consistency in the chase behind the Ibrox team, attendances buck all the trends in the High Street and the new League set-up emerge as an unqualified success. But first to Walter Smith and his players, who once again placed their priorities in the correct order and made sure of the domestic top prize, before allowing their focus to stray toward Europe too early.

Their triumph in this, the marathon game, was earned through persistently churning out positive results, even when thrown down a realistic challenge by Motherwell, particularly in the first half of the season.

There were hiccups along the way of course, not the least of which were three defeats inside one week from A.E.K. Athens in the Champions Cup, Celtic in the League and Falkirk in The Coca-Cola Cup.

That was the stuff that the critics dreamed of, and before October was through, there were further losses against Motherwell and Hibernian, to offer the suggestion that perhaps the title flag was not destined to fly in the south side of Glasgow after all. But it was then that the mettle of the

Champions was pushed to the fore with an unbeaten League sequence that stretched from the last week in October, with a 3-1 away victory over their Old Firm rivals, Celtic, until mid February, when a 2-0 defeat at Pittodrie ended a 14 match unbeaten run that had finished all rivals off.

As well as the consistency that marked their efforts, it is impossible to over stress the impact of the great Brian Laudrup, in his first excursion into football on this side of the North Sea. His elegant, fluid style of running, close control and willingness to play the team game for a player with so much natural ability, made him a joy to watch. Even for opposition fans, who would squirm under the cosh that we call the Great Dane, there was the recognition that we were watching one of the World's top players. Indeed, this dual Player of the Year, from the Scottish Football Writers and the Scottish Professional Footballers' Association, was just as much a hit off the pitch as he was on it.

At a time when the game needs to keep its image clear of the blemishes of other places, his contribution in the media and his sense of fair play on the field, was a credit to him, his club and to the game in Scotland. Such was his impact, that many observers were foreseeing the name Laudrup etched on the major award's trophies for many seasons to come, but Smith may have seen to it, that there is an alternative for this season.

If Rangers should be pleased with their winter's work, then so too should Alex McLeish and his Motherwell players who qualified for another tilt at Europe by finishing runners-up in a bunch finish behind the winners. Theirs had been the task of giving chase to Rangers for much of the campaign and despite being overhauled by Hibernian at a late stage, still battled back to win the one remaining place in the U.E.F.A. Cup after Raith Rovers stunning victory over Celtic in The Coca-Cola Cup Final.

Moving to Fir Park was a high risk strategy for the former Aberdeen and Scotland defender, for newcomers to the managerial business traditionally steer clear of the less affluent clubs who have performed well, on the basis that taking them a stage further was difficult if not impossible.

Therefore, when Tommy McLean left the Lanarkshire club in a more than healthy third place, having already won the Scottish Cup in his decade at the club, the signs were not good for this fledgling team boss. So when all the kudos are being dispensed for the season, McLeish must have his place. It might have been so different but for just one victory from eight games in a December-January spell, just when Rangers were building up their decisive head of steam.

Hibernian, under Alex Miller, were just a point behind in third place and the part-time Scotland coach was left to bemoan a lack of consistency that let the Easter Road team down at crucial times during the season.

They were unable to defeat Celtic and Falkirk during their schedule of games, costing them vital ground, but there was great celebration from their three wins against city rivals Hearts, having struggled for more than a decade in this private battle between the Capital clubs. Having brought Pat McGinlay back from Celtic during the winter and with so much capital being consumed by stadium work, Miller goes into the new campaign with the same seasoned squad which could still have improvement left to find.

Like Motherwell, Falkirk must also have their share of the reflective glory when Jim Jefferies transformed them from being a team constantly looking over their shoulder, into a combination with the confidence and results to look

up the way and now contemplate some reward for their efforts.

Still only six points clear of bottom place in the table with eight weeks left to go, Falkirk fairly sprinted to the line with just one defeat in an eight game March-April rush that had them within sight of European football, but in any case, in a comfortable fifth placing.

There is no doubt that the dabbling by Jefferies in the transfer market mid-season, which saw Mo Johnston, Steve Kirk and Paul McGrillen swell his squad, was a crucial intervention by a man whose controversial move to Heart of Midlothian in the summer, should not eradicate the value of a solid season's graft.

Locked on 43 points, five adrift of the Bairns, were Heart of Midlothian, Kilmarnock and Partick Thistle, and there is little doubt that the Edinburgh club will be reproaching themselves most for that finish, just one defeat away from the trauma of the Play-Off matches. They went into the first month of the season, with a new Board, led by Chris Robinson, who had recruited Tommy McLean from Motherwell and with a share issue planned for the autumn, optimism was sky high in the Gorgie area of town.

The reality, as is so often the case in this sometimes unkind game, was so different as the Edinburgh club moved from crisis to crisis starting with the removal of four senior members of staff and culminating with the sacking of McLean in July. While the share issue failed to create the funds for reinvestment that predictions indicated, ground improvements went on at good pace and in the end, Hearts won safety and a chance to regroup and try again.

Their cause was not helped by the loss of two of Scotland's finest prospects, striker Kevin Thomas and Stephen Frail, who are both recuperating from knee ligament injuries that will require a year out of action.

Perhaps too much activity and the destabalising effect that can have, was the problem, but Kilmarnock coped well with change in a period when Alex Totten replaced Tommy Burns, their stadium was transformed and lingering skirmishes with Celtic also provided an unwelcome diversion. Killie flirted on the edge of the relegation issue for long spells but the closest they came to terminal trouble was towards the end of the campaign, but by then, security and progress were confirmed.

Child's play for Mark Hateley

It was below them that all the anxiety was created when the unthinkable prospect of Aberdeen and Dundee United filled the bottom two places of the Bell's Premier Division with United falling down a division automatically, and Aberdeen facing Dunfermline in a two leg Play-Off for a continued place in the top ten.

United, like so many others, had made changes as danger loomed, with last season's Scottish Cup hero, Ivan Golac, making way for former player Billy Kirkwood, who saw just one victory in his nine games in charge, as United were relegated a conclusive five points behind the Dons.

Aberdeen and Dunfermline Athletic were left to create Scottish football history in the Play-Off matches, which the First Division team found a grade too good for them, but not for the fist time it was proved that there is cash in adversity. With full houses at Pittodrie and East End Park and live coverage of both matches by Grampian Television, both sides took away in excess of £100,000 each by way of compensation for facing two such

tension laden matches.

Left till last, Celtic, who perhaps established their fourth placing in the final table, amid more tumult than the rest of the clubs in this Championship contest added together.

A new Chief Executive, Fergus McCann, hired a new management team of Tommy Burns and Billy Stark. Their share issue was fully subscribed, freeing millions to be spent on players and the impressive new structure now presiding over Glasgow's east end.

Finishing eighteen points behind their rivals, Rangers, seemed to signal a termination of a meaningful challenge for the big prizes, but in the overall picture that is the Scottish game, that first trophy for five years when they defeated Airdrieonians in the Tennents Scottish Cup Final, may well spell good news for the Bell's Scottish League. With club accountants scrutinising their side of the story ever more significantly, the prospect of Celtic, Hibernian, Motherwell and the rest wrestling with the stadium responsibilities and still producing the goods on the pitch is a mouth watering prospect.

This would not be an accurate reflection on a season, unless there was a meeting of a band of dissidents to recall. Last season, they met in South Queensferry at the invitation of the Hearts new man, Chris Robinson, under the agenda that "the product was not right." Record sponsorship, increased attendances, brand new stadia sprouting throughout the country, Paul Gascoigne, Andreas Thom and Oleg Salenko, to name but a few, to attract paying customers, and European action for our best finishing clubs. The product is fine.

**RAY HEPBURN
(Freelance)**

Alex McLeish (Motherwell)

Alex Miller (Hibernian)

9

ABERDEEN

Pittodrie Stadium, Pittodrie Street,
Aberdeen AB2 1QH

CHAIRMAN
Ian R. Donald

VICE-CHAIRMAN
Denis J. Miller

DIRECTORS
Gordon A. Buchan & Stewart Milne

SECRETARY
Ian J. Taggart

MANAGER
Roy Aitken

ASSISTANT MANAGER
Tommy Craig

COACH
Drew Jarvie

PLAYER/COACH
Neil Cooper

TRAINER
Teddy Scott

CLUB DOCTOR
Dr. Derek Gray

PHYSIOTHERAPISTS
David Wylie & John Sharp

S.F.A. COMMUNITY COACH
Chic McLelland

CHIEF SCOUT
Jimmy Carswell

GROUNDSMAN
Jim Warrender

GENERAL MANAGER
David Johnston
(01224) 633267

TELEPHONES
Ground/Ticket Office
(01224) 632328
Fax (01224) 644173
Donsline (0898) 121551

CLUB SHOP
c/o Crombie Sports, 23 Bridge Street,
Aberdeen, Tel (01224) 593866
and Ticket Office, c/o Aberdeen F.C.,
Pittodrie Stadium, Aberdeen

OFFICIAL SUPPORTERS CLUB
Association Secretary:
Mrs. Susan Scott, 32 Earns Heugh
Crescent, Cove, Aberdeen AB1 4RU

TEAM CAPTAIN
Stewart McKimmie

SHIRT SPONSOR
Northsound Radio

LIST OF PLAYERS 1995-96

SURNAME	FIRST NAME	MIDDLE NAME	DATE OF BIRTH	PLACE OF BIRTH	DATE OF SIGNING	HEIGHT FT INS	WEIGHT ST LBS	PREVIOUS CLUB
Aitken	Robert	Sime	24/11/58	Irvine	27/06/92	6 0.0	13 0	St. Mirren
Bell	Robert		11/03/76	Springburn	05/10/94	5 9.5	10 12	Crombie Sports
Booth	Scott		16/12/71	Aberdeen	28/07/88	5 9.5	11 10	Deeside B.C.
Brown	Robert		04/08/79	Aberdeen	24/08/95	5 10.0	10 13	Hall Russells
Buchan	Martin	James	03/04/77	Manchester	26/08/95	5 10.0	10 10	Stonehaven
Christie	Kevin		01/04/76	Aberdeen	05/10/94	6 1.0	12 3	Lewis United
Cooper	Neil		12/08/58	Aberdeen	23/09/91	5 11.0	12 7	Hibernian
Craig	David	Charles	23/06/77	Dundee	05/10/94	5 8.0	10 9	Banks O'Dee
Craig	Michael		20/09/77	Glasgow	13/09/95	5 7.0	10 2	East End
Dodds	William		05/02/69	New Cumnock	25/07/94	5 8.0	10 10	St. Johnstone
Gilbert	Kenneth		08/03/75	Aberdeen	07/06/91	5 6.5	11 4	East End "A"
Glass	Stephen		23/05/76	Dundee	06/10/94	5 9.5	10 11	Crombie Sports
Grant	Brian		19/06/64	Bannockburn	15/08/84	5 9.0	11 6	Stirling Albion
Gray	Mark		26/08/77	Aberdeen	24/08/95	5 5.0	9 6	Hall Russells
Hetherston	Peter		06/11/64	Bellshill	04/07/94	5 9.0	10 7	Raith Rovers
Houston	Peter		20/10/77	Dingwall	04/04/95	5 7.5	10 12	Lewis United
Inglis	John		16/10/66	Edinburgh	28/10/94	6 0.5	13 0	St. Johnstone
Ireland	Craig		29/11/75	Dundee	05/10/94	6 3.0	13 9	Aberdeen Lads Club
Irvine	Brian	Alexander	24/05/65	Bellshill	19/07/85	6 2.5	13 7	Falkirk
Jess	Eoin		13/12/70	Aberdeen	13/11/87	5 9.5	11 6	Rangers
Kane	Paul	James	20/06/65	Edinburgh	22/11/91	5 9.5	11 0	Oldham Athletic
Kpedekpo	Malcolm		27/08/76	Aberdeen	08/10/94	6 0.0	12 13	Hermes
Matheson	David		27/06/78	Elgin	04/04/95	5 8.0	10 12	Lewis United
McCulloch	Greig		18/04/76	Girvan	05/10/94	5 8.0	10 7	Banchory St. Ternans
McKimmie	Stewart		27/10/62	Aberdeen	12/12/83	5 8.0	11 4	Dundee
McKinnon	Raymond		05/08/70	Dundee	07/02/94	5 10.0	11 10	Nottingham Forest
Miller	Joseph		08/12/67	Glasgow	30/07/93	5 8.0	10 7	Celtic
Morgan	Kevin	Drummond	31/01/77	Aberdeen	05/10/94	5 8.5	11 4	Hermes
Reeley	Derek		26/12/74	Glasgow	08/08/91	5 8.0	11 0	"S" Form
Robertson	Hugh	Scott	19/03/75	Aberdeen	24/08/93	5 9.0	13 11	Lewis United
Rowson	David	A.	14/09/76	Aberdeen	05/10/94	5 10.5	11 10	F. C. Stoneywood
Shearer	Duncan		28/08/62	Fort William	09/07/92	6 0.0	13 8	Blackburn Rovers
Smith	Gary		25/03/71	Glasgow	06/08/95	6 0.0	12 3	Falkirk
Snelders	Theodorus	G. A.	07/12/63	Westervoort	22/07/88	6 2.0	14 12	F. C. Twente
Stillie	Derek		03/12/73	Irvine	03/05/91	6 0.0	12 0	Notts County
Thomson	Scott	Munro	29/01/72	Aberdeen	05/11/91	5 10.0	11 10	Brechin City
Verveer	Etienne	Evert	22/09/67	Paramaribo	18/08/95	6 0.0	12 12	Millwall
Watt	Michael		27/11/70	Aberdeen	02/07/87	6 1.0	12 9	Cove Rangers "A"
Woodthorpe	Colin		13/01/69	Liverpool	19/07/94	6 1.0	12 4	Norwich City
Wyness	Dennis	Middleton	22/03/77	Aberdeen	05/10/94	5 10.5	11 4	F. C. Stoneywood
Yeats	Paul		15/08/76	Aberdeen	05/10/94	5 9.5	10 4	Hermes

MILESTONES

YEAR OF FORMATION: 1903
MOST CAPPED PLAYER: Alex McLeish
NO. OF CAPS: 77
MOST LEAGUE POINTS IN A SEASON: 64 (Premier Division - Season 1992/93) (44 games)
MOST LEAGUE GOALS SCORED BY A PLAYER IN A SEASON: Benny Yorston (Season 1929/30)
NO. OF GOALS SCORED: 38
RECORD ATTENDANCE: 45,061 (-v- Heart of Midlothian – 13.3.1954)
RECORD VICTORY: 13-0 (-v- Peterhead – Scottish Cup 9.2.1923)
RECORD DEFEAT: 0-8 (-v- Celtic - Division 1, 30.1.65)

SEASON TICKET INFORMATION

Seated
Main Stand Centre Adult £225
Wing Stand Adult £210
South Stand Adult £160
South Stand OAP £75
Merkland Stand Parent & Juvenile £200
Merkland Stand Juvenile/OAP...............................£60
Richard Donald Stand £210/185/160

LEAGUE ADMISSION PRICES

Seated
Main Stand Centre Adult £16
Main Stand Wing Adult...£14.50
South Stand Home Support £10
South Stand East (Visitors) Adult £10
                                   Juvenile/OAP £4
Merkland Stand Adult £9
                                   Juvenile/OAP £4
Richard Donald Stand £10

CLUB FACTFILE 1994/95

RESULTS . . APPEARANCES . . SCORERS

The DONS

Date	Venue	Opponents	Result	Snelders T.	McKimmie S.	Winnie D.	Grant B.	Irvine B.	Wright S.	Jess E.	Shearer D	Kane P.	Dodds W.	Robertson H.	Hetherston P.	Booth S.	Miller J.	Woodthorpe C.	McKinnon R.	Smith G.	Watt M.	Glass S.	Inglis J.	Thomson S.	Aitken R.	Kpedekpo M.
Aug 13	H	Heart of Midlothian	3-1	1	2	3	4	5	6	7	8	9	10^1	11^1	12	14^1										
20	H	Falkirk	2-2	1	2	3	4	5	6	14	8	9	10	11^1		7^1	12									
27	A	Dundee United	1-2	1	2		4^1	5	6	7	8	9	10				14	3	11							
Sep 10	A	Hibernian	2-2	1	2	11	4^1		6	7			10^1			9		3	8	5						
17	H	Partick Thistle	1-1		2		4	5	6	7			10^1			9	14	3	11	8	1					
24	H	Rangers	2-2		2		4	5	6	7			10^1		12	9^1	14	3	11	8	1					
Oct 1	A	Kilmarnock	1-2		2	8	4	5	6				10		7	9^1	12	3	11		1					
8	A	Celtic	0-0		2		4	5	6			8	10			9		3	11	7	1					
15	H	Motherwell	1-3		2		4	5	6			8	10^1		11	9	14	3		7	1					
22	A	Heart of Midlothian	0-2		2	12	4	5	6			8	10	14	11	9		3		7	1					
29	H	Dundee United	3-0	1	2	5	4		6			8^2	10		12	9^1		3	11	7		14				
Nov 5	A	Falkirk	1-2	1	2	5	4		6		12	8	10			9^1		3	11	7			14			
9	H	Hibernian	0-0	1	2	14					8	4	10			9		3	11	6			5	7		
19	A	Partick Thistle	1-2	1	2				14	8		4	10^1		12			3	11	6		9	5	7		
25	A	Rangers	0-1	1	2		8		6	11		4	10		12			3		7		14	5	9		
Dec 3	H	Kilmarnock	0-1	1	2		8		6	7		4	10		12		9	3				11	5	14		
10	A	Motherwell	†1-0	1	2		8		3			4	10		6		9			7		11	5			
26	H	Celtic	0-0	1	2		8		3	14	12	4	10		6		9			7		11	5			
31	H	Heart of Midlothian	3-1	1	2		11		3		8^2	4	10		7		9		12	6			5^1			
Jan 2	A	Dundee United	0-0	1	2		7		3	14	8	4	10				9		11	6			5		12	
7	H	Falkirk	0-0	1			7		3	14	8	4	10				9		11	6		2	5			
14	H	Partick Thistle	†3-1	1	2		11		3	7^1	8^1	4	10				9			6		14	5	12		
21	A	Hibernian	2-4	1	2		11			7	8	4	10^2				9		14	6		3	5			
Feb 4	A	Kilmarnock	1-3	1	2^1		8		3		14	4	10				9			6		11	5	7	12	
12	H	Rangers	2-0	1	2				3	7	8^1	4	10^1				9		11	6		14	5			
25	H	Motherwell	0-2	1				5	2	7	8	4	10		12		9		11	6	13	3		14		
Mar 5	A	Celtic	0-2		2		4	5	3	7	12		10		14		9		11	6	1	8				
11	A	Partick Thistle	2-2	1	2		4	5	3^1	14			10^1		12		9		11	6		8		7		
18	H	Hibernian	0-0	1	2		11		3	12	8	4	10		7		9			6	13		5	14		
Apr 1	H	Kilmarnock	0-1		2		11		3	14	8	4	10		7		9			6	1		5			
8	A	Rangers	2-3		2		11		3	14	8^1	4	10^1		7		9			6	1		5			
15	H	Celtic	2-0		2		11	5^1	3	12	8^1	4	10		7		9			6	1	14				
18	A	Motherwell	1-2		2		11	5	3	12	8	4	10^1		7		9			6	1	14				
29	A	Heart of Midlothian	2-1		2		4	5	3	11	8		10^2		7		9		12	6	1	14				
May 6	H	Dundee United	2-1	1	2		4	5	3	11	8^1		10^1		7		9			6		14				
13	A	Falkirk	2-0	1	2		4	5	3		8						9		10	6		11^1		7^1		14
TOTAL FULL APPEARANCES				24	34	6	32	17	33	15	19	27	35	2	13	11	21	14	17	31	12	11	16	6		
TOTAL SUB APPEARANCES						(2)			(1)	(10)	(4)			(1)	(9)	(1)	(6)		(3)		(2)	(8)	(1)	(4)	(2)	(1)
TOTAL GOALS SCORED					1		2	1	1	1	7	2	15	2		6						1	1	1		

Small bold figures denote goalscorers. † denotes opponent's own goal.

PITTODRIE STADIUM

CAPACITY: 21,634 (All seated)

PITCH DIMENSIONS: 109 yds x 72 yds

FACILITIES FOR DISABLED SUPPORTERS: Wheelchair section in front of Merkland Stand and in front row of Richard Donald Stand and also front row of Main Stand Section F. (Please telephone Ticket Office and reserve place(s) in advance).

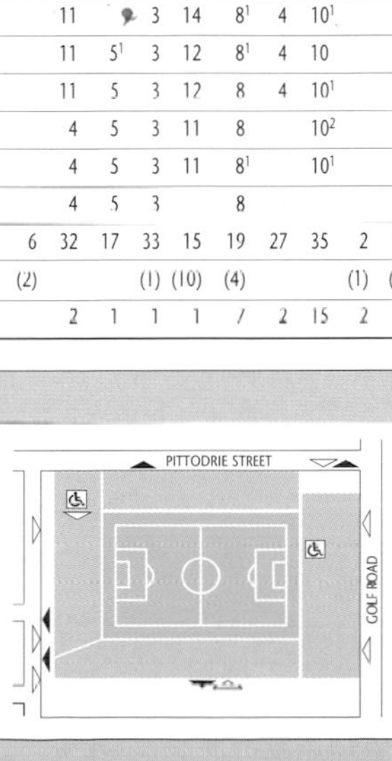

HOW TO GET THERE

You can reach Pittodrie Stadium by these routes:

BUSES: The following buses all depart from the city centre to within a hundred yards of the ground:Nos. 1, 2, 3 and 11.

TRAINS: The main Aberdeen station is in the centre of the city and the above buses will then take fans to the ground.

CARS: Motor vehicles coming from the city centre should travel along Union Street, then turn into King Street and the park will be on your right, about half a mile further on.

Parking on Beach Boulevard, King Street and Golf Road.

CELTIC

LIST OF PLAYERS 1995-96

SURNAME	FIRST NAME	MIDDLE NAME	DATE OF BIRTH	PLACE OF BIRTH	DATE OF SIGNING	HEIGHT FT INS	WEIGHT ST LBS	PREVIOUS CLUB
Adams	John		04/02/78	Motherwell	11/08/95	5 11.0	11 0	Celtic B.C.
Anthony	Marc		28/03/78	Edinburgh	25/07/95	5 6.0	10 3	Celtic B.C.
Bonner	Patrick	Joseph	24/05/60	Donegal	06/08/94	6 2.0	13 1	Keadue Rovers
Borland	Paul		28/06/79	Rutherglen	12/07/95	5 9.0	9 4	Celtic B.C.
Boyd	Thomas		24/11/65	Glasgow	06/02/92	5 11.0	11 4	Chelsea
Boyle	Charles	Declan	12/02/74	Donegal	21/02/95	6 0.0	12 9	Sligo Rovers
Carberry	Garrett		01/11/75	Glasgow	27/05/93	5 11.0	10 7	Celtic B.C.
Collins	John	Angus Paul	31/01/68	Galashiels	13/07/90	5 7.0	10 10	Hibernian
Coughlin	Martin		12/04/77	Paisley	09/06/95	5 6.0	10 5	"X" Form
Culkin	Craig		31/01/79	Jersey	25/07/95	5 10.0	11 2	Jersey Scottish B.C.
Dalglish	Paul	Kenneth	18/02/77	Glasgow	20/07/95	5 9.0	10 0	"X" Form
Docherty	Kevin		06/06/78	Glasgow	15/08/95	6 1.0	12 4	Celtic B.C.
Donnelly	Simon		01/12/74	Glasgow	27/05/93	5 9.0	10 12	Celtic B.C.
Elliot	Barry	Robert	24/10/78	Carlisle	11/08/95	5 10.0	9 5	Celtic B.C.
Falconer	William	Henry	05/04/66	Aberdeen	10/02/94	6 1.0	13 0	Sheffield United
Galloway	Michael		30/05/65	Oswestry	16/06/89	6 0.0	13 0	Heart of Midlothian
Gilligan	Kevin	Paul	04/01/79	Guernsey	25/07/95	5 7.0	10 4	Guernsey Rovers
Grant	Peter		30/08/65	Bellshill	27/07/82	5 9.0	10 3	Celtic B.C.
Gray	Stuart	Edward	18/12/73	Harrogate	07/07/92	6 1.0	12 0	Giffnock North A.F.C.
Hamill	Stephen		17/05/77	Glasgow	09/06/95	5 8.5	9 9	"X" Form
Hay	Christopher	Drummond	28/08/74	Glasgow	27/05/93	5 11.0	11 7	Giffnock North A.F.C.
Hughes	John		09/09/64	Edinburgh	07/08/95	6 0.0	13 7	Falkirk
Kelly	Patrick		26/04/78	Kirkcaldy	03/08/95	6 2.0	11 9	Celtic B.C.
Kerr	James	Stewart R.	13/11/74	Bellshill	27/05/93	6 2.0	13 0	Celtic B.C.
Lyttle	Gerard		27/11/77	Belfast	09/12/94	5 7.0	11 2	Star of the Sea
MacDonald	Peter		14/08/77	Glasgow	11/08/95	6 1.0	11 7	Celtic B.C.
Mackay	Malcolm	George	19/02/72	Bellshill	06/08/93	6 1.0	12 7	Queen's Park
Marshall	Gordon	George B.	19/04/64	Edinburgh	12/08/91	6 2.0	13 0	Falkirk
Martin	Lee	Andrew	05/02/68	Hyde	19/01/94	5 11.0	12 8	Manchester United
McBride	John	Paul	28/11/78	Hamilton	11/08/95	5 10.0	10 2	Celtic B.C.
McCondichie	Andrew		21/08/77	Glasgow	09/06/95	5 10.5	11 9	Celtic B.C.
McGrath	Timothy		16/08/79	Dublin	30/08/95	6 0.0	11 1	Town Celtic
McKinlay	Thomas	Valley	03/12/64	Glasgow	04/11/94	5 10.0	11 9	Heart of Midlothian
McLaughlin	Brian		14/05/74	Bellshill	07/07/92	5 4.0	8 7	Giffnock North A.F.C.
McNally	Mark		10/03/71	Motherwell	15/05/87	5 9.0	11 7	Celtic B.C.
McQuilken	James		03/10/74	Glasgow	31/03/93	5 9.0	10 7	Giffnock North B.C.
McStay	Paul	Michael L.	22/10/64	Hamilton	20/02/81	5 10.0	10 7	Celtic B.C.
Morrison	Graeme		29/10/76	Falkirk	24/12/94	6 0.0	12 9	Celtic B.C.
Mowbray	Anthony	Mark	22/11/63	Saltburn	08/11/91	6 1.0	13 2	Middlesbrough
O'Brien	Andrew		30/04/78	Bellshill	15/08/95	5 5.0	10 0	Celtic B.C.
O'Donnell	Philip		25/03/72	Bellshill	09/09/94	5 10.0	10 5	Motherwell
O'Neil	Brian		06/09/72	Paisley	10/07/91	6 1.0	12 4	Porirua Viard United
O'Neill	John	Joseph	03/01/74	Glasgow	16/05/94	5 10.0	10 4	Queen's Park
Slavin	James		18/01/75	Lanark	24/12/92	6 2.0	14 0	Giffnock North A.F.C.
Smith	Barry	Martin	19/02/74	Paisley	21/06/91	5 10.0	12 0	Giffnock North A.F.C.
Thom	Andreas		07/09/65	Rudersdorf	04/08/95	5 8.5	11 10	TSV Bayer 04 Leverkusen
Van Hooijdonk	Pierre		29/11/69	Steenbergen	11/01/95	6 4.5	13 5	NAC Breda
Vata	Rudi		13/02/69	Schroder	18/08/92	6 1.0	12 5	Dinamo Tirana
Vaugh	Brian		22/08/78	Belfast	11/08/95	5 11.0	10 13	Celtic B.C.
Walker	Andrew	Francis	06/04/65	Glasgow	01/07/94	5 8.0	10 7	Bolton Wanderers
Wilson	Thomas	Charles	13/06/77	Aberdeen	28/11/94	5 9.0	10 8	Celtic B.C.

MILESTONES

YEAR OF FORMATION: 1888
MOST CAPPED PLAYER: Paul McStay
NO. OF CAPS: 72
MOST LEAGUE POINTS IN A SEASON: 72 (Premier Division – Season 1987/88)
MOST LEAGUE GOALS SCORED BY A PLAYER IN A SEASON: Jimmy McGrory (Season 1935/36)
NO. OF GOALS SCORED: 50
RECORD ATTENDANCE: 92,000 (-v- Rangers – 1.1.1938)
RECORD VICTORY: 11-0 (-v- Dundee – Division 1, 26.10.1895)
RECORD DEFEAT: 0-8 (-v- Motherwell – Division 1, 30.4.1937)

SEASON TICKET AND LEAGUE ADMISSION PRICES

NORTH STAND		Season Ticket	League Ticket
Centre Upper Rear	Adult	£259	£12-14
Centre Upper Front	Adult	£309	£15-18
Centre Lower Rear (East & West)	Adult	£279	£12-15
Centre Lower Middle	Adult	£329	£16-19
	Juvenile	£199	—
Centre Lower Front	Adult	£279	£9-12
	Juvenile/OAP	£169	—
West Lower	Adult	£199	£9-12
	Juvenile/OAP	£120	£6-9
West Upper Rear	Adult	£229	£11-13
West Upper Front	Adult	£259	£12-14
West Lower	Adult	£199	£9-12
	Juvenile	—	£6-9

SOUTH STAND		Season Ticket	League Ticket
Rear	Adult	£305	£15-17
	Juvenile	£199	—
Front (West)	Family (2)	£298	£15-19
	Additional Juvenile	£120	£6
Front (East)		—	£11-13

Celtic Park, 95 Kerrydale Street, Glasgow G40 3RE

CHAIRMAN
Fergus McCann

DIRECTORS
Eric J. Riley; William Haughey

SECRETARY
Dominic W. Keane

MANAGER
Thomas Burns

ASSISTANT MANAGER
William Stark

CHIEF SCOUT
David Hay

RESERVE TEAM MANAGER
Frank Connor

RESERVE TEAM COACH
Tom McAdam

YOUTH TEAM COACH
William McStay

CLUB DOCTOR
Jack Mulhearn

PHYSIOTHERAPIST
Brian Scott

RESERVE TEAM PHYSIOTHERAPIST
Gerry McElhill

GROUNDSMAN
John Hayes

MARKETING DIRECTOR
Patrick Ferrell

PUBLIC RELATIONS MANAGER
Peter McLean

MANAGING DIRECTOR CELTIC POOLS
John McGuire

TELEPHONES
Ground 0141-556 2611
Fax 0141-551 8106
Ticket Office 0141-551 8654
Ticket Enquiries 0141-551 8653
Celtic Hotline 0891-121888
Celtic View 0141-551 8103
Walfrid Restaurant 0141-551 9955

CLUB SHOPS
18/20 Kerrydale Street, Glasgow
G40 3RE Tel 0141-554 4231
(9.00 a.m. to 5.00 p.m. Mon-Sat),
40 Dundas Street, Glasgow G1 2AQ
Tel 0141-332 2727
(9.00 a.m. to 5.00 p.m. Mon-Sat)
and 21 High Street, Glasgow,
G1 1LX Tel 0141-552 7630
(9.30 a.m. to 5.30 p.m. Mon-Sat)

OFFICIAL SUPPORTERS CLUB
Celtic Supporters Association,
1524 London Road, Glasgow G40 3RJ
Tel 0141-556 1882

TEAM CAPTAIN
Paul McStay

SHIRT SPONSOR
C.R. Smith

CLUB FACTFILE 1994/95
RESULTS .. APPEARANCES .. SCORERS

The BHOYS

Date	Venue	Opponents	Result	Marshall G.	Martin L.	Boyd T.	McNally M.	Mowbray A.	Grant P.	Galloway M.	McStay P.	Falconer W.	Walker A.	Collins J.	Nicholas C.	Donnelly S.	McGinlay	O'Neil B.	O'Donnell P.	McLaughlin B.	Smith B.	Byrne ?	McKinlay ?	O'Neil J.	Gray S.	Bonner P.	Hay C.	Slavin J.	Van Hooijdonk P.	Vata R.	Mackay M.
Aug 13	A	Falkirk	1-1	1	2	3	4	5	6	7	8	9	10¹	11																	
20	H	Dundee United	2-1	1	2	3	4	5¹	6		8	9	10¹	11	7	12	14														
27	A	Rangers	2-0	1		3	4	5	2	7	8¹		10	11¹	12	9	6	14													
Sep 10	A	Partick Thistle	2-1	1		3	4	5	2	7			10	11	12	9	6		8²	14											
17	H	Kilmarnock	1-1	1	2	3	4	5	6		8	9		11			14	7¹	10												
24	H	Hibernian	2-0	1		3	4	5	6	2			10	11¹	9	12	7	14	8¹												
Oct 1	A	Motherwell	1-1	1		3	4		6	2	12	14	10¹	11	9			7	5	8											
8	H	Aberdeen	0-0	1		3	4			2	8	14	10	11	9			7	5	6											
15	A	Heart of Midlothian	0-1	1		3	4		6	2	8	14	10	11	12	9			7	5											
22	H	Falkirk	0-2	1	2	3	4		6		9	12	11	10	14		7	5	8												
30	H	Rangers	1-3	1		3	4				8	14	10	11	12	9		5	6			2	7¹								
Nov 5	A	Dundee United	2-2	1		2	4		6		8	9	10	11²	12	14		5					7		3						
9	H	Partick Thistle	0-0	1		2	12	5	6		8			11	10	9		4					7		3		14				
19	A	Kilmarnock	0-0	1		2	4		6		8	9	10	11		12		5	7						3						
30	A	Hibernian	1-1	1		2	4			6	8	9	10	11¹				5	7						3				12		
Dec 3	H	Motherwell	†2-2	1		2	4		6		8	9¹	10		12			5		7					3		11				
26	A	Aberdeen	0-0			2		5	6		8		10	11	14			4	9						3	1	7				
31	H	Falkirk	2-0			2			6¹		8		10¹	11				4	9	5					3	1	14	7			
Jan 4	A	Rangers	1-1			2		5			8		10	11				4	6	9			7¹		3	1	12				
7	H	Dundee United	1-1			2					8	12	10	11¹				4	6	9			7		3	1	14	5			
11	H	Heart of Midlothian	1-1			2	4				8	12		11					6	10			7		3	1		5	9¹		
14	H	Kilmarnock	2-1			2	4				8	10¹		11¹					6	7					3	1	14	5	9		
21	A	Partick Thistle	0-0			2		5		6			10	11				4	8	7					3	1			9		
Feb 4	A	Motherwell	0-1			2		5		6	8		10	11				4	7	14					3	1			9		
11	H	Hibernian	2-2			2		5		6			10¹	11¹				4	8	7					3	1			9		
25	A	Heart of Midlothian	1-1				2	5		6		12	10	11				4	8¹	7					3	1			9		
Mar 5	H	Aberdeen	2-0			2		5		6	8		10		12			4	11	7					3	1			9²		
21	A	Kilmarnock	1-0			2		5		12	8	14¹	10	11					6	7					3	1			9	4	
Apr 1	H	Motherwell	1-1			2		5			8	12	10¹	11					6	7					3	1			9	4	
15	A	Aberdeen	0-2			2				6	8	9	10	11	12			5	14	7					3	1				4	
19	A	Heart of Midlothian	0-1			3		5		6		9	10	11	12			4	8	7						1					2
29	A	Falkirk	2-1			2¹		5		6	8	9	10	11				4	7¹						3	1			14		
May 2	H	Partick Thistle	1-3			2		5		6¹	8	9		11				4	7						3	1			10		
7	H	Rangers	†3-0			2				6	8	12	10	11				5	14	7					3	1			9¹	4¹	
10	A	Hibernian	1-1			2				6	8	10¹						5	11	7					3	1			9	4	
13	A	Dundee United	1-0			2				6	8	11			12				10¹	7					3	1	14		9	4	5
TOTAL FULL APPEARANCES				16	4	35	19	15	27	11	28	19	22	33	5	7	7	24	25	19	3	6	17		8	20	2	3	13	7	1
TOTAL SUB APPEARANCES							(1)			(1)		(1)			(7)	(4)	(1)	(7)	(10)	(1)	(2)	(2)	(2)	(1)	(3)		(3)		(1)		
TOTAL GOALS SCORED						1		1		2	1	4	6	8				1	6				2						4	1	

Small bold figures denote goalscorers. † denotes opponent's own goal.

CELTIC PARK

CAPACITY: 34,000 (Approx) (All Seated)
PITCH DIMENSIONS: 120 yds x 74 yds
FACILITIES FOR DISABLED SUPPORTERS:
77 Wheelchair spaces for Celtic Supporters front of lower tier. 9 Wheelchair spaces for visiting supporters-max number could be reduced for different segregation conditions. 18 Chair spaces for ambulant disabled supporters allocated at Celtic's discretion in the stand. 54 Chair spaces for helpers. 43 Chair seats at front row adjacent to wheelchair spaces. 11 Chairs allocated at Celtic's discretion in the stand. 22 Chair spaces for blind party-located at the South Stand behind dugouts; induction loop facilities being provided for this area only. Toilet facilities also available.

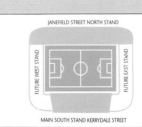

JANEFIELD STREET NORTH STAND
FUTURE WEST STAND
FUTURE EAST STAND
MAIN SOUTH STAND KERRYDALE STREET

HOW TO GET THERE

The following routes may be used to reach Celtic Park:
BUSES: The following buses all leave from the city centre and pass within 50 yards of the ground. Nos. 61, 62, and 64.
TRAINS: There is a frequent train service from Glasgow Central Low Level station to Bridgeton Cross Station and this is only a ten minute walk from the ground. Belgrove Rail Station is approximately 1.5 miles from the ground.
CARS: From the city centre, motor vehicles should travel along London Road and this will take you to the ground. Parking space is available in front of the Main Stand and also on the vacant ground adjacent to the park.

LIST OF PLAYERS 1995-96

SURNAME	FIRST NAME	MIDDLE NAME	DATE OF BIRTH	PLACE OF BIRTH	DATE OF SIGNING	HEIGHT FT INS	WEIGHT ST LBS	PREVIOUS CLUB
Clark	John		22/09/64	Edinburgh	16/09/94	6 0.0	14 1	Stoke City
Corrigan	Martyn		14/08/77	Glasgow	02/08/95	5 9.0	10 9	Gairdoch United
Elliot	David		13/11/69	Glasgow	18/08/95	5 9.0	11 0	St. Mirren
Ferguson	Derek		31/07/67	Glasgow	07/09/95	5 8.5	11 6	Sunderland
Fulton	Stephen		10/08/70	Greenock	12/08/94	5 10.0	11 0	Bolton Wanderers
Hamilton	Graeme	John	22/01/74	Stirling	19/06/91	5 10.0	10 10	Gairdoch United
Henderson	Nicholas	Sinclair	08/02/69	Edinburgh	04/03/94	5 10.0	11 1	Cowdenbeath
Inglis	Neil	David	10/09/74	Glasgow	03/08/95	6 1.0	12 2	Rangers
James	Kevin	Francis	03/12/75	Edinburgh	17/11/93	6 0.0	12 0	Musselburgh Athletic
Johnston	Forbes	Duthie S.	03/08/71	Aberdeen	08/09/90	5 10.0	9 12	Musselburgh Athletic
Johnston	Maurice	Thomas	13/04/63	Glasgow	01/03/95	5 9.0	11 4	Heart of Midlothian
Kirk	Stephen	David	03/01/63	Kirkcaldy	24/02/95	5 11.0	11 4	Motherwell
McKenzie	Scott		07/07/70	Glasgow	08/09/90	5 9.0	10 5	Musselburgh Athletic
McDonald	Colin		10/04/74	Edinburgh	08/07/93	5 7.0	10 8	Hibernian
McDonald	Craig		30/01/77	Bellshill	12/08/95	5 6.0	11 0	Cambuslang Juniors
McGlynn	David	John	26/06/75	Edinburgh	24/07/95	6 0.0	11 3	Musselburgh Athletic
McGowan	Jamie		05/12/70	Morecambe	02/03/94	6 0.0	11 1	Dundee
McGraw	Mark	Robertson	05/01/71	Rutherglen	18/08/95	5 11.5	11 2	Hibernian
McGrillen	Paul		19/08/71	Glasgow	24/02/95	5 8.0	10 5	Motherwell
McLaughlin	Joseph		02/06/60	Greenock	12/09/92	6 1.0	12 0	Watford
Napier	Craig	Cameron	14/11/65	East Kilbride	18/08/95	5 9.0	12 0	Kilmarnock
Oliver	Neil		11/04/67	Berwick-upon-Tweed	07/08/91	5 11.0	11 10	Blackburn Rovers
Parks	Anthony		28/01/63	Hackney	23/10/92	5 10.0	13 2	Rotherham United
Paterson	Jamie		26/04/73	Dumfries	20/12/94	5 4.0	10 0	Halifax Town
Rice	Brian		11/10/63	Bellshill	09/08/91	6 1.0	11 7	Nottingham Forest
Weir	David	Gillespie	10/05/70	Falkirk	01/08/92	6 2.0	13 7	Celtic B.C.

MILESTONES

YEAR OF FORMATION: 1876
MOST CAPPED PLAYER: Alex H. Parker
NO. OF CAPS: 14
MOST LEAGUE POINTS IN A SEASON: 59 (Division 2 – Season 1935/36)
MOST LEAGUE GOALS SCORED BY A PLAYER IN A SEASON: E. Morrison (Season 1928/29)
NO. OF GOALS SCORED: 43
RECORD ATTENDANCE: 23,100 (-v- Celtic – 21.2.1953)
RECORD VICTORY: 12-1 (-v- Laurieston – Scottish Cup 23.3.1893)
RECORD DEFEAT: 1-11 (-v- Airdrieonians – Division 1, 28.4.1951)

SEASON TICKET INFORMATION

Seated
Adult ....£195/£180
Juvenile/O.A.P. ....£150/£95
Husband and Wife £345
Standing
South Enclosure   Adult £160
                    Juvenile/O.A.P. £80
Ground   Adult £150
                    Juvenile/O.A.P. £80

LEAGUE ADMISSION PRICES

Seated
Adult ....£11 and £10
Juvenile/O.A.P. ....£6 (Wing Stand)
Standing
Enclosure   Adult £9.50
Ground   Adult £9
              Juvenile/OAP.........................£5

Brockville Park, Hope Street,
Falkirk, FK1 5AX

CHAIRMAN
George J. Fulston

DIRECTOR
Alexander D. Moffat

SECRETARY
Alexander D. Moffat

TECHNICAL DIRECTOR
John Lambie

ASSISTANT MANAGER/ COACH
Gerry Collins

CLUB DOCTOR
Dr. R. G. Sinclair

PHYSIOTHERAPIST
Bob McCallum

CHIEF SCOUT
John Murray

S.F.A. COMMUNITY COACH
Peter Houston

GROUNDSMAN
James Dawson

COMMERCIAL EXECUTIVE
George Miller
(01324) 624121

STADIUM MANAGER
James Hendry
(01324) 624121

TELEPHONES
Ground/Ticket Office/Information
Service (01324) 624121/632487
Fax (01324) 612418

OFFICIAL SUPPORTERS CLUB
Association of Falkirk F.C.Supporters
Clubs–Chairman : Alex Hastings
Tel (01324) 627793

CLUB SHOP
47 Glebe Street, Falkirk, FK1 1HX

TEAM CAPTAIN
Joe McLaughlin

SHIRT SPONSOR
Beazer Homes

Est. 1876

CLUB FACTFILE 1994/95
RESULTS .. APPEARANCES .. SCORERS

The BAIRNS

Small bold figures denote goalscorers.   † denotes opponent's own goal.

Date	Venue	Opponents	Result	Parks A.	Weir D.	McGowan J.	Hughes J.	Oliver N.	McKenzie S.	May E.	Fulton S.	Cacette R.	McCall I.	Johnston F.	Hamilton G.	McDonald C.	McLaughlin J.	Rice B.	McStay I.	Henderson N.	Cramb C.	Lamont W.	Clark J.	McAvennie F.	James K.	Shaw G.	Burridge J.	Paterson J.	McQueer T.	Kirk S.	McGillier P.	Johnston M.
Aug 13	H	Celtic	1-1	1	2	3	4	5	6	7	8	9	10¹	11	12	14																
20	A	Aberdeen	2-2	1	2	3		4	6	7	8	9¹				11¹	5	10	14													
27	H	Partick Thistle	2-1	1	2	3		4	6	7	8¹	9¹				11	5	10														
Sep 10	A	Kilmarnock	1-1	1	2	3		4	6	7	8	9¹				11	5	10	12	13												
17	H	Rangers	0-2		2	12		3	6	7	8	9				11	5	10			1		4	14								
24	A	Dundee United	0-1	1	2			3	6	7	8	9				11	5	10		14				4								
Oct 1	H	Heart of Midlothian	2-1	1	2	12		3	6	7	8	9					5¹	10		14			4	11								
8	A	Motherwell	3-5	1	2			3	6	7	8	9				11	5	10					4²	14¹								
15	H	Hibernian	0-0	1	2	3		4	6	7	10					11	5		12	14	9		8									
22	A	Celtic	2-0	1	2	3		4	6	7	14					11	5	10¹		9			8¹									
29	A	Partick Thistle	2-1	1	2	3		4	6	7¹						11	5	10			9		8¹									
Nov 5	H	Aberdeen	2-1	1	2	3¹		4	6	7						11	5	10	13		9¹		8									
8	H	Kilmarnock	3-3		2	3		4	6	7	14					11	5	10¹	12		9	1	8²									
19	A	Rangers	1-1		2	3		4	6	7	9					11	5	10¹					8				1					
26	H	Dundee United	1-3		2	3	12	4	6		9					7	5	11	14	10¹			8				1					
Dec 3	A	Heart of Midlothian	1-1		2	3	14	4	6	7	9					11¹	5		10				8				1					
10	A	Hibernian	2-2		2	3	14	4	6	7	9					11¹	5	12¹		10		1	8									
26	H	Motherwell	0-1		2	3	5	4	6	7	9					11		12		10		1	8						14			
31	A	Celtic	0-2		2	3	14	4	6	7	9						5	12		10		1	8					11				
Jan 7	A	Aberdeen	0-0	1	2	12		3	6	7	10					9	5				6		8									14
14	H	Rangers	2-3	1		3	5	4	11	7¹	10					9¹					6		8		2	12						
17	A	Partick Thistle	1-3	1				4	11¹	7	10					2	5	12			6		8						3		9	
21	A	Kilmarnock	1-2	1	2		5	4	11	7						9		12		14	6¹		8						3			10
Feb 4	H	Heart of Midlothian	2-0	1	2		8	4	11	7	10¹					9	5	12¹			6								3			
21	A	Dundee United	0-1	1	2		3	4	11	7	10					9	5				6		8						14			
25	H	Hibernian	1-0	1	2		3	4	11		10						5	12	13		6		8							7¹	9	
Mar 7	A	Motherwell	2-2	1	2	3		4	11		8						5¹	12			6									7¹	9	10
11	A	Rangers	2-2	1		3		4	11							9²	5	12		14	6		8		2					7		10
25	A	Kilmarnock	2-0	1	2	3		4	11								5				6		8¹							7¹	9	10
Apr 1	A	Heart of Midlothian	1-0	1	2	3	14	4	11							12	5				6		8							7	9¹	10
8	H	Dundee United	3-1	1	2	3		4	11		14					12¹	5				6		8							7¹	9	10¹
15	H	Motherwell	3-0	1	2¹	3		4	11		12¹					9	5				6		8							7¹		
19	A	Hibernian	2-0	1	2	3		4	11		12					14¹	5				6¹		8							7	9	10
29	H	Celtic	1-2	1	2	3		4	11		8					9	5		14		6¹									7		10
May 6	A	Partick Thistle	0-0	1	2	3		4	11		8					9	5				6									7		10
13	H	Aberdeen	0-2	1	2	3		4	11		9					12	5				6		8							7		10
TOTAL FULL APPEARANCES				28	32	27	17	26	36	24	25	8	3	3	2	26	28	19		14	6	5	31	1	1		3	1	3	11	6	10
TOTAL SUB APPEARANCES						(4)	(3)	(1)			(3)		(2)		(1)	(5)		(7)	(1)	(1)	(2)	(3)		(2)		(3)		(3)	(1)			
TOTAL GOALS SCORED					1	1		1	2	3	3	1				9	2	2		5	1		8	2						5	1	1

BROCKVILLE PARK

CAPACITY: 13,401; Seated 2,661, Standing 10,740

PITCH DIMENSIONS: 110 yds x 72 yds

FACILITIES FOR DISABLED SUPPORTERS: Disabled Enclosure opposite Main Stand - takes 7 disabled fans in wheelchairs plus 1 helper each.

WATSON STREET · HOPE STREET · COOPERAGE LANE

HOW TO GET THERE

Brockville Park can be reached by the following routes:

TRAINS: The main Edinburgh-Glasgow railway line passes by the ground and passengers can alight at Grahamston Station. They will then have a walk of 100 yards to the ground.

BUSES: All buses departing from the city centre pass by Brockville.

CARS: Car parking facilities are available in the Meeks Road car park for coaches and cars and also in a local shopping car park which can hold 500 cars. Supporters coaches and cars will be directed to the appropriate parking area by the police on duty.

HEART OF MIDLOTHIAN

LIST OF PLAYERS 1995-96

SURNAME	FIRST NAME	MIDDLE NAME	DATE OF BIRTH	PLACE OF BIRTH	DATE OF SIGNING	HEIGHT FT INS	WEIGHT ST LBS	PREVIOUS CLUB
Barnes	Derek		20/09/77	Glasgow	05/01/95	6 0.0	11 3	Edinburgh United
Barr	Anthony		11/09/77	Bellshill	19/11/94	5 9.0	10 1	Royal Albert
Berry	Neil		06/04/63	Edinburgh	05/12/84	6 0.0	12 7	Bolton Wanderers
Bradley	Mark		10/08/76	Glasgow	02/03/95	5 6.0	9 7	Ashfield
Burns	John	Paul	11/03/78	Kirkcaldy	21/11/94	5 6.0	10 9	Newtongrange Star
Callaghan	Stuart		20/07/76	Calderbank	03/08/92	5 8.0	10 3	Blantyre B.C.
Colquhoun	John	Mark	14/07/63	Stirling	27/07/93	5 8.0	11 2	Sunderland
Cramb	Colin		23/06/74	Lanark	01/03/95	6 0.0	11 7	Falkirk
Duncan	Grant		04/04/77	Edinburgh	02/03/95	5 7.0	10 7	Bathgate Thistle
Frail	Stephen	Charles	10/08/69	Glasgow	31/03/94	6 0.0	11 13	Dundee
Hagen	David		05/05/73	Edinburgh	01/12/94	5 11.0	13 0	Rangers
Hamilton	Brian		05/08/67	Paisley	04/01/95	6 0.0	12 6	Hibernian
Holmes	Derek		18/10/78	Lanark	05/01/95	6 0.0	12 2	Royal Albert
Horn	Robert		03/08/77	Edinburgh	13/05/95	5 9.0	11 0	Edinburgh United
Jamieson	William	George	27/04/63	Barnsley	01/12/94	5 11.0	12 0	Partick Thistle
Johnston	Allan		14/12/73	Glasgow	23/06/90	5 11.0	11 0	Tynecastle Boys Club
Kidd	Walter	Joseph	10/03/58	Edinburgh	12/08/94	5 11.0	12 3	Airdrieonians
Lawrence	Alan		19/08/62	Edinburgh	24/08/95	5 7.0	10 0	Airdrieonians
Leitch	Donald	Scott	06/10/69	Motherwell	06/08/93	5 9.0	11 8	Dunfermline Athletic
Levein	Craig	William	22/10/64	Dunfermline	25/11/83	6 2.0	13 0	Cowdenbeath
Locke	Gary		16/06/75	Edinburgh	31/07/92	5 10.0	11 8	Whitehill Welfare
Mackay	Gary		23/01/64	Edinburgh	16/06/80	5 9.0	11 8	Salvesen B.C.
Mathieson	Peter	David	18/10/77	Edinburgh	21/11/94	5 5.0	9 1	Edinburgh United
McManus	Allan	William	17/11/74	Paisley	03/08/92	6 0.0	12 0	Links United
McNicol	Grant		07/09/77	Edinburgh	20/07/94	5 9.0	10 1	Yett Farm B.C.
McPherson	David		28/01/64	Paisley	25/10/94	6 3.0	11 11	Rangers
Millar	John		08/12/66	Bellshill	26/07/91	5 10.0	11 10	Blackburn Rovers
Miller	Colin	Fyfe	04/10/64	Lanark	18/11/94	5 7.0	12 2	St. Johnstone
Murie	David		02/08/76	Edinburgh	31/07/92	5 8.0	10 4	Tynecastle B.C.
Murray	Grant	Robert	29/08/75	Edinburgh	02/03/95	5 10.0	12 0	Bonnyrigg Rose
Nelson	Craig	Robert	28/05/71	Coatbridge	30/11/94	6 1.0	12 3	Partick Thistle
O'Connor	Gary		07/04/74	Newtongrange	23/02/94	6 2.0	12 4	Berwick Rangers
Queen	Kevin		16/08/78	Bellshill	19/08/94	5 8.0	10 6	Yett Farm
Ritchie	Paul	Simon	21/08/75	Kirkcaldy	31/07/92	5 11.0	12 0	Links United
Robertson	John	Grant	02/10/64	Edinburgh	09/12/82	5 6.0	11 4	Newcastle United
Smith	Henry	George	10/03/56	Lanark	05/08/81	6 2.0	13 2	Leeds United
Storrar	Andrew	David	06/10/77	Stirling	21/11/94	5 5.0	10 6	Dunipace Juniors
Thomas	Kevin	Roderick	25/04/75	Edinburgh	31/07/92	5 11.0	12 5	Links United
Winnie	David		26/10/66	Glasgow	30/08/95	6 1.5	12 7	Aberdeen
Wishart	Fraser		01/03/65	Johnstone	10/03/95	5 8.0	10 0	Rangers
Wright	George		22/12/69	South Africa	04/07/87	5 9.0	11 4	Hutchison Vale B.C.

MILESTONES

YEAR OF FORMATION: 1874
MOST CAPPED PLAYER: Bobby Walker
NO. OF CAPS: 29
MOST LEAGUE POINTS IN A SEASON: 63 (Premier Division - Season 1991/92)
MOST LEAGUE GOALS SCORED BY A PLAYER IN A SEASON: Barney Battles (Season 1930/31)
NO. OF GOALS SCORED: 44
RECORD ATTENDANCE: 53,396 (-v- Rangers – 13.2.1932)
RECORD VICTORY: 21-0 (-v- Anchor – EFA Cup 1880)
RECORD DEFEAT: 1-8 (-v- Vale of Leven – Scottish Cup 1883)

SEASON TICKET PRICES

Main Stand
Centre Stand   Adult....£215
North Stand   Adult....£200
North Enclosure   Adult....£180

School End Stand
Adult & 1 Juvenile £240
Adult & 2 Juveniles..........£295
Adult & 3 Juveniles..........£350
Adult, OAP & 2 Juveniles.£350
Juvenile/OAP £75
Disabled/Carer £75

Wheatfield Stand
Prime Stand   Adult £230
Front Section Adult £200
Wing Section   Adult £200

LEAGUE ADMISSION PRICES

	Cat A Matches	Cat B Matches
Main Stand		
Centre Stand	£12	£11
North Stand	£11	£10
North Enclosure	£10	£9
Wheatfield Stand		
Prime Stand	£13	£12
Front Section	£11	£10
Wing Section	£11	£10

School End Stand
(All Concession Prices are in the School Stand)
Adult £10
Juvenile/Disabled/Carer/OAP ..£5
Adult & Juvenile £15
Adult & 2 Juveniles................£20
Adult & 3 Juveniles................£25
Adult, OAP & 2 Juveniles £25

Heart of Midlothian F.C.,
Tynecastle Park, Gorgie Road,
Edinburgh EH11 2NL

CHAIRMAN
Christopher P. Robinson

VICE-CHAIRMAN
Leslie G. Deans

DIRECTORS
Fraser S. Jackson & Colin G. Wilson

SECRETARY
Leslie W. Porteous

GENERAL MANAGER
Sally Robinson

MANAGER
James Jefferies

ASSISTANT MANAGER
Billy Brown

COACHES
Walter Kidd & Paul Hegarty

CLUB DOCTOR
Dr. Melvin

PHYSIOTHERAPIST
Alan Rae

S.F.A. COMMUNITY OFFICER
Bobby Jenks

CHIEF SCOUT
Douglas Dalgleish

GROUNDSMAN
Ronnie Blair

COMMERCIAL DEPARTMENT
Gary Mackay, Shirley Twist
& Brian Whittaker
Tel 0131-337 9011

TICKET MANAGER
Neil Hunter

TELEPHONES
Ground 0131-337 6132
Fax 0131-346 0699
Telex 72694
Ticket Office 0131-337 9011
Information Service 0131-346 8556

CLUB SHOP
Heart of Midlothian Sport & Leisure,
Tynecastle Park, McLeod Street,
Edinburgh. Tel 0131-346 8511.
Open 9.30 a.m. – 5.30 p.m.
Mon. to Sat. and match days.

OFFICIAL SUPPORTERS CLUB
Heart of Midlothian Federation,
John N. Borthwick, 80 Slateford
Road, Edinburgh, EH11 1QU

TEAM CAPTAIN
Craig Levein

SHIRT SPONSOR
Strongbow

CLUB FACTFILE 1994/95
RESULTS .. APPEARANCES .. SCORERS

The JAM TARTS

Player columns (left to right): Smith H., Frail S, McKinlay T., Locke G., Weir J., McLaren A., Colquhoun J., Mackay G., Robertson J., Leitch S., Millar J., Johnston A., Thomas K, Walker J N., Levein C, Johnston M., Berry N., Hogg G., Bett J., McPherson C., Wright G., Miller C., Kidd W., Nelson C., Jamieson W., Hagen D., Hamilton B., Grant C., Wishart F.

Date	Venue	Opponents	Result	Smith H.	Frail S	McKinlay T.	Locke G.	Weir J.	McLaren A.	Colquhoun J.	Mackay G.	Robertson J.	Leitch S.	Millar J.	Johnston A.	Thomas K	Walker J N.	Levein C	Johnston M.	Berry N.	Hogg G.	Bett J.	McPherson C.	Wright G.	Miller C.	Kidd W.	Nelson C.	Jamieson W.	Hagen D.	Hamilton B.	Grant C.	Wishart F.
Aug 13	A	Aberdeen	1-3	1	2	3	4	5	6	7¹	8	9	10	11	12	14																	
20	A	Motherwell	1-1		2	3		5	6	7	8	9	14	11	12		1	4	10¹														
27	H	Hibernian	0-1		2	3			6	7	8	9		11	14	12	1	4	10	5													
Sep 11	A	Rangers	0-3	1		3	2		6	7		11	8	10	12	14		4	9	5													
17	H	Dundee United	2-1	1	2¹	3			6	7		9	8	10	14	11¹		4	12	5													
24	H	Kilmarnock	3-0	1	2	3			6¹	7	14¹	9	8	10¹	12	11		4		5													
Oct 1	A	Falkirk	1-2	1	2	3			6	7	14	9¹	8	10	12	11		4		5													
8	A	Partick Thistle	1-0	1	2	3			6	7	12	9¹		10	14	11		4		5		8											
15	H	Celtic	1-0	1	2	3			6	12	7	9¹	10	14		11		4		5		8											
22	H	Aberdeen	2-0	1	2¹	3			6	12	7	9¹	14	10		11		4		5		8											
29	A	Hibernian	1-2	1	2	3				12	7	9¹	10	14		11		4		5		8	6										
Nov 5	H	Motherwell	1-2	1	2					7	8	9¹	10	3	11	12				5		4	6										
9	H	Rangers	1-1	1	2					7¹	4	9	10	3	11	12				5		8	6		14								
19	A	Dundee United	2-5	1		14				7	4	9	10	3		11²				5		8	6		2								
26	A	Kilmarnock	1-3	1		2				7	4	9¹	12	10	14	11						8	6		3	5							
Dec 3	A	Falkirk	1-1		2					7	12	9	10			11¹				5		8	6		3		1			4	14		
26	H	Partick Thistle	3-0		2					7	14	9¹	10		12					5		8¹	6		3		1			4	11¹		
31	A	Aberdeen	1-3		2					7	10	9			12¹					5		8	6	14	3		1			4	11		
Jan 8	A	Motherwell	2-1		2						14	12	10		9					5		8	6		3¹		1			4	11	7¹	
11	A	Celtic	1-1		2						14	12	10		9					5		8¹	6		3		1			4	11	†	
14	H	Dundee United	2-0		2						12	9	10¹							5		8	6		3		1			4¹	11	7	
18	H	Hibernian	2-0		2					14	12	9	10¹					4				8	6¹		3		1			5	11	7	
21	A	Rangers	0-1		2						9	14	12	10				4				8	6		3		1			5	11	7	
Feb 4	A	Falkirk	0-2		2					12	10	9				14		4		5		8	6		3		1				11	7	
11	H	Kilmarnock	2-2		2					7	12¹	9			10¹			4		3		5	6				1				14	8	
25	H	Celtic	1-1		2					12	8		3	10	9	14		4					6				1			5¹	11	7	
Mar 18	H	Rangers	2-1		2					14	7	9¹	3	10¹	12			4				8	6				1			5	11		
21	A	Dundee United	1-1		2		14			7			3	10	9¹			4		6		8					1			5	11		12
Apr 1	H	Falkirk	0-1	13						7		9	10	3	11			4		5		8	6				1				12	14	2
4	A	Partick Thistle	1-3	1						7	14	9		10¹	12			4				5	6	3			1				11	8	2
12	A	Kilmarnock	2-3			14				7	8			10	11			4		5			6	3			1		12¹			9¹	2
15	H	Partick Thistle	0-1			14				7	8		3	10	11			4	6								1		5	12		9	2
19	A	Celtic	1-0			14					12	10						4	6			8	3				1		5	11¹	7	9	2
29	H	Aberdeen	1-2							9	10	12						4	5			8	6¹	3			1	14		11	7		2
May 6	A	Hibernian	1-3							7	12	9			14			4	5			8	6	3			1			11¹	10		2
13	H	Motherwell	2-0			14				7	2	9¹						4	5			8	6				1			11	10¹	12	3
TOTAL FULL APPEARANCES				14	25	11	3	2	10	23	21	27	18	25	9	11	2	24	3	29	26	23	16	1	20	13	16	13	3	8		
TOTAL SUB APPEARANCES				(1)		(6)				(8)	(13)	(4)	(3)	(3)	(12)	(7)		(1)				(1)		(2)			(2)	(4)			(3)	
TOTAL GOALS SCORED						2				1	2	2	10		6	1	5		1			2	2		1			3	3	2	1

Small bold figures denote goalscorers. † denotes opponent's own goal.

TYNECASTLE PARK

CAPACITY: 17,000 (Approx) (All seated)
PLEASE NOTE: STADIUM UNDER RECONSTRUCTION
PITCH DIMENSIONS: 108 yds x 72 yds
FACILITIES FOR DISABLED SUPPORTERS: There are 10 spaces for visiting fans at South end of the Enclosure (must be pre-booked). Regarding facilities for home supporters, see Season Ticket and League Admission Price information

WHEATFIELD ROAD
GORGIE ROAD
McLEOD STREET

HOW TO GET THERE

Tynecastle Park can be reached by the following routes:

BUSES: A frequent service of buses leaves from the city centre, Nos. 1, 2, 3, 4, 33, 34, 35 and 44 all pass the ground

TRAINS: Haymarket Station is about half a mile from the ground.

CARS: Car Parking facilities exist in the adjacent side streets in Robertson Avenue and also the Westfield area.

HIBERNIAN

LIST OF PLAYERS 1995-96

SURNAME	FIRST NAME	MIDDLE NAME	DATE OF BIRTH	PLACE OF BIRTH	DATE OF SIGNING	HEIGHT FT INS	WEIGHT ST LBS	PREVIOUS CLUB
Anderson	Steven		18/09/78	Bangour	18/07/95	5 8.0	9 7	Hutchison Vale B.C.
Bannerman	Scott		21/03/79	Edinburgh	18/07/95	5 6.0	9 4	Hutchison Vale B.C.
Cook	Paul		05/08/78	Broxburn	18/07/95	5 10.0	10 0	Hutchison Vale B.C.
Dods	Darren		07/06/75	Edinburgh	03/08/92	6 1.0	12 13	Hutchison Vale B.C.
Donald	Graeme	Still	14/04/74	Stirling	12/06/91	6 0.0	12 1	Gairdoch United
Edgar	Scott		07/09/78	Paisley	18/07/95	5 7.0	9 8	Duntocher B.C.
Evans	Gareth	John	14/01/67	Coventry	06/02/88	5 7.5	11 0	Rotherham United
Farrell	David		29/10/69	Glasgow	12/08/88	5 9.0	11 4	Oxford United
Gardiner	Jason	Stanley	30/10/73	Edinburgh	14/05/91	6 0.0	13 3	Salvesen B.C.
Harper	Kevin	Patrick	15/01/76	Oldham	03/08/92	5 6.0	10 13	Hutchison Vale B.C.
Hunter	Gordon		03/05/67	Wallyford	10/08/83	5 10.0	12 3	Musselburgh Windsor
Jackson	Christopher		29/10/73	Edinburgh	14/05/91	5 7.0	10 11	Salvesen B.C.
Jackson	Darren		25/07/66	Edinburgh	14/07/92	5 10.0	11 0	Dundee United
Leighton	James		24/07/58	Johnstone	14/07/93	6 0.0	13 6	Dundee
Lockhart	Darren	Derek	06/09/77	Edinburgh	03/06/94	5 10.0	10 9	Hutchison Vale B.C.
Love	Graeme		07/12/73	Bathgate	14/05/91	5 10.0	12 0	Salvesen B.C.
Martin	John		29/01/79	Edinburgh	18/07/95	5 10. 0	10 2	Hutchison Vale B.C.
McAllister	Kevin		08/11/62	Falkirk	29/07/93	5 5.0	11 0	Falkirk
McDonald	Ian		07/03/78	Newcastle	19/07/94	6 0.0	12 13	Salvesen B.C.
McGinlay	Patrick	David	30/05/67	Glasgow	01/11/94	5 10.0	11 10	Celtic
McNab	Ross		12/12/78	Glasgow	18/07/95	5 6.5	9 3	Duntocher B.C.
Millen	Andrew	Frank	10/06/65	Glasgow	21/03/95	5 11.0	11 2	Kilmarnock
Miller	Graeme		21/02/73	Glasgow	11/06/90	5 7.0	10 3	Tynecastle B.C.
Miller	Greg		01/04/76	Glasgow	29/07/94	5 7.5	9 6	Hutchison Vale B.C.
Miller	William		01/11/69	Edinburgh	14/03/87	5 8.0	11 2	Edina Hibs B.C.
Mitchell	Graham		02/11/62	Glasgow	31/12/86	5 10.0	11 12	Hamilton Academical
Newman	Andrew		03/10/78	Paisley	18/07/95	5 6.5	10 10	Duntocher B.C.
O'Neill	Michael	Andrew M.	05/07/69	Portadown	20/08/93	5 11.5	11 3	Dundee United
Paton	Eric	John	01/08/78	Glasgow	19/07/94	5 8.5	11 3	Hutchison Vale B.C.
Reid	Christopher	Thomas	04/11/71	Edinburgh	20/06/88	5 11.0	13 7	Hutchison Vale B.C.
Renwick	Michael		29/02/76	Edinburgh	03/08/92	5 9.0	11 0	Hutchison Vale B.C.
Riley	Paul		07/08/75	Edinburgh	03/08/92	5 7.0	9 11	Hutchison Vale B.C.
Tortolano	Joseph		06/04/66	Stirling	29/08/85	5 8.0	11 6	West Bromwich Albion
Tweed	Steven		08/08/72	Edinburgh	25/08/90	6 3.0	15 0	Hutchison Vale B.C.
Weir	Michael	Graham	16/01/66	Edinburgh	14/01/88	5 4.0	10 3	Luton Town
Wright	Keith		17/05/65	Edinburgh	01/08/91	5 11.0	12 6	Dundee

MILESTONES

YEAR OF FORMATION: 1875
MOST CAPPED PLAYER: Lawrie Reilly
NO. OF CAPS: 38
MOST LEAGUE POINTS IN A SEASON: 57 (First Division – Season 1980/81)
MOST LEAGUE GOALS SCORED BY A PLAYER IN A SEASON: Joe Baker (Season 1959/60)
NO. OF GOALS SCORED: 42
RECORD ATTENDANCE: 65,860 (-v- Heart of Midlothian – 2.1.1950)
RECORD VICTORY: 22-1 (-v- 42nd Highlanders 3.9.1881)
RECORD DEFEAT: 0-10 (-v- Rangers – 24.12.1898)

SEASON TICKET INFORMATION

Seated

Centre Stand	Adult	£215
	Juvenile/OAP	£160
Wing Stand	Adult	£180
	Juvenile/OAP	£140
North Enclosure	Adult Only	£165
East Seated Terrace	Adult	£165
	Juvenile/OAP	£90
Family Section	Parent and 1 Juvenile	£210
	Family of 3	£250
	Family of 4	£280
	Family of 5	£300

LEAGUE ADMISSION PRICES

Seated

Centre Stand	Adult	£12
Wing Stand North	Adult	£10.50
Seated Enclosure	Adult	£9
Family Enclosure	Adult	£8
	Juvenile	£4
Seated Terrace	Adult	£9
	Juvenile/OAP	£5

Please note: No Concessions in all ticket games -v- Celtic, Heart of Midlothian and Rangers (No Juvenile/OAP gates)

Easter Road Stadium,
64 Albion Road,
Edinburgh EH7 5QG

CHAIRMAN
Douglas W. M. Cromb

DIRECTORS
Robert Huthersall
Allan Munro
Thomas J. O'Malley
Ian Brennan

SECRETARY
Cecil F. Graham, F.F.A.

MANAGER
Alexander Miller

FIRST TEAM COACH
Jocky Scott

RESERVE TEAM COACH
Donald Park

CLUB DOCTOR
James Ledingham

PHYSIOTHERAPIST
Stuart Collie

S.F.A. COMMUNITY COACH
John Ritchie

COMMERCIAL MANAGER
Ian Erskine
0131-661 2159

CATERING MANAGER
Keith J. C. Donaldson

MARKETING EXECUTIVE
Alan Wardrop

STADIUM MANAGER
David C. Brown

TELEPHONES
Ground 0131-661 2159
Fax 0131-659 6488
Ticket Office 0131-652 0630
Information Service
(0891) 121189

CLUB SHOP
178A Easter Road, Edinburgh

OFFICIAL SUPPORTERS CLUB
11 Sunnyside Lane, Off Easter Road,
Edinburgh EH7

TEAM CAPTAIN
Gordon Hunter

SHIRT SPONSOR
Calor Gas (Scotland)

CLUB FACTFILE 1994/95
RESULTS . . APPEARANCES . . SCORERS

The HIBEES

Date	Venue	Opponents	Result	Leighton J.	Miller W.	Mitchell C.	Findlay W.	Tweed S.	Hunter G.	McAllister K.	Hamilton B.	Evans G.	Jackson D.	O'Neill M.	Harper K.	Tortolano J.	Beaumont D.	Farrell D.	McGraw M.	Love G.	Weir M.	McGinlay P.	Wright K.	Millen A.	Dods D.	Renwick M.
Aug 13	H	Dundee United	5-0	1	2	3	4^1	5	6	7	8	9	10^2	11^1	14^1											
20	H	Kilmarnock	0-0	1	2	3	4	5	6	7	8	9	10	11	14	12										
27	A	Heart of Midlothian	1-0	1	2		4	5	6^1	12	8	9	10	11	7	14	3									
Sep 10	H	Aberdeen	2-2	1			4	5		7	8	9	10^1	11^1			3	6	2	12	14					
17	A	Motherwell	1-1	1	2		7	5	6	12	8	9	10	11^1			4	3			14					
24	A	Celtic	0-2	1	2		7	5	6	12	8	14	10	11	9			4			3					
Oct 1	H	Partick Thistle	3-0	1	2			5	6		8	9	10^2	11	7			4	14^1		3	12				
8	H	Rangers	2-1	1	2			5	6^1		8	9	10	11	7^1			4	14		3	12				
15	H	Falkirk	0-0	1	2			5	6		8	9		11	7			4	10		3	12				
22	A	Dundee United	0-0	1	2		12	5	6		8	9		11	10	14		4			3	7				
29	H	Heart of Midlothian	2-1	1	2		9	5			8	12	10^1	11^1	14	6	4				3	7				
Nov 5	A	Kilmarnock	0-0	1	2		9	5	6		8	14	10	11	12						3	7	4			
9	A	Aberdeen	0-0	1	2			5	6	7	8	12	10	11	9						3		4			
19	H	Motherwell	2-2	1	2			5	6	7^1	8		10	11^1	9						3	12	4			
30	H	Celtic	1-1	1	2		14	5	6	7	8		10^1	11	12						3	9	4			
Dec 3	H	Partick Thistle	2-2	1	2		8	5	6		14		10	11^1	9	7	3					12	4^1			
10	H	Falkirk	2-2	1	2		8		6	7		9	10^1	11^1				5			3	12	4			
26	A	Rangers	0-2	1	2		14	5	6	12	4	8	10	11	7								3	9		
31	H	Dundee United	4-0	1		3	12	5	6	7	8	14	10	11^1					2				4	9^3		
Jan 7	H	Kilmarnock	2-1	1	2	3	8	5	6	7		12	10	11^1		14							4^1	9		
13	A	Motherwell	0-0	1	2	3		5	6	7			10	11				8					4	9		
18	A	Heart of Midlothian	0-2	1	2	3	14	5	6	7			10	11				12			8		4	9		
21	H	Aberdeen	4-2	1	2	3	12	5		7		8	10^2		11			6				14	4^1	9^1		
Feb 4	H	Partick Thistle	1-2	1	2	3	11	5	6	7		8	10			12	14						4^1	9		
11	A	Celtic	2-2	1	2	3			6				10		8	11		5		14^1		7	4^1	9		
25	A	Falkirk	0-1	1	2	3		5	6				10	11				8	7				4	9		
Mar 4	H	Rangers	1-1	1	2	3		5	6	7			10			8		4	12					9^1		
18	A	Aberdeen	0-0	1	2	3		5	6				10	11		7	8		14			12	4	9		
22	H	Motherwell	2-0	1	2			5	6				10	11		7	8			14		12	4	9^2	3	
Apr 1	A	Partick Thistle	2-2	1	2			5	6			12		11	7^1	10		8				14	4	9^1	3	
16	A	Rangers	1-3	1	2	3				14		7	10	11^1		12		8					4	9	6	
19	H	Falkirk	0-2	1	2	3		5		7			10	11		14		8					4	9	6	
29	A	Dundee United	1-0	1	2	3			6	7		8		11	12	10		14					4^1	9	5	
May 6	H	Heart of Midlothian	3-1	1	2	3		5		7		12		11	14^1	6					10^1		4	9^1	8	
10	H	Celtic	1-1	1	2	3		5	6			14		11	10^1	12						7	4	9	8	
13	A	Kilmarnock	2-1	1	2	3		5		12		7	10	11									4^1	9^1	8	14
TOTAL FULL APPEARANCES				36	34	18	12	33	29	17	17	16	30	33	15	11	7	15	2	11	8	24	19	8	1	
TOTAL SUB APPEARANCES							(6)			(6)	(1)		(8)	(1)	(8)	(7)		(4)	(6)	(1)			(11)			(1)
TOTAL GOALS SCORED							1		2	1			10	10	5			2		1	7	10			

Small bold figures denote goalscorers. † denotes opponent's own goal.

EASTER ROAD

CAPACITY: 16,218 (All seated)

PITCH DIMENSIONS: 112 yds x 74 yds

FACILITIES FOR DISABLED SUPPORTERS: Area in South Seated Enclosure, new North Stand and new South Stand.

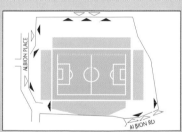

HOW TO GET THERE

Easter Road Stadium can be reached by the following routes:

BUSES: The main bus station in the city is served by buses from all over the country and the following local buses departing from Princes Street all stop near the ground. Nos. 4, 15, 42 and 44.

TRAINS: Edinburgh Waverley Station is served by trains from all parts of the country and the above buses all stop near the ground.

KILMARNOCK

Rugby Park, Rugby Road,
Kilmarnock KA1 2DP

CHAIRMAN
Robert Fleeting

VICE-CHAIRMAN
James H. Moffat

DIRECTORS
Mrs. Laurel J. Chadwick
John Paton
Ronald D. Hamilton

SECRETARY
Kevin D. Collins

MANAGER
Alexander Totten

FIRST TEAM COACH
Kenneth Thomson

RESERVE COACH
Bobby Williamson

GOALKEEPING COACH
Jim Stewart

YOUTH COACHES
Stuart McLean & Alan Robertson

HON. MEDICAL OFFICER
Dr. Robin Magee

CROWD DOCTOR
Dr. Zaidi

PHYSIOTHERAPIST
Hugh Allan M.B.E.

S.F.A. COMMUNITY OFFICER
Jim Clark

CHIEF SCOUT
Alec Wright

COMMERCIAL MANAGER
Denny Martin
(01563) 525184

STADIUM MANAGER
Angus Hollas

TELEPHONES
Ground (01563) 525184
Fax (01563) 522181
Matchday/Ticket Information
(01563) 542999

CLUB SHOP
Killie Sports, 36 Bank Street,
Kilmarnock. Tel (01563) 534210.
Open Mon to Sat
9.00 a.m. – 5.00 p.m.
Also shop situated at ground.

OFFICIAL SUPPORTERS CLUB
c/o Rugby Park, Kilmarnock KA1 2DP

TEAM CAPTAIN
Raymond Montgomerie

SHIRT SPONSOR
A.T. Mays, Travel Agents

LIST OF PLAYERS 1995-96

SURNAME	FIRST NAME	MIDDLE NAME	DATE OF BIRTH	PLACE OF BIRTH	DATE OF SIGNING	HEIGHT FT INS	WEIGHT ST LBS	PREVIOUS CLUB
Anderson	Derek	Christopher	15/05/72	Paisley	15/11/94	6 0.0	11 0	Kilwinning Rangers
Black	Thomas		11/10/62	Lanark	08/11/91	5 11.5	13 3	St. Mirren
Brown	Thomas		01/04/68	Glasgow	27/08/93	5 7.0	10 7	Glenafton Athletic
Burke	Alexander		11/11/77	Glasgow	18/08/95	5 7.5	9 11	Kilmarnock B.C.
Connor	Robert		04/08/60	Kilmarnock	11/08/94	5 11.0	11 4	Aberdeen
Davidson	Stuart		03/08/79	Glasgow	18/08/95	5 7.5	9 2	Glasgow City B.C.
Doig	Kevin		06/11/75	Glasgow	15/05/95	6 0.0	12 5	Troon Juniors
Findlay	William	McCall	29/08/70	Kilmarnock	21/03/95	5 10.0	12 13	Hibernian
Fitzpatrick	Iain		20/09/69	Edinburgh	26/01/95	5 11.0	11 3	Kilbirnie Ladeside
Geddes	Alexander	Robert	12/08/60	Inverness	25/05/90	6 0.0	12 8	Dundee
Hamilton	Steven	James	19/03/75	Baillieston	26/08/94	5 9.0	12 10	Troon Juniors
Hay	Gary		07/09/77	Irvine	18/08/95	5 7.5	10 0	Kilmarnock B.C.
Henry	John		31/12/71	Vale of Leven	15/08/94	5 10.0	10 5	Clydebank
Holt	Gary		09/03/73	Irvine	18/08/95	5 11.5	11 3	Stoke City
Jack	Alan		11/11/76	Glasgow	22/12/94	5 6.0	10 9	Troon Juniors
Kerr	Alan		07/05/76	Irvine	11/05/95	5 8.0	10 9	Troon Juniors
Lauchlan	James	Harley	02/02/77	Glasgow	20/07/94	6 1.0	10 13	Kilmarnock B.C.
Lekovic	Dragoje		21/11/67	Sivac	26/11/94	6 2.5	12 9	Buducnost Podgorica
MacPherson	Angus	Ian	11/10/68	Glasgow	10/06/86	5 11.0	11 8	Rangers
Maskrey	Stephen	William	16/08/62	Edinburgh	11/08/94	5 7.5	9 10	St. Johnstone
McCutcheon	Gary		08/10/78	Dumfries	18/08/95	5 4.5	9 11	Kilmarnock B.C.
McKee	Colin		22/08/73	Glasgow	06/09/94	5 10.0	11 3	Manchester United
Meldrum	Colin	George	26/11/75	Kilmarnock	03/09/93	5 10.5	13 4	Kilwinning Rangers
Mitchell	Alistair	Robert	03/12/68	Kirkcaldy	05/07/91	5 7.0	11 8	East Fife
Montgomerie	Samuel	Raymond	17/04/61	Irvine	12/08/88	5 8.0	11 12	Dumbarton
Reilly	Mark		30/03/69	Bellshill	05/07/91	5 8.0	10 10	Motherwell
Roberts	Mark	Kingsley	29/10/75	Irvine	07/02/92	5 9.5	10 12	Bellfield B.C.
Ryan	Alexander		07/09/79	Glasgow	18/08/95	5 5.0	9 9	Highbury B.C.
Skilling	Mark	James	06/10/72	Irvine	01/10/91	5 9.5	11 2	Saltcoats Victoria
Whitworth	Neil		12/04/72	Wigan	02/09/94	6 0.5	12 9	Manchester United
Williamson	Robert		13/08/61	Glasgow	15/11/90	5 7.5	12 9	Rotherham United
Wright	Paul	Hamilton	17/08/67	East Kilbride	31/03/95	5 8.0	11 7	St. Johnstone

MILESTONES

YEAR OF FORMATION: 1869
MOST CAPPED PLAYER: Joe Nibloe; **NO. OF CAPS:** 11
MOST LEAGUE POINTS IN A SEASON: 58 (Division 2 - Season 1973/74)
MOST LEAGUE GOALS SCORED BY A PLAYER IN A SEASON: Harry "Peerie" Cunningham (Season 1927/28) and Andy Kerr (Season 1960/61)
NO. OF GOALS SCORED: 34
RECORD ATTENDANCE: 34,246 (-v- Rangers – August 1963)
RECORD VICTORY: 13-2 (-v- Saltcoats – Scottish Cup 12.9.1896)
RECORD DEFEAT: 0-8 (-v- Rangers and Hibernian - Division 1)

SEASON TICKET INFORMATION

West
Adult £200
Juvenile/O.A.P £100
East
Adult £180
Juvenile/O.A.P. £90

Moffat Stand
Adult £160 Juvenile/OAP £80

(Family) Moffat Stand
Adult £160 Juvenile £40 plus £20 for each additional
Juvenile
PLEASE NOTE: Juvenile prices apply to 15 year olds and under (proof of age may be required)

LEAGUE ADMISSION PRICES

West Centre
Adult £12
Wing Adult £10 Juvenile/O.A.P. £5
Family Enclosure (Moffat Stand South)
Adult £9 Juvenile/OAP £4.50
(Juvenile must be accompanied by an Adult)
East
Adult £9
Juvenile/O.A.P. £5
North (Chadwick Stand)
Visitors
Adult £9
Juvenile/O.A.P £4.50

CLUB FACTFILE 1994/95
RESULTS . . APPEARANCES . . SCORERS

KILLIE

Small bold figures denote number of goals;

Date	Venue	Opponents	Result	Geddes R.	MacPherson A.	Black T.	Montgomeri R.	Reilly M.	Millen A.	Mitchell A.	Napie C.	Williamson R.	Connor R.	Maskrey S.	McCluskey C.	Henry J.	McSkimming	Brown T.	Whitworth N.	McKee C.	Meldrum	Skilling M	Anderson D.	Lekovic D.	Roberts M.	Lauchar J.	McCarrison D	Findlay W.	Wright P.
Aug 13	A	Partick Thistle	0-2	1	2	3	4	5	6	7	8	9	10	11	14														
20	A	Hibernian	0-0	1	2	3	4	5	6	7		14	11	9	10	8													
27	H	Motherwell	0-1	1	2	3	4	5	6	7		12	10	9	8			11	14										
Sep 10	H	Falkirk	1-1	1	2	3	4		6	7		9[1]	10			12	11	14		5	8								
17	A	Celtic	1-1	1	2		12	11	6	7		9[1]	10					4	3	5	8								
24	A	Heart of Midlothian	0-3	1		12	2	11	6	7		9	10					4	3	14	5	8							
Oct 1	H	Aberdeen	† 2-1	1		3	2	12	6			9	4	14		8	11	10[1]	5	7									
8	A	Dundee United	0-2	1	2	3	4	11	6	12		9	14			8		10	5	7									
15	A	Rangers	0-2	1	2	3		4	6	7		9				8	11	10	5	14									
22	H	Partick Thistle	2-0		2	3		4	6	7						8	11	10[1]	5	9[1]	1								
29	A	Motherwell	2-3		2	3		4	6	7		12	14			8[1]	11	10	5	9[1]	1								
Nov 5	H	Hibernian	0-0	1	2	3	11		6	7		12	14			8		10	5	9		4							
8	A	Falkirk	3-3	1	2	3[1]	11		6	7		12	14			8[1]		10	5	9		4[1]							
19	H	Celtic	0-0		2	3	11			7			12			8		10	5	9	1	4	6						
26	H	Heart of Midlothian	3-1		2	3	11			7[1]		12	14			8		10	5	9[1]		4[1]	6	1					
Dec 3	A	Aberdeen	1-0		2		4			7	3	12	10	11[1]					5	9		8	6	1	14				
10	H	Rangers	1-2		2	3	4			7		14	10	11		12			5	9[1]		8	6	1					
26	A	Dundee United	† 2-2		2	3	4			7[1]		14	10	11		8			5	9		12	6	1					
31	A	Partick Thistle	2-2		2[1]	3	4			7			10	11[1]		8	14			9		5	6	1					
Jan 7	A	Hibernian	1-2		2	3	4			7	12		10	11		8		14	5	9[1]			6	1					
14	A	Celtic	1-2		2	3[1]	4			7			10	14		8		11		9		5	6	1					
17	H	Motherwell	2-0		2	3[2]	4			7			10			8			9	5	11		6	1					
21	H	Falkirk	2-1		2	3[1]	4	6		7			10	14		8			9		11[1]			1		5			
Feb 4	H	Aberdeen	3-1		2	3	4			7			10	11[1]		8			9[1]	5			6	1			14[1]		
11	H	Heart of Midlothian	2-2		2	3	4			7			10	11[1]		8			9[1]	5			6	1			14		
25	A	Rangers	0-3		2	3	12			7			10	11		8			5	9			6	1			14		
Mar 4	H	Dundee United	2-0		2	3	4			7[2]			10	11		8			5	9		12	6	1				14	
21	H	Celtic	0-1		2	3	4			7			10	11					9	5	14	8	6	1				12	
25	A	Falkirk	0-2		2	3	4			7			10	11		8			5	9			6	1				12	
Apr 1	A	Aberdeen	1-0		2	3	4			7			11	14				10	5			8[1]	6	1				17	9
12	H	Heart of Midlothian	3-2		2	3	12			7			10	11		8[1]			5[2]				6	1				4	9
15	A	Dundee United	2-1		2	3				7			10	11		8[1]		14	5[1]			4	6	1				12	9
20	H	Rangers	0-1		2	3				7			10	11				14	5			4	6	1				8	9
29	H	Partick Thistle	0-0		2	3				7			10	11				14	5			12	6	1				4	9
May 6	A	Motherwell	0-2	1	2		4	3		7			14			8		12	5	11		10						6	9
13	H	Hibernian	1-2				4	3		14			10	11		6			9	5	1	12					2	7	8[1]
TOTAL FULL APPEARANCES				12	33	31	9	31	13	33	2	7	27	19	2	28	8	18	30	22	4	13	20	20	2			5	7
TOTAL SUB APPEARANCES					(1)		(3)	(1)		(2)	(1)	(8)		(1)	(11)	(1)	(2)		(9)		(3)		(4)		(4)	(1)	(4)		
TOTAL GOALS SCORED					1	5				4		2		4		4			4	3		6	3				1		1

Small bold figures denote goalscorers. † denotes opponent's own goal.

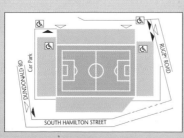

MOTHERWELL

Fir Park, Firpark Street,
Motherwell ML1 2QN

CHAIRMAN
John C. Chapman O.B.E. A.R.A.gS

VICE-CHAIRMAN
William H. Dickie, R.I.B.A.

GENERAL MANAGER/SECRETARY
Alan C. Dick

PLAYER/MANAGER
Alexander McLeish

ASSISTANT MANAGER
Andrew Watson

COACH
Jim Griffin

HON. MEDICAL OFFICERS
Mr. Ian Kerr & Dr. Robert Liddle

PHYSIOTHERAPIST
John Porteous

S.F.A. COMMUNITY OFFICER
William McLean

**YOUTH DEVELOPMENT OFFICER/
CHIEF SCOUT**
John Park

GROUNDSMAN
Christopher Westwood

COMMERCIAL MANAGER
John Swinburne
(01698) 261437

TELEPHONES
Ground (01698) 261437
Fax (01698) 276333
Ticket Office (01698) 263396
Information Service 0891 121553

CLUB SHOP
Motherwell Football & Athletic Club,
Firpark Street, Motherwell ML1 2QN
Tel (01698) 261437.
Open 9.00 a.m. – 4.30 p.m. Mon. to
Fri. (Open Saturdays from 10.00
a.m. to 5.00 p.m. on first team
home match days only)

OFFICIAL SUPPORTERS CLUB
c/o Fir Park, Firpark Street,
Motherwell ML1 2QN.

TEAM CAPTAIN
Chris McCart

SHIRT SPONSOR
Motorola

LIST OF PLAYERS 1995-96

SURNAME	FIRST NAME	MIDDLE NAME	DATE OF BIRTH	PLACE OF BIRTH	DATE OF SIGNING	HEIGHT FT INS	WEIGHT ST LBS	PREVIOUS CLUB
Arnott	Douglas		05/08/61	Lanark	29/10/86	5 7.0	10 7	Pollok Juniors
Burns	Alexander		04/08/73	Bellshill	06/08/91	5 8.0	10 0	Shotts Bon–Accord
Coyne	Thomas		14/11/62	Glasgow	30/11/93	6 0.0	10 7	Tranmere Rovers
Craigan	Stephen		21/10/76	Newtonards	07/09/95	5 10.0	10 9	Blantyre Vics
Davies	William	McIntosh	31/05/64	Glasgow	12/03/94	5 6.0	10 9	Dunfermline Athletic
Denham	Greig	Paterson	05/10/76	Glasgow	19/08/93	6 0.0	12 2	Cumbernauld United
Dolan	James		22/02/69	Salsburgh	13/06/87	5 9.0	10 7	Motherwell B.C.
Essandoh	Roy		17/02/76	Belfast	09/12/94	6 0.0	12 3	Cumbernauld Juniors
Ferguson	Paul		12/03/75	Dechmont	25/08/93	5 7.0	9 12	Stoneyburn United
Hendry	John		06/01/70	Glasgow	12/07/95	5 11.0	10 0	Tottenham Hotspur
Howie	Scott		04/01/72	Glasgow	13/10/94	6 3.0	13 5	Norwich City
Krivokapic	Miodrag		06/09/59	Niksic Crna Gora	10/07/93	6 1.0	12 6	Dundee United
Lambert	Paul		07/08/69	Glasgow	07/09/93	5 11.0	9 10	St. Mirren
Martin	Brian		24/02/63	Bellshill	14/11/91	6 0.0	13 0	St. Mirren
May	Edward		30/08/67	Edinburgh	24/02/95	5 7.5	10 3	Falkirk
McCart	Christopher		17/04/67	Motherwell	19/12/84	6 1.0	12 10	Motherwell B.C.
McCulloch	Lee		14/05/78	Bellshill	17/08/95	5 11.0	12 5	Cumbernauld United
McKinnon	Robert		31/07/66	Glasgow	08/01/92	5 10.0	11 12	Hartlepool United
McLeish	Alexander		21/01/59	Glasgow	15/07/94	6 1.5	13 4	Aberdeen
McMillan	Stephen		19/01/76	Edinburgh	19/08/93	5 10.0	11 0	Troon Juniors
McSkimming	Shaun	Peter	29/05/70	Stranraer	03/11/94	5 11.0	10 8	Kilmarnock
Philliben	John		14/03/64	Stirling	05/09/86	5 11.5	12 7	Doncaster Rovers
Rae	Derek		02/08/74	Glasgow	02/09/94	5 10.0	10 10	Rangers
Ritchie	Innes		24/08/73	Edinburgh	14/08/93	6 0.0	12 7	Bathgate Thistle
Roarty	David	Francis	19/08/77	Glasgow	02/08/95	5 11.0	11 4	Motherwell B.C.
Roddie	Andrew	Robert	04/11/71	Glasgow	20/08/94	5 10.5	11 6	Aberdeen
Ross	Ian		27/08/74	Broxburn	14/08/93	5 10.0	10 7	Bathgate Thistle
Shields	Alan		27/04/77	Banbury	17/08/95	5 10.0	10 7	Cumbernauld United
Van Der Gaag	Mitchell		27/10/71	Zutphen	22/03/95	6 2.0	12 4	PSV Eindhoven
Williamson	David		15/12/75	Hong Kong	07/09/95	5 8.0	10 2	Irvine Vics
Woods	Stephen	Gerard	23/02/70	Glasgow	22/07/94	6 2.0	12 0	Preston North End

MILESTONES

YEAR OF FORMATION: 1886
MOST CAPPED PLAYER: George Stevenson
NO. OF CAPS: 12
MOST LEAGUE POINTS IN A SEASON: 66 (Division 1 - Season 1931/32)
MOST LEAGUE GOALS SCORED BY A PLAYER IN A SEASON: William McFadyen (Season 1931/32)
NO. OF GOALS SCORED: 52
RECORD ATTENDANCE: 35,632 (-v- Rangers – Scottish Cup 12.3.1952)
RECORD VICTORY: 12-1 (-v- Dundee United – Division 2, 23.1.1954)
RECORD DEFEAT: 0-8 (-v- Aberdeen - Premier Division, 26.3.1979)

SEASON TICKET INFORMATION

Main Stand (Members) Adult £175
Juvenile/OAP £100
Main Stand Family Section
Parent & Juvenile £205 plus an additional £30 for every
other Juvenile
David Cooper Stand Adult £160
Juvenile/OAP £95
David Cooper Stand Family Section
Parent & Juvenile £190, plus an additional £30 for every
other Juvenile
East Stand Adult £145
Juvenile/OAP £80

LEAGUE ADMISSION PRICES

Main Stand (Members) Adult....................£11
Juvenile/OAP..........£6
Main Stand Family Section Parent & Juvenile £13 plus
an additional £2 for every other Juvenile
David Cooper Stand Adult....................£10
Juvenile/OAP..........£6
David Cooper Stand (Family Section) Parent & Juvenile
£12, plus an additional £2 for every other Juvenile
East Stand Adult....................£9
Juvenile/OAP..........£5
South Stand (Visiting Fans Only) Adult....................£10
Juvenile/OAP..........£6
South Stand (Family Section) Parent & Juvenile £12
plus an additional £2 for every other Juvenile

The WELL

Small bold figures denote goalscorers. † denotes opponent's own goal.

Date	Venue	Opponents	Result	Woods S	Shannon R	McKinnon R	Philliben J	Martin E	McCart C	Lambert P	Davies W	Coyne T	O'Donnell P	Kirk S	Dolan J	Roddie A	Burns A	Arnott D	McGrillen P	McLeish A	McSkimming S	Krivokapic M	Howie S	McMillan S	May E	Van Der Gaag M	Ritchie I
Aug 13	A	Rangers	1-2	1	2	3	4	5	6	7	8	9^1	10	11													
20	H	Heart of Midlothian	1-1	1	2		3	5	6	7		9^1	10	8	4	11	14										
27	A	Kilmarnock	1-0	1	2		3	5	6	7	8	9^1	10	12	4	11	14										
Sep 10	A	Dundee United	1-1	1		3	2	5	6	7	11	9		4^1	8			10	14								
17	H	Hibernian	1-1	1	2^1	3	4	5	6	7	11	9	12		8			10	14								
24	A	Partick Thistle	2-2	1	2	3	4	5	6	7	11^1	9^1	12		8			10	14								
Oct 1	A	Celtic	1-1	1	2	3	4	5	6	7	11	9	12		8		14	10^1									
8	H	Falkirk	5-3	1	7	3	4	5		7	11^1	9^2			8		14	10^2	6								
15	A	Aberdeen	3-1	1	2	3^1	4	5	6	7	11	9^1	12^1		8		14	10									
22	H	Rangers	2-1	1	2	3	4	5	6	7	11	9			8		14	10^2									
29	H	Kilmarnock	3-7	1	2	3	4	5^1		7	11	9^2	12		8			10	6								
Nov 5	A	Heart of Midlothian	2-1	1	2^1	3	4	5	6	7	11	9^1	12		8		14	10									
8	H	Dundee United	1-1	1	2	3	4	5^1	6	7	11	9	12		8		14	10									
19	A	Hibernian	2-2	1	2	3	4	5	6	7	11^1	9^1			8			10				14					
26	H	Partick Thistle	3-1	1	2	3	4	5	6	7	11^1	9^1	12		8		14	10^1									
Dec 3	A	Celtic	2-2	1	2	3	4	5	6	7	11	9^2			8			10									
10	H	Aberdeen	0-1	1	2	3	4	5	6	7	11	9	12		8		14	10									
26	A	Falkirk	1-0	1	2^1	3	4		6	7	11	9						10			8			5			
31	H	Rangers	1-3	1	2	3	4		6	7	11	9	12					10		14^1	8			5			
Jan 8	H	Heart of Midlothian	1-2	1	2	3	4		6	7	11	9					14			10^1	8			5			
13	H	Hibernian	0-0		7	3		5	6	7	10	9	12		8						11	4	1				
17	A	Kilmarnock	0-2		7	3		5	6	7	11	9	10		8						14	4	1				
21	A	Dundee United	1-6		2	3		5		7	11	9^1	10		8			14			12	6	4				1
Feb 4	H	Celtic	1-0	1		3^1	2	5	6	7	11	9			8			10			12	4			14		
25	A	Aberdeen	2-0	1	12	3^1		5	6	7					8		14	9^1	10		11	4			2		
Mar 7	H	Falkirk	2-2	1		3	2	5	6	7^1					8		14	9	10		4				11^1		
14	A	Partick Thistle	0-0	1		3		5	6	7	11				8			9	10		4				2		
18	H	Dundee United	2-1	1			6	5		7	11				8	12		9^1	10^1		4				3	2	
22	H	Hibernian	0-2	1	14		6			7	11	12			8			9	10		4				3	2	
Apr 1	A	Celtic	1-1	1		3		5		7	11	9^1			8	12		10			14	4			2	6	
8	H	Partick Thistle	1-2	1		3	14	5		7	11	9			8	2		10^1			12	4				6	
15	A	Falkirk	0-3	1	2	3	6	5		7		9			8			12	10		11	4					
18	H	Aberdeen	2-1	1		3	6	5		7		9			8	14		12	10^1		11^1	4			2		
29	A	Rangers	2-0	1		3	4	5		7	11	9			8		14	10^1			6^1				2		
May 6	H	Kilmarnock	2-0	1		3	4	5		7	11	9			8		14	10^1			6				2^1		
13	A	Heart of Midlothian	0-2	1			3	4	5	7	11				12			9	10		6				2		8
TOTAL FULL APPEARANCES				33	23	32	30	32	24	36	31	30	3	6	31	4	7	26	2	2	10	16	3	2	10	2	1
TOTAL SUB APPEARANCES					(2)		(1)				(1)		(12)	(15)		(7)	(1)	(5)			(4)			(1)			
TOTAL GOALS SCORED					3	3		2		1	4	16	2					3			10	2			2		

FIR PARK

CAPACITY: 13,741 (All seated)

PITCH DIMENSIONS: 110 yds x 75 yds

FACILITIES FOR DISABLED SUPPORTERS: Area between Main Stand and South Stand. Prior arrangement must be made with the Secretary and a ticket obtained.

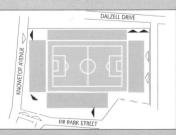

HOW TO GET THERE

The following routes can be used to reach Fir Park:

BUSES: Fir Park is less than a quarter of a mile from the main thoroughfare through the town and numerous buses serving Lanarkshire and Glasgow all pass along this road. De-bus at the Civic Centre.

TRAINS: Motherwell Station is a main-line station on the Glasgow–London (Euston) route, and the station is particularly well served by trains running from numerous points throughout the Strathclyde Region. Motherwell station is a twenty minute walk from Fir Park, while the new station at Airbles is only fifteen minutes away.

CARS: Car Parking is only available in the many side streets around the ground. There is no major parking area close to Fir Park.

PARTICK THISTLE

Firhill Stadium, 80 Firhill Road,
Glasgow G20 7BA

CHAIRMAN
James Oliver

VICE-CHAIRMAN
T. Brown McMaster

DIRECTORS
Angus MacSween, Harry F. Scott,
Robert G.S. McCamley

PRESIDENT
James R. Aitken

SECRETARY
Robert W. Reid

MANAGER
Murdo MacLeod

ASSISTANT MANAGER
Gordon Chisholm

CLUB DOCTOR
Alan W. Robertson

PHYSIOTHERAPIST
Frank Ness

S.F.A. COMMUNITY COACH
Graham Diamond

CHIEF SCOUT
Robert Dinnie

CHIEF OF SECURITY
Bill McPhie

GROUNDSMAN
David Lyle

COMMERCIAL MANAGER
Tommy Dickson
0141-945 4811

TELEPHONES
Ground/Ticket Office/Commercial
0141- 945 4811
Fax 0141-945 1525

CLUB SHOP
c/o 90 Firhill Road, Glasgow G20 7AL
Tel 0141-945 4811. Open Tues-Thurs
12.30-5.30 p.m. and Fri 12.30-
5.00p.m. and matchdays/evenings

OFFICIAL SUPPORTERS CLUB
Ms. Morag McHaffie
99 Somerville Drive, Glasgow,
G42 9BH. Tel 0141-632 3604

TEAM CAPTAIN
Albert Craig

SHIRT SPONSOR
Texstyle World

LIST OF PLAYERS 1995-96

SURNAME	FIRST NAME	MIDDLE NAME	DATE OF BIRTH	PLACE OF BIRTH	DATE OF SIGNING	HEIGHT FT INS	WEIGHT ST LBS	PREVIOUS CLUB
Adams	Charles	Stuart	21/03/76	Irvine	12/09/95	5 10.0	11 5	Kilwinning Rangers
Archibald	Alan	Maxwell	13/12/77	Glasgow	13/06/94	5 9.0	11 7	Possilpark Y.M.C.A.
Ayton	Stuart		19/10/75	Glasgow	01/07/94	5 8.0	10 12	Rangers
Budinauckas	Kevin		16/09/74	Bellshill	10/08/92	5 10.0	11 0	Armadale Thistle
Cairns	Mark	Henry	25/09/69	Edinburgh	28/10/94	6 0.0	13 2	Gala Fairydean
Cameron	Ian		24/08/66	Glasgow	30/07/92	5 9.0	10 4	Aberdeen
Craig	Albert	Hughes	03/01/62	Glasgow	28/08/92	5 8.0	11 5	Dundee
Curran	Henry		09/10/66	Glasgow	29/07/95	5 8.0	11 8	St. Johnstone
Dinnie	Alan		14/05/63	Glasgow	27/08/94	5 10.0	11 5	Dundee
Docherty	Stephen		18/02/76	Glasgow	25/08/93	5 8.0	10 10	Pollok Juniors
Foster	Wayne	Paul	11/09/63	Tyldesley	02/12/94	5 10.0	12 3	Heart of Midlothian
Gibson	Andrew		02/02/69	Dechmont	18/12/93	5 9.5	11 10	Aberdeen
Gormill	Steven	David	16/02/78	Lanark	01/07/94	5 6.0	9 9	Possilpark Y.M.C.A.
Gray	Donal		22/05/77	Newry	22/09/94	5 8.0	12 0	Portadown
Hutton	Mark	Stephen	29/11/75	Falkirk	25/08/95	5 11.0	12 5	Shettleston Juniors
McDonald	Rodney		20/03/67	London	23/09/94	5 10.5	12 2	Walsall
McKee	Kevin	George	10/06/66	Edinburgh	13/09/94	5 8.0	11 11	Hamilton Academical
MacLeod	Murdo	Davidson	24/09/58	Glasgow	16/08/95	5 9.0	12 4	Dumbarton
McWilliams	Derek		16/01/66	Broxburn	02/08/94	5 10 .0	12 0	Dunfermline Athletic
Milne	Callum		27/08/65	Edinburgh	04/09/93	5 8.5	10 7	Hibernian
Pittman	Stephen	Lee	18/07/67	North Carolina	09/09/94	5 10.0	12 0	Dundee
Ramsay	Scott	McKenna	02/10/75	Glasgow	30/08/95	5 7.0	11 5	Shettleston Juniors
Smith	Thomas	William	12/10/73	Glasgow	12/01/95	5 8.5	11 7	Portadown
Stirling	Jered		13/10/76	Stirling	29/09/93	6 0.0	11 6	St. Rochs
Tierney	Peter	Grant	11/10/61	Falkirk	17/07/90	6 0.5	13 13	Dunfermline Athletic
Turner	Thomas	Gibson	11/10/63	Johnstone	31/12/94	5 10.0	10 7	St. Johnstone
Walker	Joseph	Nicol	29/09/62	Aberdeen	02/12/94	6 2.0	12 7	Heart of Midlothian
Watson	Gregg		21/09/70	Glasgow	14/08/93	5 9.5	10 9	Aberdeen
Welsh	Steven	George	19/04/68	Glasgow	26/12/94	6 0.0	12 2	Peterborough United
West	Joseph		02/08/78	Glasgow	02/08/94	5 5.0	9 0	Wolves B.C.

MILESTONES

YEAR OF FORMATION: 1876
MOST CAPPED PLAYER: Alan Rough
NO. OF CAPS: 53
MOST LEAGUE POINTS IN A SEASON: 57 (First Division - Season 1991/92)
MOST LEAGUE GOALS SCORED BY A PLAYER IN A SEASON: Alec Hair (Season 1926/27)
NO. OF GOALS SCORED: 41
RECORD ATTENDANCE: 49,838 (-v- Rangers – 18.2.1922)
RECORD VICTORY: 16-0 (-v- Royal Albert – Scottish Cup 17.1.1931)
RECORD DEFEAT: 0-10 (-v- Queen's Park - Scottish Cup 3.12.1881)

SEASON TICKET INFORMATION

Seated
Adult £180
OAP/Under 16/Student £100
Under 12 ....£50

LEAGUE ADMISSION PRICES

Seated
Adult £10
Juvenile/OAP £5
Standing
Adult £8
Juvenile/OAP £4

CLUB FACTFILE 1994/95
RESULTS .. APPEARANCES .. SCORERS

The JAGS

Small bold figures denote goalscorers. † denotes opponent's own goal.

Date	Venue	Opponents	Result	Nelson C.	Byrne D.	Law R.	Jamieson M.	Tierney P.S.	McWilliams D.	Tayor A.	Craig A.	Grant R.	English I.	Charnley J.	Cameron I.	Smith T.	Dinnie A.	Docherty S.	Pittman S.	Watson G.	Gibson A.	McKee K.	McDonald R.	Murdoch A.	Walker J.N.	Milne C.	Foster W.	Welsh S.	Turner T.	Gray D.	Cairns M.	Eli R.	Ayton S.
Aug 13	H	Kilmarnock	2-0	1	2	3	4	5	6[1]	7	8	9	10[1]	11																			
20	A	Rangers	0-2	1	2	3	4	5	6	7	8	9	10	11	12		14																
27	A	Falkirk	1-2	1	2		4	5	6	7	8	9[1]	10	11	12	3	14																
Sep 10	H	Celtic	1-2	1	2		5		6	11	8	9[1]			12	7			3	4		10											
17	A	Aberdeen	1-1	1	2		5		6	11[1]		7	12		3				4	10	14												
24	H	Motherwell	2-2	1			5		6		8	9[1]		11	14	10	2		3	1	12	7[1]											
Oct 1	A	Hibernian	0-3		2		5		6		8	12	10	11	14	9			3	4		7	1										
8	H	Heart of Midlothian	0-1		2		5		6	12		9		11	10	8			3	4	14	7	1										
15	A	Dundee United	1-0	1	2		5		6	8		14	10	11[1]		12			3	4	9	7											
22	A	Kilmarnock	0-2	1	2	14	5					12	10	11	6	8			3	4	9	7											
29	H	Falkirk	1-2	1		14	5		6	8		9[1]	12	11		10			3	4	7	2											
Nov 5	A	Rangers	0-3	1			5	11		8		12	14	10	6				3	4	9	2	7										
9	A	Celtic	0-0	1			5		6	8		9	14	11	7				3	4	10	2											
19	A	Aberdeen	2-1	1			5		6	8[1]				11	10	3				4	9[1]	2	7										
26	A	Motherwell	1-3	1	12		5		6	8		14		11	10[1]	3				4	9	2	7										
Dec 3	H	Hibernian	2-2		4			6		8		12[1]	11	10	3						2	7	1	5	9[1]								
26	A	Heart of Midlothian	0-3		14					8	12		11	10	6				4		2	7	1	3	9	5							
31	H	Kilmarnock	2-2	2	14					8	12		11		6	3			4		7[2]	1		9	5	10							
Jan 7	H	Rangers	1-1				9	11[1]	8				10	12	2				3	4	7	1		5	6								
14	A	Aberdeen	1-3				9	11	8				10	12	2	3[1]	4				7	1		5	6	14							
17	A	Falkirk	3-1				9[1]	11	8				10	12	2[1]	3	4				1	7[1]		5	6								
21	H	Celtic	0-0				9	11	8				10	12	2	3	4		14		7		5	6									
Feb 4	A	Hibernian	2-1				14	11	8				10		2	3	4			7[1]	1	12	9	5	6[1]								
25	A	Dundee United	0-7				14	12	11	8			10		2	3	4			7	9	5	6	1									
Mar 7	H	Dundee United	2-0					11	8				10	14[1]		3	4		2	7	1	9[1]		5	6								
11	A	Aberdeen	2-2					11	8	14			10	12		3[1]	4		2	7	1	9		5	6[1]								
14	H	Motherwell	0-0					11	8	7			10			2	3	4	2	14	1	9		5	6								
Apr 1	H	Hibernian	2-2					11	12	8			10			3	4		2	7	1	9[2]		5	6					14			
4	H	Heart of Midlothian	3-1					11[1]	12	8			10			3[1]	4		2	7[1]	1	9		5	6					14			
8	A	Motherwell	2-1					11	12	8[1]	14		10[1]			3	4		2	7	1	9		5	6								
15	A	Heart of Midlothian	1-0				9	11	8	12			10		14[1]	3	4		2	7	1			5	6								
18	H	Dundee United	1-3				9	11	8	7			10			3[1]	4		12		1			5	6								
29	A	Kilmarnock	0-0					6	8	9			11	10	7	2	3		4		1			5									
May 2	A	Celtic	3-1					14	8	9[1]			11	10	3	2					1	7[2]		5									
6	H	Falkirk	0-0					6	8	9			11	10	2	4	3				1	7		5									
13	A	Rangers	1-1				5	11[1]		14			10	8	3	4			7		1	2	9	6									12
TOTAL FULL APPEARANCES				13	11	2	15	4	27	17	30	14	6	19	27	8	23		27	29	9	16	22	2	20	3	16	20	15				1
TOTAL SUB APPEARANCES				(1)	(3)		(1)	(2)	(6)			(9)	(5)	(1)	(7)	(6)	(2)	(1)		(2)	(1)	(3)			(1)			(1)		(2)	(1)		
TOTAL GOALS SCORED										3		2	2	5	2	1	3		1	2		4		1			5	7	2			

FIRHILL STADIUM

CAPACITY: 21,776; Seated 9,076 Standing 12,700

PITCH DIMENSIONS: 110 yds x 74 yds

FACILITIES FOR DISABLED SUPPORTERS: Covered places available in North Enclosure. 10 Wheelchair spectators, 10 attendants, 10 ambulant disabled. Telephone call in advance to Office Secretary for arrangements.

FIRHILL ROAD

HOW TO GET THERE

The following routes may be used to reach Firhill Stadium:

TRAINS: The nearest railway stations are Glasgow Queen Street and Glasgow Central and buses from the centre of the city pass within 100 yards of the ground.

BUSES: The following from the city centre all pass by the park. Nos. 1, 18, 21, 21A, 57, 60, 61 and 61R and the frequency of the buses is just over 12 minutes.

UNDERGROUND: The nearest GGPTE Underground station is St.George's Cross and supporters walking from here should pass through Cromwell Street into Maryhill Road and then walk up this road as far as Firhill Street. The ground is then on the right. The Kelvinbridge Underground Station is also not far from the park and supporters from here should walk along Great Western Road as far as Napiershill Street and then follow this into Maryhill Road.

RAITH ROVERS

LIST OF PLAYERS 1995-96

SURNAME	FIRST NAME	MIDDLE NAME	DATE OF BIRTH	PLACE OF BIRTH	DATE OF SIGNING	HEIGHT FT INS	WEIGHT ST LBS	PREVIOUS CLUB
Black	Derek	John	15/12/77	Uphall	26/08/94	5 11.0	10 4	Livingston U'15
Broddle	Julian		01/11/64	Sheffield	14/07/93	5 9.0	12 8	Partick Thistle
Buist	Mark		13/09/75	Kirkcaldy	20/07/93	6 0.0	11 12	Glenrothes Strollers
Cameron	Colin		23/10/72	Kirkcaldy	30/04/92	5 5.5	9 6	Sligo Rovers
Cochrane	Matthew		06/04/77	Bellshill	20/08/94	5 11.0	11 4	Bothkennar B.C.
Coyle	Ronald		04/08/64	Glasgow	08/01/88	5 11.0	12 9	Rochdale
Crawford	Stephen		09/01/74	Dunfermline	13/08/92	5 10.0	10 7	Rosyth Recreation
Dair	Jason		15/06/74	Dunfermline	03/07/91	5 11.0	10 8	Castlebridge
Dennis	Shaun		20/12/69	Kirkcaldy	03/08/88	6 1.0	13 7	Lochgelly Albert
Drummond	John	George	12/12/77	Dunfermline	21/07/94	5 10.0	9 8	Inverkeithing Utd. 'U16
Forrest	Gordon	Iain	14/01/77	Dunfermline	21/07/93	5 6.0	8 2	Rosyth Recreation
Fridge	Leslie	Francis	27/08/68	Inverness	05/07/95	5 11.0	11 10	Clyde
Graham	Alastair		11/08/66	Glasgow	23/09/93	6 3.0	12 7	Motherwell
Kirkwood	David	Stewart	27/08/67	St. Andrews	10/08/94	5 10.0	11 7	Airdrieonians
Lennon	Daniel	Joseph	06/04/69	Whitburn	31/03/94	5 5.0	10 8	Hibernian
McAnespie	Stephen		01/02/72	Kilmarnock	25/01/94	5 9.0	10 7	Vasterhaninge I.F.
McInally	James	Edward	19/02/64	Glasgow	07/07/95	5 8.5	11 4	Dundee United
McKinlay	Craig		19/10/76	Edinburgh	13/08/93	5 9.5	11 6	I.C.I. Grangemouth
McMillan	Ian		09/06/76	Broxburn	31/03/93	5 10.0	11 4	Armadale Thistle
McPherson	Dean		07/06/78	Aberdeen	06/08/94	5 10.0	9 9	Hutchison Vale B.C.
Nicholl	James	Michael	20/12/56	Hamilton, Canada	27/11/90	5 10.0	11 10	Dunfermline Athletic
Potter	Brian		26/01/77	Dunfermline	13/08/93	5 10.5	11 5	Rosyth Recreation
Quinn	Mark		14/05/75	Broxburn	27/02/93	5 8.0	10 2	Strathbrock U18's
Raeside	Robert		07/07/72	South Africa	13/09/90	6 0.0	11 10	St.Andrews United
Robertson	Graham		02/11/76	Edinburgh	03/08/93	5 11.0	10 10	Balgonie Colts U16
Rougier	Anthony	Leo	17/07/71	Trinidad & Tobago	13/03/95	6 0.0	14 1	Trinity Pros
Sellars	Neil	Andrew	09/05/77	Kirkcaldy	03/08/94	5 8.0	9 11	Kirkcaldy Y.M.
Sinclair	David		06/10/69	Dunfermline	11/02/92	5 11.0	12 10	Portadown
Taylor	Alexander		13/06/62	Baillieston	05/07/95	5 9.5	11 7	Partick Thistle
Thomson	Scott	Yuill	08/11/66	Edinburgh	08/09/93	6 0.0	11 9	Forfar Athletic
Wilson	Barry	John	16/02/72	Kirkcaldy	03/09/94	5 11.0	12 4	Ross County

MILESTONES

YEAR OF FORMATION: 1883
MOST CAPPED PLAYER: David Morris
NO. OF CAPS: 6
MOST LEAGUE POINTS IN A SEASON: 65 (First Division - Season 1992/93) – 2 points for a win
69 (First Division - Season 1994/95) – 3 points for a win
MOST LEAGUE GOALS SCORED BY A PLAYER IN A SEASON: Norman Heywood (Season 1937/38)
NO. OF GOALS SCORED: 42
RECORD ATTENDANCE: 31,306 (-v- Heart of Midlothian – Scottish Cup 7.2.1953)
RECORD VICTORY: 10-1 (-v- Coldstream – Scottish Cup 13.2.1954)
RECORD DEFEAT: 2-11 (-v- Morton – Division 2 18.3.1936)

SEASON TICKET INFORMATION

Seated
A & B Stands   Adult £205
                   Juvenile/OAP £95
New Stand   Adult £185
                   Juvenile/OAP £85
Standing
Enclosure   Adult £150
                   Juvenile/OAP £80
Ground   Adult £140
                   Juvenile/OAP £70

LEAGUE ADMISSION PRICES

Seated
A & B Stands   Adult £10
                   Juvenile/OAP £5
New Stand   Adult £9
                   Juvenile/OAP £5
Standing
Enclosure   Adult £8.50
                   Juvenile/OAP £4.50
Ground   Adult £8
                   Juvenile/OAP £4

Stark's Park, Pratt Street,
Kirkcaldy, Fife KY1 1SA

CHAIRMAN
Alexander A. Penman

VICE-CHAIRMAN
William Shedden

DIRECTORS
Charles A. Cant
William H. Gray

GENERAL MANAGER
William McPhee

PLAYER/MANAGER
James M. Nicholl

ASSISTANT MANAGER
Martin Harvey

YOUTH COACHES
Jimmy Thomson & Derek Smith

CLUB DOCTOR
Dr. G. K. N. Hall

PHYSIOTHERAPIST
Gerry Docherty

GROUNDSMAN
Scott Paterson

COMMERCIAL DEPARTMENT
Lynn Penman
(01592) 263514

TELEPHONES
Ground (01592) 263514
Fax (01592) 642833
Ticket Office (01592) 263514
Club Call 0891 884479

CLUB SHOP
16 Links Street, Kirkcaldy
Tel (01592) 201993.
Open Mon-Fri 9.00 am – 5.00 pm
(Early closing Wed at 1.00 pm).
Sat 9.00 am – 3.00 pm on Home
Match Days and 9.00 am – 5.00 pm
on Away Match Days.

OFFICIAL SUPPORTERS CLUB
c/o Fraser Hamilton,
22 Tower Terrace, Kirkcaldy, Fife

TEAM CAPTAIN
Shaun Dennis

SHIRT SPONSOR
Kelly's Copiers

CLUB FACTFILE 1994/95
RESULTS .. APPEARANCES .. SCORERS

The ROVERS

Small bold figures denote goalscorers. † denotes opponent's own goal.

Date	Venue	Opponents	Result	Thomson S.	Rowbotham J.	Kirkwood D.	Coyle R.	Dennis S.	Sinclair C.	Lennon D.	Dalziel G.	Graham A.	Cameron C.	Dair J.	Crawford S.	Raeside F.	Broddle J.	McAnespie S.	Redford I.	Narey D.	Wilson B.	Nichol J.	Allan R.	McMillan I.	Rougier A.
Aug 13	H	St. Johnstone	1-1	1	2	3	4	5	6	7	8	9	10^{1}	11	12	14									
20	H	Hamilton Academical	1-1	1	2		4		6	7	8	9^{1}	10	11	12	5	3	14							
27	A	Dunfermline Athletic	0-1	1			4		5	7	12	9	8	10	11		3	2	6						
Sep 3	H	Clydebank	1-1	1	4				6	7	8	9	10^{1}		12		3	2	11	5					
10	A	Stranraer	0-0	1	4	12			6	7	8	9	10				3	2	11	5	14				
24	A	St. Mirren	2-1	1	4			5		7	12	9^{1}	10	11	8^{1}		3	2	6		14				
Oct 1	H	Ayr United	3-0	1				5	6	4	12^{2}	9	10	11	8^{1}		3	2				7			
8	A	Airdrieonians	0-0	1		12		5	6	4	8	9	10		11		3	2			14	7			
15	H	Dundee	1-1	1	14			5	6	7	8	9	10^{1}	12	11		3	2	4						
22	A	St. Johnstone	1-3	1		7		5	4		8^{1}	9	10	11	12		3	2	6		14				
29	H	Dunfermline Athletic	2-5		14			5	4	7	12	9	10		8		3	2	6			11^{2}	1		
Nov 5	A	Hamilton Academical	3-0	1		12		5			8^{1}	9	10	14	11^{2}		3	2	6	7					
12	H	Stranraer	4-2	1	14			5		4	8^{3}	9^{1}	10	12	11		3	2	6	7					
19	A	Clydebank	3-0	1	4			5			8^{1}	9^{1}	10	12	11		3	2	7	6^{1}				14	
Dec 3	A	Ayr United	1-1	1	12	14		5	4		8^{1}		10		9		3	2	7	6	11				
6	H	St. Mirren	1-1	1	12	14		5	4		8^{1}		10		9		3	2	7	6	11				
10	A	Dundee	1-2	1	4				6		8^{1}		10		9		3	2	11	5	12	7			
26	A	Airdrieonians	3-2	1				5	12^{1}		8^{1}	9	10^{1}		11		3	2	6	4		7			
31	A	St. Johnstone	2-0	1		12		5	4		8^{1}	9	10		11		3^{1}	2	7	6		14			
Jan 7	H	Hamilton Academical	2-0	1		11		5	4^{1}		8	9	10^{1}				3	2	6	14		7			
11	A	Dunfermline Athletic	1-0	1	3	11		5	6		8	9^{1}	10					2	4	14		7			
14	H	Clydebank	1-0	1	3			5^{1}		4	8		10	14	9			2	6	11		7			
24	A	Stranraer	4-2	1		12			4	10	8^{1}				9^{1}	5	3	2	6	11^{2}		7			
Feb 4	A	Ayr United	2-1	1	14		4	5	7^{1}	10	8	12			9^{1}	6	3	2		11					
11	A	St. Mirren	2-1	1			4	5	8	11		9	14		10^{2}	6	3	2		7					
25	H	Dundee	0-0	1	3		4	5	6		12	9	8	11	10		14	2		7					
Mar 6	A	Airdrieonians	2-1	1	3			5	6	4		9^{1}	8	11^{1}	10			2		7					
18	H	Stranraer	1-1	1	3	2		5			8^{1}	9	6		10				4	14		7			11
Apr 1	H	Ayr United	1-0	1	3	10^{1}	4	5	11			14	12	7	9	6		2							8
4	A	Clydebank	†2-1	1	3	7	4	5	6	10		8	11		9^{1}			2				14			
8	H	St. Mirren	2-1	1		3	4	5	6	11		9	7^{2}		10		14	2		12					8
15	H	Airdrieonians	0-1	1		3		5	6	4	12	9	8	11	10		2	14		7					
22	A	Dundee	2-0	1		12			4		8		10	14	9^{1}	5	3	2	6	11^{1}	7				
29	A	St. Johnstone	†2-1	1	12				6		8		10		9^{1}	5	3	2	4	11	7				14
May 6	H	Dunfermline Athletic	0-0	1		14			6	12	8		10	11	9	5	3	2	4	7					
13	A	Hamilton Academical	0-0	1				5	11		8		10	9		6	3	2	4	14	7				
TOTAL FULL APPEARANCES				35	14	9	9	26	31	19	25	25	32	12	28	9	26	33	11	21	14	13	1		3
TOTAL SUB APPEARANCES					(6)	(10)			(1)	(1)	(6)	(2)	(2)	(6)	(4)	(1)	(2)	(1)	(1)		(12)			(1)	(1)
TOTAL GOALS SCORED						1			1	3	15	6	7	1	11		1			1	5				

STARK'S PARK

CAPACITY: 9,300; Seated 2,939, Standing 6,361

PITCH DIMENSIONS: 113 yds x 70 yds

FACILITIES FOR DISABLED SUPPORTERS: By prior arrangement with the Secretary.

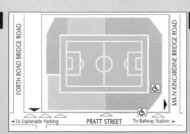

FORTH ROAD BRIDGE ROAD — MAN KINCARDINE BRIDGE ROAD
◄ To Esplanade Parking · PRATT STREET · To Railway Station ►

HOW TO GET THERE

The following routes may be used to reach Stark's Park:

TRAINS: Kirkcaldy railway station is served by trains from Dundee, Edinburgh and Glasgow (via Edinburgh) and the ground is within walking distance of the station.

BUSES: The main bus station in Kirkcaldy is also within 15 minutes walking distance of the ground, but the Edinburgh, Dunfermline and Leven services pass close by the park.

CARS: Car parking is available in the Esplanade, which is on the south side of the ground, in Beveridge Park, which is on the north side of Stark's Road, and in ground adjacent to the railway station.

Ibrox Stadium, Glasgow G51 2XD

CHAIRMAN
David E. Murray
VICE-CHAIRMAN
Donald R. Findlay Q.C., LL.B.
DIRECTORS
Hugh R. W. Adam, John Gillespie,
R. Campbell Ogilvie,
Walter Smith, Ian Skelly
SECRETARY
R. Campbell Ogilvie
MANAGER
Walter Smith
ASSISTANT MANAGER
Archie Knox
FIRST TEAM COACH
Davie Dodds
RESERVE COACH
John McGregor
YOUTH COACH
John Chalmers
S.F.A. COMMUNITY OFFICER
Ewan Chester
CLUB DOCTOR
Dr. Donald Cruickshank
PHYSIOTHERAPIST
Grant Downie
PUBLIC RELATIONS EXECUTIVE
John Greig M.B.E.
FINANCIAL CONTROLLER
Douglas Odam
OPERATIONS EXECUTIVE
Alistair Hood Q.P.M.
RANGERS CATERING MANAGER
Peter Kingstone
MANAGER, MARKETING & PUBLICATIONS DEPARTMENT
Brian Main
COMMERCIAL SALES EXECUTIVE
John Lawson
STADIUM ACCESS ADMINISTRATOR
Ian Hosie
PITCH SUPERINTENDENT
Alan Ferguson
COMMERCIAL MANAGER
Bob Riley 0141-427 8822
STADIUM PROPERTY MANAGER
Tom Onions
TELEPHONES
Ground/Public Relations Department
Tel 0141-427 8500 Fax 0141-427 2676
Stadium Access Administration (Tickets)
Tel 0141-427 8800 Fax 0141-427 8504

CLUB SHOPS
The Rangers Shop,
150 Copland Road, Glasgow G51.
Open 10.00 a.m.–5.00 p.m. Matchdays Only.
The Rangers Shop, 103 St. Vincent Street,
Glasgow G2. Open 10.00 a.m.–5.30 p.m.
The Rangers Shop,
100 Edmiston Drive, Glasgow G51. Open
9.45 a.m.–5.00 p.m. Mon to Sat.
OFFICIAL SUPPORTERS CLUB
Rangers F.C. Supporters' Association,
250 Edmiston Drive, Glasgow G51 1YU
TEAM CAPTAIN
Richard Gough
SHIRT SPONSOR
McEwan's Lager

RANGERS

LIST OF PLAYERS 1995-96

SURNAME	FIRST NAME	MIDDLE NAME	DATE OF BIRTH	PLACE OF BIRTH	DATE OF SIGNING	HEIGHT FT INS	WEIGHT ST LBS	PREVIOUS CLUB
Bollan	Gary		24/03/73	Dundee	27/01/95	5 11.0	12 12	Dundee United
Boyack	Steven		04/09/76	Edinburgh	01/07/93	5 10.0	10 7	Rangers B.C.
Brown	John		26/01/62	Stirling	15/01/88	5 11.0	11 2	Dundee
Cleland	Alexander		10/12/70	Glasgow	27/01/95	5 8.5	11 7	Dundee United
Dair	Lee		28/05/77	Dunfermline	01/07/93	5 10.0	11 10	Rangers B.C.
Davidson	William		09/07/78	Glasgow	06/07/94	5 8.0	10 0	Rangers S.A.B.C.
Douglas	John		05/09/77	Belfast	06/07/94	5 8.0	11 7	Rangers S.A.B.C.
Durie	Gordon	Scott	06/12/65	Paisley	24/11/93	5 10.0	12 13	Tottenham Hotspur
Durrant	Ian		29/10/66	Glasgow	27/07/84	5 8.0	9 7	Glasgow United
Ferguson	Barry		02/02/78	Glasgow	06/07/94	5 7.0	9 10	Rangers S.A.B.C.
Ferguson	Ian		15/03/67	Glasgow	15/02/88	5 10.0	10 11	St. Mirren
Fitzgerald	Darren		13/10/78	Belfast	06/07/94	5 8.0	10 0	St. Andrews B.C.
Fotheringham	Kevin	George	13/08/75	Dunfermline	06/05/92	5 10.0	11 4	Rangers B.C.
Galloway	Andrew		12/03/77	Glasgow	01/07/93	5 10.0	11 5	Rangers B.C.
Gascoigne	Paul		27/05/67	Gateshead	10/07/95	5 9.0	11 10	Lazio Societa Sportiva
Goram	Andrew	Lewis	13/04/64	Bury	27/06/91	5 11.0	12 13	Hibernian
Gough	Charles	Richard	05/04/62	Stockholm	02/10/87	6 0.0	11 12	Tottenham Hotspur
Graham	David		06/10/78	Edinburgh	03/07/95	5 10.0	10 10	Rangers S.A.B.C.
Haggarty	Francis		16/11/78	Glasgow	03/07/95	5 7.0	9 3	Rangers S.A.B.C.
Hateley	Mark		07/11/61	Wallasey	19/07/90	6 2.5	13 0	A.S. Monaco
Jardine	Christopher		26/11/78	Dumfries	03/07/95	5 6.0	8 10	Rangers S.A.B.C.
Juttla	Jaswinder	Singh	02/08/77	Glasgow	06/07/94	5 6.0	9 13	Rangers S.A.B.C.
Kerr	Roddy		04/05/77	Bellshill	09/07/93	5 8.0	9 7	"S" Form
Laudrup	Brian		22/02/69	Vienna	21/07/94	6 0.0	13 0	Fiorentina AC
Matheson	Ross		15/11/77	Greenock	06/07/94	5 6.0	9 10	Rangers S.A.B.C.
McCall	Stuart		10/06/64	Leeds	15/08/91	5 8.0	11 12	Everton
McCoist	Alistair		24/09/62	Bellshill	09/06/83	5 10.0	12 0	Sunderland
McGinty	Brian		10/12/76	East Kilbride	03/07/95	6 1.0	11 4	Rangers B.C.
McKnight	Paul		08/02/77	Belfast	05/08/93	5 7.0	11 4	St. Andrews B.C.
McLaren	James		04/01/71	Edinburgh	26/10/94	6 0.0	13 0	Heart of Midlothian
McShane	Paul		13/04/78	Alexandria	06/07/94	5 8.0	10 7	Rangers S.A.B.C.
Mikhailitchenko	Alexei		30/03/63	Kiev	05/07/91	6 2.5	13 3	UC Sampdoria SpA
Miller	Charles		18/03/76	Glasgow	02/07/92	5 9.0	10 8	Rangers B.C.
Milligan	Ross		02/06/78	Dumfries	03/07/95	6 0.0	12 6	Maxwellton Thistle
Moore	Craig	Andrew	12/12/75	Canterbury, Aus.	16/09/93	6 1.0	12 0	Australian Institute
Morrow	John		20/11/71	Belfast	29/07/88	5 7.0	10 0	Linfield
Murray	Neil		21/02/73	Bellshill	23/08/89	5 9.0	10 10	Rangers Amateurs F.C.
Nicholson	Barry		24/08/78	Dumfries	03/07/95	5 7.0	9 1	Rangers S.A.B.C.
Nicoll	Mark	Charles	20/11/77	Dumfries	06/07/94	5 7.0	10 12	Rangers S.A.B.C.
Nicolson	Iain		13/10/76	Glasgow	04/06/93	5 10.0	10 4	Rangers B.C.
Petric	Gordan		30/07/69	Belgrade	29/07/95	6 2.5	13 9	Dundee United
Rae	Michael		24/11/76	Inverness	06/07/94	5 10.0	12 4	Mayburgh A.F.C.
Reid	Brian	Robertson	15/06/70	Paisley	25/03/91	6 2.0	11 12	Greenock Morton
Robertson	David		17/10/68	Aberdeen	02/07/91	5 11.0	11 0	Aberdeen
Robertson	Lee		25/08/73	Edinburgh	23/06/90	5 7.0	9 6	Salvesen B.C.
Robson	Barry		07/11/78	Aberdeen	10/07/95	5 11.0	12 0	Rangers S.A.B.C.
Salenko	Oleg		25/10/69	St. Pietroburg	11/08/95	5 11.0	12 9	Valencia
Scott	Colin		19/05/70	Glasgow	21/08/87	6 1.0	12 4	Dalry Thistle
Shields	Greg		21/08/76	Falkirk	01/07/93	5 9.0	10 10	Rangers B.C.
Steven	Trevor		21/09/63	Berwick upon Tweed	29/07/92	5 9.0	10 12	Olympique de Marseille
Stone	Michael		15/01/79	Stirling	03/07/95	6 0.0	13 3	Rangers S.A.B.C.
Thomson	William	Marshall	10/02/58	Linwood	27/07/94	6 2.0	12 3	Motherwell
Watt	James		09/02/79	Dunfermline	03/07/95	5 11.0	11 7	Rangers S.A.B.C.
Wilson	Scott		19/03/77	Edinburgh	01/07/93	6 1.0	11 4	Rangers B.C.
Wright	Stephen		27/08/71	Bellshill	05/07/95	5 10.5	11 2	Aberdeen

MILESTONES

YEAR OF FORMATION: 1873
MOST CAPPED PLAYER: George Young
NO. OF CAPS: 53
MOST LEAGUE POINTS IN A SEASON: 76 (Division 1 - Season 1920/21)
MOST LEAGUE GOALS SCORED BY A PLAYER IN A SEASON: Sam English (Season 1931/32)
NO. OF GOALS SCORED: 44
RECORD ATTENDANCE: 118,567 (-v- Celtic – 2.1.1939)
RECORD VICTORY: 14-2 (-v- Blairgowrie – Scottish Cup 20.1.1934)
RECORD DEFEAT: 2-10 (-v- Airdrieonians – 1886)

SEASON TICKET INFORMATION

	Adult	OAP	Juvenile
Main Stand Sections A,B,F,G,O,P,S,T	£200	£120	£105
Main Stand Sections C,D,Q,R	£220	£130	£105
Main Stand Sections E,J,K,M,N	£260	£155	£105
Main Stand Section H	£370	£220	£105
Main Stand Section W	£575	£345	£105
PREMIER CLUB	**Adult**	**OAP**	**Juvenile**
GR1/GR7	£295	£175	£120
GR2/GR6	£325	£195	£120
GR3,4,5	£360	£215	£120
	Adult	**OAP**	**Juvenile**
Govan Stand Front	£230	£140	£105
Copland Stand Front	£210	£125	£105
Copland Stand Rear	£220	£130	£105
Seated Enclosure	£220	£130	£105

LEAGUE ADMISSION PRICES

Main Stand Front & Govan Rear ....(Adult) £15
....(Juvenile) £6
....(OAP) £8
Club Deck ....(Adult) £18
....(Juvenile) £9
....(OAP) £12
Broomloan Rear, Copland Rear, Govan Front ....(Adult) £11
& Seated Enclosure ....(Juvenile) £6
....(OAP) £8
Broomloan Front, Copland Front & Main Stand Rear ....(Adult) £10
....(Juvenile) £6
....(OAP) £8

CLUB FACTFILE 1994/95
RESULTS .. APPEARANCES .. SCORERS

The GERS

Small bold figures denote goalscorers. † denotes opponent's own goal.

Date	Venue	Opponents	Result	Goram A.	Murray N.	Roberson D.	Gough R.	Boli B.	McPherson D.	Durrant I.	McCall S.	McCoist A.	Hateley M.	Laudrup B.	Ferguson J.	Brown J.	Moore C.	Ferguson .	Pressley S.	Durie G.	Mikhailitchenko A.	Miller C.	Huistra P.	Hager D.	Wishart F.	McLaren A.	Scott C.	McGinty B.	Maxwell A.	Steven T.	Bollan G.	Cleland A.	Thomson W.	Roberson L.	Caldwell N.	McKnight P.
Aug 13	H	Motherwell	2-1	1	2	3	4	5	6	7	8	9	10¹	11	14¹																					
20	A	Partick Thistle	†2-0	1			4	5	6		2		10¹	11	9	3	7	8																		
27	H	Celtic	0-2	1			4	5	6	7	2		10	11	12					8	3	9														
Sep 11	H	Heart of Midlothian	3-0	1		7	3	4			5	9	2		10²	11	14			6	8	12¹														
17	A	Falkirk	2-0	1			3	4	5¹	7	2		10	11¹						6	8	9														
24	A	Aberdeen	2-2	1		7	3	4	6	5	12	8	10¹	11¹						2¹		9														
Oct 1	H	Dundee United	2-0	1	12	3	4	6	5		7	14	10¹	11¹						2		8	9													
8	A	Hibernian	1-2	1	12	3	4	6¹	5		7	14	10	11						2		9	8													
15	H	Kilmarnock	2-0	1		7	3¹		5		4		10	11						2	6	9¹	8													
22	A	Motherwell	†1-2	1		7	3		6	5	4		10	11						7		9	8	14												
30	A	Celtic	3-1	1	8	3		6			4	14	10²	11¹								9	7	12	2	5										
Nov 5	H	Partick Thistle	3-0	1	8	3		6		12	4		10¹	11¹								9¹	7		2	5										
9	A	Heart of Midlothian	1-1	1	8	3		6		9	4	14	10¹	11						2			7			5										
19	H	Falkirk	1-1	1		3		6		12	4	9	10¹	11						2		14	8	7		5										
25	H	Aberdeen	1-0	1		3		6			4	9¹	10	11								14	8	7	2	5										
Dec 4	A	Dundee United	3-0	1		3	4	6		12¹	2	9		11¹								10	8	7¹		5										
10	A	Kilmarnock	2-1	1	6	3	4			10	2			11¹			14					9	8	7		3¹										
26	H	Hibernian	2-0			3	4¹	6			2		10¹	11			12					9	8	7		5	1									
31	A	Motherwell	3-1			3	4	6			2¹			11¹			10	12				9¹	8	7		5	1									
Jan 4	H	Celtic	1-1			3	4	6		14	2			11	12					8¹		9	10	7		5	1									
7	A	Partick Thistle	1-1	1	11	3¹				9	4				6	2	8					7				5	13	10								
14	A	Falkirk	3-2	10	3			11	4¹						6	2	8			9	/²	14	5			1	12									
21	H	Heart of Midlothian	1-0	10		4	6			12	2			11	3	14	8			9¹		5				1	7									
Feb 4	A	Dundee United	1-1			3¹	4	5			6	14	10	11	12	2				9		8				1	7									
12	A	Aberdeen	0-2			3	4	5		12	8		10	11		2				14		9				1					6	7				
25	H	Kilmarnock	3-0			3	4	6		14¹	2			11¹	12					10¹		9				5	1	7	8							
Mar 4	A	Hibernian	1-1		8		4	6		12	10			11	2	14	9¹					5				1	7	3								
11	H	Falkirk	2-2				4	6		7	2			11¹	10¹		8	9	14			5				1	3									
18	A	Heart of Midlothian	1-2		14		4	6		12	10			11¹		8	9					5				1	7	3	2							
Apr 1	A	Dundee United	2-0				4	6		10	7			11	3		9¹	12	8			5¹						14	2	1						
8	H	Aberdeen	3-2		12¹		4	6		9¹			10¹	11	3		14	8				5				7		2	1							
16	H	Hibernian	3-1		12		4		6¹				10	11	3		9¹	14¹	8			5				7		2	1							
20	A	Kilmarnock	1-0		6		4			9				11		2	8			10¹		5				1		3	7				14			
29	H	Motherwell	0-2				4	6		9			10	11			8			3		5				7		2	1							
May 7	A	Celtic	0-3		14		4			9			10	11	6	2	8			12		5				13	7	3	1							
13	H	Partick Thistle	1-1	13			9						10	11		4¹				8	6	5				1	7	3						2	14	
TOTAL FULL APPEARANCES				18	14	23	25	28	9	16	30	4	23	33	1	10	19	13	2	16	4	21	15		3	24	3	1	10	10	5	10	5			1
TOTAL SUB APPEARANCES				(1)	(6)					(10)		(5)			(3)	(3)	(2)	(3)		(4)	(5)				(2)	(1)		(1)		(1)	(1)	(1)		(1)		(1)
TOTAL GOALS SCORED						1	3	1	2		4	2	1	13	10	1	1	2	1		6	2	3	3		2									

EDMISTON DRIVE

IBROX STADIUM

CAPACITY: 46,888 (All seated)

PITCH DIMENSIONS: 115 yds x 78 yds

FACILITIES FOR DISABLED SUPPORTERS: Special area within stadium and also special toilet facilities provided. We also have a Rangers Disabled Supporters' Club. Contact: David Milne, Secretary, Disabled Supporters' Club, c/o Ibrox Stadium, Glasgow G51 2XD.

HOW TO GET THERE

You can reach Ibrox Stadium by these routes:

BUSES: The following buses all pass within 300 yards of the Stadium and can be boarded from Glasgow city centre. Nos. 4, 9A, 23, 23A, 52, 53, 53A, 54A, 54B, 65, 89 and 91.

UNDERGROUND: GGPTE Underground station is Ibrox, which is two minutes walk from the Stadium.

CARS: Motor Vehicles can head for the Stadium from the city centre by joining the M8 Motorway from Waterloo Street. Take the B768 turn-off for Govan. This will then take you to the ground. There are parking facilities available at the Albion car park.

Raith's Manager, Jimmy Nicholl, with the two trophies

Test of Nerve

It is the dearest wish of every sponsor throughout world League football that the championship goes to the last day of the season.

But Scottish League backers Bell's would have been forgiven in reaching for a stiff drink of their own product as the First Division Championship reached its most thrilling conclusion.

Picture the scene: David Thomson of the Scottish League, is sitting in his office with a colleague at 4.20 p.m. on Saturday, 13th May, the First Division Championship trophy sitting nearby and a decision on whether to travel east, south or west must be made.

To the south, third place Dundee were playing Stranraer and eventually ran out comfortable 5-0 winners. To the east, second placed Dunfermline Athletic were narrowly overcoming Clydebank 2-1 at East End Park to put all the pressure on leaders Raith Rovers.

Jimmy Nicholl's side had gone into the final Saturday of the season knowing even a draw at Hamilton, playing temporarily at Firhill, would be enough to hand them their second title in three years. However, defeat would have relegated the Stark's Park club to third place and have forced them out of the Play-Off place with the team which finished second bottom of the Premier Division.

The nerves were frayed at Maryhill as the score remained goalless deep into the second half. It was then that the League made the decision to take the 10 minute trip with the trophy from their city centre offices to the west end and discard, for one afternoon at least, any impartiality in the hope of a Raith win.

"As you'd imagine, it was a quite nerve racking time," David Thomson recalled. "We knew we couldn't hold on much longer and eventually opted for Firhill because Raith Rovers were still in the driving seat at that time. It made for a thrilling climax to the season, but as you can imagine, it was pretty hairy for everyone involved!"

The quandry which League officials had to suffer was nothing to what player–boss Nicholl was going through in his usual midfield berth as his side eventually held out for the draw which handed them another title.

He said, "The last weeks of the season were really nervous. The week before the game with Hamilton Academical, we played Dunfermline Athletic at home and knew a win would give us the title, whilst a Dunfermline victory would hand them the initiative for the final game. That

match ended 0-0 and I'm not sure anyone enjoyed it, even the fans who crammed into the ground!"

"Hamilton was probably our most nervous display of the season though. Near the end, they sent in a couple of crosses along the six yard line and all it needed was a toe poke to give them victory. But thankfully, the chances went begging.

"When the final whistle ended, I remember my first reaction was a feeling of relief and being glad it was all over because the margin of error was so slight."

At least second placed Dunfermline had the consolation of a Play-Off place over two legs with Aberdeen to look forward to. But for Jim Duffy's Dundee, pipped for the runners-up spot by only two goals, there was only the prospect of another season in the First Division and that was especially cruel on the Dens Park club as they had led the division for much of the year.

Ultimately, fate decreed they would be joined by the Pars, who met a rejuvenated Aberdeen in the first ever Play-Off at the end of May. In the first leg at Pittodrie, Bert Paton's side gave themselves valid hopes for the return with a 3-1 defeat.

However, the Dons were in no

mood to give up the chance of salvaging something from the wreck of their worst ever season and ran out winners at East End Park four days later by the same scoreline, giving arguably their finest performance of the campaign.

Without doubt, the season belonged to Raith, a fact recognised at the SPFA Annual Awards in May when Nicholl was named Manager of the Year and striker Stevie Crawford, who made his full Scotland debut on the tour of Japan, voted First Division Players' Player of the Year.

The Kirkcaldy fairy tale was one Hans Christian Anderson would have struggled to pen. Raith were, in the words of Nicholl, "absolutely shocking", in the opening stages of the season, but that was all to change in one afternoon at Ibrox in November.

Raith had battled through to the Final of The Coca-Cola Cup, but were underdogs to Celtic, who were looking to end their long barren spell without a trophy. But, in an afternoon which will go down in Scottish football folklore, they battled for a 2-2 draw – with goals from Crawford and a late equaliser from Gordon Dalziel – before taking Tommy Burns' men to a penalty kick shoot-out, where Raith held their nerve to capture the first major honour in their history.

"That was the turning point for us as we lost only two games between then and the end of the season," added Nicholl. "Until the Cup Final, I hadn't been happy with our form and we only seemed to play well in the Cup at night under floodlights with a decent atmosphere.

"After the previous season in the Premier Division, I think the players found it hard to motivate themselves playing in front of 1,500 fans away from home, but the result against Celtic gave us real satisfaction. It showed the players what they had to do to be a success. It proved they could be, and from that moment, I couldn't fault the grit and determination of the squad."

Dundee apart, the greatest hard luck story of the season concerned Airdrieonians. They proved Scotland's Cup specialists, lifting The B & Q Cup, reaching the Semi-Finals of The Coca-Cola Cup and were beaten finalists in the Tennents Scottish Cup, with Celtic making amends for the disappointment against Raith with a 1-0 win at Hampden.

The heavy burden of Cup encounters eventually took its toll on the League

Stevie Crawford (Raith Rovers)

challenge of Alex MacDonald's side as they faltered badly in the final stages after pressing hard on the leaders for much of the previous eight months.

The season was one of transition for St. Johnstone boss Paul Sturrock, in his first full term in charge. However, too many draws cost Saints their chance of mounting a prolonged challenge at the top.

Hamilton Academical boss Iain Munro can take a great deal of credit from moulding his young side into one of the attractive sides in the division, although inevitably with youth comes inconsistency and they finished mid-table.

St. Mirren suffered the same fate. They languished near the bottom of the table, but a surge at the right time

towards the end of the season enabled them to escape the relegation zone.

The season held only bad memories for Clydebank. They suffered the tragic loss of player/coach Davie Cooper, who was still entertaining crowds throughout Scotland up until his untimely death from a brain haemorrhage at the age of 38.

Cooper was instrumental in coaxing former Rangers team-mate Terry Butcher out of retirement for a four week spell, but not even the influence of the former England skipper could prevent Brian Wright's side from slipping near the bottom of the table as the season entered its final few vital weeks. However, dogged determination enabled the Bankies to escape relegation and they will be hoping for a big improvement in what could be their last season at Kilbowie before moving to a newly constructed stadium on the outskirts of the town.

Ayr United and Stranraer will play their football in the Second Division this season after falling victim to the most intense division in Scotland. But no doubt the players of both United and Stranraer will be ambitious to bounce back again immediately to prove they can maintain a place in arguably the most entertaining and competitive division in the country.

GARY RALSTON
(Scottish Daily Express)

Raith winning First Division

AIRDRIEONIANS

Broadwood Stadium, Cumbernauld G68 9NE

ALL CORRESPONDENCE SHOULD BE ADDRESSED TO:
G. W. PEAT, C.A., Esq.,
32 Stirling Street, Airdrie ML6 0AH

CHAIRMAN
George W. Peat, C.A.

VICE-CHAIRMAN
David W. Smith, C.Eng., M.I.C.E.

DIRECTORS
Joseph M. Rowan
Alexander P. Bryce
Alexander MacDonald

SECRETARY
George W. Peat, C.A.

MANAGER
Alexander MacDonald

ASSISTANT MANAGER
John McVeigh

COACH
John Binnie

CLUB DOCTOR
Brian Dunn, M.B.,C.L.B.,M.R.C.P.(UK)

PHYSIOTHERAPIST
Ian Constable

YOUTH DEVELOPMENT OFFICER
Roy Tomnay

COMMERCIAL MANAGER
George Watson
Tel 01236-747255

TELEPHONES
Ground
(01236) 451511 (Match Days Only)
Office (01236) 762067
Fax (01236) 760698
Ticket Office (01236) 747255
Information Service (01236) 762067

CLUB SHOP
93 Graham Street, Airdrie, ML6 6DE.
Tel (01236) 747255. Open Mon-Fri.
10.00 a.m. till 1.00 p.m. and 2.00 p.m.
till 4.00 p.m. (Closed Wednesday)
Sat 9.00 a.m. – 3.00 p.m.

OFFICIAL SUPPORTERS CLUB
c/o David Johnstone,
16 Deveron Street, Coatbridge
Tel (01236) 423812

TEAM CAPTAIN
James Sandison

SHIRT SPONSOR
John C. Dalziel (Airdrie) Limited

LIST OF PLAYERS 1995-96

SURNAME	FIRST NAME	MIDDLE NAME	DATE OF BIRTH	PLACE OF BIRTH	DATE OF SIGNING	HEIGHT FT INS	WEIGHT ST LBS	PREVIOUS CLUB
Balfour	Evan	William	09/09/65	Edinburgh	12/05/89	5 11.0	12 6	Whitburn Juniors
Black	Kenneth	George	29/11/63	Stenhousemuir	12/09/91	5 9.0	11 10	Portsmouth
Bonar	Paul		28/12/76	Glasgow	11/08/95	5 11.0	10 7	Milngavie Wanderers
Borland	Gerald		08/09/76	Glasgow	11/08/95	5 11.0	11 7	Milngavie Wanderers
Boyle	James		19/02/67	Glasgow	11/08/89	5 6.0	11 2	Queen's Park
Connelly	Gordon		01/11/76	Glasgow	11/08/95	6 0.0	12 0	Milngavie Wanderers
Cooper	Stephen		22/06/64	Birmingham	30/09/94	5 11.0	12 2	York City
Davies	John		25/09/66	Glasgow	09/09/94	5 7.0	10 0	St. Johnstone
Duffield	Peter		04/02/69	Middlesbrough	21/07/95	5 6.0	10 4	Hamilton Academical
Harvey	Paul	Edward	28/08/68	Glasgow	25/01/94	5 8.0	10 7	Clydebank
Hay	Graham	Stuart	27/11/65	Falkirk	25/01/94	6 0.0	12 7	Clydebank
Jack	Paul	Dunn	15/05/65	Malaya	05/08/89	5 10.0	11 7	Arbroath
Martin	John	Galloway K.	27/10/58	Edinburgh	30/04/80	6 1.0	12 0	Tranent Juniors
McClelland	John	Stephen	26/04/77	Glasgow	11/08/95	5 9.0	10 4	Milngavie Wanderers
McCulloch	William		02/04/73	Baillieston	11/09/92	6 6.0	12 6	Rutherglen Glencairn
McIntyre	James		24/05/72	Alexandria	23/09/93	5 11.0	11 5	Bristol City
McIntyre	Thomas		26/12/63	Bellshill	29/07/94	6 0.0	12 5	Hibernian
McKenna	Gerard		02/02/77	Bellshill	11/08/95	5 8.0	10 9	Milngavie Wanderers
McPeak	Anthony		22/05/74	Glasgow	10/08/95	6 0.0	12 0	Knightswood Juveniles
Sandison	James	William	22/06/65	Edinburgh	27/07/91	5 10.5	10 10	Heart of Midlothian
Smith	Anthony		28/10/73	Bellshill	02/06/93	5 8.0	9 7	Heart of Midlothian
Stewart	Alexander		14/10/65	Bellshill	14/10/89	5 8.0	11 0	Kilmarnock
Sweeney	Sean	Brian	17/08/69	Glasgow	10/08/95	6 0.0	11 0	Clydebank
Tait	Stephen	James	15/10/76	Glasgow	11/08/95	6 0.0	11 8	Milngavie Wanderers
Wilson	Marvyn		01/12/73	Bellshill	22/07/92	5 7.5	10 0	Heart of Midlothian

MILESTONES

YEAR OF FORMATION: 1878
MOST CAPPED PLAYER: Jimmy Crapnell
NO. OF CAPS: 9
MOST LEAGUE POINTS IN A SEASON: 60 (Division 2 - Season 1973/74) (2 Points for a Win)
    61 (First Division - Season 1994/95) (3 Points for a Win)
MOST LEAGUE GOALS SCORED BY A PLAYER IN A SEASON: Hugh Baird (Season 1954/55)
NO. OF GOALS SCORED: 53
RECORD ATTENDANCE: 24,000 (-v- Heart of Midlothian – 8.3.1952)
RECORD VICTORY: 15-1 (-v- Dundee Wanderers – Division 2. 1.12.1894)
RECORD DEFEAT: 1-11 (-v- Hibernian - Division 1, 24.10.1959)

SEASON TICKET INFORMATION

Seated
Adult £125
Juvenile/OAP...£65

LEAGUE ADMISSION PRICES

Seated
Adult £8
Juvenile/OAP £4

CLUB FACTFILE 1994/95
RESULTS .. APPEARANCES .. SCORERS

The DIAMONDS

Date	Venue	Opponents	Result	Martin J.	Stewart A.	Smith Anthony	Sandison J.	McIntyre T.	Black K.	Boyle	Wilson M.	Smith Andrew	Harvey P.	Lawrence A.	McIntyre J.	Hay G.	Ferguson I.	Jack P.	Davies J.	Honor C.	Cooper S.	McCulloch W.	Connelly G.	McClelland J.	Tait S.	McKenna G.
Aug 13	H	Dunfermline Athletic	0-0	1	2	3	4	5	6	7	8	9	10	11	12											
20	H	St. Johnstone	0-0	1		3	4	5	10	2	8	9	7	11	14	6	12									
27	A	Hamilton Academical	6-2	1	8	3	4	5	10	12		9^2	7^1	11^3		6		2								
Sep 3	A	Dundee	1-1	1	2	12	4	5	6	7	8	9	10	11^1		14		3								
10	H	Ayr United	0-0	1	2		4	5	6	7		9	10	11		14		3	8							
24	H	Clydebank	2-0	1	2				6	7	12	9^1	10	11^1		14		5	3		8	4				
Oct 1	A	Stranraer	1-0	1	2		4	14		7	6	9	10	11^1				5	3		8			12		
8	H	Raith Rovers	0-0	1	2		4	5	6	7		14	10	11				5	3		9					
15	A	St. Mirren	1-0	1	2		4	5	6	7		12	10	11		14		3	8^1		9					
22	A	Dunfermline Athletic	2-2	1	2		4		6	7	12		10	11^1		14		5	3		9^1					
29	H	Hamilton Academical	1-0	1	2	14	4		6	7	8	12^1		11				5	3	10	9					
Nov 12	A	Ayr United	3-0	1	3	14	4		10	2	12		7	11^1				5	6		9^2					
19	H	Dundee	2-1	1	2	11^1	4		6	7	14	12^1	10	8				5	3		9			13		
22	A	St. Johnstone	0-4	1		11	4	14	6	2	12		7	10				5	3		9					
26	A	Clydebank	1-0	1	2	12	4		6	7	14^1		10	11				5	3		9					
Dec 3	H	Stranraer	8-1	1	2	14			6	7^2		11^1	10^1	12		5		3	8^2		9^2					
26	A	Raith Rovers	2-3	1	2	14			6	7^1	8	11	10	12				5	3		9^1					
31	H	Dunfermline Athletic	0-0	1	2	14			6	7	12		10	11				5	3		9					
Jan 2	A	Hamilton Academical	0-3	1	2	3	4		6	7	12			11				5	8		9					
7	H	St. Johnstone	0-2	1	2	14	4		6	7	8	12		11				5	3	10	9					
10	H	St. Mirren	2-0	1	2	3	12	5	6	7		11^1	10					4	8		9^1		14			
14	A	Dundee	1-0	1	2		4	5	6	7		11^1	10			14		3	8		9					
24	H	Ayr United	2-2	1	2	14	4	5	6^1	7^1		11	10	12				3	8		9					
Feb 4	A	Stranraer	4-1	1	2	3^1	4		6	7	8	9	10	11^2		14		5^1			12					
14	A	Clydebank	1-2	1	2	14			6^1	7	8	9	10	11				5	3		12					
25	A	St. Mirren	1-0	1	2		4	5	6	7		12^1	10	11		14		3	8		9					
Mar 6	H	Raith Rovers	1-2	1	2	12	4	5	6	7			10	11		14		3	8		9^1					
18	A	Ayr United	2-0	1	2	14	4	5	6	7		11	10	12^2				3	8		9					
25	H	Dundee	0-3	1	2		4		6	7		11	10	12		14		5	3		9					
Apr 1	H	Stranraer	2-0	1	2		4		6	7	8	12^1	10	11				5	3		9^1			14		
11	A	Clydebank	1-1	1	2	14	4		6	7		11	10	12				5	3		9					
15	A	Raith Rovers	1-0	1	2	14	4		6	7		11	10	12				5	3		9^1					
22	H	St. Mirren	1-0	1	2	3	4			7	6		10	11		14^1		5	8		9					
29	A	Dunfermline Athletic	0-0	1	2		4			7	6		10	11	12			5	3		9					
May 6	H	Hamilton Academical	0-1	1	2	11	4			8	6		10			7		3			9			12	5	
13	A	St. Johnstone	1-2	1	2^1	14	4		6		9		10	11				3			1			7	8	12
TOTAL FULL APPEARANCES				35	32	12	32	15	31	33	12	24	33	24	2	25		29	25	1	26	1	1	2	1	
TOTAL SUB APPEARANCES					(15)	(1)	(2)		(1)	(3)	(12)		(8)	(10)	(1)	(3)			(3)		(1)	(3)				(1)
TOTAL GOALS SCORED					1	2			2	4		12	2	11	1	1			3		11					

Small bold figures denote goalscorers. † denotes opponent's own goal.

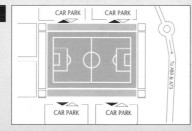

BROADWOOD STADIUM

CAPACITY: 6,300 (All seated)

PITCH DIMENSIONS: 112 yds x 76 yds

FACILITIES FOR DISABLED SUPPORTERS: Facilities available in both Home and Away Stands.

HOW TO GET THERE

Broadwood Stadium can be reached by the following routes:

BUSES: From Buchanan Street Bus Station, Glasgow. Bus No. 36A (Glasgow to Westfield).

TRAINS: From Queen Street Station, Glasgow to Croy Station. The Stadium is a 15 minute walk from here.

CARS: From Glasgow City Centre via Stepps By Pass joining A80 towards Stirling. Take Broadwood turn-off to Stadium.

YOUNGER'S TARTAN SPECIAL

CLYDEBANK

Kilbowie Park, Arran Place,
Clydebank G81 2PB

CHAIRMAN
C. Graham Steedman

DIRECTORS
William Howat
John S. Steedman, C.B.E.
Colin L. Steedman, B.Acc, C.A.
Charles A. Steedman
James H. Heggie

MANAGING DIRECTOR
Ian C. Steedman C.A.

SECRETARY
Andrew Steedman

COACH
Brian Wright

ASSISTANT COACH
Ken Eadie

CLUB DOCTOR
Stuart Hillis

PHYSIOTHERAPIST
Peter Salila

S.F.A. COMMUNITY COACH
Tony Gervaise

CHIEF SCOUT
Robert Gallie

GROUNDSMAN
George Furze

COMMERCIAL MANAGER
David Curwood
0141-952 2887

TELEPHONES
Ground 0141-952 2887
Fax 0141-952 6948

OFFICIAL SUPPORTERS CLUB
c/o Bankies Club, Kilbowie Park,
Clydebank

TEAM CAPTAIN
Scott Murdoch

SHIRT SPONSOR
Wet Wet Wet

LIST OF PLAYERS 1995-96

SURNAME	FIRST NAME	MIDDLE NAME	DATE OF BIRTH	PLACE OF BIRTH	DATE OF SIGNING	HEIGHT FT INS	WEIGHT ST LBS	PREVIOUS CLUB
Agnew	Paul		28/06/72	Coatbridge	14/06/94	5 7.0	10 10	Arthurlie Juniors
Bowman	Gary		12/08/74	Glasgow	30/03/94	5 11.0	11 4	Knightswood Juveniles
Connell	Graham		31/10/74	Glasgow	03/07/95	5 11.0	11 10	Ipswich Town
Connelly	Dean		06/01/70	St. Helier	25/08/95	5 8.0	10 10	Stockport County
Crawford	Derek		18/06/74	Glasgow	05/07/93	5 8.0	10 0	Rangers
Currie	Thomas		06/11/70	Vale of Leven	29/08/92	6 1.0	12 7	Shettleston Juniors
Dunn	Raymond		29/12/75	Glasgow	31/03/95	5 7.0	10 10	Rutherglen Glencairn
Eadie	Kenneth	William	26/02/61	Paisley	16/01/88	5 10.0	11 8	Falkirk
Flannigan	Craig		11/02/73	Dumfries	13/03/92	5 6.0	10 2	Rangers
Grady	James		14/03/71	Paisley	14/06/94	5 7.0	10 0	Arthurlie Juniors
Jack	Stephen	J.	27/03/71	Bellshill	28/05/92	5 11.0	10 0	Queen's Park
Keane	Gary		18/07/73	Glasgow	09/06/95	5 11.0	11 7	Calton U'21
Kerrigan	Steven	John	09/10/72	Bellshill	11/02/94	6 0.0	11 8	Albion Rovers
Lansdowne	Alan		08/04/70	Glasgow	13/06/89	5 11.0	11 4	Drumchapel Amateurs
Lovering	Paul		25/11/75	Glasgow	31/03/95	5 10.0	10 0	Neilston Juniors
Matthews	Gary		15/03/70	Paisley	21/03/94	6 3.5	16 2	Kilmarnock
McLaughlin	Ian		24/08/73	Glasgow	21/06/95	5 6.0	9 10	Knightswood Juveniles
Miller	Scott	Kerr	04/05/75	Glasgow	11/08/95	5 9.0	10 5	Possil Y.M.
Monaghan	Allan		06/10/72	Glasgow	10/08/93	6 0.0	12 7	Rutherglen Glencairn
Murdoch	Scott	McKenzie	27/02/69	Glasgow	22/10/92	5 7.0	10 7	St. Rochs
Nicholls	David	Clarkson	05/04/72	Bellshill	11/08/95	5 8.0	12 6	Cork City
Prior	Peter		07/10/73	Glasgow	29/06/95	5 7.5	11 3	Dundee United
Robertson	Joseph		12/04/77	Glasgow	15/05/95	5 8.0	11 5	Clydebank B.C.
Sutherland	Colin		15/03/75	Glasgow	24/02/95	5 11.0	11 10	Kilpatrick Juveniles
Tomlinson	Craig		01/06/74	Bellshill	06/09/94	5 11.0	11 0	Shotts Bon Accord
Wright	Brian	Vincent	05/10/58	Glasgow	09/05/95	5 11.0	11 3	Queen of the South

MILESTONES

YEAR OF FORMATION: 1965
MOST LEAGUE POINTS IN A SEASON: 58 (Division 1 – Season 1976/77)
MOST LEAGUE GOALS SCORED BY A PLAYER IN A SEASON: Ken Eadie (Season 1990/91)
NO. OF GOALS SCORED: 29
RECORD ATTENDANCE: 14,900 (-v- Hibernian – 10.2.1965)
RECORD VICTORY: 8-1 (-v- Arbroath – Division 1, 3.1.1977)
RECORD DEFEAT: 1-9 (-v- Gala Fairydean – Scottish Cup 15.9.1965)

SEASON TICKET INFORMATION

Seated
Adult ....£100 and £90
Juvenile/OAP...............................£50 and £45

LEAGUE ADMISSION PRICES

Seated
Adult ....£8 and £7
Juvenile/OAP..................................£4 and £3.50

CLUB FACTFILE 1994/95
RESULTS .. APPEARANCES .. SCORERS

The BANKIES

Date	Venue	Opponents	Result	Matthews C.	Lansdowne 4	Bowman G.	Murdoch S.	Sweeney S.	Currie T.	Cooper D.	Harris C.	Eadie K.	Grady J.	Ferguson G.	Flannigan C.	Jack S.	Kerrigan S.	Sutherland C.	Crawford D.	Walker J.	Keane G.	Butcher T.	Tomlinson C.	Agnew P.	McStay J.	Connolly D.	Robertson J.	Lovering P.	Dunn R.
Aug 13	H	Stranraer	2-0	1	2	3	4	5	6	7¹	8	9¹	10	11	12														
20	H	Dunfermline Athletic	0-1	1	2	3	4	5	6	7	8	9	10	14		11	12												
27	A	St. Mirren	1-2	1	2	3	4		5¹	7	8		9	14	10	11	12	6											
Sep 3	A	Raith Rovers	1-1	1	2		4		5¹	7			12	8	10	11	9	6	3	14									
10	H	Dundee	5-2	1	2		4	5¹	6	7			9¹		10²	11¹		3	12	8									
24	A	Airdrieonians	0-2	1	2	3	4	5	6	7		12	10	9		11				8	14								
Oct 1	H	St. Johnstone	0-0	1			4	5	6	7		9	10	12		11			3	8									
8	H	Ayr United	3-0	1		3	4	5	6	7	11	9²	10¹	12	2					8									
15	A	Hamilton Academical	0-0	1		3	4	5		7	11	9	10	12	2			14	8	6									
22	A	Stranraer	1-0	1	12	3	4	5		7		9	11¹	10	2				8	6									
29	H	St. Mirren	1-1	1	11	3	4	5¹	6	7		9	10	12	2			14	8										
Nov 5	A	Dunfermline Athletic	1-4	1	11	3	4		5	7	14	9	10	12	2¹				8		6								
12	A	Dundee	0-2	1		3	4		5	7	12	9	10	11					8		6		2	14					
19	H	Raith Rovers	0-3	1		3			5	7	4	9	10		11	12			8		6		2	14					
26	H	Airdrieonians	0-1	1		11			5	7		9	10	12	2			3			6	4	8						
Dec 3	A	St. Johnstone	1-1	1		11		5	6	12		9¹	8			14	10	3				4	7	2					
26	A	Ayr United	1-1	1		11	4	5	6¹	7		9	10	14	12			3					8	2					
31	H	Stranraer	2-3	1		3	4¹	5	6	7	8	9	12	10¹	11				14					2					
Jan 2	A	St. Mirren	0-0	1		3	4	5	6	12			14	10	11	9			7				8	2					
7	H	Dunfermline Athletic	1-2	1	14	3	4	5	6			9¹	8		11	10			7					2					
10	H	Hamilton Academical	0-0	1		11	4	5	6			9	10	14	8			3	7					2					
14	A	Raith Rovers	0-1	1		11	4	5	6	7		9	12	10	8			3	14					2					
21	H	Dundee	0-3	1	14	11	4	5		7		9	12	10	6			3	8					2					
Feb 4	H	St. Johnstone	0-0	1	8	3	4	5	6			9	14	10	11									2	7				
14	A	Airdrieonians	2-1	1	7	11	4	5	6			9¹	10¹	3		8	12							2	14				
25	A	Hamilton Academical	†1-0	1	7	11		5	6			9	10	3		8		14				4		2					
Mar 11	H	Ayr United	1-1	1	7	11		5	6			9	10¹	3		8						4		2					
18	A	Dundee	2-3	1	7	11		5	6			9¹	10¹	3		8	12	4						2					
Apr 1	A	St. Johnstone	0-1	1	*15	11		5	6				10			8	9	3	12			4		2		14			
4	H	Raith Rovers	1-2	1	*15	14	4	5					10			8	9	6	3	12				2		11¹			
11	A	Airdrieonians	1-1	1	*15	14	4	5				9	10¹			8		6	3					2		11			
15	A	Ayr United	0-1	1	*15		4	5				9	10			8	12	6	3					2		11			
22	H	Hamilton Academical	1-4	1	*15	11	4	5				9¹	10	12	14	8		3			6			2					
29	A	Stranraer	1-0	1	*15	6			5			9	10	2		8						4				14	11¹	3	
May 6	H	St. Mirren	2-1	1		8¹	6¹						10	2		5	9					4			12	*15	11	3	14
13	A	Dunfermline Athletic	1-2	1		6						12¹	10	2		5	9	14				4			8	*15	11	3	
TOTAL FULL APPEARANCES				36	20	30	27	27	27	19	7	26	30	9	11	33	8	9	12	14	3	3	10	4	19	3	6	3	
TOTAL SUB APPEARANCES					(3)	(2)				(2)	(1)	(3)	(6)	(3)	(10)	(2)	(6)		(4)	(7)					(2)	(1)	(2)	(1)	(1)
TOTAL GOALS SCORED						1	2	2	3	1		9	7	3	2											2			

Small bold figures denote goalscorers. † denotes opponent's own goal.

KILBOWIE PARK

CAPACITY: 9,950 (All Seated)

PITCH DIMENSIONS: 110 yds x 68 yds

FACILITIES FOR DISABLED SUPPORTERS: Accommodation for about eight Wheelchairs by prior arrangement with Club Secretary.

(Stadium plan: Pavilion, Social Club, ARGYLE ROAD, ARRAN PLACE)

HOW TO GET THERE

The following routes may be used to reach Kilbowie Park:

TRAINS: The train service from Glasgow Queen Street and Glasgow Central Low Level both pass through Singer Station, which is a two minute walk from the ground.

BUSES: A number of SMT buses pass down Kilbowie Road, which is two minutes walk from the ground. The buses are bound for Faifley, Duntocher and Parkhall and passengers should alight at Singer Station.

CARS: Car Parking is available in side streets adjacent to the park. The private car park in front of Kilbowie is reserved on match days for Directors, Players, Officials, Referee and certain Social Club members.

YOUNGER'S TARTAN SPECIAL

DUMBARTON

Boghead Park, Miller Street,
Dumbarton G82 2JA

CHAIRMAN
Douglas S. Dalgleish

VICE–CHAIRMAN
Gilbert R. Lawrie A.R.I.C.S.

DIRECTORS
David Wright
G. James Innes
Alistair G. Paton
William J. Walker
Neil Rankine

HON. PRESIDENT
Robert Nisbet

PRESIDENT
Ian A. Bell

COMPANY SECRETARY
Alistair Paton

CLUB SECRETARY
Graham Casey

ASSISTANT SECRETARY
Colin Hosie

MANAGER
Jim Fallon

RESERVE TEAM COACH
Alastair MacLeod

CLUB DOCTORS
James Goldie & Paul Jackson

PHYSIOTHERAPIST
David Stobie

GROUNDSMAN
Martin Mooney

KIT MAN
Richard Jackson

COMMERCIAL MANAGER
Ian Sinclair
(01389) 762569

TELEPHONES
Ground (01389) 762569/767864
Sec. Bus. (01563) 525151
Fax (01389) 762629

CLUB SHOP
Situated in ground –
open on matchdays and
10.00 a.m. – 4.00 p.m. Mon-Fri

OFFICIAL SUPPORTERS CLUB
c/o Boghead Park, Miller Street,
Dumbarton

TEAM CAPTAIN
James Meechan

SHIRT SPONSOR
Allied Distillers Ltd.

LIST OF PLAYERS 1995-96

SURNAME	FIRST NAME	MIDDLE NAME	DATE OF BIRTH	PLACE OF BIRTH	DATE OF SIGNING	HEIGHT FT INS	WEIGHT ST LBS	PREVIOUS CLUB
Burns	Hugh		13/12/65	Lanark	11/08/95	6 0.0	11 7	Ayr United
Campbell	Calum		07/11/65	Erskine	11/02/94	6 1.0	12 0	Kilmarnock
Charnley	James	Callaghan	11/06/63	Glasgow	28/07/95	5 9.0	11 12	Partick Thistle
Dallas	Stephen		02/11/74	Glasgow	31/03/95	5 7.0	10 4	Hibernian
Fabiani	Roland		24/11/71	Greenock	20/08/93	5 11.0	10 2	St. Mirren
Foster	Alan		10/03/71	Glasgow	20/02/91	5 8.0	10 8	Kilsyth Rangers
Gibson	Charles		12/06/61	Dumbarton	09/06/89	5 10.0	10 10	Stirling Albion
Gow	Stephen		06/12/68	Dumbarton	23/07/87	6 0.0	11 1	Dumbarton United
Granger	Alan		16/09/71	Glasgow	09/08/95	5 9.0	11 0	Pollok Juniors
Hamilton	James	Michael	09/12/66	Duntocher	24/02/95	5 9.0	11 0	Stirling Albion
King	Thomas	David	23/01/70	Dumbarton	30/09/94	5 9.0	11 0	Arbroath
MacFarlane	Ian		05/12/68	Bellshill	12/07/91	6 1.0	12 7	Hamilton Academical
Marsland	James		28/08/68	Dumbarton	15/06/90	5 8.0	10 12	Kilpatrick Juveniles
Martin	Paul	John	08/03/65	Bellshill	30/01/91	5 11.5	11 0	Hamilton Academical
McGarvey	Martin		16/01/72	Glasgow	20/02/91	5 8.0	11 0	Irvine Meadow
McGivern	Samuel		09/10/63	Kilwinning	11/08/95	5 8.0	10 10	Ayr United
McKinnon	Colin		29/08/69	Glasgow	30/09/94	6 0.0	11 7	Arbroath
McLaren	Christopher		06/09/74	Halifax	31/03/95	5 10.0	11 2	Musselburgh Athletic
Meechan	James		14/10/63	Alexandria	05/10/90	5 9.0	11 7	Irvine Meadow
Melvin	Martin		07/08/69	Glasgow	22/12/ 90	5 11.0	11 6	Falkirk
Mooney	Martin	James	25/09/70	Alexandria	24/09/92	5 7.5	9 11	Falkirk
Ward	Hugh		09/03/70	Dumbarton	05/11/93	5 8.0	9 12	Greenock Juniors

MILESTONES

YEAR OF FORMATION: 1872
MOST CAPPED PLAYERS: J. Lindsay and J. McAulay
NO. OF CAPS: 8 each
MOST LEAGUE POINTS IN A SEASON: 53 (First Division – Season 1986/87) (2 Points for a Win)
60 (Second Division – Season 1994/95) (3 Points for a Win)
MOST LEAGUE GOALS SCORED BY A PLAYER IN A SEASON: Kenneth Wilson (Season 1971/72)
NO. OF GOALS SCORED: 38
RECORD ATTENDANCE: 18,001 (-v- Raith Rovers – 2.3.1957)
RECORD VICTORY: 13-2 (-v- Kirkintilloch – Scottish Cup)
RECORD DEFEAT: 1-11 (-v- Ayr United and Albion Rovers)

SEASON TICKET INFORMATION

Seated
Presidents Club
Adult £290
Juvenile/OAP...£235
Stand
Adult £150
Juvenile/OAP...£100
Standing
Adult £110
Juvenile/OAP...£35
Parent/Juvenile £125

LEAGUE ADMISSION PRICES

Seated
Adult..£9.50
Juvenile/OAP £6
Standing
Adult..£7
Juvenile/OAP..£3.50
Parent/Juvenile...£9

The SONS

Small bold figures denote goalscorers.   † denotes opponent's own goal.

Date	Venue	Opponents	Result	MacFarlane I.	Marsland J.	Fabiani R.	Melvin V.	Martin ?.	MacLeod M.	Mooney M.	Meechan J.	Gibson C.	McGarvey M.	Foster A.	Campbell C.	Ward H.	Boyd J.	Gow S.	McKinnon C.	Hendry M.	Burridge J.	King T.	Mooney S.	McConville R.	Farrell G.	Hamilton J.	Dallas S.
Aug 13	A	Queen of the South	1-4	1	2	3	4	5	6	7¹	8	9	10	11	12	14											
20	A	Stirling Albion	1-1	1	2	3	4		6	7¹	8	9	10		11	14	5										
27	H	Greenock Morton	2-1	1	2	3	4		6	7¹	8	9	10		11	14¹	5										
Sep 3	H	Meadowbank Thistle	0-1	1	2	3	4		6	7	8	9	10		12	11	5										
10	A	Berwick Rangers	0-1	1		3	4		6	7	8	9	10		11	12	5	2									
24	H	Clyde	2-1	I		3	4		6	7		9	10		11		5²	2									
Oct 1	A	Brechin City	2-1	1		3	4	5¹	6	7	8	9	10¹		12	2		11	14								
8	A	East Fife	3-2	1	6	3	4	5		7¹	8	9²	10		12	2		11	14								
15	H	Stenhousemuir	1-2		6	3	4	5		7¹	8	9	10			2		11	12	1		14					
22	H	Queen of the South	0-0			3	4	5	6	7	12					10		2	11	9	1	8		14			
29	A	Greenock Morton	0-1			3	4	5	6	7			8		12	11	2	9		1		10		14			
Nov 5	H	Stirling Albion	1-0	1		3	4	5	6	14		9	12		7	11	2	10¹				8					
12	H	Berwick Rangers	3-2	1		3	4	5	6	12¹		9	11¹		7		2	10				8¹					
19	A	Meadowbank Thistle	0-0	1		3	4		6	7		12	10	5		11	14	2	9			8					
26	A	Clyde	1-3	1			4	5		7¹		9	8	3		14	6	2	11			10					
Dec 3	H	Brechin City	6-0	1			4	5		7¹	12		8²	3	14¹	11	6	2	9¹			10¹					
26	H	East Fife	4-0	1	6	3		5		7¹	4¹		10¹		12	11¹		2	9			8			14		
31	A	Stenhousemuir	0-1	1	6	3		5		7	4		10		12	11		2	9			8					
Jan 14	A	Queen of the South	0-0	1	6	3		5		7	4		10			11		2	9			8					
21	H	Stirling Albion	2-2	1	2	3		5	6	7¹	4		10		14	11¹		12	9			8					
24	H	Greenock Morton	2-1	1	4	3		5	6	7	10	9¹	14			11¹		2				8					
Feb 4	A	Berwick Rangers	2-1	1	6	3		5		12	4¹	9¹				11		2	10			8			7		
11	H	Meadowbank Thistle	4-0	1	6	3		5		7¹	4	9¹	10¹			11¹		2	12			8					
18	H	Clyde	2-2	1	6	3		5¹		7¹	4		10		12	11		2	9			8					
25	A	Brechin City	0-0	1	3			5	6	7	4				12	11		2	9			8					10
Mar 4	A	East Fife	2-0	1	3			5	6	7	4	9	10		14	11²		2	12			8					
14	H	Stenhousemuir	5-1	1	3	14		5	6	7¹		9	10		12	11³		2	8¹								4
21	H	Berwick Rangers	1-0	1	6	3		5		7	12	9				11¹		2	10			8					4
25	A	Meadowbank Thistle	0-1	1	6	3		5		7	12	9	14			11		2	10			8					4
Apr 1	H	Brechin City	4-1	1	5	3¹			6	7²	10¹		14			11		2	9			8				4	12
8	A	Clyde	0-1	1	5	3			6	7	10	14	12			11		2	9			8				4	
15	H	East Fife	2-0	1	5	3			6	7¹	10	9	14			11		2	12¹			8				4	
22	A	Stenhousemuir	0-0	1	4	3		5	6	7	10		14			11		2	9			8					
29	H	Queen of the South	2-2	1	4	3		5	6	7¹	10¹	12				11		2	9			8					
May 6	A	Greenock Morton	0-2	1	4	3		5	6	7	10	14	11			12		2	9			8					
13	A	Stirling Albion	2-0	1	4			5	6	7	10	9¹		3		11¹		12				8					2
TOTAL FULL APPEARANCES				33	29	27	16	28	24	33	25	21	23	5	4	24	10	30	25	1	3	25	1			1	9
TOTAL SUB APPEARANCES						(1)				(3)	(3)	(5)	(7)		(10)	(9)	(1)	(1)	(4)		(3)	(1)	(2)	(1)			(1)
TOTAL GOALS SCORED						1		2		17	4	6	6		1	12	2					4					2

BOGHEAD PARK

CAPACITY: 5,503; Seated 303, Standing 5,200

PITCH DIMENSIONS: 110 yds x 68 yds

FACILITIES FOR DISABLED SUPPORTERS: Wheelchairs are accommodated on the track

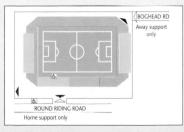

BOGHEAD RD
Away support only

ROUND RIDING ROAD
Home support only

HOW TO GET THERE

Boghead Park can be reached by the following routes:

TRAINS: The train service from Glasgow Queen Street and Glasgow Central Low Level both pass through Dumbarton East Station (away fans best choice) and Dumbarton Central Station, both of which are situated just under a ten minute walk from the ground.

BUSES: There are two main services which pass close to the ground. These are bound for Helensburgh and Balloch from Glasgow.

CARS: Car parking is available in certain side streets around the ground. Supporters buses should follow Police signposts to designated parking area.

DUNDEE

Dens Park Stadium,
Sandeman Street,
Dundee DD3 7JY

CHAIRMAN
Ronald N. Dixon

VICE-CHAIRMAN
Malcolm Reid

DIRECTORS
Robert W. Hynd
John F. Black
Nigel R. Squire

SECRETARY
Andrew P. Drummond
LL.B. (Hons) Dip., L.P., N.P.

PLAYER/MANAGER
James Duffy

ASSISTANT MANAGER/COACH
John McCormack

SPRINT COACH
Harry Hay

CLUB DOCTOR
Dr. Phyllis Windsor

PHYSIOTHERAPIST
James Crosbie

GROUNDSMAN
Brian Robertson

TELEPHONES
Ground/Ticket Office
(01382) 889966
Fax (01382) 832284

CLUB SHOP
Contact Dens Park Stadium

OFFICIAL SUPPORTERS CLUB
The Dee Club, Taylor Street,
Lochee, Dundee

TEAM CAPTAIN
Cornelius Duffy

SHIRT SPONSOR
Auto Windscreens

LIST OF PLAYERS 1995-96

SURNAME	FIRST NAME	MIDDLE NAME	DATE OF BIRTH	PLACE OF BIRTH	DATE OF SIGNING	HEIGHT FT INS	WEIGHT ST LBS	PREVIOUS CLUB
Anderson	Iain		23/07/77	Glasgow	10/08/94	5 8.0	9 7	"X" Form
Bain	Kevin		19/09/72	Kirkcaldy	28/06/89	6 0.0	11 9	Abbey Star
Binnie	Kenneth		16/10/77	Aberdeen	01/09/95	5 8.0	10 3	Deveronvale Jnrs
Britton	Gerard	Joseph	20/10/70	Glasgow	11/01/94	6 1.0	11 0	Partick Thistle
Cadger	Graham		22/05/77	Aberdeen	22/07/95	5 9.0	11 5	"S" Form
Cargill	Andrew		02/09/75	Dundee	23/09/94	5 6.5	10 8	Dundee United
Dailly	Marcus	Graham	01/10/75	Dundee	06/07/94	5 9.0	11 6	Dundee United
Duffy	Cornelius		05/06/67	Glasgow	01/03/94	6 1.0	11 13	Falkirk
Duffy	James		27/04/59	Glasgow	03/06/94	5 10.0	11 11	Partick Thistle
Farningham	Raymond	Paul	10/04/61	Dundee	06/06/94	5 8.0	11 5	Partick Thistle
Hamilton	James		09/02/76	Aberdeen	31/01/94	6 0.0	10 10	Keith
Hutchison	Mark	George	13/07/73	Edinburgh	10/09/94	5 10.0	10 7	Meadowbank Thistle
Magee	Darren		14/04/77	Glasgow	27/06/95	5 10.0	12 0	Ferguslie Juveniles
Manley	Roderick		23/07/65	Glasgow	10/08/95	5 11.0	11 4	Instant Dict
Mathers	Paul		17/01/70	Aberdeen	06/10/86	5 11.0	11 6	Sunnybank "A"
Matheson	Andrew	McRae	20/08/75	Dunfermline	16/06/95	5 10.0	11 0	Forres Mechanics
McBain	Roy		07/11/74	Aberdeen	12/09/95	5 11.0	11 5	Hermes Jnrs
McCann	Neil	Docherty	11/08/74	Greenock	14/05/92	5 10.0	10 0	Greenock Morton B.C.
McKeown	Gary		19/10/70	Oxford	31/07/92	5 10.5	11 8	Arsenal
McQueen	Thomas	Feeney	01/04/63	Glasgow	10/08/95	5 9.0	11 7	Falkirk
O'Driscoll	Jerry		04/04/78	Aberdeen	01/09/95	6 0.0	11 9	Crombie Jnrs
Pageaud	Michel		30/08/66	Paris	26/02/94	6 0.0	12 9	Valenciennes
Rae	Gavin		28/11/77	Aberdeen	01/09/95	5 11.0	10 4	Hermes Jnrs
Shaw	George		10/02/69	Glasgow	11/01/94	5 7.0	10 9	Partick Thistle
Tannock	Gordon		11/06/74	Kilmarnock	14/05/92	5 11.0	10 10	Bellfield B.C.
Teasdale	Michael	Joseph	28/07/69	Elgin	11/01/94	6 0.0	13 0	Elgin City
Thompson	Barry	Crawford	12/07/75	Glasgow	13/08/93	6 1.0	12 5	Aviemore Thistle
Tosh	Paul	James	18/10/73	Arbroath	04/08/93	6 0.0	11 10	Arbroath
Tully	Craig		07/01/76	Stirling	18/04/94	5 11.0	11 0	Victoria Juveniles
Vrto	Dusan		29/10/65	Banksa Stiavnica	07/08/92	6 0.0	10 12	Banik Ostrava
Wieghorst	Morten		25/02/71	Glostrup	02/12/92	6 3.0	14 .0	Lyngby

MILESTONES

YEAR OF FORMATION: 1893
MOST CAPPED PLAYER: Alex Hamilton
NO. OF CAPS: 24
MOST LEAGUE GOALS SCORED BY A PLAYER IN A SEASON: Alan Gilzean (Season 1963/64)
NO. OF GOALS SCORED: 52
RECORD ATTENDANCE: 43,024 (-v- Rangers – 1953)
RECORD VICTORY: 10-0 (-v- Fraserburgh, 1931; -v- Alloa, 1947; -v- Dunfermline Athletic, 1947;
        -v- Queen of the South, 1962)
RECORD DEFEAT: 0-11 (-v- Celtic – Division 1 26.10.1895)

SEASON TICKET INFORMATION

Seated
Centre Stand   Adult £175
            Juvenile/OAP £100
South Enclosure   Adult £135
            Juvenile/OAP £65

LEAGUE ADMISSION PRICES

Seated
Stand   Adult £9
      Juvenile/OAP £5
South Enclosure   Adult £7
       Juvenile/OAP ...£3.50
West Enclosure   Adult £7
       Juvenile/OAP ...£3.50
Wing Stand   Adult £8
       Juvenile/OAP £4
East Terracing   Adult £7
       Juvenile/OAP ...£3.50

CLUB FACTFILE 1994/95
RESULTS .. APPEARANCES .. SCORERS

The DARK BLUES

Date	Venue	Opponents	Result	Pageaud M.	McQuillan J	Pittman S.	Duffy C	Blake N	Duffy J.	Shaw G	Dinnie A.	Wieghorst W.	Britton G.	McCann N	Tosh P.	Farningham R.	Anderson I	Vrto D.	McKeown G.	Teasdale V.	Hutchison M.	Hamilton Bj	Mathers P.	Bain K	Cargill A.	Daily M.	Ritchie P.
Aug 13	H	St. Mirren	2-0	1	2	3	4	5	6	7^1	8	9	10^1	11	14												
20	H	Stranraer	†3-1	1	2		6	5		7		9	10^2	11	14	3	4		8	12							
27	A	St. Johnstone	1-0	1	2	3^1	6	5		7		9	10	11	12	4			8	14							
Sep 3	H	Airdrieonians	1-1	1	2	3	4	5	6	7		9	10	11	14	8^1											
10	A	Clydebank	2-5	1	2		4	5		7		9	10^2	11	12	6	14		8		3						
24	A	Ayr United	2-3	1	2		6	5		7		9	10^1	11			4		8		3	14^1					
Oct 1	H	Dunfermline Athletic	4-4		3			5	6	7^2	8		10^1		9^1		2			12		11		1	4		
8	H	Hamilton Academical	2-0	1	2			5		7	6		10^1		9							11^1		3	4		
15	A	Raith Rovers	1-1	1	2			5		7	6		10	12	9	4	14^1		8			11		3			
22	A	St. Mirren	2-1	1	2		14	5			6		10	11^2	12	4	7		8			9		3			
29	H	St. Johnstone	1-0	1	2		12	5		7^1			10	11	9	4					3	14		6	8		
Nov 12	H	Clydebank	2-0	1	2			5		7^1	6		10	11	12				8	14		9		3^1	4		
19	A	Airdrieonians	1-2	1	2			5	6	7		9	10^1	11	12	4			8			14				3	
23	A	Stranraer	2-0	1	2			5	6	7	8			11	9^1					3		10			4^1		
26	H	Ayr United	1-1	1	2			5		7	8		10	11	9^1					3		12		6	4		
Dec 3	H	Dunfermline Athletic	1-0	1	2			5		7				11	9	4	12			3		10		6	8		14^1
10	H	Raith Rovers	2-1	1	2		14	5				8^1		11	9	4	12			3		10^1		6			
26	A	Hamilton Academical	1-0	1	2			5		7	6			11	9	4			8	3		10^1			12		14
31	H	St. Mirren	4-0		2			5		7^3		9	12	11					8	3		10^1		6			14
Jan 7	H	Stranraer	2-0	1	14		2^1	5		7			12	11					8	3		10		6	4		9^1
11	A	St. Johnstone	2-2	1	14		2	5		7			12^1	11					8	3		10^1		6	4		9
14	H	Airdrieonians	0-1	1	2			5		7			10	11		3			8			9		6	4		12
21	A	Clydebank	†3-0	1	2		3^1	5		7			10	11		12			8			9^1		6			14
Feb 4	H	Dunfermline Athletic	2-3	1	2		3	5				4	10^1	11	7^1		14		8			9	13	6			
11	A	Ayr United	0-1		2			5		7		4	10	11	12			6	8			9	1	3			14
25	A	Raith Rovers	0-0	1	2					7		9	10	11		4			8	3		12		6	5		14
Mar 4	H	Hamilton Academical	2-0	1	2					14		9	10^1	12		4			8	5^1	3	11		6			7
18	H	Clydebank	3-2	1	2			5	3	7^2			10	11	12	4^1			8			9		6			
25	A	Airdrieonians	3-0	1	2		4	5		7^2	6			11	14	10^1			8	3							9
Apr 1	A	Dunfermline Athletic	1-1	1	2		4		3	7^1			10	11		6			8	12					5		9
8	H	Ayr United	1-1	1	2		4^1	5	6	7		9		11	12	14			8		3						10
15	H	Hamilton Academical	4-1	1	2		4	5	6	7^1	8			11	9	12					3	10^3					14
22	A	Raith Rovers	0-2	1	2		6	5	4	7^1		8		11	12				8		3	10					
29	A	St. Mirren	0-1	1	2		4	5	6	7		9		11					8	3		10				14	12
May 6	A	St. Johnstone	2-1	1	2		4	5	6	7^1		9		11		8	14			3		10^1				12	
13	A	Stranraer	5-0	1	2		4	5	3	7^1		9^2		11	12^1	8			6			10^1				14	
TOTAL FULL APPEARANCES				34	30	3	23	29	16	33	1	29	23	29	13	25	4		22	13	7	23	2	20	10	1	6
TOTAL SUB APPEARANCES					(2)		(1)	(2)		(1)			(3)	(3)	(14)	(2)	(6)	(1)	(4)	(5)	(1)				(4)		(9)
TOTAL GOALS SCORED						1		3		16		3	12	2	5	3	1		1			12		1	1		2

Small bold figures denote goalscorers.   † denotes opponent's own goal.

DENS PARK

CAPACITY: 14,177; Seated 10,877, Standing 3,300

PITCH DIMENSIONS: 110 yds x 72 yds

FACILITIES FOR DISABLED SUPPORTERS: East End of Stand Enclosure.

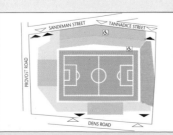

HOW TO GET THERE

You can reach Dens Park by the following routes:

BUSES: There is a frequent service of buses from the city centre. Nos. 1A and 1B leave from Albert Square and Nos. 18, 19 and 21 leave from Commercial Street.

TRAINS: Trains from all over the country pass through the mainline Dundee station and fans can then proceed to the ground by the above buses from stops situated close to the station.

CARS: Car may be parked in the car park and local streets adjacent to the ground.

DUNDEE UNITED

LIST OF PLAYERS 1995-96

SURNAME	FIRST NAME	MIDDLE NAME	DATE OF BIRTH	PLACE OF BIRTH	DATE OF SIGNING	HEIGHT FT INS	WEIGHT ST LBS	PREVIOUS CLUB
Bett	James		25/11/59	Hamilton	29/08/95	5 11.5	13 4	Heart of Midlothian
Black	Paul	Alexander	30/10/77	Aberdeen	27/07/94	5 9.5	11 6	Dundee United B.C.
Bowman	David		10/03/64	Tunbridge Wells	21/05/86	5 10.0	11 6	Coventry City
Brewster	Craig	James	13/12/66	Dundee	05/08/93	6 1.0	12 9	Raith Rovers
Caldwell	Neil		25/09/75	Glasgow	18/07/95	5 6.0	10 2	Rangers
Canning	Stephen		31/10/77	Motherwell	27/07/94	5 7.0	10 3	Dundee United B.C.
Connolly	Patrick		25/06/70	Glasgow	02/08/86	5 9.5	11 0	"S" Form
Crabbe	Scott		12/08/68	Edinburgh	03/10/92	5 8.0	11 5	Heart of Midlothian
Craig	David	William	11/06/69	Glasgow	09/06/94	6 1.5	12 8	East Stirlingshire
Dailly	Christian	Eduard	23/10/73	Dundee	02/08/90	6 1.0	12 12	"S" Form
Devine	Christopher		21/02/79	Bellshill	31/08/95	5 6.0	9 3	Dundee United B.C.
Easton	Craig		26/02/79	Bellshill	31/08/95	5 9.0	9 8	Dundee United B.C.
Fallon	Steven		08/05/79	Paisley	31/08/95	5 8.5	10 7	Dundee United B.C.
Ferreri	Juan	Francisco	13/07/70	Florida, Uruguay	06/01/95	5 10.0	12 4	Defensor Sporting Club
Gilmour	Stuart	John	17/08/77	Broxburn	27/07/94	5 7.0	10 11	Dundee United B.C.
Gomes	Sergio	Henrique	27/07/69	Juiz De Fora, Brazil	20/01/95	5 10.0	12 3	Amora
Gray	Dale	Ronald J.	27/07/94	Edinburgh	27/07/94	6 0.5	10 8	Dundee United B.C.
Hannah	David		04/08/73	Airdrie	04/09/91	5 11.5	11 8	Hamilton Thistle
Hegarty	Ryan	Michael	08/03/76	Edinburgh	27/07/94	5 11.0	10 0	Dundee United B.C.
Honeyman	Ben		14/02/77	Adelaide	27/07/94	5 9.0	10 3	Dundee United B.C.
Hughes	John	Paul	03/10/76	Bellshill	27/07/94	5 10.0	10 12	Dundee United B.C.
Johnson	Ian	Grant	24/03/72	Dundee	07/09/90	5 11.0	11 2	Broughty Ferry
Kennedy	Grahame	David	07/07/77	Dundee	27/07/94	6 0.0	10 6	Dundee United B.C.
Lamb	John		12/08/77	Bellshill	27/07/94	5 10.5	11 4	Dundee United B.C.
Malpas	Maurice	Daniel R.	03/08/62	Dunfermline	14/08/79	5 8.0	11 6	"S" Form
Maxwell	Alastair	Espie	16/02/65	Hamilton	27/06/95	5 10.0	10 12	Rangers
McKinlay	William		22/04/69	Glasgow	24/06/85	5 8.0	11 7	Hamilton Thistle
McLaren	Andrew		05/06/73	Glasgow	20/06/89	5 10.5	11 7	Rangers B.C.
Mitchell	David		24/09/76	Irvine	27/07/94	5 11.5	11 11	Dundee United B.C.
Moule	Andrew	Gareth	16/04/77	Neath	29/05/94	5,11.5	11 5	Dyce Juniors
Munro	Graeme		23/09/78	Motherwell	16/08/95	5 8.0	11 0	Dundee United B.C.
Myers	Chris		01/04/69	Yeovil	05/08/93	5 10.0	12 6	Torquay United
O'Hanlon	Kelham		16/05/62	Cleveland	14/09/94	6 0.5	13 12	Preston North End
Perry	Mark	George	07/02/71	Aberdeen	09/08/88	6 1.0	12 7	Cove Rangers
Pressley	Steven		11/10/73	Elgin	28/07/95	6 0.0	11 0	Coventry City
Robertson	Alexander		26/04/71	Edinburgh	28/07/95	5 9.0	10 7	Coventry City
Shannon	Robert		20/04/66	Bellshill	04/07/95	5 11.0	11 8	Motherwell
Stewart	Andrew	Thomas	02/01/78	Dumfries	31/08/95	6 1.0	12 4	Dundee United B.C.
Stirling	Anthony		07/09/76	Glasgow	27/07/94	6 0.0	11 5	Dundee United B.C.
Thomson	Richard	James	11/08/77	Perth	31/08/95	6 0.0	11 4	Elwood Juniors
Walker	Paul		20/08/77	Kilwinning	27/07/94	5 5.5	9 7	Dundee United B.C.
Welsh	Brian		23/02/69	Edinburgh	24/06/85	6 2.0	13 8	Tynecastle B.C.
Winters	Robert		04/11/74	East Kilbride	11/01/92	5 10.0	11 10	Muirend Amateurs

MILESTONES

YEAR OF FORMATION: 1923 (1909 as Dundee Hibs)
MOST CAPPED PLAYER: Maurice Malpas
NO. OF CAPS: 55
MOST LEAGUE POINTS IN A SEASON: 60 (Premier Division - Season 1986/87)
MOST LEAGUE GOALS SCORED BY A PLAYER IN A SEASON: John Coyle (Season 1955/56)
NO. OF GOALS SCORED: 41
RECORD ATTENDANCE: 28,000 (-v- Barcelona – 16.11.1966)
RECORD VICTORY: 14-0 (-v- Nithsdale Wanderers – Scottish Cup 17.1.1931)
RECORD DEFEAT: 1-12 (-v- Motherwell – Division 2, 23.1.1954)

SEASON TICKET INFORMATION

George Fox Stand
Top Tier
Adult £190
Juvenile/OAP £100
Middle Tier
Adult £200
Juvenile/OAP £120
Lower Tier
Adult £144
Juvenile/OAP £75

East Stand
Top Tier
Adult £190
Juvenile/OAP £100
Lower Tier
Adult £144
Juvenile/OAP £75
Family Section
1 Adult & 1 Juvenile £180

LEAGUE ADMISSION PRICES

George Fox Stand
Top Tier   Adult ....£10   Juvenile/OAP.......£6
Lower Tier   Adult ....£8   Juvenile/OAP.......£4
East Stand
Top Tier   Adult ....£10   Juvenile/OAP.......£6
Lower Tier   Adult ....£8   Juvenile/OAP.......£4
Family Section   1 Adult & 1 Juvenile............£12
Each Additional Juvenile.......................£4

South Stand
(Away Supporters)   Adult...£10
Juvenile/OAP..................................£6

West Stand
(Away Supporters)   Adult................................,.........£8
Juvenile/OAP..................................£4

Tannadice Park, Tannadice Street,
Dundee DD3 7JW

CHAIRMAN/MANAGING DIRECTOR
James Y. McLean

VICE-CHAIRMAN
Douglas B. Smith

DIRECTORS
Alistair B. Robertson
William M. Littlejohn
John H. McConnachie

SECRETARY
Miss Priti Trivedi

MANAGER
William Kirkwood

ASSISTANT PLAYER/MANAGER
Maurice Malpas

COACHING STAFF
Gordon Wallace, Kenny Cameron,
Ian Campbell, Graeme Liveston

CLUB DOCTOR
Dr. Derek J. McCormack

PHYSIOTHERAPIST
David Rankine

CHIEF SCOUT
Kenny Cameron

S.F.A. COMMUNITY OFFICER
John Holt

COMMERCIAL MANAGER
Stuart Turnbull
(01382) 833166

TELEPHONES
Ground (01382) 833166
Fax (01382) 889398

CLUB SHOP
The United Shop, Unit 2,
5/15 Victoria Road, Dundee
Tel (01382) 204066 - Open 9.00 a.m.
to 5.30 p.m. Mon-Sat
Souvenir shops are also situated
within the ground and are open
on match days

TEAM CAPTAIN
Christian Dailly

SHIRT SPONSOR
Rover

The TERRORS

Date	Venue	Opponents	Result	Jorgensen H.	Cleland A.	Perry M.	Hannah D.	Petric G.	Welsh B.	Bowman D.	Connolly P.	Ristic D.	Brewster C.	Nixon J.	Bollan C.	Main A.	McInally J.	McKinlay W.	McLaren A.	Dailly C.	Malpas M.	Myers C.	Johnson I.G.	O'Hanlon K.	Moule A.	Craig D.	Winters R.	Gomes S.	Ferreri J.	Crabbe S.
Aug 13	A	Hibernian	0-5	1	2	3	4	5	6	7	8	9	10	11	12															
20	A	Celtic	1-2		2		4	5	6	7		9	10	14¹		1		3		8	11									
27	H	Aberdeen	2-1		2		4	5	6¹	7		9	10¹	14		1		3		8	11	12								
Sep 10	H	Motherwell	1-1		2		4	5	6		10	9¹		14		1		3		8	11	7								
17	A	Heart of Midlothian	1-2		2		4	5		7		9	10	14¹		1	6	11		8	3	12								
24	H	Falkirk	1-0		2		4	5¹	6		10			11		1		8		9	7	3								
Oct 1	A	Rangers	0-2	13				5	6	7		10	14	2		1	4	8	9	11	3	12								
8	A	Kilmarnock	2-0		2		4	5	6¹	7	9¹		11	12		14	8	10		3		1					1			
15	A	Partick Thistle	0-1		2		4	5	6	7	9		11			8	10	14	3			1					1			
22	H	Hibernian	0-0		2		4	5	6	/	9		14			8		10	3		11	1	12							
29	A	Aberdeen	0-3		2		4	5	6	7		14		12		8	9	10	3		11	1								
Nov 5	H	Celtic	2-2		2			5	6	7		10¹	14			8	9	11¹	3		4	1	12							
8	A	Motherwell	1-1		2		14	5	6	7		10¹				8	9	11	3		4	1								
19	H	Heart of Midlothian	5-2		2		4	5	6	7		10¹		8¹	12	9²	3		11¹		1						14			
26	A	Falkirk	3-1				4	5	6	7		10¹	12¹	2		8¹	9	3			11	1					14			
Dec 4	H	Rangers	0-3		2		4		6	7		10	5			8	9	3			11	1					14			
26	A	Kilmarnock	2-2				4¹	5		7	12	10	14	2		8		6	3		11	1					9¹			
31	A	Hibernian	0-4		2		4	5		7		10	14			8	6	3			11	1					9			
Jan 2	H	Aberdeen	0-0		2		4	5		7	9	10	14	6		8	²11	3			1	12								
7	A	Celtic	1-1		2¹		4	5	6	7	12	10	14			8		11	3		1		9							
14	H	Heart of Midlothian	0-2		2		4	5	6	7	9	10				8	12	11	3		1		14							
21	H	Motherwell	6-1				4	5	6	/		10¹	14²	2		8²		11¹	3		1						9	12		
Feb 4	A	Rangers	1-1				4	5		7		10	11¹	2		8	6	3			1					12	14	9		
21	H	Falkirk	1-0				4	5	6	7	12	10	14	2		8		11	3¹		1						9			
25	H	Partick Thistle	2-0				4	5	6	7		10¹	14	2		8		11	3		1						9¹	12		
Mar 4	A	Kilmarnock	0-2				4	5	6	7	14	10	8	2				11	3		1						9	12		
7	A	Partick Thistle	0-2				4	5	6	7	14	10		2				11	3		1				8		9	12		
18	A	Motherwell	1-2				4	5	6	7	14	12		2		8		11	3¹		1						9	10		
21	H	Heart of Midlothian	1-1			4		5		7	10	14		2		8		11	3		1			6			9¹			
Apr 1	H	Rangers	0-2		11	4		5	6	7		10		2		8	9	12	3		1						14			
8	A	Falkirk	1-3			4		5	6	7	12			2		8	10	11	3		1						9¹			
15	A	Kilmarnock	1-2			2	10	5¹	12	6			11			3	8	14	4		1						9		7	
18	A	Partick Thistle	3-1			2	10¹	4	5²	7			6			8	12	11	3		1						14		9	
29	H	Hibernian	0-1			2	11	4				12				6	10	5	3		8	1		14	9				7	
May 6	A	Aberdeen	1-2			2	11				10			8		12		4	3		6	1		5	14¹	9			7	
13	H	Celtic	0-1			2	10				9			6			7	5	3		8	1		4	11	14		12	
TOTAL FULL APPEARANCES				1	18	9	31	33	26	31	4	8	25	8	5	6	23	25	16	30	31		12	29		3	6	11		5
TOTAL SUB APPEARANCES				(1)		(1)					(1)	(2)	(2)	(20)	(2)		(2)	(1)	(4)	(3)		(1)	(1)		(1)	(3)	(7)	(3)	(1)	(4)
TOTAL GOALS SCORED					1		2	2	4			2	7	6			4	4		1							2	3		

Small bold figures denote goalscorers. † denotes opponent's own goal.

TANNADICE PARK

CAPACITY: 12,616 (All seated)

PITCH DIMENSIONS: 110 yds x 72 yds

FACILITIES FOR DISABLED SUPPORTERS: Lower Tier – George Fox Stand – Cover for home supporters only on request.

SANDEMAN STREET

NOT IN USE

TANNADICE STREET

HOW TO GET THERE

Tannadice Park can be reached by the following routes:

BUSES: The following buses leave from the city centre at frequent intervals. Nos. 18, 19 and 21 from Commercial Street and No. 20 from Reform Street.

TRAINS: Trains from all over the country pass through the main Dundee station and fans can then proceed to the ground by the above bus services situated within walking distance of the station.

CARS: There is parking in the streets adjacent to the ground.

DUNFERMLINE ATHLETIC

East End Park, Halbeath Road,
Dunfermline, Fife, KY12 7RB

CHAIRMAN
C. Robert Woodrow

DIRECTORS
William M. Rennie
Gavin G. Masterton F.I.B. (Scot)
Joseph B. Malcolm B.Sc. Eng.
Andrew T. Gillies
David A.G. Grant C.A.

SECRETARY
Paul A. M. D'Mello

MANAGER
Robert Paton

ASSISTANT MANAGER
Richard Campbell

COACHING STAFF
Joe Nelson

CLUB DOCTOR
Hugh Whyte

PHYSIOTHERAPIST
Philip Yeates, M.C.S.P.

S.F.A. COMMUNITY COACH
Graeme Robertson

YOUTH DEVELOPMENT MANAGER
David McParland

SAFETY/SECURITY ADVISOR
William Nellies

COMMERCIAL MANAGER
Mrs. Audrey M. Kelly
(01383) 724295

TELEPHONES
Ground/Ticket Office
(01383) 724295/721749
Fax (01383) 723468

CLUB SHOP
Intersport, Kingsgate, Dunfermline.
Open 9.00 – 5.00 p.m.
Mon to Sat

OFFICIAL SUPPORTERS CLUB
c/o Mrs. J. Malcolm, Secretary,
Dunfermline Athletic
Supporters Club,
15 Meadowfield, Leuchatsbeath,
Cowdenbeath, KY4 9BF

TEAM CAPTAIN
Norman McCathie

SHIRT SPONSOR
Landmark Home Furnishing

LIST OF PLAYERS 1995-96

SURNAME	FIRST NAME	MIDDLE NAME	DATE OF BIRTH	PLACE OF BIRTH	DATE OF SIGNING	HEIGHT FT INS	WEIGHT ST LBS	PREVIOUS CLUB
Cooper	Neale	James	24/11/63	Darjeeling	29/11/91	6 0.0	12 7	Reading
Corkan	Thomas	Charles	28/04/77	Aberdeen	14/08/95	5 11.0	10 7	Rosyth Recreation
Den Bieman	Ivo	Johannes	04/02/67	Wamel	05/08/93	6 2.0	12 10	Dundee
Fenwick	Paul	Joseph	25/08/69	London	21/03/95	6 2.0	12 7	Birmingham City
Ferguson	Steven		18/05/77	Edinburgh	15/08/95	5 8.0	11 6	Rosyth Recreation
Fleming	Derek		05/12/73	Falkirk	07/10/94	5 7.0	10 2	Meadowbank Thistle
French	Hamish	Mackie	07/02/64	Aberdeen	23/10/91	5 10.5	11 7	Dundee United
Hawkins	Andrew		12/10/75	Cambridge	13/08/94	5 9.0	10 4	Hutchison Vale B.C.
Higgins	Gary		15/09/72	Stirling	10/06/94	5 11.0	11 5	Rosyth Recreation
Kinnaird	Paul		11/11/66	Glasgow	27/07/95	5 8.0	11 11	Partick Thistle
McCathie	Norman		23/03/61	Edinburgh	17/08/81	6 0.0	12 10	Cowdenbeath
McCulloch	Mark	Ross	19/05/75	Inverness	02/08/94	5 11.0	12 0	Inverness Clachnacuddin
McKeever	Mark	John	11/07/75	Motherwell	15/08/95	5 8.0	10 10	Bonnybridge Juniors
McNamara	Jackie		24/10/73	Glasgow	17/09/91	5 8.0	9 7	Gairdoch United
Millar	Marc		10/04/69	Dundee	14/10/94	5 9.0	10 12	Brechin City
Moore	Allan		25/12/64	Glasgow	26/03/94	5 7.0	10 0	St. Johnstone
Petrie	Stewart	James John	27/02/70	Dundee	27/08/93	5 10.0	11 11	Forfar Athletic
Robertson	Craig	Peter	22/04/63	Dunfermline	30/08/91	5 10.0	12 0	Aberdeen
Shaw	Gregory		15/02/70	Dumfries	31/03/95	6 0.0	10 12	Falkirk
Smith	Andrew	Mark	22/11/68	Aberdeen	21/07/95	6 1.0	12 7	Airdrieonians
Smith	Paul	McKinnon	02/11/62	Edinburgh	06/01/93	5 11.0	12 0	Falkirk
Tod	Andrew		04/11/71	Dunfermline	04/11/93	6 3.0	12 0	Kelty Hearts
Van De Kamp	Guido		08/02/64	S-Hertogewbosch	21/01/95	6 2.5	12 12	Dundee United
Ward	Kenneth		16/06/63	Blairhall	05/08/94	5 7.0	11 4	Hamilton Academical
Westwater	Ian		08/11/63	Loughborough	30/03/94	6 2.0	14 8	Dundee

MILESTONES

YEAR OF FORMATION: 1885
MOST CAPPED PLAYER: Istvan Kozma
NO. OF CAPS: Hungary 29 – (13 whilst with Dunfermline Athletic)
MOST LEAGUE POINTS IN A SEASON: 65 (First Division – Season 1993/94) (2 Points for a Win)
68 (First Division – Season 1994/95) (3 Points for a Win)
MOST LEAGUE GOALS SCORED BY A PLAYER IN A SEASON: Bobby Skinner (Season 1925/26)
NO. OF GOALS SCORED: 53
RECORD ATTENDANCE: 27,816 (-v- Celtic – 30.4.1968)
RECORD VICTORY: 11-2 (-v- Stenhousemuir – Division 2. 27.9.1930)
RECORD DEFEAT: 0-10 (-v- Dundee – Division 2. 22.3.1947)

SEASON TICKET INFORMATION

Seated
Centre Stand
Adult £170
Juvenile/OAP £95
West Enclosure
Adult £130
Juvenile/OAP £75
Family West Wing Stand Parent & Juvenile............£235
Extra Parent....................£150
Extra Juvenile...................£85
OAP & Juvenile £170

Standing
Adult £130
Juvenile/OAP.......................................£75

LEAGUE ADMISSION PRICES

Seated
Stand
Adult £9
Juvenile/OAP £5
West Enclosure
Adult £7
Juvenile/OAP £4

Standing
Ground
Adult £7
Juvenile/OAP £4

CLUB FACTFILE 1994/95
RESULTS .. APPEARANCES .. SCORERS

The PARS

Small bold figures denote goalscorers. † denotes opponent's own goal.

Date	Venue	Opponents	Result	Westwater I.	Den Bieman I.	Bowes M.	McCathie N.	Cooper N.	Smith ?.	Moore A.	Robertson C.	Petrie ?.	Laing D.	Tod A.	McCulloch M.	McNamara J.	Ward K.	French H.	Will J.	McQueen J.	Sharp R.	Sinclair C.	Hawkins A.	Fleming C.	Millar M.	Higgins G.	Paterson G.	Harrison T.	Van De Kamp G.	Shaw C.	Fenwick F.
Aug 13	A	Airdrieonians	0-0	1	2	3	4	5	6	7	8	9	10	11	14																
20	A	Clydebank	1-0	1	2	3	4	5	6		8	9[1]		11				7	10	12											
27	H	Raith Rovers	1-0	1	2	3	4	5	6		8	10	12	11				7	9[1]	13											
Sep 3	A	St. Mirren	1-1		2	3	4	5	6		8	10	12	11				7	9[1]	1											
10	H	Hamilton Academical	4-0		7		2	4[1]	5	6	8	10[2]						11	9[1]	1	3										
24	H	Stranraer	1-0	1	7		2	4		6	8	10[1]	12	5				11	9		3	14									
Oct 1	A	Dundee	4-4	1	7		2	4[1]		6[1]	8	10[1]	12	5		3	11	9[1]					14								
8	H	St. Johnstone	3-0	1	7		4		6[1]		8	10[1]		5[1]		2	11	9					3								
15	A	Ayr United	0-0	1	7		4		6		10			5		2	11	9					3	8							
22	H	Airdrieonians	2-2	1	14				6		8	10	7	5	4	2	12	9[2]					3	11							
29	A	Raith Rovers	5-2	1	12		4		6		8	10[2]		5	2		7[2]	9[1]					3	11	14						
Nov 5	H	Clydebank	4-1	1	12[1]		4		6		8[1]	10[2]		5		2	7	9					3	11							
12	A	Hamilton Academical	1-3	1	12		4	14	6		8	10[1]		5		2	7	9					3	11							
19	H	St. Mirren	1-0	1	12		4	5	6[1]		8	10		14		2	7	9					3	11							
26	A	Stranraer	0-0	1	12		4	5	6		8	10		7		2		9					3	11							
Dec 3	H	Dundee	0-1	1			4	5	6		8	10		14		2	7	9					3	11							
10	H	Ayr United	6-0	1	7[1]		4	5	6		8	10		14[1]		2[1]	11	9[3]					3	12							
26	A	St. Johnstone	2-3	1	7[2]			5	6		8	14		10		2	11	9					3	12			4				
31	A	Airdrieonians	0-0		7			5	6		8	10		12		2	14	9	1				3	11			4				
Jan 7	A	Clydebank	2-1		7		4		6		8[1]	14		12		2		9	1				3	11[1]	10	5					
11	H	Raith Rovers	0-1		14		4		6		8	10		5		2	7	9	1				3	11							
14	A	St. Mirren	2-2				4	5	6		8	10[2]		9		2	7		1				3	11			14				
21	H	Hamilton Academical	2-1		7			5	6		8	10[1]		9[1]		2	11						3				4	1			
Feb 4	A	Dundee	3-2		7		4		6[2]		8	10		11		2	14	9					3[1]		5		1				
14	H	Stranraer	3-1		14		4		6		8	10		9[1]		2[1]	12[1]	7			11	3			5		1				
25	A	Ayr United	2-1		12		4	5	6[1]	7	8	10		2			11[1]					3	9			1					
Mar 11	A	St. Johnstone	1-1				4		7	8				5	6	2	11	9			12	3	10[1]			1					
22	A	Hamilton Academical	3-1		7		4		11[1]	8				5	6	2	9[2]				12	3	10			1					
25	H	St. Mirren	1-1	1	12		4		6	7	8	10		5[1]		2	9					3	11								
Apr 1	H	Dundee	1-1		14[1]		4		6	7	8	10		5		2						3	11					1	9	
8	A	Stranraer	1-0				4		6	7	8[1]	10		5	12	2						3	11					1	9	
15	A	St. Johnstone	1-1				4		6	9	8[1]	10		5	7	2					12	3	11					1	9	14
22	H	Ayr United	3-0		12		4[1]		6	7	8[1]	10		5[1]		2						3	11					1	9	
29	H	Airdrieonians	0-0		7			6	11	8	10			5	14	2						3						1	9	12
May 6	A	Raith Rovers	0-0		10		4		6	7	8			5		2						3	11					1	9	
13	H	Clydebank	2-1		7		4[1]		6	12	8[1]	10		5	14	2						3	11					1	9	
TOTAL FULL APPEARANCES				17	19	7	32	14	34	11	35	31	2	30	5	30	19	24	5	1	2	1	29	22	1	5	1		13	6
TOTAL SUB APPEARANCES					(12)		(1)		(1)		(2)	(4)	(5)	(4)		(4)	(1)	(1)			(1)	(4)		(2)	(1)		(1)			(2)
TOTAL GOALS SCORED					5		4		6	1	6	14		6		2	4	12					1		2					

EAST END PARK

CAPACITY: 18,328; Seated 4,008, Standing 14,320

PITCH DIMENSIONS: 115 yds x 68 yds

FACILITIES FOR DISABLED SUPPORTERS: Special ramped area in West Enclosure.

HALBEATH ROAD

HOW TO GET THERE

East End Park may be reached by the following routes:

TRAINS: Dunfermline Station is served by trains from both Glasgow and Edinburgh and the ground is a 15 minute walk from here.

BUSES: Buses destined for Kelty, Perth, St. Andrews and Kirkcaldy all pass close to East End Park.

CARS: Car Parking is available in a large car park adjoining the East End of the ground and there are also facilities in various side streets. Multi-storey car parking approximately 10 minutes walk from ground.

GREENOCK MORTON

Cappielow Park, Sinclair Street,
Greenock, PA15 2TY

CHAIRMAN
John Wilson

DIRECTORS
Duncan D. F. Rae
Kenneth Woods
Andrew Gemmell

SECRETARY
Mrs Jane W. Rankin

MANAGER
Allan McGraw

ASSISTANT MANAGER
Peter Cormack

SENIOR COACH
John McMaster

CLUB DOCTOR
Dr. R. Craig Speirs

CROWD DOCTOR
Dr. F. Gray

PHYSIOTHERAPIST
John Tierney

S.F.A. COMMUNITY COACH
David Provan

GROUNDSMAN
Ian Lyle

KIT MANAGER
William Gray

SALES & MARKETING MANAGER
Ms. Sandra Fisher

LOTTERY MANAGER
Stuart Rafferty

STADIUM MANAGER
Alex Renfrew

TELEPHONES
Ground/Ticket Office
(01475) 723571
Fax (01475) 781084

CLUB SHOP
Situated under Main Stand –
Open Home matchdays only

OFFICIAL SUPPORTERS CLUB
Greenock Morton Supporters Club,
Regent Street, Greenock

TEAM CAPTAIN
Derek McInnes

SHIRT SPONSOR
Buchanans Toffees

LIST OF PLAYERS 1995-96

SURNAME	FIRST NAME	MIDDLE NAME	DATE OF BIRTH	PLACE OF BIRTH	DATE OF SIGNING	HEIGHT FT INS	WEIGHT ST LBS	PREVIOUS CLUB
Aitken	Stephen	Smith	25/09/76	Glasgow	17/12/93	5 6.0	9 7	Erskine B.C.
Alexander	Rowan	Samuel	28/01/61	Ayr	09/08/86	5 7.0	11 10	Brentford
Anderson	John	Patton	02/10/72	Greenock	25/01/94	6 2.0	12 2	Gourock Y.A.C.
Blaikie	Alan		25/08/72	Greenock	30/12/94	6 1.0	12 0	Greenock Juniors
Blair	Paul		05/07/76	Greenock	21/06/94	5 7.0	10 8	Ferguslie United
Collins	Derek	J.	15/04/69	Glasgow	23/07/87	5 8.0	10 7	Renfrew Waverley
Cormack	Peter	Robert	08/06/74	Liverpool	11/08/94	6 0.0	11 5	Newcastle United
Fanning	Ross	Stewart	04/09/76	Vale of Leven	01/09/95	5 9.5	10 11	Duntocher B.C.
Flannery	Patrick		23/07/76	Glasgow	10/08/94	5 11.0	10 12	Eadie Star U'18
Gibson	Lorn		06/07/76	Paisley	05/07/94	5 11.0	10 12	Clydebank U'18
Hawke	Warren		20/09/70	Durham	28/07/95	5 10.5	11 4	Berwick Rangers
Hunter	James	Addison	20/12/64	Johnstone	18/09/85	5 9.0	10 10	Glentyan Thistle
Johnstone	Douglas	Iain	12/03/69	Irvine	31/08/91	6 2.0	12 8	Glasgow University
Laing	Derek	James	11/11/73	Haddington	20/02/95	5 10.0	11 7	Dunfermline Athletic
Lilley	Derek	Symon	09/02/74	Paisley	13/08/91	5 10.5	12 7	Everton B.C.
Lindberg	Janne		24/05/66	Finland	11/11/94	5 7.0	11 0	MyPa–47 (Finland)
Mahood	Alan	Scott	26/03/73	Kilwinning	23/03/92	5 8.0	10 10	Nottingham Forest
Mason	Barry		06/09/76	Glasgow	31/08/95	5 8.5	11 0	Bearsden B.C.
McArthur	Scott		28/02/68	Johnstone	26/12/92	5 11.0	11 10	Heart of Midlothian
McCahill	Stephen	Joseph	03/09/66	Greenock	02/10/92	6 2.0	12 0	Celtic
McCann	Mark		26/01/76	Kilwinning	29/06/94	5 9.0	10 10	Tass Thistle B.C.
McGhee	Dennis		01/04/75	Greenock	07/06/93	5 6.0	10 0	Clyde Thistle
McInnes	Derek	John	05/07/71	Paisley	13/08/88	5 7.0	11 4	Gleniffer Thistle
McPherson	Craig		27/03/71	Greenock	07/10/94	5 9.0	11 3	Gourock Amateurs
Rajamaki	Marko		03/10/68	Finland	11/11/94	5 7.0	11 3	MyPa–47 (Finland)
Simpson	Mark		04/11/75	Aberdeen	10/04/95	6 0.0	12 2	Greenock Juniors
Wylie	David		04/04/66	Johnstone	01/08/85	6 0.0	13 0	Ferguslie United

MILESTONES

YEAR OF FORMATION: 1874
MOST CAPPED PLAYER: Jimmy Cowan
NO. OF CAPS: 25
MOST LEAGUE POINTS IN A SEASON: 69 (Division 2 – Season 1966/67)
MOST LEAGUE GOALS SCORED BY A PLAYER IN A SEASON: Allan McGraw (Season 1963/64)
NO. OF GOALS SCORED: 58
RECORD ATTENDANCE: 23,500 (-v- Celtic – 1922)
RECORD VICTORY: 11-0 (-v- Carfin Shamrock – Scottish Cup, 13.11.1886)
RECORD DEFEAT: 1-10 (-v- Port Glasgow Athletic – Division 2, 5.5.1884)

SEASON TICKET INFORMATION

Seated
Adult £140
Juvenile/OAP.......................................£90
Standing
Adult £120
Juvenile/OAP.......................................£60

LEAGUE ADMISSION PRICES

Seated
Adult £9
Juvenile/OAP £4
Standing
Adult £7
Juvenile/OAP £3

The TON

Small bold figures denote goalscorers. † denotes opponent's own goal.

Date	Venue	Opponents	Result	Wylie D.	Collins J.	Cormack P.	Hunter J.	McCahill S.	Johnstone D.	Lilley D.	Anderson J.	Alexander R.	McArthur S.	Flannery P.	Blair P.	Fowler J.	Mahood A.	Pickering M.	Gibson L.	McPherson C.	McCann M.	Lindberg J.	McInnes D.	Rajamaki M.	Laing J.
Aug 13	H	Berwick Rangers	1-1	1	2	3	4	5	6	7	8	9^{1}	10	11	14										
20	A	Meadowbank Thistle	1-0	1	2	3	4	5	6	7^{1}		9	11		14	8	10								
27	A	Dumbarton	1-2	1	2	3	4	5	6	7^{1}		9	11		14	8	10	12							
Sep 3	A	Stirling Albion	0-2	1	2	3	4	5	6	7	14	9	11			8	10	12							
10	H	Brechin City	2-0	1	2	12	4	5	6	7		9^{1}	11^{1}			8	10		3						
24	H	East Fife	2-1	1	2	3	4	5	6	7^{1}		9^{1}	11			8	10								
Oct 1	H	Stenhousemuir	3-2	1	2	3		5	6	7	4^{1}	9^{2}	11		14	8	10	12							
8	A	Clyde	0-1	1	2	3		5	6	7	4	9	10	11		8									
15	A	Queen of the South	0-3	1	2	3		5	6	7	4	9	10	11	14	8		12							
22	A	Berwick Rangers	1-2	1	2			5		7^{1}	4	9	3			8						6	10	11	
29	H	Dumbarton	1-0	1	2	3		5		7	4	9^{1}				8						6	10	11	
Nov 5	H	Meadowbank Thistle	4-0	1	2	3		5		7^{2}	4	9			14	8		12				6	10	11^{2}	
12	A	Brechin City	3-1	1	2			5^{1}		7	4	9^{1}	3		14	8						6^{1}	10	11	
22	A	Stirling Albion	1-1	1	2			5		7	4	9^{1}	3		14	8		12				6	10	11	
26	H	East Fife	3-0	1	2			5		7	4^{1}	9	3			8		12				6	10	11^{2}	
Dec 3	A	Stenhousemuir	0-0	1	2			5		7	4	9	3		14	8						6	10	11	
26	H	Clyde	0-0	1	2			5		7	4	9	3			8		12				6	10	11	
31	H	Queen of the South	1-1	1	2			5		7	4	9	3			8		12				6	10	11^{1}	
Jan 14	H	Berwick Rangers	2-1	1	2	3		5		7^{1}	4	9	12		14	8						6	10	11^{1}	
21	A	Meadowbank Thistle	0-1	1	2			5		7	4	9	3			8		12				6	10	11	
24	A	Dumbarton	1-2	1	2			5		7	4	9	3			8		12				6	10	11^{1}	
Feb 4	H	Brechin City	1-0	1	2			5		7	4	9^{1}	3		14	8				12		6	10	11	
11	A	Stirling Albion	3-0	1	2			5		7^{1}	4	9	3		14			12		8^{1}		6	10^{1}	11	
25	H	Stenhousemuir	1-0	1	2			5		7	4	9	3			8						6	10	11^{1}	12
28	A	East Fife	†1-1	1	2			5		7	4	9	3			8				14		6	10	11	12
Mar 11	A	Queen of the South	0-1	1	2			5			4	9	3			8		12				6	10	11	7
14	A	Clyde	4-1	1	2			5		7^{2}	4	9	3			8				14		6	10^{1}	11^{1}	12
18	A	Brechin City	1-1	1	2			5		7	4	9	3			8				12		6	10	11^{1}	14
25	A	Stirling Albion	2-2	1	2			5		7	4	9	3					12				6	10	11^{2}	8
Apr 1	H	Stenhousemuir	1-1	1	2			5		7^{1}	4		3			8				14		6	10	11	9
8	H	East Fife	4-1	1	2			5^{1}		7^{1}	4^{1}		3			8		12		14		6	10	11	9^{1}
15	A	Clyde	3-1	1	2			5		7	4		3^{1}			8				12		6	10^{1}	11	9^{1}
22	H	Queen of the South	0-0	1	2			5		7	4		3			8		12		14		6	10	11	9
29	A	Berwick Rangers	4-3	1	2			5		7^{2}	4		3							8^{1}		6	10	11	9
May 6	H	Dumbarton	2-0	1	2			5		7^{1}	4		3			8				12		6	10	11^{1}	9
13	H	Meadowbank Thistle	1-0	1	2			5		7^{1}	4		3		14			12		8		6	10	11	9
TOTAL FULL APPEARANCES				36	33	12	6	27	22	34	28	26	30	2	8	9	18	6	3	9	2	25	26	25	9
TOTAL SUB APPEARANCES							(2)		(2)	(1)	(2)	(6)	(3)	(1)	(8)	(5)	(3)	(2)	(1)	(7)					(3)
TOTAL GOALS SCORED					1			2		16	3	9	2				1					1	3	14	2

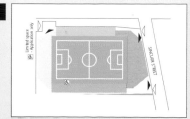

CAPPIELOW PARK

CAPACITY: 14,267; Seating 5,257, Standing 9,010

PITCH DIMENSIONS: 110 yds x 71 yds

FACILITIES FOR DISABLED SUPPORTERS: Seating facilities below Grandstand.

HOW TO GET THERE

Cappielow Park may be reached by the following routes:

BUSES: Services from Glasgow stop just outside the park. There are also services from Port Glasgow and Gourock.

TRAINS: The nearest local station is Cartsdyke and it is a five minute walk from here to the ground. There are two to three trains every hour from Glasgow and from Gourock.

CARS: Car parking is available in James Watt Dock which is on the A8 road just next to the ground and on adjacent ground nearby.

HAMILTON ACADEMICAL

Douglas Park, Douglas Park Lane,
Hamilton ML3 0DF

GROUND ADDRESS
Firhill Stadium, 80 Firhill Road,
Glasgow G20 7BA

CHAIRMAN
David Campbell

CHIEF EXECUTIVE
Alistair R. Duguid

DIRECTORS
David Campbell Jnr.
James W. Watson C.A.
William Whitelaw

SECRETARY
Scott A. Struthers B.A.

HON. LIFE PRESIDENT
Dr. Alexander A. Wilson

MANAGER
Iain Munro

**ASSISTANT MANAGER/
COMMERCIAL MANAGER**
Alexander Clark

HON. MEDICAL OFFICER
Dr. Brian Lynas

HON. ORTHOPAEDIC SURGEON
Mr. S. K. Mukherjee

PHYSIOTHERAPIST
Douglas Lauchlan

S.F.A. COMMUNITY COACH
Jim Chapman

TELEPHONES
Office (01698) 286103
Ground 0141-945 4811
(Matchdays Only)
Fax (01698) 285422
Information Service
(0891) 666492

CLUB SHOP
"The Acciesshop",
c/o Accies Stand Club,
51 Burnbank Road,
Hamilton ML3

OFFICIAL SUPPORTERS CLUB
The Stand Club,
c/o 51 Burnbank Road,
Hamilton ML3

TEAM CAPTAIN
Paul McKenzie

SHIRT SPONSOR
Wilson Homebuilders

LIST OF PLAYERS 1995-96

SURNAME	FIRST NAME	MIDDLE NAME	DATE OF BIRTH	PLACE OF BIRTH	DATE OF SIGNING	HEIGHT FT INS	WEIGHT ST LBS	PREVIOUS CLUB
Baptie	Crawford	Bowie	24/02/59	Glasgow	11/08/95	6 1.0	11 7	Falkirk
Burns	Thomas	Brian	06/08/77	Bellshill	25/08/95	5 11.0	11 8	Dundee United
Clark	Gary		13/09/64	Glasgow	25/06/91	5 10.0	11 10	Clyde
Cormack	David		29/11/70	Lanark	01/11/93	6 2.0	13 7	Vale of Clyde
Ferguson	Allan	Thomas	21/03/69	Lanark	31/12/87	5 10.5	12 6	Netherdale Com A.F.C
Hartley	Paul		19/10/76	Glasgow	09/09/94	5 8.0	10 0	Mill United B.C.
Hillcoat	Christopher	Patrick	03/10/69	Glasgow	19/05/87	5 10.0	11 3	St. Bridget's B.G.
Lorimer	David	James	26/01/74	Bellshill	04/08/93	5 9.5	11 0	Hamilton Accies B.C.
McCarrison	Dugald		22/12/69	Lanark	18/08/95	5 8.0	12 0	Kilmarnock
McCormick	Steven	Walter	10/11/75	Bellshill	02/06/94	5 6.0	9 10	Mill United
McCulloch	Scott	Anderson J.	29/11/75	Irvine	24/03/95	5 11.0	11 12	Rangers
McEntegart	Sean	David	01/03/70	Dublin	24/07/92	6 0.0	11 7	Queen's Park
McIntosh	Martin	Wylie	19/03/71	East Kilbride	01/02/94	6 2.0	12 4	Clydebank
McInulty	Stephen	James	22/09/71	Bellshill	30/01/93	5 11.0	11 0	Larkhall Thistle
McKenzie	Paul	Vincent	22/09/64	Glasgow	30/01/91	5 11.0	12 4	Dumbarton
McParland	John	Ian	04/10/61	Edinburgh	23/08/95	5 9.0	11 4	Eastern Athletic
McQuade	John		08/07/70	Glasgow	31/08/93	5 9.0	10 4	Dumbarton
McStay	Raymond		16/05/70	Hamilton	10/01/95	5 11.0	11 0	Celtic
Murphy	David		08/09/76	Lanark	18/08/95	5 10.5	11 0	"X" Form
Paterson	Craig	Stewart	02/10/59	South Queensferry	10/08/95	6 2.5	13 10	Kilmarnock
Renicks	Steven	John	28/11/75	Bellshill	01/06/94	5 7.0	10 4	Hamilton Accies B.C.
Sherry	James	Cunningham	09/09/73	Glasgow	19/05/92	5 8.0	11 9	Hamilton Accies B.C.
Tennant	Gary		16/08/75	Bellshill	15/11/94	6 1.0	12 0	Cumnock Juniors
Thomson	Steven		19/04/73	Glasgow	06/01/95	6 0.0	10 12	Kirkintilloch Rob Roy
Tighe	Martin	Charles	11/06/76	Bellshill	30/09/94	5 9.0	11 0	Dundee United

MILESTONES

YEAR OF FORMATION: 1874
MOST CAPPED PLAYER: Colin Miller (Canada)
NO. OF CAPS: 29
MOST LEAGUE POINTS IN A SEASON: 57 (First Division – Season 1991/92)
MOST LEAGUE GOALS SCORED BY A PLAYER IN A SEASON: David Wilson (Season 1936/37)
NO. OF GOALS SCORED: 34
RECORD ATTENDANCE: 28,690 (-v- Heart of Midlothian – Scottish Cup 3.3.1937)
RECORD VICTORY: 10-2 (-v- Cowdenbeath – Division 1, 15.10.1932)
RECORD DEFEAT: 1-11 (-v- Hibernian – Division 1, 6.11.1965)

SEASON TICKET INFORMATION

Seated
Adult £120
Youth/OAP £70
Child (U-14) £25

LEAGUE ADMISSION PRICES

Seated
Adult £7
U-16/OAP £4

CLUB FACTFILE 1994/95
RESULTS .. APPEARANCES .. SCORERS

The ACCIES

Date	Venue	Opponents	Result	Ferguson A.	McKerzie P.	McNulty S.	McEntagart S.	Baptie C.	McIntosh M.	McQuade J.	Sherry J.	Chalmers ?.	Duffield P.	Lorimer D.	Campbell D.	McLean C.	Hartley P.	Nicholls D.	Cormack D.	Clark P.	McGill D.	McStay J.	Rennicks S.	Clark G.	Tichie M.	McCormick S.	Hillcoat C.	McStay R.	Water M.	McCall I.	McCulloch S.A.J.
Aug 13	A	Ayr United	1-1	1	2	3	4	5	6	7	8	9	10	11¹	12																
20	A	Raith Rovers	1-1	1	2	3	4	5	6	7	8	9¹	10	11	14																
27	H	Airdrieonians	2-6	1	2	3	4	5	6¹	7	8	9	10¹	11	12	14															
Sep 3	H	Stranraer	1-0	1	2	3	4	5	6	12	8	9	10¹				7	14	11												
10	A	Dunfermline Athletic	0-4	1	2	3	4	5	6	11	8	9	10				7														
24	A	St. Johnstone	1-1		2	3	4	5	6	7			10		12				11	1	8	9¹									
Oct 1	H	St. Mirren	7-2		2	3	4	5	6	7¹			10¹							1	11	9	8								
8	A	Dundee	0-2		2	3	4	5	6	7	11		10		14					1		9	8								
15	H	Clydebank	0-0		2	3	4	5	6	7	14	12	10						11	1				8	9						
22	A	Ayr United	2-0		2	3	4	5	6	7	12		10¹	14					11	1				8¹	9						
29	A	Airdrieonians	0-1		2	3	4	5	6	7	12		10	9			14			1				8		11					
Nov 5	H	Raith Rovers	0-3		2	3	4	5	6	7	12		10	9						1				8		11					
12	H	Dunfermline Athletic	3-1		5		4	12	6	7	2	9	10²	11						1			14	3	8¹						
19	A	Stranraer	0-2		5		4	12	6	7	2	9	10	11						1				3	8						
26	H	St. Johnstone	3-1		5	3	4		6	8¹		9	10²	11			7			1				2	14						
Dec 3	A	St. Mirren	1-0		5	3	4		6	8		9	10¹	11						1			14	2	7						
26	H	Dundee	0-1		5	3			6	8		9	10	11				4	1				14	2	12	7					
31	A	Ayr United	2-1	1	5	3¹	4	12	6	8		9	10	11										2	7¹	14					
Jan 2	H	Airdrieonians	3-0	1	5	3	4	8	6¹			9¹	10¹	11										2	7	12	14				
7	A	Raith Rovers	0-2	1	5	3	4	8	6			9	10	11	12									2	7		14				
10	A	Clydebank	0-0	1		3		8	6			9	10	11	14									2	7		5	4	12		
14	H	Stranraer	1-0	1		3		12	6			9	10¹						8					2	14		5	4	7	11	
21	A	Dunfermline Athletic	1-2	1		3	14	9	6	8			10	12										2	7¹		5	4		11	
Feb 4	H	St. Mirren	2-0	1	5		4		6	11		9	10¹	14										2	7¹		3	8	12		
18	A	St. Johnstone	0-3	1	9		4	5	6	8			10	11					14					2	7		3	12			
25	H	Clydebank	0-1	1	5		4	6		9	2	14	10	12										7			3	8		11	
Mar 4	A	Dundee	0-2	1	5	3	4		6	8		9	10											2	7		14	12		11	
22	H	Dunfermline Athletic	1-3	1	5	3	4	12		9			10¹	14										2	7	8	11	6			
25	A	Stranraer	5-0	1	5	3		6		12			10²	14	9¹									2	4¹	7		8¹		11	
Apr 1	A	St. Mirren	2-3	1	5	3	14¹	6		8			10	12	9	7								2	4					11¹	
8	H	St. Johnstone	1-0	1	5		4	12		8			10¹	14	9	7		2						3	6					11	
15	H	Dundee	1-4	1	5		4			8	14		10¹		9	7		2						12	3	6				11	
22	H	Clydebank	4-1	1		3	4	5	6		8		10³	14		7								12	9¹	2				11	
29	H	Ayr United	1-0	1		3	4	5	6	12	8		10	14		7								9	2					11	
May 6	A	Airdrieonians	1-0	1		3	4	5	6		8		10	14		7								12¹	9	2				11	
13	H	Raith Rovers	0-0	1		3	4	5	6	8	7		10	14										12	9	2				11	
TOTAL FULL APPEARANCES				24	29	29	30	24	30	27	12	18	36	15		5	10	3	12	4	4	2	19	12	7	5	15	9	2	5	8
TOTAL SUB APPEARANCES							(2)		(6)		(3)	(2)		(5)	(12)	(3)	(2)	(6)				(3)		(5)	(3)	(3)	(2)	(1)	(1)	(1)
TOTAL GOALS SCORED						1	1		2	2		2	20	2		1			1				1	4	1	1		1		1	1

Small bold figures denote goalscorers. † denotes opponent's own goal.

FIRHILL STADIUM

CAPACITY: 21,776 Seated 9,076 Standing 12,700

PITCH DIMENSIONS: 110 yds x 74 yds

FACILITIES FOR DISABLED SUPPORTERS: Covered places available in North Enclosure. 10 Wheelchair spectators, 10 attendants, 10 ambulant disabled. Telephone in advance to Club Secretary for arrangements.

FIRHILL ROAD

HOW TO GET THERE

The following routes may be used to reach Firhill Stadium:

TRAINS: The nearest railway stations are Glasgow Queen Street and Glasgow Central and buses from the centre of the city pass within 100 yards of the ground.

BUSES: The following buses from the city centre all pass by the park. Nos. 1, 18, 21, 21A, 57, 60, 61 and 61B and the frequency of buses is just over 12 minutes.

UNDERGROUND: The nearest GGPTE Underground station is St. George's Cross and supporters walking from here should pass through Cromwell Street into Maryhill Road and then walk up this road as far as Firhill Street. The ground is then on the right. The Kelvinbridge Underground Station is also not far from the park and supporters from here should walk along Great Western Road as far as Napiershill Street and then follow this into Maryhill Road.

ST. JOHNSTONE

McDiarmid Park, Crieff Road
Perth PH1 2SJ

CHAIRMAN
Geoffrey S. Brown

DIRECTORS
Douglas B. McIntyre
Henry S. Ritchie
David F. Sidey
Alexander Hay
Henry G. Stewart

**MANAGING DIRECTOR/
SECRETARY**
A. Stewart M. Duff

MANAGER
Paul W. Sturrock

FIRST TEAM COACH
John Blackley

RESERVE TEAM COACHES
John Blackley
Alastair Stevenson

YOUTH COACH
Alastair Stevenson

CLUB DOCTOR
Alistair McCracken

PHYSIOTHERAPIST
David Henderson

S.F.A. COMMUNITY OFFICER
Atholl Henderson

STADIUM MANAGER
Jimmy Hogg

SALES EXECUTIVE
Helen Harcus
(01738) 626961

LOTTERY MANAGER
Alastair Cameron

CATERING MANAGER
Scott Ritchie

TELEPHONES
Ground/Ticket Office
(01738) 626961
Fax (01738) 625771
Information Service 0891 121559

CLUB SHOP
Mon-Fri Ticket Office at Ground
and Sat. Matchdays.
Situated at South Stand

OFFICIAL SUPPORTERS CLUB
c/o McDiarmid Park,
Crieff Road, Perth

TEAM CAPTAIN
David Irons

SHIRT SPONSOR
The Famous Grouse

LIST OF PLAYERS 1995-96

SURNAME	FIRST NAME	MIDDLE NAME	DATE OF BIRTH	PLACE OF BIRTH	DATE OF SIGNING	HEIGHT FT INS	WEIGHT ST LBS	PREVIOUS CLUB
Baillie	Robert		04/04/78	Edinburgh	15/06/94	5 10.0	11 8	"S" Form
Cherry	Paul	Robert	14/10/64	Derby	02/07/88	6 0.0	11 6	Cowdenbeath
Davidson	Callum	Ian	25/06/76	Stirling	08/06/94	5 10.0	11 0	"S" Form
Donaldson	Euan	Gordon	20/08/75	Falkirk	16/05/95	5 10.0	10 7	Stenhousemuir
English	Isaac		12/11/71	Paisley	31/12/94	5 9.0	10 11	Partick Thistle
Farquhar	Gary	Robert	23/02/71	Wick	14/10/94	5 7.0	11 4	Brora Rangers
Ferguson	Ian		05/08/68	Dunfermline	30/11/93	6 1.0	13 12	Heart of Midlothian
Freedman	Gordon	James	27/11/78	Glasgow	22/07/95	5 10.0	10 4	Celtic B.C.
Grant	Roderick	John	16/09/66	Gloucester	29/07/95	5 11.0	11 0	Partick Thistle
Griffin	Daniel	Joseph	10/08/77	Belfast	18/02/94	5 10.0	10 5	St. Andrews Belfast
Irons	David	John	18/07/61	Glasgow	15/07/93	6 0.0	11 4	Partick Thistle
Main	Alan	David	05/12/67	Elgin	05/01/95	5 11.5	12 13	Dundee United
Mathieson	David	James	18/01/78	Dumfries	10/08/94	5 11.0	10 13	Rangers
McCluskey	Stuart	Campbell	29/10/77	Bellshill	07/07/94	5 11.0	10 3	"S" Form
McGowne	Kevin		16/12/69	Kilmarnock	26/06/92	6 0.0	12 3	St. Mirren
McLean	Scott	James	17/06/76	East Kilbride	01/08/95	5 11.5	12 5	East Kilbride Thistle
McQuillan	John		20/07/70	Stranraer	04/07/95	5 10.0	11 7	Dundee
Mullen	Martynn		23/05/78	Glasgow	27/03/95	5 10.0	11 0	West Ham United
Munro	Kenneth	Neil	08/08/77	Edinburgh	06/05/94	5 10.0	11 0	Possil Y.M.
O'Boyle	George		14/12/67	Belfast	24/07/94	5 8.0	11 9	Dunfermline Athletic
O'Neil	John		06/07/71	Bellshill	04/08/94	5 7.0	11 7	Dundee United
Preston	Allan		16/08/69	Edinburgh	26/03/94	5 10.0	11 4	Dunfermline Athletic
Proctor	Mark	Gerard	30/01/61	Middlesbrough	22/08/95	5 9.0	11 8	Tranmere Rovers
Reynolds	Craig	Robert John	03/10/77	Dunfermline	06/05/94	5 8.0	9 9	Possilpark Y.M.C.A.
Rhodes	Andrew	Charles	23/08/64	Doncaster	02/07/92	6 1.0	14 2	Oldham Athletic
Rice	Paul	William	25/08/77	Glasgow	18/02/94	5 9.0	11 6	Possil Y.M.
Robertson	Stephen		16/03/77	Glasgow	16/09/94	5 10.0	11 13	Ashfield Juniors
Scott	Peter		24/11/78	Vale of Leven	10/12/94	5 5.5	10 12	Gleniffer Thistle
Scott	Philip	Campbell	14/11/74	Perth	30/07/91	5 9.0	11 1	Scone Thistle
Sturrock	Paul	Whitehead	10/10/56	Ellon	26/11/93	5 8.5	12 2	Dundee United
Tosh	Steven	William	27/04/73	Kirkcaldy	22/07/95	5 9.0	10 2	Arbroath
Twaddle	Kevin		31/10/71	Edinburgh	08/10/94	6 3.0	12 2	Dunbar United
Weir	James	McIntosh	15/06/69	Motherwell	18/11/94	6 1.0	12 5	Heart of Midlothian
Whiteford	Andrew		22/08/77	Bellshill	09/06/94	5 10.0	11 4	Possil Y.M.C.A.
Young	Scott	Robertson	05/04/77	Glasgow	22/09/93	5 8.0	9 0	West Park United

MILESTONES

YEAR OF FORMATION: 1884
MOST CAPPED PLAYER: Sandy McLaren
NO. OF CAPS: 5
MOST LEAGUE POINTS IN A SEASON: 59 (Second Division – Season 1987/88)
MOST LEAGUE GOALS SCORED BY A PLAYER IN A SEASON: Jimmy Benson (Season 1931/32)
NO. OF GOALS SCORED: 38
RECORD ATTENDANCE: 29,972 (-v- Dundee 10.2.1951)
RECORD VICTORY: 8-1 (-v- Partick Thistle – League Cup 16.8.1969)
RECORD DEFEAT: 0-12 (-v- Cowdenbeath – Scottish Cup 21.1.1928)

SEASON TICKET INFORMATION

Seated
West Stand
Adult..£180
Juvenile/OAP................................£108
East Stand
Adult..£140
Juvenile/OAP..................................£90
South Stand
Adult..£125
Female/Juvenile/OAP......................£50

LEAGUE ADMISSION PRICES

Seated
West Stand
Adult £10
Juvenile/OAP £6
East Stand
Adult £8
Juvenile/OAP £5
North Stand (Visitors)
Adult £8
Juvenile/OAP £5
South Stand
(Family Section)
Adult Male...............................£7
Female/Juvenile/OAP £3

CLUB FACTFILE 1994/95
RESULTS .. APPEARANCES .. SCORERS

The SAINTS

Small bold figures denote goalscorers. † denotes opponent's own goal.

Date	Venue	Opponents	Result	Rhodes A.	Miller C.	Davidson C.	Turner T.	McGinnis G.	McGowne K.	O'Nei J.	Davies J.	Davenport P.	O'Boyle G.	Irons D.	Ramsey P.	Scott ?	Inglis I.	Cherry P.	Preston A.	McAuey S.	McMartin G.	Morgan A.	Curran H.	Twaddle E.	Farquhar G.	Norer P.	Deas P.	Walemark J.	Wright P.	Weir J.	Englis I	Main A.	McCluskey S.	Griffin D.	Young S.
Aug 13	A	Raith Rovers	1-1	1	2	3	4	5	6	7	8	9	10	11¹	12	14																			
20	A	Airdrieonians	0-0	1	3		4	2		7	12	9	10	11	8	14		5	6																
27	H	Dundee	0-1	1	3	11	8		6	7	12	9	10	4		14		5	2																
Sep 3	A	Ayr United	4-3	1	3		8	6		7		9	10³	11¹	4			5	2	12															
10	H	St. Mirren	1-1	1	3		8	6		7		9	10¹	2	4			5			11	12	14												
24	H	Hamilton Academical	1-1	1	3		8		2	7		9	10¹	6				5			11	4	12	14											
Oct 1	H	Clydebank	0-0	1	3			8	5	7		9	10	6	4			2			11	12	14												
8	A	Dunfermline Athletic	0-3	1	3				5	7		9	10	6	4			2			11	12	8	14											
15	H	Stranraer	3-0	1		3	12		6	7		14	10²	4	5			2			11	8	9¹												
22	H	Raith Rovers	3-1	1		3			6	7		14	10²	4				7	11¹		8					5	9								
29	A	Dundee	0-1	1		3			6	7			10	4	12			2	11		8					5	9	14							
Nov 12	A	St. Mirren	2-2	1		3	12	4	6	7		9¹		8	2			11	10	14				5¹											
19	H	Ayr United	1-0	1		7¹	8		6			9	10	5	3	2		11	14										4						
22	A	Airdrieonians	4-0	1			8	6	7			10¹	4	2¹	3¹			11	9	12¹									14	5					
26	A	Hamilton Academical	1-3	1			8	6¹			10	4	2	3	12			11	9	7									14	5					
Dec 3	H	Clydebank	1-1	1			12	6			10	4	2	3	8			11¹	14	7									9	5					
10	A	Stranraer	2-2	1				6	7	14¹	4	12	2	3	11			10¹	8										9	5					
26	H	Dunfermline Athletic	3-2	1				6	7¹	14¹	4		2	3	8¹			11	10	12									9	5					
31	A	Raith Rovers	0-2	1				6	7	14	4		2	3	8			11		12									9	5	10				
Jan 7	A	Airdrieonians	2-0					6	7	10	4		2¹	3	8			9¹				11							5	12	1				
11	H	Dundee	2-2					6	7¹	14	10	4	2	3	8¹							11							5	12	1				
14	A	Ayr United	3-1					6	7	14¹	10	4	2	3	12¹			8¹	9			11							5		1				
21	H	St. Mirren	5-1					6	7	14	10¹	4	2¹	3¹	12			8	9			11							5		1				
Feb 4	A	Clydebank	0-0					6	7	12	4		2	3	11			8	14										9	5	1				
18	H	Hamilton Academical	3-0					6		14	10²	4	8	7	2¹			3				12	9						5	11	1				
25	H	Stranraer	3-0						11	10¹	4	8	7	2	3			12	9¹									14¹	5		1				
Mar 11	A	Dunfermline Athletic	1-1					6	11	10	4	8	7	2	3			12	9¹									14	5		1				
21	A	St. Mirren	0-0						10	4	8	7	3	12	6			9										14	5	11	1				
25	A	Ayr United	†1-1			6	11	10	4		7	3	2	12	9													14	5		1	8			
Apr 1	A	Clydebank	1-0			6	11	10¹	4		7	3	2		9	8													1				5		
8	A	Hamilton Academical	0-1		12	11	10	4	8		3	2	9		7													14	1			6	5		
15	H	Dunfermline Athletic	1-1		5	6	10	4	7		2	3	12	8	9	14¹												11	1						
22	A	Stranraer	6-2		5	6	7¹	10³	4		2¹	3	11	9¹	12													14	1					8	
29	H	Raith Rovers	1-2		6	5	12	10	4		2	3	7¹	11	9	8												1							
May 6	A	Dundee	1-2		5	6	7	10¹	4		2	3	12	11	9	8												1						14	
13	H	Airdrieonians	2-1		11	6	10	4	7¹		3	2	9¹	8	14													1				5			
TOTAL FULL APPEARANCES				19	12	4	10	10	30	26	1	12	32	34	9	9	5	27	24	7	12	22	21	11	1	7	2	5	17	4	17	2	3	1	
TOTAL SUB APPEARANCES						(3)	(1)		(1)	(2)	(10)			(2)	(3)			(2)	(1)	(10)	(2)	(4)	(4)	(6)				(7)		(5)				(1)
TOTAL GOALS SCORED								1		1	3	4	19	2		1		5	2		3	4	6	2		1		1				1		

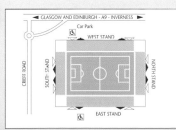

McDIARMID PARK

CAPACITY: 10,721 (All Seated)
PITCH DIMENSIONS: 115 yds x 75 yds
FACILITIES FOR DISABLED SUPPORTERS: Entrance via south end of West Stand and south end of East Stand. Visiting disabled fans should contact the club in advance. Headphones available in West and North Stands for blind and partially sighted supporters.

HOW TO GET THERE

The following routes can be used to reach McDiarmid Park:

TRAINS: Perth Station is well served by trains from all parts of the country. The station is about 40 minutes walk from the park.

BUSES: Local services nos. 1 and 2 pass near the ground. Both leave from Mill Street in the town centre.

CARS: The car park at the park holds 1,500 cars and 100 coaches. Vehicles should follow signs A9 to Inverness on Perth City by-pass, then follow "Football Stadium" signs at Inveralmond Roundabout South onto slip road adjacent to McDiarmid Park. Vehicle charges are £1.00 for cars and £5.00 for coaches.

ST. MIRREN

LIST OF PLAYERS 1995-96

SURNAME	FIRST NAME	MIDDLE NAME	DATE OF BIRTH	PLACE OF BIRTH	DATE OF SIGNING	HEIGHT FT INS	WEIGHT ST LBS	PREVIOUS CLUB
Archdeacon	Paul		11/10/76	Greenock	22/04/94	5 9.0	11 5	St. Mirren B.C.
Baker	Martin		08/06/74	Govan	16/09/92	6 0.0	10 12	St. Mirren B.C.
Bone	Alexander	Syme Frew	26/02/71	Stirling	22/10/92	5 9.0	10 7	Fallin
Boyd	John	Robertson	01/01/69	Greenock	07/12/94	6 0.0	12 4	Dumbarton
Combe	Alan		03/04/74	Edinburgh	07/08/93	6 1.0	12 2	Cowdenbeath
Dawson	Robert	McQuillan	01/08/63	Stirling	05/06/87	5 9.0	11 5	Stirling Albion
Dick	James		21/06/72	Bellshill	06/07/93	5 11.0	10 8	Airdrieonians
Fullarton	James		20/07/74	Bellshill	13/06/91	5 11.0	11 12	Motherwell B.C.
Gillies	Richard	Charles	24/08/76	Glasgow	12/12/92	5 10.0	11 0	St. Mirren B.C.
Hetherston	Brian		23/11/76	Bellshill	26/03/94	6 0.0	10 6	St. Mirren B.C.
Hewitt	John		09/02/63	Aberdeen	04/09/92	5 9.0	11 7	Deveronvale
Inglis	Grant	Hugh	29/12/66	Corby	06/01/95	5 7.0	11 1	Shotts Bon Accord
Kennedy	Andrew	John	08/10/64	Stirling	19/08/95	6 2.0	13 7	Portadown
Lavety	Barry		21/08/74	Johnstone	10/08/91	6 0.0	12 12	Gleniffer Thistle
Law	Robert		24/12/65	Bellshill	05/07/95	5 9.5	11 12	Partick Thistle
McGrotty	Gary		26/09/76	Glasgow	28/04/94	5 6.0	8 10	St. Mirren B.C.
McIntyre	Paul		18/01/67	Girvan	27/03/91	6 0.0	12 11	Maybole Juniors
McLaughlin	Barry	John	19/04/73	Paisley	01/08/91	6 1.0	12 7	St. Mirren B.C.
McMillan	John	David	09/08/76	Irvine	04/08/95	5 8.0	10 12	Motherwell
McWhirter	Norman		04/09/69	Johnstone	16/09/85	5 10.0	11 4	Linwood Rangers B.C.
Money	Israel	Campbell	31/08/60	Maybole	08/06/78	5 11.0	13 10	Dailly Amateurs
Pollock	Christopher		06/11/77	Kilwinning	04/08/95	5 8.0	10 12	Rangers
Scrimgour	Derek		29/03/78	Glasgow	06/09/95	6 3.0	12 7	Largs Thistle
Smith	Brian		26/10/76	Paisley	10/08/95	5 11.0	10 2	"S" Form
Taylor	Stuart		26/11/74	Glasgow	16/09/92	6 1.0	11 4	St. Mirren B.C.
Watson	Stephen		04/04/73	Liverpool	28/07/94	6 1.0	13 0	Rangers

MILESTONES

YEAR OF FORMATION: 1877
MOST CAPPED PLAYERS: Iain Munro & Billy Thomson
NO. OF CAPS: 7
MOST LEAGUE POINTS IN A SEASON: 62 (Division 2 – Season 1967/68)
MOST LEAGUE GOALS SCORED BY A PLAYER IN A SEASON: Dunky Walker (Season 1921/22)
NO. OF GOALS SCORED: 45
RECORD ATTENDANCE: 47,438 (-v- Celtic 7.3.1925)
RECORD VICTORY: 15-0 (-v- Glasgow University – Scottish Cup 30.1.1960)
RECORD DEFEAT: 0-9 (-v- Rangers – Division 1, 4.12.1897)

Sidebar

St. Mirren Park, Love Street, Paisley PA3 2EJ

CHAIRMAN/CHIEF EXECUTIVE
Robert Earlie

VICE-CHAIRMAN
William W. Waters, F.R.I.C.S.

HON. PRESIDENT
William Todd M.B.E. J.P.

DIRECTORS
Allan W. Marshall, LL.B.
J. Yule Craig, J.P., C.A.
Charles G. Palmer
George P. Campbell
John F. Paton
Stewart G. Gilmour

GENERAL MANAGER/SECRETARY
Jack Copland

MANAGER
James Bone

CLUB DOCTOR
Stuart McCormick, M.B., Ch.B.

PHYSIOTHERAPIST
Andrew Binning B.Sc., M.C.S.P.

S.F.A. COMMUNITY OFFICER
Tony Fitzpatrick

CHIEF SCOUT
Joe Hughes

GROUNDSMAN
Tom Docherty

COMMERCIAL MANAGER
Bill Campbell
0141-840 1337

CATERING MANAGER
Mrs. Sally A. MacDonald

TELEPHONES
Ground 0141-889 2558/840 1337
Fax 0141-848 6444

CLUB SHOP
Situated at Ground
Open 10.30 a.m. – 2.30 p.m.
Mon to Fri
and 10.00 a.m. – 3.00 p.m.
on Saturdays

OFFICIAL SUPPORTERS CLUB
St. Mirren Supporters Club,
11 Knox Street, Paisley

TEAM CAPTAIN
Norman McWhirter

SHIRT SPONSOR
Phoenix Honda

SEASON TICKET INFORMATION

Seated		
Main Stand	Adult	£155
	Juvenile/OAP	£95
North Stand	Adult	£140
	Juvenile/OAP	£85
Enclosure	Adult	£140
	Juvenile/OAP	£85

LEAGUE ADMISSION PRICES

Seated		
Main Stand	Adult	£9
	Juvenile/OAP	£4.50
Lower Enclosure	Adult	£8
	Juvenile/OAP	£4
North Stand	Adult	£8
	Juvenile/OAP	£4
	1 Parent & Juvenile	£10
Family Enclosure	1 Parent & Juvenile	£8
	Each additional Juvenile	£3
Standing		
Adult	£7 Juvenile/OAP	£3.50

CLUB FACTFILE 1994/95
RESULTS .. APPEARANCES .. SCORERS

The BUDDIES

Date	Venue	Opponents	Result	Combe A.	Dawson F.	Watson S.	McLaughlin B.	Taylor S.	Arondaeson P.	McIntyre P.	Bone A.	Lavety B.	Gardner	Elliot D.	Hick M.	Gillies R.	Gillies K.	Baker M.	Dick J.	Money C.	Fularton J.	McWhirter N.	Scott J.	Orr N.	McGrafty G.	McAvenne F.	Hewitt J.	Oxone E.	Smith B.	Boyd J.	Hetherston B	Inglis G.	Byrne L.	Galloway G.	Scrimgour B.
Aug 13	A	Dundee	0-2	1	2	3	4	5	6	7	8	9	10	11	12	14																			
20	A	Ayr United	1-1	1		3	4	5		6	8	9¹	10	11					2	14	7	12													
27	H	Clydebank	2-1	1	2	3	4	5		8	9¹	10	11							14¹	7	12	6												
Sep 3	H	Dunfermline Athletic	1-1		2	3	4	14	5	9¹	10	11		8	7			6	1	12																
10	H	St. Johnstone	1-1		2	3	4	5		9	10	11		8	7¹	12		6	1	14																
24	H	Raith Rovers	1-2		2	3	5		6	7	9¹	10	11		14	12		8	1		4															
Oct 1	H	Hamilton Academical	2-2		2	3	5		12	7	9	10	11¹					8	6¹	1			4	14												
8	A	Stranraer	1-1		2		5	12	4	7	9	10	11					3¹	8	1			6	14												
15	H	Airdrieonians	0-1	1	2	12	5		4		9	10	11					14	3	7			6	8												
22	H	Dundee	1-2	1	2	3	5			8	11	12	11¹	10					7		4	6	9													
29	A	Clydebank	1-1	1		6¹	5			8		9	14	11	2	12			3	7		4	10													
Nov 5	H	Ayr United	1-0	1	2¹	6	5			8	14	9		11					3	7	12	4	10													
12	H	St. Johnstone	2-2	1	2	6	5			14		9	11		7¹			3		8¹	4	10	12													
19	A	Dunfermline Athletic	0-1	1	2	6	5			14	9	11		7			3		8	4	10	12														
Dec 3	H	Hamilton Academical	0-1	1		6	5			9	14	7	11	12			3		8	10	2	4														
6	A	Raith Rovers	1-1	1	2		5			9	11	8	14	3	7			12	10¹	6	4															
26	H	Stranraer	1-0	1	2	12	5			9	11¹	8	3	7	4	10	6	14																		
31	A	Dundee	0-4	1	2	8	5	12		9	11	14	3	7	4	10	6																			
Jan 2	H	Clydebank	0-0	1	2	5				9	11	8	3	7	4	10	6	12																		
7	A	Ayr United	0-2	1	2	5				9	11	8	10	3	7	4	14	6	12																	
10	A	Airdrieonians	0-2	1	2	5	8			14	9	11	3	7	4	12	6	10																		
14	H	Dunfermline Athletic	2-2	1		5	6¹			8	9	3	7	11	4	10	2	12	14¹																	
21	A	St. Johnstone	1-5	1		5	6			8¹	9	11	12	2	10	4	14	3	7																	
Feb 4	A	Hamilton Academical	0-2	1	2	5	12	3	8	9		14	7	6	4	10	11																			
11	H	Raith Rovers	1-2		2	6	5	8	7	9		3	12	1	11	4¹	10	14																		
25	H	Airdrieonians	0-1		2	4	5	14	9	11		10	3	8	1	6	12	7																		
Mar 11	A	Stranraer	3-1		2¹	6¹	5	8	9	14¹		11	10	3	1	12	4	7																		
21	H	St. Johnstone	0-0		2	6	5	7	9	10	14	11	3	1	8	4	12																			
25	A	Dunfermline Athletic	1-1		2	12	6	5	7	9	10¹	11	3	1	8	4	14																			
Apr 1	H	Hamilton Academical	3-2		2	6	5	7	9	10¹	11	14	3¹	1	8	4	12¹																			
8	A	Raith Rovers	1-2		2	12	6	9	10¹	11	7	14	5	1	4	8	3																			
15	H	Stranraer	2-0		2	6	9	10	11	7	14	5¹	1	4	12	8¹	3																			
22	A	Airdrieonians	0-1	13	2	3	6	9	10	14	5	1	4	11	8	7																				
29	H	Dundee	1-0		2	5	6	7	9	10	14	1	4	11¹	8	12	3																			
May 6	A	Clydebank	1-2	1		6¹	5	9	10	3	4	14	12	8	7	2	11																			
13	H	Ayr United	2-1		6	5	9	10¹	3	11	4	12¹	14	2	8	7	1																			
TOTAL FULL APPEARANCES				20	29	25	31	10	1	19	19	29	17	26	2	13	5	23	24	15	13	23		4		7	9	2	4	10	1	7	6	1	1
TOTAL SUB APPEARANCES				(1)		(4)		(3)	(1)	(1)	(6)	(2)	(3)	(2)	(1)	(11)	(4)	(3)	(1)			(4)		(1)		(1)	(2)		(7)		(1)	(2)	(2)	(8)
TOTAL GOALS SCORED					2	3		1			2	7		3				3	1	2	2			1		1				1		2			3

Small bold figures denote goalscorers. † denotes opponent's own goal.

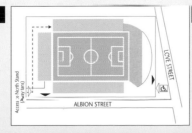

ST. MIRREN PARK

CAPACITY: 15,410; Seated 9,395, Standing 6,015
PITCH DIMENSIONS: 112 yds x 73 yds
FACILITIES FOR DISABLED SUPPORTERS: Full wheelchair facilities available for visiting supporters in the West Stand.

ALBION STREET — *Access to North Stand (Away fans)* — *LOVE STREET*

HOW TO GET THERE

St. Mirren Park can be reached by the following routes.

TRAINS: There is a frequent train service from Glasgow Central Station and all coastal routes pass through Gilmour Street. The ground is about 400 yards from the station.

BUSES: All SMT coastal services, plus buses to Johnstone and Kilbarchan, pass within 300 yards of the ground.

CARS: The only facilities for car parking are in the streets surrounding the ground.

CK MORTON ◆ FOOTBAL

Finnish Finale

It was the Finnish connection that ultimately provided the impetus for Greenock Morton to gain promotion along with Dumbarton from the highly competitive Bell's League Championship Second Division. In October, the Greenock club splashed out £165,000 to attract the Finnish international players, Janne Lindberg and Marko Rajamaki.

While both players were crucially involved in their country's European Championship challenge, including ironically, Scotland, the two refused to be deflected from their endeavours on the Tail O' the Bank. Both carried out important roles to help their new club finally lift the championship after a titanic struggle that involved as many as seven clubs during the season.

The skills of Lindberg in midfield combined with the home grown talent of Derek McInnes – the Players' Player of the Year for the Second Division – Alan Mahood, as well as striker Rajamaki, provided a constant threat to opposition defences. The outcome was promotion to the First Division – a relief to manager Allan McGraw, who, before the season began, had promised to resign if his side had not achieved promotion.

McGraw admitted when the season had been completed however, that this threat had been a mistake. "I put too

much pressure on my players," he declared.

Looking over the entire campaign, McGraw remembers two outstanding results as being crucial to the final outcome.

"They came near the end of the season. To me, our best performance was when we travelled to Forthbank and beat Stirling Albion and then followed this result by defeating Clyde, who were another of the Second Division promotion hopefuls. The inclusion of the two Finns had a telling effect, however. We were unfortunate in that we had to bear a number of injuries, but these two arrived just at the right time to strengthen our squad of players.

"Janne is a competitive player, but he also has that little bit of class which enables him to rise above others and Marko, even when he is not firing on all cylinders, can do what all good strikers can do – he can score goals. He can never be ignored. In my opinion, Derek thoroughly deserved to be the Player of the Year in our division. He had an outstanding season and played his part magnificently. But we had important contributions from all the departments in the team, and that was what was extremely important to us.

" The Second Division was highly

competitive, but it took a little bit of flair – that extra touch of class – and I felt that in the end we had it."

Dumbarton, meanwhile, clinched their place on the final day of the season with an outstanding win against rivals Stirling Albion. After a ten match unbeaten run, the Forthbank club only needed to draw in front of their own support to gain promotion, under manager Kevin Drinkell. Albion had pursued a policy of operating with a number of full-time players during the course of the season, however, despite this gamble, a crowd of over 3,000 witnessed a Dumbarton victory by two goals to nil. The Sons' fans celebrated and their manager, Murdo MacLeod, praised the players for the hard work they had put in during the season.

The Boghead club had a number of players who gave sterling performances throughout the course of an arduous season. They also had the exciting skills of winger Hugh Ward, who often provided that little extra touch of class on many occasions to earn the Sons vital points.

Stirling Albion, to their credit, have overcome their disappointment and after serious consideration, have decided to continue with their full-time policy for the 1995/96 campaign, with their

Scott McArthur with the Bell's Second Division Trophy

Chairman, Peter McKenzie, explaining, "It is too early after one season to change a policy which almost earned us promotion."

That competitive element throughout the entire campaign saw many clubs record increased average attendances. Greenock Morton, for example, attracted considerably more spectators to their matches in the new ten club Second Division than the previous season, when they played in the old twelve club First Division. Supporter interest was maintained throughout virtually the entire 36 match League card with several clubs retaining a realistic expectation of promotion until late in the campaign.

Stenhousemuir, under their manager Terry Christie, not only captured the imagination by their defeats of First Division St. Johnstone and Premier Division Aberdeen in the Tennents Scottish Cup, but also by rising to their highest ever position in League football.

The exciting striker, Warren Hawke, led Berwick Rangers, under manager Tom Hendrie, to the top of the League at one stage before injuries to important players, and the resultant affect this had on their small squad of players, finally ended their brave challenge.

Clyde set up a new soccer academy at their new Broadwood Stadium home in Cumbernauld. Their manager, Alex Smith, and backroom staff, although being disappointed at not sustaining their challenge, continued to unearth exciting young talent with Martin O'Neill forcing his way into the Scotland Under-21 squad.

Former Scotland international striker, Steve Archibald, had East Fife jostling for a top position at one stage, while Queen of the South, with manager Billy McLaren guiding their fortunes, have not only carried out several impressive ground developments at Palmerston Park, but have put in place a youth development programme which promises to be beneficial to the Dumfries club in the years to come.

Meadowbank Thistle's season started full of hope after winning their opening League fixture at Brechin by five goals to one. However, it was noticed that Meadowbank had fielded an ineligible player in this match and after the League Management Committee had deducted three points and expunged the goals from this match from their records, their season disintegrated and ironically, along with Brechin, were relegated to the Third Division.

Despite being the poorest supported side in the Second Division, the Edinburgh club pulled off an imaginative double signing of Barbadian international players and in the hope that progress can be made, the club will be moving to their new base at a newly constructed stadium in Livingston and will employ full-time players under new manager Jim Leishman.

Ambition continues to flower even in the lower divisions.

BILL MARWICK
(Freelance)

Morton celebrate Marko Rajamaki's goal against Dumbarton.

AYR UNITED

Somerset Park, Tryfield Place,
Ayr, KA8 9NB

CHAIRMAN
William J. Barr

VICE-CHAIRMAN
Donald R. Cameron

DIRECTORS
Donald McK. MacIntyre
David McKee
George H. Smith
John E. Eyley B.A., A.C.M.A.
Kenneth W. MacLeod
Roy G. Kennedy

SECRETARY
John A. Eyley B.A., A.C.M.A.

ADMINISTRATOR
Brian Caldwell

MANAGER

ASSISTANT MANAGER

CLUB DOCTORS
Dr. Faith Gardner, M.B.B.S. Dip.
Sports Medicine (London & SRC)
Dr. Marion McNaught, M.B., CH.B.

CROWD DOCTOR
Dr. Robert Paterson M.B., CH.B.

PHYSIOTHERAPIST
Ayr Sports Medical Centre

GROUNDSMAN
David Harkness

COMMERCIAL MANAGER
Sandy Kerr
(01292) 263435

LOTTERY MANAGER
Andrew Downie

TELEPHONES
Ground/Ticket Office
(01292) 263435
Fax (01292) 281314

CLUB SHOP
Ayr United Enterprises, Tryfield Place,
Ayr, KA8 9NB. (01292) 280095.
Open 9.00 a.m.-3.30 p.m. Mon-Fri
and 1.00 p.m.-3.00 p.m. on all first
team matchdays.

OFFICIAL SUPPORTERS CLUB
c/o Ayr United F.C., Somerset Park,
Ayr, KA8 9NB

TEAM CAPTAIN
John Sharples

SHIRT SPONSOR
What Everyone Wants

LIST OF PLAYERS 1995-96

SURNAME	FIRST NAME	MIDDLE NAME	DATE OF BIRTH	PLACE OF BIRTH	DATE OF SIGNING	HEIGHT FT INS	WEIGHT ST LBS	PREVIOUS CLUB
Agnew	Steven	James	07/10/75	Irvine	24/02/95	5 7.0	10 5	Dundee United
Biggart	Kevin		10/11/73	Kilmarnock	13/01/94	5 8.5	11 1	Dundee United
Bilsland	Brian		06/08/71	Glasgow	11/02/94	5 10.0	10 0	Hunter Clark A.F.C.
Boyce	David		13/06/73	Paisley	10/08/95	5 11.0	12 0	Kilpatrick Juniors
Burns	Gordon		02/12/78	Glasgow	05/09/95	5 11.75	10 13	'S' Form
Byrne	David	Stuart	05/03/61	London	25/08/95	5 9.0	10 9	Tottenham Hotspur
Chalmers	Paul		31/10/63	Glasgow	08/09/95	5 10.0	11 4	Hamilton Academical
Connelly	Stuart		05/07/78	Birmingham	01/09/95	5 10	11 0	'X' Form
Connie	Cameron		03/01/71	Paisley	17/02/94	5 10.0	12 0	Kilbirnie Ladeside
Coyle	Thomas		06/08/77	Glasgow	31/08/95	5 10.0	10 9	Pollok B.C
Dalziel	Gordon		16/03/62	Motherwell	09/08/95	5 10.5	10 13	Raith Rovers
Dowe	Julian		09/09/75	Manchester	25/11/94	6 2.0	13 0	Athletico Marbella
Duncan	Cameron		04/08/65	Coatbridge	23/03/91	6 1.0	12 4	Partick Thistle
George	Duncan	Henry	04/12/67	Paisley	29/03/91	5 10.0	10 7	Stranraer
Gorgues	Regis		06/05/72	St. Malo	09/09/94	5 9.0	11 10	Caldas Da Rainha
Gribben	Kevin		30/08/75	Irvine	04/11/94	5 6.0	10 0	Maybole Juniors
Grierson	George		28/03/77	Kirkcaldy	24/05/95	6 3.0	12 10	Ayr United B.C.
Hood	Gregg		29/05/74	Bellshill	01/07/91	6 0.0	12 7	Ayr United B.C.
Jackson	Justin		10/12/74	Nottingham	21/07/94	5 10.0	11 0	Lancaster
Kerr	John		26/05/79	London	01/09/95	5 3.5	8 0	'S' Form
Lamont	William	Fleming	24/07/66	Falkirk	11/08/95	5 11.5	13 12	Falkirk
MacFarlane	Colin		03/07/70	Bellshill	15/07/94	6 3.0	12 3	Baillieston Juniors
McIntosh	Gordon		17/08/78	Ayr	05/09/95	5 8.5	11 8	'S' Form
McIntosh	Stuart	Russell	06/02/74	Ayr	16/08/94	6 1.0	12 7	Maybole Juniors
McKay	Kenneth		19/10/78	Irvine	31/08/95	5 7.0	10 5	'S' Form
McKilligan	Neil		02/01/74	Falkirk	31/03/94	5 10.0	11 0	Partick Thistle
McNeil	Scott		24/04/79	Ayr	05/09/95	5 9.25	10 0	'S' Form
Moore	Vincent		21/08/64	Scunthorpe	28/09/93	5 11.0	12 0	Stirling Albion
Rolling	Frank		23/08/68	Colnar	08/08/94	6 2.0	13 6	F.C. Pau
Sharples	John	Benjamin	26/01/73	Bury	13/07/94	6 1.0	12 8	Heart of Midlothian
Shepherd	Anthony		16/11/66	Glasgow	11/08/95	5 9.0	10 0	Portadown
Stewart	David		14/08/78	Irvine	01/09/95	6 0.0	11 2	'S' Form
Tannock	Ross		30/04/71	Kilmarnock	03/09/94	6 0.0	11 2	Ostende
Traynor	John	Francis C.	10/12/66	Glasgow	07/11/91	5 10.0	11 0	Clydebank
Wilson	Stuart		27/08/76	Girvan	13/07/95	5 10.0	12 4	Aberdeen

MILESTONES

YEAR OF FORMATION: 1910
MOST CAPPED PLAYER: Jim Nisbett
NO. OF CAPS: 3
MOST LEAGUE POINTS IN A SEASON: 61 (Second Division – Season 1987/88)
MOST LEAGUE GOALS SCORED BY A PLAYER IN A SEASON: Jimmy Smith (Season 1927/28)
NO. OF GOALS SCORED: 66
RECORD ATTENDANCE: 25,225 (-v- Rangers – 13.9.1969)
RECORD VICTORY: 11-1 (-v- Dumbarton – League Cup, 13.8.1952)
RECORD DEFEAT: 0-9 (-v- Rangers, Heart of Midlothian, Third Lanark – Division 1)

SEASON TICKET INFORMATION

Seated
Centre Stand Adult..........................£150
             OAP £125
Wing Stand   Adult..........................£130
             Juvenile/OAP.................£110
Family Stand Adult/Juvenile £130
Standing
Ground/Enclosure Adult..................£100
             Juvenile/OAP.................£50

LEAGUE ADMISSION PRICES

Seated
Main Stand   Adult ....£10 (Centre)
             Adult ....£9 (Wing)
Family Stand Adult/Juvenile £8
(Plus £2.00 for each additional Juvenile)
Standing
Enclosure   Adult £6.50
Ground   Adult £6
             Juvenile/OAP £3

The HONEST MEN

Date	Venue	Opponents	Result	Duncan C.	Burns H.	McVicar D.	Paterson G.	Rolling F.	Sharples J.	Moore V.	McGilligan N.	McGiverin S.	Glizean I.	Bilsland B.	Traynor J.	Woods T.	Connie C.	Stainrod J.	McIntosh S.	Biggart K.	Tannock R.	George D.	Gorgues R.	Jackson J.	Hood G.	Spence W.	Lamont L.	Nylen N.	Valetta C.	Murray B.	Forbes .	Dowe . J.	Grierson G.	Cribben K.	MacFarlane C.	Agnew S.	Okorie K.	Connelly S.
Aug 13	H	Hamilton Academical	1-1	1	2	3	4	5	6	7	8	9	10	11	12¹	14																						
20	H	St. Mirren	1-1	1	2	3	4	5	6		8	9	10	12¹	7			11	14																			
27	A	Stranraer	1-2	1	2	3	4	5	14	6	9¹	10	8	7	12	11		13																				
Sep 3	H	St. Johnstone	3-4		2	3	12	5	4		8		9¹	14	6¹			10¹	1	7	11																	
10	A	Airdrieonians	0-0	1	2	3	4	5			9	11	12	8				10			6	7																
24	H	Dundee	3-2	1	2		4	5		8			7					3	10		6¹	11	9²															
Oct 1	A	Raith Rovers	0-3	1	7		4	5		8	10			2	12	3			14		6	11	9															
8	A	Clydebank	0-3	1	7		4	5		8	2	14						10		3	6	11	9															
15	H	Dunfermline Athletic	0-0	1	7			5		8	14	9						10		3	6	11	12	4														
22	A	Hamilton Academical	0-2		7		6	5		8	14							10		2	11	3	12	4	1	9												
29	H	Stranraer	2-1	1	7²		9	5		8	2							14		3	6	11	10	4														
Nov 5	A	St. Mirren	0-1	1	7		9	5		8	14	12						3		6	11					2	4	10										
12	H	Airdrieonians	0-3	1	7			5	4		12	9		14				3		6	11					2	8	10										
19	A	St. Johnstone	0-1	1	7			5	6		11	9						10		2	8	3		4		12	14											
26	A	Dundee	1-1	1	7			5	6	14	11	9						3		2	8		10	4¹		12												
Dec 3	H	Raith Rovers	1-1	1	7			5	6	11	2	9						3	14		8		10	4¹														
10	A	Dunfermline Athletic	0-6		2			5	6		11		12					3	10	1	8		9					4			7	13						
26	H	Clydebank	1-1	1	7			5	6		2		9					3			8	11¹	12	4				10										
31	H	Hamilton Academical	1-2	1				5	6		2		9					3		7	14	8	11	12	4			10¹										
Jan 2	A	Stranraer	0-2	1				5	6	14	2		9					3			8	11	12	4				10	7									
7	H	St. Mirren	2-0	1				5¹	6	12	2		9	14¹				3			8	11	10	4					7									
14	H	St. Johnstone	1-3	1				5	6		2		9	12				3				11	10¹	4				14				7	8					
24	A	Airdrieonians	2-2	1				5¹	4	8	2		9¹	12				3			14		11	10								7	6					
Feb 4	A	Raith Rovers	1-2	1				5	4	8¹	2		9	7				3	14		11			10									6					
11	H	Dundee	1-0	1				5	6	8¹	2		9	7					10		3		11		12	4												
25	H	Dunfermline Athletic	†1-2	1				5	6		2		9	7				12	10		3	8	11		14	4												
Mar 11	A	Clydebank	1-1	1				5	6		2		9	7					10		3	12	11		8	4¹												
18	H	Airdrieonians	0-2	1				5	6		2		9	/	14				10		3	12	11		8	4												
25	A	St. Johnstone	1-1	1	7				6		2		9	10	5		11				3	4¹	8		14											12		
Apr 1	H	Raith Rovers	0-1	1	7				6		2		9	10	5						3	4	8		14												11	12
8	A	Dundee	1-1	1	2¹			5	6		7		9				13			3	8	4	11	10													
15	H	Clydebank	1-0		2			5	6		7		9¹					11		1	3	8	4														12
22	A	Dunfermline Athletic	0-3		2			6	5		9			11				1	3	8	4	12	10						14								7
29	A	Hamilton Academical	0-1					5	6		7							3	10		2	4	8	11	9				14								
May 6	H	Stranraer	3-0					5	6		7			11				3	10¹	1	2	8¹	4		9¹												14
13	A	St. Mirren	1-2					5	6	11	7			14	9¹			3	10	1	2	8	4														12
TOTAL FULL APPEARANCES				29	23	5	10	33	27	13	30	9	21	11	9			20	15	6	22	11	29	18	18	15		1	1	2	3	1	1	4		4	3	1	1
TOTAL SUB APPEARANCES					(1)			(4)	(4)	(2)	(2)	(7)	(2)	(3)		(1)	(4)	(2)	(1)	(4)		(1)	(9)		(2)		(1)	(3)	(1)				(1)		(1)	(3)	
TOTAL GOALS SCORED					3			2		2			1	3	3	2			2					2	1	1	4	3					1					

Small bold figures denote goalscorers. † denotes opponent's own goal.

SOMERSET PARK

CAPACITY: 13,918; Seated 1,450, Standing 12,468
PITCH DIMENSIONS: 110 yds x 72 yds
FACILITIES FOR DISABLED SUPPORTERS: Enclosure and toilet facilities for wheelchairs. Match commentary available for blind persons at all first team matches.

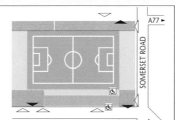

HOW TO GET THERE

Somerset Park can be reached by the following routes.

TRAINS: There is a half hourly train service from Glasgow to either Ayr or Newton-on-Ayr. The ground is a ten minute walk from both stations.

BUSES: There are several buses from the town centre with a frequency approximately every five minutes. Fans should board buses bound for Dalmilling, Whitletts or any bus passing Ayr Racecourse. The ground is only a ten minute walk from the town centre.

CARS: Car parking facilities are available at Craigie Park and at Ayr Racecourse.

BERWICK RANGERS

SURNAME	FIRST NAME	MIDDLE NAME	DATE OF BIRTH	PLACE OF BIRTH	DATE OF SIGNING	HEIGHT FT INS	WEIGHT ST LBS	PREVIOUS CLUB
Banks	Alan		25/02/70	Edinburgh	27/07/93	5 11.0	11 0	Meadowbank Thistle
Clegg	Neil		03/01/77	Berwick	13/05/94	5 9.0	11 0	Berwick H.S.
Cole	Anthony	Richard	18/09/72	Gateshead	09/08/94	6 1.0	12 13	Gateshead
Coughlin	John	Joseph	11/04/63	New York	27/07/93	5 11.0	13 10	Meadowbank Thistle
Cowan	Mark		16/01/71	Edinburgh	15/07/93	6 0.0	12 7	Armadale Thistle
Donaldson	Greig	William	01/04/71	Dunfermline	30/03/94	5 10.0	12 0	Rosyth Recreation
Forrester	Paul		03/11/72	Edinburgh	30/03/94	5 9.0	12 0	Middlesbrough
Fraser	Graeme	William	07/08/73	Edinburgh	31/03/94	5 11.0	11 8	Dunfermline Athletic
Gallacher	John	Anthony	26/01/69	Glasgow	26/08/94	5 10.0	10 10	Falkirk
Graham	Thomas	Newlands	25/08/65	Edinburgh	03/07/87	5 8.0	11 7	Edina Hibs
Irvine	William		28/12/63	Stirling	09/10/92	5 10.0	11 3	Meadowbank Thistle
Kane	Kevin		30/12/69	Edinburgh	01/03/93	5 10.0	12 0	Meadowbank Thistle
King	Thomas	Richard	07/03/76	St. Albans	26/01/95	5 11.0	11 7	Dundee North End
Leadbetter	Kevin		18/06/79	Edinburgh	15/07/95	5 7.0	10 0	"S" Form
McDowell	Murray	John L.	17/02/78	Dundee	26/06/95	5 6.0	9 6	North Muirton B.C.
Morrell	Anthony		10/10/77	Sunderland	05/07/95	5 8.0	10 4	Oxclose Juniors
Murray	Marc	Andrew	08/12/78	Berwick	05/07/95	5 8.5	10 7	Lowick
Neil	Martin		16/04/70	Ashington	17/11/94	5 8.0	11 7	Bolton Wanderers
Nixon	Andrew		24/02/78	Sunderland	05/07/95	5 9.0	10 10	Oxclose Juniors
Petrucci	Massimo		16/05/78	Edinburgh	06/08/95	5 7.0	10 9	Heart of Midlothian
Reid	Alastair		16/12/68	Edinburgh	15/02/95	6 1.0	11 6	Ormiston Primrose
Robertson	Greig		17/02/78	Edinburgh	18/08/95	5 7.0	10 3	Musselburgh Athletic
Rowan	Graham	Mark	20/12/78	Broxburn	05/07/95	5 7.0	10 7	Muirieston B.C.
Rutherford	Paul		23/02/67	Sunderland	30/12/94	5 11.0	11 0	Scarborough
Valentine	Craig		16/07/70	Edinburgh	03/08/92	5 8.0	11 0	Easthouses B.C.
Walton	Kevin		02/05/75	Durham City	05/07/95	5 10.0	11 2	Edinburgh University
Wilson	Mark		31/07/74	Dechmont	17/02/93	5 11.0	10 8	Fauldhouse Utd B.C.
Windram	Mark	John	11/01/78	Edinburgh	05/07/95	5 8.0	10 7	Eyemouth Legion Amateurs
Young	Neil	Andrew	14/10/67	Beverley	31/03/94	5 10.0	11 8	Goole Town

Sidebar

Shielfield Park,
Shielfield Terrace, Tweedmouth,
Berwick Upon Tweed, TD15 2EF

CHAIRMAN
Robert W. McDowell

VICE-CHAIRMAN
Thomas Davidson

DIRECTORS
John H. Hush
Peter McAskill
William M. McLaren
James M.S. Rose

CLUB SECRETARY
Dennis J. McCleary

COMPANY SECRETARY
Miss Sheila Stoddart

MANAGER
Thomas Hendrie

ASSISTANT MANAGER
John Coughlin

COACHING STAFF
Ian Smith
Ian Oliver

KIT MAN
Ian Oliver

PHYSIO STAFF
Ian Oliver
Glynn Jones

GROUNDSMAN
Jim Sim

COMMERCIAL MANAGER
Conrad I. Turner
(01289) 307969

TELEPHONES
Ground/Ticket Office/Fax
(01289) 307424
Club Sec. Home/Fax
(01289) 307623
Information Service
0891 800697

CLUB SHOP
Supporters Shop situated within
the ground. Open during first
team matchdays.

OFFICIAL SUPPORTERS CLUB
c/o Shielfield Park, Tweedmouth,
Berwick Upon Tweed, TD15 2EF

TEAM CAPTAIN
Craig Valentine

SHIRT SPONSOR
Federation Brewery (L.C.L. Pils)

MILESTONES

YEAR OF FORMATION: 1881
MOST LEAGUE POINTS IN A SEASON: 54 (Second Division – Season 1978/79) (2 Points for a Win)
55 (Second Division – Season 1994/95) (3 Points for a Win)
MOST LEAGUE GOALS SCORED BY A PLAYER IN A SEASON: Ken Bowron (Season 1963/64)
NO. OF GOALS SCORED: 38
RECORD ATTENDANCE: 13,365 (-v- Rangers – 28.1.1967)
RECORD VICTORY: 8-1 (-v- Forfar Athletic (H) – Division 2, 25.12.1965)
8-1 (-v- Vale of Leithen – Scottish Cup at Innerleithen Dec. 1966)
RECORD DEFEAT: 1-9 (-v- Hamilton Academical – First Division, 9.8.1980)

SEASON TICKET INFORMATION

Seated
Adult £115
Juvenile/OAP..£70
Standing
Adult £90
Juvenile/OAP..£50
(Family Tickets available on request-
prices depend on numbers)

LEAGUE ADMISSION PRICES

Seated
Adult £7
Juvenile/OAP £4
N.B. Admission to seated area is by transfer **via ground**.
Standing
Adult £6
Juvenile/OAP £3
For League matches only under-10's are admitted for £1
and over-70's are admitted free.
President's Box Tickets - Prices on application

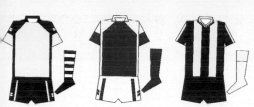

CLUB FACTFILE 1994/95
RESULTS .. APPEARANCES .. SCORERS

The BORDERERS

Date	Venue	Opponents	Result	Young N.	Valentine C.	Banks A.	Cole A.	Cowan M.	Bel D.	Forrester P.	Neil M.	Hawke W.	Irvine W.	Wilson M.	Kane K.	Fraser J.	Gallacher J.	Graham T.	Osborne M.	Rutherford P.	Greenwood F.	King T.	Reid A.	Robinson A.	Macaulay L.
Aug 13	A	Greenock Morton	1-1	1	2	3	4	5	6	7	8	9	10^1	11	12	14									
20	A	Brechin City	2-1	1	2	3	4	5		7	8	9	10^1	6	11	14^1	12								
27	H	Queen of the South	1-0	1	2	3^1	4	5		7	8	9	10	6				11							
Sep 3	H	Clyde	4-3	1	2	3^1	4	5	12	7^1	8	9^1	10^1	6			14	11							
10	H	Dumbarton	1-0	1	2	3^1	4			7	6	9	10	8		5		11	14						
24	A	Stenhousemuir	1-1	1	2	3	4	5		7	8	9	10^1	6	12	14		11							
Oct 1	H	East Fife	1-1	1	2	3	4	5		7	8	9	10	6		14		11							
8	H	Meadowbank Thistle	2-1	1	2	3	4	5		7	8^1	9^1	10	6		14		11							
15	A	Stirling Albion	2-3	1	2	3	4	5		7	8	9^1	10^1	6	12	14		11							
22	H	Greenock Morton	2-1	1	2	3	4	5		7	8	9^2	10	6	12	14		11							
29	A	Queen of the South	4-5	1	2	3	4	5		7	8^1	9^2	10^1	6		14		11							
Nov 5	H	Brechin City	2-1		2	3^2	4	5		7	8	9	10	6		14		11	12	1					
12	A	Dumbarton	2-3		2	3	4	5			8	9^1	10^1	6			7	11			1				
19	H	Clyde	2-1		2	3	4	5		7	8	9^2	10	6		14		11	12		1				
26	H	Stenhousemuir	0-0		2	3	4	5		6	8	9	10	11		14		7	12		1				
Dec 3	A	East Fife	0-3		2	3	4	5		7	8	9	10	6		14		12	11		1				
10	A	Meadowbank Thistle	1-2		2	3	4	5^1	12		8	9	10	6		14		7	11		1				
31	H	Stirling Albion	1-0		2	3^1	4	5			8	9	10	6					7		1	11			
Jan 10	H	Queen of the South	3-1			3	4	5		12	8	9	10^1	6				7^1	11		1		2^1		
14	A	Greenock Morton	1-2		2	3	4	5			8	9	10	6	14			7^1	11		1	12			
21	A	Brechin City	0-1			3	4	5		7	8	9	10	6	12			11			1		2	14	
Feb 4	H	Dumbarton	1-2		2	3	4	5		7	8^1	9	10	6	12			11			1		14		
11	A	Clyde	3-1	1	2	3		5		12	8^1	9^1	10	6	7			11					4^1		
25	H	East Fife	0-0	1	4	3				12	8	9	10	6	7			11					5	2	
Mar 4	H	Meadowbank Thistle	1-0	1	2	3		5			8	9^1	10	6	7			11					4		
7	A	Stenhousemuir	2-2	1	2	3		5		12	8^1	9	10	6	7			11					4^1		
11	A	Stirling Albion	2-2	1	2	3		5		14	8	9^1	10^1	11	7			12					4	6	
21	A	Dumbarton	0-1	1	2	3		5		12	8	9	10	11	4			7					14	6	
25	H	Clyde	1-1	1		3		5		12	8	9	10	11	6			7^1					2	4	
Apr 1	A	East Fife	1-0	1		3		5		12	8	9	10^1	11	6			7					2	4	
8	H	Stenhousemuir	0-0	1	2	3		5			8	9	10	11	6			7					4		
15	H	Meadowbank Thistle	3-0	1	2	3		5			8	9^2	10	11	6^1			7					4		
22	A	Stirling Albion	0-0	1	2	3		5		7	8	9	10	11	6								4		
29	H	Greenock Morton	3-4	1	2	3		5		7	8	9^3	10	14	11			12	13				4		
May 6	A	Queen of the South	0-2		2	3		5		7	8	9	10	14	11			12			1		4		
13	H	Brechin City	2-0	1	5	3^1					8	9	10	12	11			6	7^1				2	4	14
TOTAL FULL APPEARANCES				24	36	32	22	33	1	23	34	35	36	17	15	20	11	23	12	1	2	3	14	2	
TOTAL SUB APPEARANCES									(1)	(9)				(3)	(4)	(11)	(8)	(7)	(1)		(1)	(3)			(1)
TOTAL GOALS SCORED						7		1		3	5	16	11				2	2	2			1	2		

Small bold figures denote goalscorers. † denotes opponent's own goal.

SHIELFIELD PARK

CAPACITY: 4,131; Seated 1,366, Standing 2,765
PITCH DIMENSIONS: 112 yds x 76 yds
FACILITIES FOR DISABLED SUPPORTERS: Supporters should enter via gate adjacent to ground turnstiles (see ground plan) or via official entrance

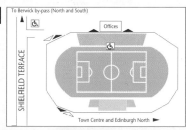

To Berwick by-pass (North and South)
Offices
SHIELFIELD TERRACE
Town Centre and Edinburgh North

HOW TO GET THERE

Shielfield Park can be reached by the following routes.
The ground is approximately 1.5 miles from the town centre (South) and is situated in Shielfield Terrace, Tweedmouth.
BUSES: The local bus route from the town centre is the Prior Park service and the nearest stop to the ground is in Shielfield Terrace. The bus stop is only yards away from the ground.
TRAINS: The only railway station is Berwick, which is situated on the East Coast line and a frequent service operates at various stages during the day. The ground is approximately 1.5 miles from the station and a taxi service operates from there or alternatively, fans can take the local bus service as detailed above.
CARS: There is a large car park at the rear of the ground. (Nominal charge).

CLYDE

LIST OF PLAYERS 1995-96

SURNAME	FIRST NAME	MIDDLE NAME	DATE OF BIRTH	PLACE OF BIRTH	DATE OF SIGNING	HEIGHT FT INS	WEIGHT ST LBS	PREVIOUS CLUB
Angus	Ian	Allan	19/11/61	Glasgow	02/08/94	5 10.0	10 3	Motherwell
Annand	Edward		24/03/73	Glasgow	28/07/95	5 11.0	11 1	Sligo Rovers
Brown	James		21/10/74	Bellshill	09/07/93	6 0.0	10 0	Rangers
Brownlie	Paul		30/08/77	Falkirk	25/08/95	5 9.0	10 4	Dunipace Juniors
Campbell	Paul		26/11/77	Bellshill	10/09/95	5 8.0	10 7	Bellshill Athletic
Dickson	John		23/12/69	Glasgow	07/08/92	5 5.0	9 7	Clydebank
Falconer	Marc		04/11/72	Glasgow	27/06/94	5 10.0	11 2	Campsie Black Watch
Fay	James		06/04/76	Glasgow	30/08/94	5 9.0	10 11	Rutherglen Glencairn
Ferguson	Graeme		03/03/71	Stirling	22/07/95	5 10.0	11 10	Clydebank
Frater	Alan		29/10/75	Paisley	24/06/94	5 7.0	10 8	Gleniffer Thistle
Gentles	Gareth		15/03/77	Glasgow	26/08/95	5 10.0	11 0	Renfrew Juniors
Gillies	Kenneth		20/07/74	Glasgow	25/07/95	5 10.0	11 10	St. Mirren
Halpin	Michael	Christopher	04/09/75	East Kilbride	19/07/94	6 0.0	11 3	Oldham B.C.
Harrison	Thomas	Edward	22/01/74	Edinburgh	04/08/95	5 9.0	11 8	Dunfermline Athletic
Hillcoat	John		16/12/70	East Kilbride	31/03/94	5 11.0	10 10	Dunfermline Athletic
Knox	Keith		06/08/64	Stranraer	16/03/88	5 10.0	12 2	Stranraer
McCarron	James		31/10/71	Glasgow	29/07/92	5 6.0	9 12	Aberdeen
McCheyne	Graeme		21/12/73	Bellshill	29/07/92	6 1.0	11 3	Dundee United
McCluskey	George	McKinlay C.J.	19/09/57	Hamilton	11/08/95	5 10.5	12 6	Kilmarnock
McConnell	Ian	Paul	06/01/75	Glasgow	04/10/93	6 1.0	12 8	Derry City
McGregor	Allan		17/10/75	Glasgow	19/08/94	5 11.0	11 10	Bathgate Thistle
McQueen	James		10/06/61	Edinburgh	04/08/95	6 3.0	13 4	Queen of the South
Muir	Jack		08/02/75	Hamilton	14/10/93	5 10.0	10 10	Dunipace Juniors
Nicholas	Charles		30/12/61	Glasgow	10/08/95	5 9.0	11 0	Celtic
Nisbet	Iain		11/05/74	Bellshill	15/08/94	5 9.0	10 2	Aberdeen
O'Neill	Martin		17/06/75	Glasgow	08/06/93	5 7.5	10 10	Clyde B.C.
Parks	Gordon	John	19/11/72	Glasgow	18/08/92	5 9.5	10 7	Shettleston Juniors
Patterson	Paul	Joseph	30/07/75	Glasgow	25/07/95	5 10.0	9 1	Motherwell
Prunty	James		21/09/74	Bellshill	08/06/93	5 8.5	10 8	Clyde B.C.
Shanks	Donald	William	12/11/76	Coatbridge	07/09/94	6 1.0	12 1	Coltness United
Thomson	James		15/05/71	Stirling	09/08/91	6 1.0	12 7	Campsie Black Watch
Watson	Graham		10/09/70	St. Andrews	03/06/94	5 9.5	11 6	Aberdeen

MILESTONES

YEAR OF FORMATION: 1878
MOST CAPPED PLAYER: Tommy Ring
NO. OF CAPS: 12
MOST LEAGUE POINTS IN A SEASON: 64 (Division 2 – Season 1956/57)
MOST LEAGUE GOALS SCORED BY A PLAYER IN A SEASON: Bill Boyd (Season 1932/33)
NO. OF GOALS SCORED: 32
RECORD ATTENDANCE: 52,000 (-v- Rangers – 21.11.1908 – at Shawfield Stadium)
    5,369 (-v- Hamilton Academical – 5.2.1994 – at Broadwood Stadium)
RECORD VICTORY: 11-1 (-v- Cowdenbeath – Division 2, 6.10.1951)
RECORD DEFEAT: 0-11 (-v- Dumbarton and Rangers, Scottish Cup)

SEASON TICKET INFORMATION

Seated
Adult £100
Juvenile/OAP..£55

LEAGUE ADMISSION PRICES

Seated
Adult £7
Juvenile/OAP £4
Parent and Juvenile £9

CLUB FACTFILE 1994/95
RESULTS .. APPEARANCES .. SCORERS

The BULLY WEE

Date	Venue	Opponents	Result	Fridge L.	Clark M.	Neill A.	Knox K.	Thomson J.	Watson G.	Dickson J.	McCheyne G.	McConnell I.	McAvay J.	MacKenzie A.	O'Neill M.	Strain B.	Wright A.	McFarlane R.	Frater A.	McCartor J.	Wylde C.	Nisbet I.	Argue I.	Tennant S.	Parks G.	Hillcoat I.	Brown J.	McGill D.	Prunty J.	Falconer M.	McCluskey C.	Muir J.	Fay J.
Aug 13	A	Stenhousemuir	0-1	1	2	3	4	5	6	7	8	9	10	11	12																		
20	A	Queen of the South	2-1	1	2		4	5	8	7^1	12^1						3		6	9		10	11	14									
27	H	Stirling Albion	1-2	1	2		4^1	5	8	7	12						3		6	9		10	11	14									
Sep 3	H	Berwick Rangers	3-4	1			6	5	2	11	9	8	14^1	7	4					10		3^1	12^1										
10	A	East Fife	0-2		2		4	5	8	3	9		11							14	10	7	1	6	12								
24	A	Dumbarton	1-2	13	2		4	5		8	14		7		11				10		6				1	9^1	3						
Oct 1	H	Meadowbank Thistle	2-1	1	2		4^2	5		8			11	7	14	10			6							9	3	12					
8	A	Greenock Morton	1-0	1	2		4^1	5	14	8			11		6	10	7		3							12	9						
15	H	Brechin City	4-0	1	2		4^1	5	6	8^1			11^1	14		10	7		3^1							12	9						
22	H	Stenhousemuir	0-0	1	2		4^1	5	6	8			11	14		10	7		3							12	9						
29	A	Stirling Albion	1-0	1	2		4^1	5	6	12	8		14	11		10	7		3								9						
Nov 5	H	Queen of the South	2-2	1	2		4	5	6	8			14^1	12^1		10	7		3							11	9						
12	H	East Fife	1-1	1	2		4		6		8	11				10	7		3					12		5	14	9^1					
19	A	Berwick Rangers	1-2	1	2		4	5	6		12					10	7		3^1		11	14			8	9							
26	H	Dumbarton	3-1	1			10	5	2	7	8^2	11			4				14			3		12		6					9^1		
Dec 3	H	Meadowbank Thistle	2-2	1			10	5	2	7^1	8	11			4				14			3^1		12		6					9		
26	H	Greenock Morton	0-0	1	2		10	5	8	7	4	11							12			3		14		6					9		
31	A	Brechin City	2-0	1			10	5	8	7	12	11^1	2		4				3			14				6					9^1		
Jan 14	A	Stenhousemuir	2-2	1			10		8	7^1	14	12	2	5					4			3		11^1		6					9		
17	H	Stirling Albion	2-0	1			10	5	8	7^2	14	9	2						4			3		11		6	12						
21	H	Queen of the South	3-4	1			10	5	8	7^2	11	14	2						4			3		9^1		6	12						
Feb 4	A	East Fife	3-1	1		11	10	5	8	7		12	2^1						4	3^1		9^1		6	14								
11	H	Berwick Rangers	1-3	1			10	5	8	7	14	12^1	2						4	3		11		6							9		
18	A	Dumbarton	2-2	1		11	10	5	8	7	12		2						4	3^1		9^1		6									
25	H	Meadowbank Thistle	4-1	1		11	10	5^1	12	7	8		2^1						14^1	4^1		3		9		6							
Mar 11	H	Brechin City	1-0	1		11	10	5	12	7^1	14		2						8	4		3		9		6							
14	A	Greenock Morton	1-4	1		11	10	5	8	7^1	9		2						12	4		3		6									14
18	H	East Fife	1-1				10	5		7	11		2		8				4^1			12	1	6		3		9					
25	A	Berwick Rangers	1-1				10	5	4	7	11		2		8				14			12	1	6		3		9^1					
Apr 1	A	Meadowbank Thistle	1-0				10	5	4	7^1	11		2		8				12				1	6		3	14	9					
8	A	Dumbarton	1-0				10	5	8	7	11		2		4				14				1	6		3	12	9^1					
15	H	Greenock Morton	1-3				10	5	8	7	14		11		2				4			12	1	6^1		3		9					
22	A	Brechin City	0-0				5		4	14	3	8	2						10			7	1	6		12	11	9					
29	H	Stenhousemuir	3-2				10	5			14	11^2	4		8	2							1	6		3		9			7^1		
May 6	A	Stirling Albion	0-2				10	5		7	11	4	12		8	2							1	6		3		9			14		
13	A	Queen of the South	0-1				5	2	14	3	4								7	10		8	1	6		12	9						11
TOTAL FULL APPEARANCES				25	18	10	30	30	28	23	13	7	8	22	20	3	9	2	2	17	2	18	24	1	11	11	23	2	11	6	18	1	1
TOTAL SUB APPEARANCES				(1)				(3)	(4)		(5)	(8)	(7)	(1)	(4)				(5)			(7)		(7)		(2)	(4)	(5)	(4)	(1)	(1)		
TOTAL GOALS SCORED							6	1		10	3	1		3	5	2				1		2	5		1	5	1		1		5		1

Small bold figures denote goalscorers. † denotes opponent's own goal.

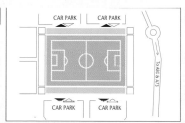

BROADWOOD STADIUM

CAPACITY: 6,300 (All Seated)
PITCH DIMENSIONS: 112 yds x 76 yds
FACILITIES FOR DISABLED SUPPORTERS: Facilities available in both Home and Away Stands.

HOW TO GET THERE

The following routes may be used to reach Broadwood Stadium:

BUSES: From Buchanan Street Bus Station, Glasgow. Bus No. 36A (Glasgow to Westfield).

TRAINS: From Queen Street Station, Glasgow to Croy Station. The Stadium is a 15 minute walk from here.

CARS: From Glasgow City Centre via Stepps By-Pass joining A80 towards Stirling. Take Broadwood turn off to Stadium.

YOUNGER'S TARTAN SPECIAL

EAST FIFE

LIST OF PLAYERS 1995-96

SURNAME	FIRST NAME	MIDDLE NAME	DATE OF BIRTH	PLACE OF BIRTH	DATE OF SIGNING	HEIGHT FT INS	WEIGHT ST LBS	PREVIOUS CLUB
Allan	Gilbert	Chapman	21/02/73	St. Andrews	16/11/93	6 0.0	9 7	Anstruther Colts
Andrew	Benjamin		05/02/73	Perth	20/08/90	5 8.0	9 6	Lochore Welfare
Archibald	Steven		27/09/56	Glasgow	22/08/94	5 10.5	11 7	Clyde
Balmain	Kenneth	John A.	08/11/73	Bellshill	31/03/95	5 9.0	12 0	Hibernian
Barron	Douglas		25/10/61	Edinburgh	31/03/93	5 11.0	10 0	Clydebank
Beaton	David	Robert	08/08/67	Bridge of Allan	24/11/90	5 11.0	11 4	Falkirk
Bell	Graham		29/03/71	St. Andrews	12/08/87	5 10.0	11 0	St. Andrews
Burns	William		10/12/69	Motherwell	07/08/91	5 10.0	11 7	Rochdale
Cusick	John	James	16/01/75	Kirkcaldy	18/03/94	5 8.0	10 0	Dundonald Bluebell
Donaghy	Mark		29/08/72	Glasgow	22/10/94	5 8.0	9 13	Shettleston Juniors
Dwarika	Arnold		23/08/73	Trinidad & Tobago	31/03/95	5 8.0	10 4	Superstar Rangers
Gartshore	Philip		02/04/76	Kirkcaldy	29/10/94	5 10.0	9 7	Methilhill Strollers
Gibb	Richard		22/04/65	Bangour	17/09/93	5 7.0	11 0	Armadale Thistle
Hamill	Alexander		30/10/61	Coatbridge	13/01/95	5 8.0	11 4	Cowdenbeath
Hamilton	Lindsay		11/08/62	Bellshill	04/08/95	6 2.0	13 4	Portadown
Hildersley	Ronald		06/04/65	Kirkcaldy	17/09/93	5 5.0	10 7	Halifax Town
Hope	Douglas		14/06/71	Edinburgh	15/08/88	5 8.0	11 0	Hutchison Vale B.C.
Hunter	Paul		30/08/68	Kirkcaldy	28/07/94	5 9.0	10 7	Cowdenbeath
Hutcheon	Stephen		20/05/70	St. Andrews	07/10/94	6 0.0	12 7	Cupar Hearts A.F.C.
Irvine	Alan	James	29/11/62	Broxburn	12/08/93	6 2.0	14 5	Portadown
Long	Derek		20/08/74	Broxburn	31/03/93	5 10.0	12 0	Newburgh Juniors
McLeod	Darren		28/06/78	Kirkcaldy	24/02/95	5 6.0	9 10	Northern Colts U'16
McStay	John		24/12/65	Larkhall	11/07/95	5 9.5	10 12	Clydebank
Rae	Gordon		03/05/58	Edinburgh	20/02/95	6 0.0	15 0	Gala Fairydean
Robertson	Dean		06/07/74	Johannesburg	20/05/95	5 11.0	12 0	Norton House
Sneddon	Alan		12/03/58	Baillieston	27/07/93	5 11.0	12 3	Motherwell
Struthers	David	Paul	21/10/74	Dunfermline	24/03/95	5 9.0	10 8	Glenrothes
Taylor	Paul	Henry	02/12/70	Falkirk	19/10/89	5 10.0	11 7	Sauchie Juniors
Williamson	Andrew		04/09/69	Kirkcaldy	10/07/93	6 0.0	11 0	Dunfermline Athletic
Wilson	Ewan		01/10/68	Dunfermline	15/04/93	6 2.0	12 0	Strathmilgo United

Bayview Park, Wellesley Road, Methil, Fife, KY8 3AG

CHAIRMAN
James W. Baxter

VICE-CHAIRMAN
Stephen Baxter

DIRECTORS
John Fleming
James Taylor
Julian S. Danskin

SECRETARY
Mrs. Leona R. G. Walker

GENERAL MANAGER
David Gorman

PLAYER/MANAGER
Steven Archibald

ASSISTANT MANAGER
Alan Sneddon

RESERVE TEAM COACHES
Ronnie Hildersley
Gordon Rae

CLUB DOCTOR
Dr. William McCrossan

PHYSIOTHERAPIST
Alex MacQueen L.V.M.C.

YOUTH DEVELOPMENT OFFICERS
John Gartshore
Don McKay
Tom Auld

GROUNDSMAN
James Hay

KIT MAN
Alexander Doig

TELEPHONES
Ground (01333) 426323
Fax (01333) 426376

CLUB SHOP
A Supporters' Club Shop
is situated within the Ground

OFFICIAL SUPPORTERS CLUB
J. Tindal, 62 Harcourt Road,
Kirkcaldy (01592) 642775

TEAM CAPTAIN
John McStay

SHIRT SPONSOR
Andrew Forrester, Leven

MILESTONES

YEAR OF FORMATION: 1903
MOST CAPPED PLAYER: George Aitken
NO. OF CAPS: 5
MOST LEAGUE POINTS IN A SEASON: 57 (Division 2 – Season 1929/30)
MOST LEAGUE GOALS SCORED BY A PLAYER IN A SEASON: Henry Morris (Season 1947/48)
NO. OF GOALS SCORED: 41
RECORD ATTENDANCE: 22,515 (-v- Raith Rovers – 2.1.1950)
RECORD VICTORY: 13-2 (-v- Edinburgh City – Division 2, 11.12.1937)
RECORD DEFEAT: 0-9 (-v- Heart of Midlothian – Division 1, 5.10.1957)

SEASON TICKET INFORMATION

Seated
Adult £112
Juvenile/OAP...£66
Standing
Adult £96
Juvenile/OAP...£54

LEAGUE ADMISSION PRICES

Seated
Adult £7
Juvenile/OAP.......................................£4.50
Standing
Adult £6
Juvenile/OAP.......................................£3.50

CLUB FACTFILE 1994/95
RESULTS .. APPEARANCES .. SCORERS

The FIFERS

Date	Venue	Opponents	Result	Wilson E.	Bell G.	Williamson A.	Barron D.	Sneddon A.	Hildersley R.	Cusick J.	Hope D.	Scott E.	Hunter P.	Gibb F.	Allan G.	Irvine A.	Beaton D.	Burns W.	Andrew J.	Dow C.	Donaghy M.	Hutcheon S.	Archibald S.	Roberson D.	Hamil A.	Struthers D.	Dwarika A.	Balmain K.
Aug 13	A	Stirling Albion	1-0	1	2	3	4	5	6	7	8	9	10	11	12	14												
20	A	Stenhousemuir	1-1	1	2		3	4		7	6	8	9	10^{1}	11	12		5	14									
27	H	Brechin City	1-1	1	2		6	4		7		11	9	10	3	14		5	8^{1}	12								
Sep 3	A	Queen of the South	2-0	1	3			2			8	9^{1}	10	11	7		12	5	4	6^{1}	14							
10	H	Clyde	2-0	1	3			2			8	9	10^{1}	11	14		12	5	4	6	7^{1}							
24	H	Greenock Morton	1-2	1				2^{1}	6	8	3	9	10	11	7		12	5	4		14							
Oct 1	A	Berwick Rangers	1-1	1	2			3			11	9^{1}	10		7		12	5	4	8	6	14						
8	H	Dumbarton	2-3	1				2	12	6		9^{1}	10	3	7		5^{1}	4		11	8	14						
15	A	Meadowbank Thistle	1-0	1	2			3			8	9^{1}	10	11			5	4		6	7	12	14					
22	H	Stirling Albion	4-3	1	2			3	7		11^{1}	9^{1}	10				5^{1}	4^{1}		6		8						
29	A	Brechin City	0-2	1				2	7		11	9	10	3			5	4	14	6	12	8						
Nov 5	H	Stenhousemuir	2-3	1				3	6	2	11	9^{1}			5	4	7	10			14^{1}	8						
12	A	Clyde	1-1	1				2		7	11	9		3		12	5	4	14	6	10	8^{1}						
19	H	Queen of the South	3-1	1	3			2		7	6	9^{1}		11		14	5	4	12	8	10^{2}							
26	A	Greenock Morton	0-3	1	3			2	14	7	11	9			12	5	4	8	6	10								
Dec 3	H	Berwick Rangers	3-0	1				2	6	7	3	9^{3}			12	14	5	4	11	10	8	13						
26	A	Dumbarton	0-4	1				2	3	7	11	9			14	12	5	4	6	10	8							
31	H	Meadowbank Thistle	2-1	1				2	3	6	11	9^{1}			7	5	4			10	14^{1}	8						
Jan 2	A	Brechin City	4-0	1				2^{1}	3^{1}	6^{1}	11	9		12	7	5	4			10^{1}	14	8						
14	A	Stirling Albion	0-3		2				8	6	11	9	12	3	7	5	4			10					1	14		
21	H	Stenhousemuir	0-2					2		6	11	9	12	3	7	5	14		8	10					1	4		
Feb 4	H	Clyde	1-3		2			4	6	5^{1}	11	9	10	3	7					12	14				1	8		
14	A	Queen of the South	3-3					5		2	11	10^{2}	6	7					4	12	8^{1}	9			1	3		
25	A	Berwick Rangers	0-0					5		2	11	10	6	7	9				4	8	14				1	3		
28	H	Greenock Morton	1-1	1				2		5	11	9	10	3	7			4		6	12	8	9^{1}					
Mar 4	H	Dumbarton	0-2	1				2		5	11	9	10	3	12			4		8						13	6	
11	H	Meadowbank Thistle	3-1					2		6	11^{1}	9	10	12	7	14	5^{2}	4		8					1	3		
18	A	Clyde	1-1					2		3^{1}	11	9	10	12	7	14	5	4		8					1	6		
25	H	Queen of the South	3-1					2		3	11	9^{2}	10^{1}		5			4		7	8				1	6	12	
Apr 1	A	Berwick Rangers	0-1					2		3	11	9	10	14	5			4			8				1	6	7	12
8	A	Greenock Morton	1-4					2		3		9	12	14	7		5	4			8				1	6^{1}	10	11
15	A	Dumbarton	0-2					2	6	4	11	12	10	7			5	14			8				1	3	9	
22	H	Meadowbank Thistle	1-1					4	6	5		9	10	3	2					12	8				1	11	14	7^{1}
29	H	Stirling Albion	1-2					2		4		9	10	11	7		5^{1}	14		12	8				1	3	6	
May 6	A	Brechin City	1-1	1				2		4	11	9^{1}		3	5			7		6	14	8	10			12		
13	A	Stenhousemuir	1-2	1				4	11		7	3	2	12	5			10		6	9^{1}		14	8				
TOTAL FULL APPEARANCES				23	12	1	3	34	17	28	31	31	24	23	18	1	29	27	10	5	23	9	12	13	15	1	5	1
TOTAL SUB APPEARANCES								(1)	(1)		(1)	(3)	(5)	(6)	(15)	(1)	(1)	(7)	(3)	(3)	(11)	(1)	(2)	(1)	(4)	(1)		
TOTAL GOALS SCORED								2	2	3	2	14	5				5	2	1	1	2	5	1		2		1	

Small bold figures denote goalscorers. † denotes opponent's own goal.

BAYVIEW PARK

CAPACITY: 5,385; Seated 600, Standing 4,785
PITCH DIMENSIONS: 110 yds x 71 yds
FACILITIES FOR DISABLED SUPPORTERS: Area available at East End of Stand.

KIRKLAND ROAD

WELLESLEY ROAD

HOW TO GET THERE

Bayview Park can be reached by the following routes:
TRAINS: The nearest railway station is Kirkcaldy (8 miles away), and fans will have to catch an inter-linking service from here to the ground.
BUSES: A regular service from Kirkcaldy to Leven passes outside the ground, as does the Leven to Dunfermline service.
CARS: There is a car park behind the ground, with entry through Kirkland Road.

FORFAR ATHLETIC

LIST OF PLAYERS 1995-96

Station Park, Carseview Road,
Forfar, DD8 3BT

CHAIRMAN
George A. Enston

VICE-CHAIRMAN
David McGregor

DIRECTORS
Donald R. Cameron
James G. Robertson
Alastair S. Nicoll

SECRETARY
David McGregor

MANAGER
Tom Campbell

ASSISTANT MANAGER
Brian McLaughlin

COACHING STAFF
Tom McCallum
Gordon Arthur
Ian McPhee

PHYSIOTHERAPIST
Jim Peacock

GROUNDSMAN
Martin Gray

COMMERCIAL DIRECTOR
James G. Robertson
(01250) 874588

TELEPHONES
Ground (01307) 463576/462259
Sec. Home (01307) 464924
Sec. Bus. (01307) 462255
Fax (01307) 466956

CLUB SHOP
45 East High Street, Forfar
(01307) 465959.
Open 9.00 a.m.-5.00 p.m.
Mon, Tue, Thur and Fri.

OFFICIAL SUPPORTERS CLUB
c/o Mrs. Yvonne Nicoll,
24 Turfbeg Drive, Forfar

TEAM CAPTAIN
Neil Irvine

SHIRT SPONSOR
Webster Contracts Ltd.

SURNAME	FIRST NAME	MIDDLE NAME	DATE OF BIRTH	PLACE OF BIRTH	DATE OF SIGNING	HEIGHT FT INS	WEIGHT ST LBS	PREVIOUS CLUB
Archibald	Eric		25/03/65	Dunfermline	23/10/93	6 0.0	12 7	Cowdenbeath
Arthur	Gordon		30/05/58	Kirkcaldy	08/09/93	5 11.0	12 5	Raith Rovers
Bingham	David	Thomas	03/09/70	Dunfermline	08/12/92	5 10.0	10 7	St. Johnstone
Bowes	Mark	John	17/02/73	Bangour	28/07/95	5 8.0	10 10	Dunfermline Athletic
Craig	Douglas	Ewing	30/01/71	London	05/11/94	5 10.0	12 9	Forfar Albion
Donegan	John	Francis J.	19/05/71	Cork	18/07/95	6 1.0	12 8	St. Johnstone
Gardner	Barry		11/06/77	Perth	06/09/95	5 9.0	10 0	Bankfoot Jnrs
Glennie	Stuart	Philip	07/10/75	Torphins	14/09/93	6 0.0	13 0	Banchory St. Ternan
Guthrie	Derek		16/08/77	Forfar	15/08/95	5 6.0	10 0	Forfar Albion
Hannigan	Paul	William	10/07/70	Perth	19/10/94	5 7.0	10 0	Jeanfield Swifts
Heddle	Ian	Alexander	21/03/63	Dunfermline	07/08/92	5 10.0	11 0	St. Johnstone
Irvine	Neil	Donald	13/10/65	Edinburgh	22/07/94	5 10.0	12 7	Montrose
Loney	James		29/08/75	Stirling	11/03/95	5 8.0	10 0	East Stirlingshire
Mann	Robert	Alexander	11/01/74	Dundee	21/07/92	6 3.0	13 7	St. Johnstone
McKillop	Alan	Robert	30/11/63	Perth	04/06/94	6 1.0	12 8	Arbroath
McPhee	Ian		31/01/61	Perth	27/09/91	5 8.0	11 10	Airdrieonians
McVicar	Donald		06/11/62	Perth	02/02/95	5 8.0	11 8	Arbroath S.C.
Morgan	Andrew	Alan	10/12/74	Glasgow	06/01/95	5 9.0	10 12	St. Johnstone
O'Neill	Hugh		03/01/75	Dunfermline	21/07/94	6 0.0	11 0	Dunfermline Athletic
Paterson	Alastair	James	20/08/75	Dundee	10/08/95	5 8.0	10 7	Celtic

MILESTONES

YEAR OF FORMATION: 1885
MOST LEAGUE POINTS IN A SEASON: 63 (Second Division – Season 1983/84) (2 Points for a Win)
80 (Third Division – Season 1994/95) (3 Points for a Win)
MOST LEAGUE GOALS SCORED BY A PLAYER IN A SEASON: Dave Kilgour (Season 1929/30)
NO. OF GOALS SCORED: 45
RECORD ATTENDANCE: 10,800 (-v- Rangers – 7.2.1970)
RECORD VICTORY: 14-1 (-v- Lindertis – Scottish Cup, 1.9.1888)
RECORD DEFEAT: 2-12 (-v- King's Park – Division 2, 2.1.1930)

SEASON TICKET INFORMATION

Seated
Adult £90
Juvenile/OAP...£45
Standing
Adult £80
Juvenile/OAP...£40

LEAGUE ADMISSION PRICES

Seated
Adult..£5.50
Juvenile/OAP £3
Standing
Adult £5
Juvenile/OAP..£2.50

CLUB FACTFILE 1994/95
RESULTS .. APPEARANCES .. SCORERS

The LOONS

Date	Venue	Opponents	Result	Arthur C.	McLaren P.	McPhee I.	Mann R.	Archibald E.	McKillop A.	O'Neill H.	Irvine N.	Lees G.	Bingham D.	Heddle I.	Kopel S.	Smith R.	Mearns G.	McCormick S.	Ross A.	Reilly J.	Glennie S.	Craig D.	Stephen C.	Hannigan P.	Morgan A.	McVicar C.	Loney J.	Guthrie D.
Aug 13	A	Queen's Park	2-1	1	2	3	4	5^1	6	7	8	9^1	10	11	12		14											
20	H	Alloa	3-2	1		3	4	5	6	7	8	9	10^2	11	2^1		14											
27	A	Arbroath	1-0	1	12	3^1	4	5	6	7	8	9	10	11	2		14											
Sep 3	H	Montrose	1-0	1		3	4	5	6	2	8	14	10^1	11				12	7	9								
10	A	Caledonian Thistle	1-3	1	2	3	4	5	6		8	9	10	11^1				14	7									
24	A	East Stirlingshire	1-3	1	2	3^1	4	5	6		11		10	8					7	9								
Oct 1	H	Albion Rovers	1-1	1		10		5	6	4	7		11^1	3	2			8	9									
8	H	Ross County	1-0	1		3^1	4	5	6	11	8		10	12	2			7	9	14								
15	H	Cowdenbeath	0-1	1		3	4	5	6	11	8	14	10	12	2			7	9									
22	H	Queen's Park	2-0	1		3	4		5	2	8	7	11^2	6				10	9		14							
29	H	Arbroath	3-0	1	14	3			5	2	8	7	11^1	6	12			10^1	9^1		4							
Nov 5	A	Alloa	1-0	1	14	3			5	2	8	12	11	6	7			10^1	9		4							
12	H	Caledonian Thistle	2-1	1	12				2	8	7		11	6	3			10^1	9^1		5	4						
19	A	Montrose	0-2	1		3	4		5	2	8		11	6				10	9					7	13	14		
26	H	East Stirlingshire	3-2	1		3	4	6	5		2	12	11	8				7	10^3					1	9			
Dec 3	A	Albion Rovers	1-0	1			4	6	5		2	12	11	8				7	10^1					3	9			
31	H	Cowdenbeath	1-1	1		3	4	5			2		11	8				6	10						9^1	7		
Jan 11	A	Ross County	1-2	1		3		5	6	4			11	8				10	9^1		2				14	7		
14	H	Queen's Park	3-0	1		3	4		5	2			11^1	8				10	9		6	14			12^1	7^1		
24	A	Alloa	2-0	1		3	4		5	14			11^1	8				10^1	9		2	6			12	7		
28	A	Arbroath	1-1	1		3	4		5		8		11^1					10	9			6			12	7	2	
Feb 4	A	Caledonian Thistle	1-1	1		3			5		8	14	11^1					10	9		4	6			12	7	2	
18	A	East Stirlingshire	2-1	1			4		5				11	8				10	9^1		2		3		12	7^1	6	
25	H	Albion Rovers	4-0	1		3			5			14	11^1	8				12	9^1		2		4		10^1	7^1	6	
Mar 4	H	Ross County	4-2	1		3	4		5				11^7	8					9^1		2		14		10^1	7	6	
11	A	Cowdenbeath	3-1	1		3			5				11	8				12	9^3		2		4		10	7	6	14
18	H	Caledonian Thistle	4-1	1		3	4^1		5				11^3	8				12	9		2		4		10	7	6	
25	A	Montrose	2-1	1		3^1	4		5				11	12				10^1	9		2		8	14		7	6	
Apr 1	H	Albion Rovers	3-0	1		3	4		5				11	8				10^1	9^2		2		14		12	7	6	
4	H	Montrose	1-3	1		3	4		5				11^1	8				10	9		2		14		12	7	6	
8	H	East Stirlingshire	1-0	1		3	4		5				11^1	12				14	9		2		8		10	7	6	
15	A	Ross County	1-0	1		3	4^1		5				11					12	9		2		8		10	7	6	
22	A	Cowdenbeath	2-2	1		3	4		5				11	14				10	9^1		2		8		12	7	6^1	2
29	A	Queen's Park	2-0	1	12		4		5				11					14	9		2		3		10^2	7	6	8
May 6	H	Arbroath	4-1	1		3	4		5				11^2					12	9^1		2		8	13	10	7^1	6	14
13	H	Alloa	2-0	1		3	4	5					11^1						14		2		8		10	7^1	12	9
TOTAL FULL APPEARANCES				35	3	32	26	16	33	15	18	7	36	25	7		3	24	28	19	17	1	12	20	15	2	2	
TOTAL SUB APPEARANCES					(4)	(1)		(1)	(7)		(5)		(3)	(2)	(2)			(7)	(1)	(1)	(1)		(5)	(2)	(11)		(1)	(2)
TOTAL GOALS SCORED						4	2	1				1	22	1	1			10	13					6	5	1		

Small bold figures denote goalscorers. † denotes opponent's own goal.

STATION PARK

CAPACITY: 8,732; Seated 739, Standing 7,993
PITCH DIMENSIONS: 115 yds x 69 yds
FACILITIES FOR DISABLED SUPPORTERS: Ramp entrance via Main Stand.

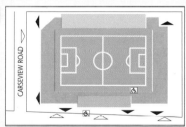

CARSEVIEW ROAD

HOW TO GET THERE

Station Park can be reached by the following routes:

BUSES: There is a regular service of buses departing from Dundee City Centre into Forfar. The bus station in the town is about half a mile from the ground. There is also a local service.

TRAINS: The nearest railway station is Dundee (14 miles away) and fans who travel to here should then board a bus for Forfar from the city centre. Arbroath station is also about 14 miles away.

CARS: There are car parking facilities in adjacent streets to the ground and also in the Market Muir car park.

MONTROSE

Links Park Stadium,
Wellington Street,
Montrose, DD10 8QD

CHAIRMAN
Bryan D. Keith

VICE-CHAIRMAN
Ronald Clark

DIRECTORS
Malcolm J. Watters
Michael G. Craig
John D. Crawford
John Archbold

HONORARY PRESIDENT
William Johnston, M.B.E., J.P.

SECRETARY
Malcolm J. Watters

MATCH DAY SECRETARY
Andrew Stephen

MANAGER
Andrew Dornan

YOUTH TEAM COACH
Walker McCall

RESERVE TEAM COACH
Colin Walker

CLUB DOCTOR
Dr. N. Piercy

PHYSIOTHERAPIST
Allan Borthwick

TELEPHONES
Ground (01674) 673200
Fax (01674) 677311
Sec. Home (01674) 830354
Sec. Bus. (01674) 674941
Sec. Fax (01674) 677830

CLUB SHOP
Situated at Stadium
(01674) 674941.
Open 10.30 a.m. – 5.00 p.m. Fri.
and on matchdays

OFFICIAL SUPPORTERS CLUB
c/o Links Park, Wellington Street,
Montrose, DD10 8QD

TEAM CAPTAIN
Mark Haro

SHIRT SPONSOR
Bon Accord Glass

LIST OF PLAYERS 1995-96

SURNAME	FIRST NAME	MIDDLE NAME	DATE OF BIRTH	PLACE OF BIRTH	DATE OF SIGNING	HEIGHT FT INS	WEIGHT ST LBS	PREVIOUS CLUB
Beedie	Stuart		16/08/60	Aberdeen	11/02/94	5 10.5	11 0	East Fife
Brown	Justin		12/02/78	Aberdeen	11/09/95	6 0.0	11 10	Bon Accord
Brown	Michael	Derek	26/10/75	Aberdeen	12/08/95	6 1.0	10 4	Bon Accord
Cooper	Craig		17/01/73	Arbroath	19/06/93	5 10.0	10 13	Portcullis
Craib	Mark		08/02/70	St. Andrews	17/07/92	5 10.0	11 12	Dundee
Dornan	Andrew		19/08/61	Aberdeen	29/01/90	5 8.5	10 13	Worcester City
Ferrie	Alistair	Alexander	13/03/78	Montrose	02/09/95	5 8.0	10 7	Stonehaven Jnrs
Garden	Mark		07/08/75	Aberdeen	02/08/93	5 11.0	11 8	Middlefield United
Grant	Derek		19/05/66	Edinburgh	12/09/92	6 2.0	12 8	Meadowbank Thistle
Haro	Mark		21/10/71	Irvine	12/07/93	6 2.0	11 7	Dunfermline Athletic
Larter	David		18/03/60	Edinburgh	27/07/87	5 10.5	11 4	Dalkeith
Lavelle	Mark		26/04/74	Hitchin	10/05/95	5 11.0	11 5	Bon Accord Juniors
MacDonald	Innes	James	19/10/62	Inverness	01/08/94	5 10.0	11 3	Luxol St. Andrews Malta
MacRonald	Colin	William	22/08/73	Aberdeen	12/08/94	5 7.5	10 0	Aberdeen
Mailer	Craig	James	27/09/67	Perth	20/02/95	5 11.0	11 7	Kinnoull Juniors
Massie	Ronald	Wilson	04/10/75	Montrose	28/08/93	5 11.0	11 5	Montrose Roselea
Masson	Christopher	Scott	05/09/77	Aberdeen	09/09/95	6 0.0	11 0	Montrose Roselea
Masson	Paul	Thomas	07/12/74	Aberdeen	27/10/93	5 9.0	10 7	Carnoustie Panmure
McAvoy	Neil		29/07/72	Stirling	08/02/95	6 2.0	11 7	Alloa
McGlashan	Colin	James	17/03/64	Perth	12/07/94	5 7.0	10 12	Ayr United
Middler	Ryan	George N.	10/03/77	Aberdeen	06/09/95	5 9.0	10 7	Lewis United
Robb	Mark	David	02/04/77	Aberdeen	11/09/95	5 11.0	11 0	Bon Accord
Robertson	Ian	William	14/10/66	Motherwell	26/07/91	5 9.0	10 10	Aberdeen
Smith	Shaun		13/04/71	Bangour	17/03/95	6 0.0	12 2	Clydebank
Stephen	Levi		19/03/74	Hastings	06/08/93	5 8.0	11 0	Clydebank
Taylor	Darren		26/06/71	Dundee	20/11/93	5 11.0	11 0	Lochee United
Taylor	Scott	A.	23/01/77	Forfar	02/08/95	5 9.0	10 0	Dundee United
Tindal	Kevin	Douglas	11/04/71	Arbroath	20/11/93	5 9.0	12 7	Arbroath
Tosh	James	David	12/09/74	Arbroath	19/06/93	6 0.0	10 11	Arbroath Lads Club
Walker	Kevin	Andrew	18/01/63	Aberdeen	30/11/94	5 10.0	11 0	Bon Accord Juniors
Wilkins	Gregg	McLean	20/11/75	Edinburgh	10/05/95	5 10.0	9 0	Bon Accord Juniors
Wood	Robert		31/08/77	Aberdeen	11/09/95	5 10.0	11 2	Banks O'Dee

MILESTONES

YEAR OF FORMATION: 1879
MOST CAPPED PLAYER: Sandy Keiller
NO. OF CAPS: 6 (2 whilst with Montrose)
MOST LEAGUE POINTS IN A SEASON: 53 (Division 2 – 1974/75 and Second Division 1984/85) (2 Points for a Win)
67 (Third Division – Season 1994/95) (3 Points for a Win)
RECORD ATTENDANCE: 8,983 (-v- Dundee – 17.3.1973)
RECORD VICTORY: 12-0 (-v- Vale of Leithen – Scottish Cup, 4.1.1975)
RECORD DEFEAT: 0-13 (-v- Aberdeen, 17.3.1951)

SEASON TICKET INFORMATION

Seated or Standing
Adult £75
Juvenile/OAP..£40
Family (1 Adult and 1 Juvenile)................................£85

LEAGUE ADMISSION PRICES

Seated or Standing
Adult £6
Juvenile/OAP £3

CLUB FACTFILE 1994/95
RESULTS .. APPEARANCES .. SCORERS

The GABLE ENDIES

Date	Venue	Opponents	Result	Larter D.	Robertson	Tindal K.	Craig M.	Grant D.	Haro M.	Garden M.	Stephen L.	McGlashan	Kennedy A.	Masson P.	Cooper C.	Milne C.	Taylor C.	MacDonald I.	Brown M.	Tosh J.	MacRorald	Beedie S.	McAvoy N.	Maier C.	Smith S.
Aug 13	H	East Stirlingshire	2-0	1	2	3	4^1	5^1	6	7	8	9	10	11	12	14									
20	A	Albion Rovers	4-2	1	2	3	4	5	6^1	7	8	9	10^2	11^1	12		14								
27	H	Cowdenbeath	2-0	1	2^1	3	4	5	6		8	9^1	10	11	7	12	14								
Sep 3	A	Forfar Athletic	0-1	1	2	3	4	5	6		8	9	10	11	7										
10	H	Ross County	0-2	1	2	3	4	5	6		12	9	10	11	7		14	8							
24	H	Queen's Park	1-1	1	2	3		5^1	6	8	12	9	10	11	7		14	4							
Oct 1	A	Arbroath	3-0	1	3	2		5	6		11^1	9^1	10^1	4	7		12	8	14						
8	A	Alloa	1-1	1	2	3			6		11	9	10	4	7				8	14		5	12^1		
15	H	Caledonian Thistle	3-1	1	2	3		5^1	6	14	8	9^1	10	4	12					7		11^1			
22	A	East Stirlingshire	2-1	1	2	3		5	6		12	9	10^2	4	7					8		11			
29	A	Cowdenbeath	1-1	1	2	3		5				9	10^1	4	7					8		11	6		
Nov 5	H	Albion Rovers	4-1	1	2	3^1	8	5	6			9^2	10^1	4						7		11			
12	A	Ross County	1-0	1	2	3	8	5	6		12	9	10^1	4			14			7		11			
19	H	Forfar Athletic	2-0	1	2	3	8	5	6			9	10^2	4						7		11			
26	H	Queen's Park	1-1	1	2	3	8	5	6^1		12	9	10	4			14			7		11			
Dec 3	H	Arbroath	3-1	1	2			5	6		12	9^3	10	4	7		14		8			11	3		
24	A	Alloa	1-2	1	2			5	6^1	8		9	10	3	7		12		4						
Jan 2	H	Cowdenbeath	1-2	1	2	3		5	6			9	10	4^1	7		12		8						
Feb 4	H	Ross County	1-1	1	2	3		5	6	4	12	9^1	10			14				7		11	8		
14	A	Caledonian Thistle	4-0	1	2	3		5	6^1		12		14	7	9^1				8			11	4^2	10	
18	A	Queen's Park	2-2	1	2	3		5^1					14^1	6	7	9			8			11	4	10	
23	A	Arbroath	1-1	1	2	3		5	6			9	10	14	7		12		11				4	0^1	
Mar 11	H	Caledonian Thistle	0-1	1		2		5	6		3	9	14	4			12			11		8	10		7
15	A	East Stirlingshire	0-1	1			2	5	6			9	10	4	7			14				3	11	8	
22	A	Albion Rovers	4-1	1			3		6^1			9^1	12	4			14			7	5	11	8	2	10^2
25	H	Forfar Athletic	1-2	1			3		6			9	12^1	4	14					7	5	11	8	2	10
28	A	Alloa	1-0	1	2		8	5	6			9^1		4	7							11	14	3	10
Apr 1	H	Arbroath	†5-0	1	2		8	5	6			9^2	12	4	7^1							11	14	3	10^1
4	A	Forfar Athletic	3-1	1	2		8^1	5	6			9^1	12	4	7							11	14	3	10^1
11	A	Queen's Park	0-1	1	2		8	5	6			9	12		7							11	4	3	10
15	H	Alloa	0-0	1	2		8	5	6			9	12	4	7							11	14	3	10
19	A	Ross County	3-0	1	2		8		6		14	9	10	4	7^1					5			11^1	3	12^1
22	A	Caledonian Thistle	3-0	1	2		8		6		14	9^1	12	4	7					5			11^1	3	10^1
29	H	East Stirlingshire	1-0	1	2		8		6			9^1		4	7		14			5			11	3	10
May 6	A	Cowdenbeath	4-0	1	2		8		6	12		9^1	14^3	4	7					5			11	3	10
13	H	Albion Rovers	4-1	1	2		8	12	6	14		9^2	10^7	4						7		5	11	3	
TOTAL FULL APPEARANCES				36	32	21	22	28	34	7	6	34	23	32	24	2	22	9	20	7	13	14	10		
TOTAL SUB APPEARANCES							(1)			(7)	(6)		(10)		(7)	(5)	(11)	(4)	(1)	(3)		(1)	(4)		(1)
TOTAL GOALS SCORED						1	1	2	4	5	1	19	17	2	2	1						2	2	3	6

Small bold figures denote goalscorers. † denotes opponent's own goal.

LINKS PARK STADIUM

CAPACITY: 4,338; Seated 1,338, Standing 3,000
PITCH DIMENSIONS: 113 yds x 70 yds
FACILITIES FOR DISABLED SUPPORTERS: Area set aside for wheelchairs and designated area in new stand.

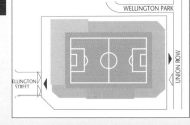

WELLINGTON PARK
ELLINGTON STREET
UNION ROW

HOW TO GET THERE

Links Park can be reached by the following routes:

TRAINS: Montrose is on the Inter-City 125 route from London to Aberdeen and also on the Glasgow-Aberdeen route. There is a regular service and the station is about 15 minutes walk from the ground.

BUSES: An hourly service of buses from Aberdeen and Dundee stop in the town centre and it is a 15 minute walk from here to the ground.

CARS: Car parking is available in the car park at the ground and there are numerous side streets all round the park which can be used if necessary.

QUEEN OF THE SOUTH

Palmerston Park, Terregles Street,
Dumfries, DG2 9BA

CHAIRMAN
Norman G. Blount

VICE-CHAIRMAN
Gordon R. McKerrow

DIRECTORS
Thomas G. Harkness
Keith M. Houliston

MATCH SECRETARY
Richard Shaw

SECRETARY
Mrs. Doreen Alcorn

MANAGER
William McLaren

ASSISTANT-MANAGER
Iain McChesney

COACHES
Graham McLean & Scott Stirling

YOUTH MANAGER
Brian Oakes

YOUTH COACHES
Trevor Wilson, Gordon Doig
Jim Grant

CHIEF SCOUT
Eddie McCulloch

CLUB DOCTORS
Dr. Phil Clayton, Dr. John Hinnie,
Dr. Steven Morris, Dr. Andrew Lyon

ORTHOPAEDIC SURGEONS
Mr. Clark Dreghorn
Miss Pat Costigan
Mr. Andrew Ogden

PHYSIOTHERAPISTS
Derek Kelly & Marion Hamilton

GROUNDSMAN
Tom Kerr

COMMERCIAL MANAGER
Robert McKinnel (01387) 258565

TELEPHONES
Ground/Ticket Office/Information
Service (01387) 254853
Fax (01387) 254853

CLUB SHOP
Palmerston Park, Terregles Street,
Dumfries (01387) 254853
Open 1.30 p.m. – 3.00 p.m.
on home matchdays.

OFFICIAL SUPPORTERS CLUB
c/o Palmerston Park, Terregles Street,
Dumfries, DG2 9BA

TEAM CAPTAIN
David Kennedy

SHIRT SPONSOR
The Open University

LIST OF PLAYERS 1995-96

SURNAME	FIRST NAME	MIDDLE NAME	DATE OF BIRTH	PLACE OF BIRTH	DATE OF SIGNING	HEIGHT FT INS	WEIGHT ST LBS	PREVIOUS CLUB
Brown	James	William	29/01/72	Dumfries	08/08/94	5 10.0	10 0	Cumnock Juniors
Bryce	Thomas	Charles	27/01/60	Johnstone	03/08/93	5 8.0	11 10	Clydebank
Brydson	Euan		13/09/73	Dumfries	03/08/95	5 8.0	9 0	Threave Rovers
Butter	James	Ross	14/12/66	Dundee	12/07/95	6 1.0	12 12	Alloa
Campbell	Colin	James	05/01/70	Edinburgh	19/09/94	5 11.0	11 0	Alloa
Campbell	Duncan	Matthew	11/09/70	Paisley	16/12/94	5 8.0	11 5	Glentoran
Cochrane	Gary		20/02/76	Dumfries	29/06/94	5 10.0	11 0	Ayr Boswell B.C.
Cody	Stephen		01/06/69	Calderbank	31/03/95	5 9.0	12 3	Stranraer
Cook	Andrew		06/11/75	Dumfries	29/06/95	5 11.0	9 8	Unattached
Friels	Gavin	David	03/08/77	Irvine	19/08/95	5 9.0	11.0	Bonnington Thistle
Harris	Colin		22/02/61	Sanquhar	29/07/95	6 0.0	12 2	Livingston
Hetherington	Kevin		23/11/63	Dumfries	09/08/94	5 10.0	12 1	Auchinleck Talbot
Jackson	David		06/12/68	Motherwell	15/06/93	5 7.0	10 6	Queen's Park
Johnston	Brian		28/10/76	Glasgow	20/07/95	5 7.0	9 7	Bellshill B.C.
Johnstone	Neil	William	21/06/79	Dumfries	07/07/95	5 6.0	11 7	"S" Form
Kennedy	David	John	07/10/66	Ayr	24/12/93	5 10.0	11 0	Ayr United
Mallan	Stephen	Patrick	30/08/67	Glasgow	03/08/93	5 11.0	12 4	Clyde
McColm	Robert	James	25/08/74	Dumfries	03/08/93	5 10.0	12 0	Annan Athletic
McCulloch	Kevin	Thomas	23/08/75	Dumfries	20/07/95	5 11.0	12 9	Unattached
McFarlane	Andrew		22/02/70	Glasgow	30/10/90	5 7.0	10 7	Arthurlie
McKeown	Brian		31/10/56	Motherwell	09/11/90	5 7.0	11 7	Airdrieonians
McKeown	Desmond	Michael	18/01/70	Glasgow	09/08/94	5 11.0	11 0	Albion Rovers
McLaren	John	Stuart	20/04/75	Glasgow	05/10/93	6 0.0	10 8	Airdrieonians
Proudfoot	Kevin	David	20/01/76	Dumfries	11/10/93	6 2.0	12 7	Dumfries H.F.P.
Purdie	David	Andrew	15/04/66	Dumfries	09/12/93	6 2.0	14 2	Ayr United
Ramsay	Steven		13/04/67	Germiston, S.A.	25/08/94	5 9.0	11 0	Alloa
Rowe	John	George	23/08/68	Glasgow	26/08/92	6 0.0	11 7	Clydebank
Sermanni	Peter	Hugh	09/09/71	Glasgow	27/08/92	5 9.0	10 0	Clydebank
Shermann	Glenn	Stuart	15/04/77	Dumfries	14/07/95	6 0.0	12 1	"S" Form
Telfer	Garry		19/01/65	Dumfries	25/02/95	6 0.0	11 0	Annan Athletic
Wilson	Stuart		21/09/65	Edinburgh	20/07/95	5 10.0	12 0	Livingston

MILESTONES

YEAR OF FORMATION: 1919
MOST CAPPED PLAYER: William Houliston
NO. OF CAPS: 3
MOST LEAGUE POINTS IN A SEASON: 55 (Division 2 – 1985/86)
MOST LEAGUE GOALS SCORED BY A PLAYER IN A SEASON: J. Gray (Season 1927/28)
NO. OF GOALS SCORED: 37
RECORD ATTENDANCE: 24,500 (-v- Heart of Midlothian – Scottish Cup 23.2.1952)
RECORD VICTORY: 11-1 (-v- Stranraer – Scottish Cup, 16.1.1932)
RECORD DEFEAT: 2-10 (-v- Dundee – Division 1, 1.12.1962)

SEASON TICKET INFORMATION

Seated
Adult £120
Juvenile/OAP/UB40's/Family Supplement £70
Junior Blues...£30
Standing
Adult £90
OAP/UB40's/Family Supplement £45
School Children £25
....
....
....

LEAGUE ADMISSION PRICES

Seated
Adult £7
School Children/UB40's/Family Supplement/OAP £5
Family Gate 1 Adult 1 Juvenile £10
       1 Adult 2 Juveniles £13
Standing
Adult £6
OAP/UB40's/Family Supplement £3
School Children £2
Family Gate 1 Adult 1 Juvenile £7
       1 Adult 2 Juveniles £8

CLUB FACTFILE 1994/95
RESULTS .. APPEARANCES .. SCORERS

The DOONHAMERS

Small bold figures denote goalscorers. † denotes opponent's own goal.

Date	Venue	Opponents	Result	Purdie D.	Mills D.	Hetherington K.	McKeown D.	Kennedy D.	McFarlane A.	McGuire D.	Cochrane G.	McLaren J.	Bryce T.	Mallan S.	Sermanni P.	Brown	McKeown B.	Ramsay S.	Jackson D.	Adams M	Leslie S	Campbell C.	Rowe G.	McQueer J.	Bell A.	Campbell D.	Cook A.	Telfer C.	Kane W.	Orr N.	Cody S.
Aug 13	H	Dumbarton	4-1	1	2	3	4	5	6	7¹	8	9¹	10²	11	12																
20	H	Clyde	1-2	1	5		2	5	6	7	8	9	10¹	11	12	3	4														
27	A	Berwick Rangers	0-1	1	2	2	3	8	6			9	7	11		12	4	10	14												
Sep 3	H	East Fife	0-2	1		3	4	5	6			7	10	12		14		8		9	11										
10	A	Meadowbank Thistle	1-0	1		2	3	5				9¹	7	11	8		4	6			10										
24	H	Brechin City	0-2	1		2	5	7	6	14		9	8	11		3	12	10				4									
Oct 1	A	Stirling Albion	0-3	1			3	5	6	14		10	8	9		12	2	11	7			4									
8	A	Stenhousemuir	0-0	1			3	5	8	11		14	9	10		12	2	6	7			4									
15	H	Greenock Morton	3-0	1			3	5¹	6			9	7	10²			4	8	11				2								
22	H	Dumbarton	0-0	1			3	5	8			7	9	10			6		11			4	2								
29	H	Berwick Rangers	5-4	1			3	5	8²	11		14	7¹	10¹			6	12	9			4	2¹								
Nov 5	A	Clyde	2-2	1			3	5	6			10¹	7	11¹			8	12	9			14	4	2							
12	H	Meadowbank Thistle	0-0	1			2	5	8	11		12	7	10		3	4	6	9												
19	A	East Fife	1-3	1		14	2	5	8			10	7	11¹		3	4	6	9			12									
26	A	Brechin City	1-0	1		2	3	5	6			10	7¹	11			4		9			8									
Dec 3	H	Stirling Albion	0-1	1		2	3	5	6			11		10		14	8	9	7			4				13					
26	H	Stenhousemuir	1-2	1			5	3	8	11		7¹		10			2	14	12			4				6	9				
31	A	Greenock Morton	1-1	1			5	3	6			10		11			2	12	7¹			4			1	14	9				
Jan 10	A	Berwick Rangers	1-3				3	6	10					11		5	2	8	7			4		1		9¹					
14	H	Dumbarton	0-0				3	5	8			7		11		2		6	10			4		1		12	9				
21	A	Clyde	4-3				3	8¹	7¹			12		10¹		5	2	6	11			4		1		9¹					
Feb 4	A	Meadowbank Thistle	2-1				3	6				12	10¹	11		5	2		7			4		1		8	9¹				
14	A	East Fife	†3-3				3	8				7¹		11		5	2	6	10			4		1		12	9¹	14			
18	A	Brechin City	0-1				3	8				14	7	11		5	2	6	10			4		1		12	9				
25	A	Stirling Albion	1-1	1			3	8				7		11		5	2	6				4				12	9¹		10		
Mar 11	H	Greenock Morton	1-0	1		12	3	8				7¹		11		5	2	6				4				9			10		
18	H	Meadowbank Thistle	2-3	1		12	3	8				7		11¹		5	2	6	14			4				9¹			10		
21	A	Stenhousemuir	2-2				5¹	2	7	14		9¹		11		3	8	6	12			4		1		10					
25	A	East Fife	1-3				2	5	8			7		11¹		3		9				4		1		12	10		6		
Apr 1	A	Stirling Albion	1-3				5	3	6			14	9	11								4		1	7	10	12¹		2		8
8	A	Brechin City	2-0				5	3	6			14	9	11			2					4		1	7²					8	10
15	H	Stenhousemuir	1-2	13			5	3	10			7		11			2		12			4		1		9				8¹	6
22	A	Greenock Morton	0-0	1			5	3	4			10		11			2	6				9								8	7
29	A	Dumbarton	†2-2	1			2	3¹	12	6		10		11			7	5	14			9								4	8
May 6	H	Berwick Rangers	2-0	1			2	3	8	6		11	9			5	10¹					7¹								4	12
13	H	Clyde	1-0	1			2	5	10¹			14	9	11		3	7	8	12			6								4	
TOTAL FULL APPEARANCES				24	3	18	34	31	28	5	2	15	32	34	1	16	30	22	18	1	4	24	4	12	3	19	3	1	7	5	
TOTAL SUB APPEARANCES				(1)		(3)		(1)	(1)	(2)		(8)	(1)	(1)	(2)	(5)	(1)	(4)	(7)			(2)			(1)	(6)		(1)	(1)		(1)
TOTAL GOALS SCORED						1	1	2	4	1		4	9	8			1	1				1				9			1	1	

PALMERSTON PARK

CAPACITY: 8,352; Seated 3,549, Standing 4,803
PITCH DIMENSIONS: 112 yds x 73 yds
FACILITIES FOR DISABLED SUPPORTERS: On application to Club Secretary.

HOW TO GET THERE

Palmerston Park can be reached by the following routes:
TRAINS: There is a reasonable service to Dumfries Station from Glasgow on Saturdays, but the service is more limited in midweek. The station is about 3/4 mile from the ground.
BUSES: Buses from Glasgow, Edinburgh, Ayr and Stranraer all pass within a short distance of the park.
CARS: The car park may be reached from Portland Drive or King Street and has a capacity for approximately 174 cars.

YOUNGER'S TARTAN SPECIAL

STENHOUSEMUIR

Ochilview Park, Gladstone Road,
Stenhousemuir, FK5 4QL

CHAIRMAN
A. Terry Bulloch

VICE-CHAIRMAN
Sidney S. Collumbine

DIRECTORS
David O. Reid
Gordon T. Cook (Treasurer)
James S. B. Gillespie
Alistair Jack
John G. Sharp
Alan J. McNeill
John Rolland

SECRETARY
David O. Reid

MANAGER
Terry Christie

ASSISTANT PLAYER/MANAGER
Graeme Armstrong

COACH
Gordon Buchanan

CLUB DOCTOR
Steven Brown

YOUTH INITIATIVE DIRECTOR
Alan J. McNeill

PHYSIOTHERAPIST
Mrs. Lee Campbell

COMMERCIAL MANAGER
John G. Sharp
Bus. (01324) 711189

TELEPHONES
Ground/Fax (01324) 562992
Sec. Home (01324) 631895
Sec. Bus. 0141-204 2511 Ext. 239

CLUB SHOP
Ochilview Park, Gladstone Road,
Stenhousemuir, FK5 4QL.
(01324) 562992
Open during first team home
matchdays between 2.00 p.m.
until 5.00 p.m. & Mon to Fri
9.00 a.m. until 4 p.m.
Contact Mrs R. Thomson.

OFFICIAL SUPPORTERS CLUB
Ochilview Park, Gladstone Road,
Stenhousemuir, FK5 4QL

TEAM CAPTAIN
Graeme Armstrong

SHIRT SPONSOR
G & J Sports

LIST OF PLAYERS 1995-96

SURNAME	FIRST NAME	MIDDLE NAME	DATE OF BIRTH	PLACE OF BIRTH	DATE OF SIGNING	HEIGHT FT INS	WEIGHT ST LBS	PREVIOUS CLUB
Aitchison	James		10/10/76	Edinburgh	25/04/95	5 10.0	10 7	Bonnyrigg Rose
Aitken	Neil		27/04/71	Edinburgh	26/01/90	6 1.0	11 7	Penicuik Athletic
Armstrong	Graeme	John	23/06/56	Edinburgh	31/10/92	5 9.0	10 12	Meadowbank Thistle
Bannon	Eamonn	John	18/04/58	Edinburgh	18/08/95	5 9.0	11 11	Heart of Midlothian
Brannigan	Kenneth		08/06/65	Glasgow	25/07/95	6 0.0	12 4	Stranraer
Buchanan	Gordon		20/10/61	Glasgow	08/08/95	6 0.0	11 12	Unattached
Christie	Martin	Peter	07/11/71	Edinburgh	04/12/93	5 6.0	10 4	Dundee
Clarke	John		23/11/70	Glasgow	04/05/92	5 11.0	11 10	Milngavie Wanderers
Fisher	James		14/10/67	Bridge of Allan	18/01/92	5 10.0	10 11	Bo'ness United
Haddow	Lloyd	Simon	21/01/71	Lanark	13/02/92	6 1.0	11 6	Fauldhouse United
Henderson	James	Charles	18/10/76	Falkirk	23/07/94	6 1.0	11 0	Bothkennar U'18
Hutchison	Gareth		04/06/72	Edinburgh	26/07/94	5 10.0	12 0	Tranent Juniors
Little	Ian	James	10/12/73	Edinburgh	06/06/95	5 6.0	8 12	Livingston
Logan	Paul	Michael	13/06/76	Sheffield	06/01/94	5 11.0	11 4	Bonnybridge Juniors
Mathieson	Miller	Stewart	19/12/64	Surrey	14/11/91	5 11.0	11 12	Edinburgh United
McAdam	William	John	22/03/72	Glasgow	25/05/95	5 10.0	13 0	Cumbernauld United
McGeachie	George		05/02/59	Bothkennar	26/07/94	5 11.5	11 12	Raith Rovers
McKenzie	Roderick		08/08/75	Bellshill	07/08/95	6 0.0	12 0	Heart of Midlothian
Montgomery	John		10/08/73	Edinburgh	25/07/95	5 9.5	11 0	Easthouses B.C.A.
Roseburgh	David		30/06/59	Loanhead	26/08/93	5 10.5	9 9	Meadowbank Thistle
Russell	Gordon	Alan	03/03/68	Falkirk	03/03/95	5 9.5	10 0	East Stirlingshire
Sprott	Adrian		23/03/62	Edinburgh	05/08/93	5 8.0	10 0	Meadowbank Thistle
Steel	Thomas	Wright	28/02/68	Kilmarnock	29/05/92	6 0.0	11 9	Hurlford United
Swanson	Darren		12/02/76	Stirling	25/06/93	5 10.0	10 11	"S" Form
Watson	William		30/08/75	Falkirk	16/01/95	5 10.0	11 0	Hibernian

MILESTONES

YEAR OF FORMATION: 1884
MOST LEAGUE POINTS IN A SEASON: 50 (Division 2 – Season 1960/61) (2 Points for a Win)
    56 (Second Division – Season 1994/95) (3 Points for a Win)
MOST LEAGUE GOALS SCORED BY A PLAYER IN A SEASON Evelyn Morrison (Season 1927/28) and
Robert Murray (Season 1936/37)
NO. OF GOALS SCORED: 31
RECORD ATTENDANCE: 12,500 (-v- East Fife – 11.3.1950)
RECORD VICTORY: 9-2 (-v- Dundee United – Division 2, 16.4.1937)
RECORD DEFEAT: 2-11 (-v- Dunfermline Athletic – Division 2, 27.9.1930)

SEASON TICKET INFORMATION

Seated
Adult £100
Juvenile/OAP...................................£50
Parent and Juvenile.......................£120
Standing
Adult £80
Juvenile/OAP...................................£40
Parent and Juvenile.......................£100

LEAGUE ADMISSION PRICES

Seated
Adult £7.50
Juvenile/OAP...................................£4.50
Standing
Adult £6
Juvenile/OAP...................................£3

CLUB FACTFILE 1994/95
RESULTS .. APPEARANCES .. SCORERS

The WARRIORS

Date	Venue	Opponents	Result	Harkness M.	Aitken N.	Haddow L.	Salton K.	McGeechie G.	Christie M.	Steel T.	Swansen D.	Hutchion G.	Sludden	Sprott A.	Mathieson M.	Fisher	Hendersor J.	Clarke J.	Godfrey	Irvine	Armstrong G.	McNiven J.	Roseburgh D.	Donaldson E.	Russell G.
Aug 13	H	Clyde	1-0	1	2	3	4	5	6	7	8	9¹	10	11											
20	H	East Fife	1-1	1	2	3	4	5	6	7	8		10¹	11	9	12	14								
27	A	Meadowbank Thistle	0-3	1		3	4		6	7	8		10	11	9	12	2	5	14						
Sep 3	A	Brechin City	1-1	1		3			6	7¹		10		11	9	8	2	5	12	4					
10	H	Stirling Albion	3-0	1		3			6¹	7¹		10¹		11	9	8	2	5	12	4					
24	H	Berwick Rangers	1-1	1		3			6	7	8	10¹	14	11	9		2	5		4					
Oct 1	A	Greenock Morton	2-3	1		3		5	6	7		10¹		11¹	9	8		2	12	4					
8	H	Queen of the South	0-0	1		3	2	5	6	7		10		11	9	8			12	4					
15	A	Dumbarton	2-1	1		3		5	6	7¹		10		11	9	8¹			12	4	2				
22	A	Clyde	0-0	1		3			6	7		10		11	9	8	2	5		4					
29	H	Meadowbank Thistle	1-1	1		3		5	6	7		10			9¹	8			12	14	4	2	11		
Nov 5	A	East Fife	3-2	1		3			6	7		10¹			9²	8		5		4	2	11		
12	A	Stirling Albion	2-0	1		3			6	7¹		10¹	12		9	8		5		4	2	11		
19	H	Brechin City	2-0	1		3			6¹	7¹		10		11	9	8		5		4	2			
26	A	Berwick Rangers	0-0	1		3			6	7		10		11	9	8		5		4	2	12		
Dec 3	H	Greenock Morton	0-0	1					6	7		10		11	9	8		5		4	2	3		
26	A	Queen of the South	2-1	1					6	7²		10		11	9	8		5		4	2	3		
31	H	Dumbarton	1-0	1				12	6	7¹		10		11	9	8		5		2	4	14	3	
Jan 10	H	Meadowbank Thistle	2-1	1					6	7		10		11	9¹	8		5	12	4	2		3¹	
14	H	Clyde	2-2	1					6	7		10¹		11¹	9	8		5		4	2		3	
21	A	East Fife	2-0	1				5	6	7		10		11¹	9¹	8			14	4	2		3	
Feb 4	H	Stirling Albion	0-2	1				5	6	7		10		11	9	8				4	2	14	3	
14	A	Brechin City	2-0	1				5	6	7		10¹		11¹	9	8			14	4	2	12	3	
25	A	Greenock Morton	0-1	1				5	6	7		10		11	9	8				4	2	12	3	
Mar 7	H	Berwick Rangers	2-2	1				5	6	7		10¹		11¹	9	8			12	4			3	2
14	A	Dumbarton	1-5	1	14				6	12		10			9	8		5	7	4			3¹	2
18	A	Stirling Albion	1-3	1	14				6	7		10		11¹	9	8		5	12	4			3	2
21	H	Queen of the South	2-2	1				5	6¹	7		10		11	9	8	8¹		12	4	2		3	
25	H	Brechin City	3-0	1					6	7		10		11	9²	8¹		5		4	2	11	3	
Apr 1	H	Greenock Morton	1-1	1				5	6	7		10		11¹	9	8			12	4	2		3	
8	H	Berwick Rangers	0-0	1				5		7		10		11	9	8				4	2	6	3	
15	A	Queen of the South	2-1	1		14		5		7¹		10		11	9	8				4		6¹	3	2
22	A	Dumbarton	0-0	1		14		5		7		10		11	9	8				4		6	3	2
29	A	Clyde	2-3	1		11¹		5		7		10¹			9	8			14	4		6	3	2
May 5	A	Meadowbank Thistle	0-1	1		11		5		7		10			9	8			14	4		6	3	2
13	H	East Fife	2-1	1		11				7		10			9¹	8¹		5		4	2	6	3	
TOTAL FULL APPEARANCES				36	2	18	4	21	28	34	3	34	4	28	35	32	1	14	17		33	19	8	16	9
TOTAL SUB APPEARANCES					(2)	(2)		(1)		(1)			(1)			(1)			(1)	(4)	(4)	(3)	(6)	(5)	(1)	(1)
TOTAL GOALS SCORED						1			3	9		10	1		7	8			3						2

Small bold figures denote goalscorers. † denotes opponent's own goal.

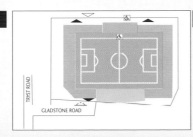

OCHILVIEW PARK

CAPACITY: 3,520; Seated 310, Standing 3,210
PITCH DIMENSIONS: 113 yds x 74 yds
FACILITIES FOR DISABLED SUPPORTERS: Accommodation for disabled in front of Stand. Toilet facilities also provided.

TRYST ROAD

GLADSTONE ROAD

HOW TO GET THERE

Ochilview Park can be reached by the following routes:
TRAINS: The nearest station is Larbert, which is about a mile away from the ground.
BUSES: Buses from Glasgow to Dunfermline, Leven, Dundee and Kirkcaldy pass through Stenhousemuir town centre and this is only a short distance from the park. There is also a regular bus service from Falkirk.
CARS: There is a large car park on the north side of the ground.

STIRLING ALBION

LIST OF PLAYERS 1995-96

SURNAME	FIRST NAME	MIDDLE NAME	DATE OF BIRTH	PLACE OF BIRTH	DATE OF SIGNING	HEIGHT FT INS	WEIGHT ST LBS	PREVIOUS CLUB
Armstrong	Paul		27/10/65	Glasgow	25/07/91	5 11.0	11 6	Cork City
Deas	Paul	Andrew	22/02/72	Perth	10/03/95	5 11.0	11 7	St. Johnstone
Drinkell	Kevin		18/06/60	Grimsby	19/03/94	5 11.5	13 4	Falkirk
Farquhar	Alastair	John	15/08/76	Aberfeldy	16/09/94	5 8.5	11 5	Coventry City
Gibson	John		20/04/67	Blantyre	26/11/93	5 10.0	10 5	Alloa
Kerr	Ross	Hutchison	19/04/76	Hamilton	16/09/94	5 11.0	10 6	Rangers
McAneny	Paul	James	11/11/73	Glasgow	11/09/93	5 11.0	12 1	Saltcoats Victoria
McCormick	Stephen		14/08/69	Dumbarton	07/07/95	6 4.0	11 4	Queen's Park
McGeown	Mark		10/05/70	Paisley	13/10/88	5 10.5	11 6	Blantyre Victoria
McInnes	Ian		22/03/67	Hamilton	09/08/90	5 8.0	10 5	Stranraer
McKechnie	Michael		10/11/74	Barrow in Furness	11/08/95	6 0.0	10 2	Barrow
McLeod	Joseph		30/12/67	Edinburgh	09/12/93	5 7.0	11 3	Portadown
McQuilter	Ronald		24/12/70	Glasgow	24/12/93	6 1.0	12 2	Ayr United
Mitchell	Colin		25/05/65	Bellshill	28/07/88	5 10.0	12 8	Airdrieonians
Monaghan	Michael	Joseph	28/06/63	Glasgow	22/02/94	6 1.0	15 2	Dumbarton
Paterson	Andrew		05/05/72	Glasgow	26/08/94	5 9.0	11 3	St. Mirren
Paterson	Garry		10/11/69	Dunfermline	07/03/95	6 5.0	15 1	Dunfermline Athletic
Reid	William	Hamilton	18/07/63	Glasgow	19/03/94	5 5.0	10 9	Hamilton Academical
Roberts	Paul		24/03/70	Glasgow	12/11/93	6 0.0	13 6	East Stirlingshire
Stewart	Raymond	Straun M.	07/09/59	Stanley	26/08/94	5 11.0	12 2	St. Johnstone
Taggart	Craig		17/01/73	Glasgow	12/08/94	5 9.0	11 6	Falkirk
Tait	Thomas		08/09/67	Ayr	12/09/92	5 10.5	12 7	Kilmarnock
Watson	Paul		16/07/68	Bellshill	08/12/90	6 0.0	12 6	Thorniewood United
Watters	William	Devlin	05/06/64	Bellshill	23/08/91	5 10.0	12 2	Queen of the South

MILESTONES

YEAR OF FORMATION: 1945
MOST LEAGUE POINTS IN A SEASON: 59 (Division 2 – Season 1964/65)
MOST LEAGUE GOALS SCORED BY A PLAYER IN A SEASON: Joe Hughes (Season 1969/70)
NO. OF GOALS SCORED: 26
RECORD ATTENDANCE: 26,400 (-v- Celtic-Scottish Cup 11.3.1959)
RECORD VICTORY: 20-0 (-v- Selkirk – Scottish Cup, 8.12.1984)
RECORD DEFEAT: 0-9 (-v- Dundee United – League, 30.12.1967)

SEASON TICKET INFORMATION

Seated
Adult £100
Juvenile/OAP...£50

LEAGUE ADMISSION PRICES

Seated
Adult £6
Juvenile/OAP £3
Standing
Adult £5
Juvenile/OAP..£2.50

The ALBION

Date	Venue	Opponents	Result	McGeown M.	Hamilton J.	Tait T.	Mitchel C.	McQuiller F.	Reid W.	McInnes I.	Roberts P.	Walters W.	Taggart C.	McLeoc J.	Gibson I.	Callaghan T.	Armstrong P.	Paterson A.	Stewart R.	Farquher A.	Drinkell K.	McAneny P.	Kerr R.	Monaghan M.	Watson P.	Paterson G.	Deas P.
Aug 13	H	East Fife	0-1	1	2	3	4	5	6	7	8	9	10	11	12	14											
20	H	Dumbarton	1-1	1	2	6	4	5	7	12	8	9	10	11¹	14			3									
27	A	Clyde	2-1	1		6¹	4	5	8	7	12	9¹	10	11	2		14	3									
Sep 3	H	Greenock Morton	2-0	1			4	5	8	7		9¹	10	11	2¹		6	3	12	14							
10	A	Stenhousemuir	0-3	1		6	4	5	8	7		9	10	11	2			3		14	12						
24	A	Meadowbank Thistle	2-1	1		6	4	5		7	14¹	9¹	10	11	3			2			8						
Oct 1	H	Queen of the South	†3-0	1		6	4	5		7	14	9¹	10	11¹	3		12	2			8						
8	A	Brechin City	2-1	1		6	4	5		7	14	9¹	10¹	11	3			2			8						
15	H	Berwick Rangers	3-2	1		6	4¹	5¹		7		9	10	11	3		12	2			8¹						
22	A	East Fife	3-4	1		6¹	4	5		7¹	14	9	10¹	11	3		12	2			8						
29	H	Clyde	0-1	1		6		5		7	14	9	10	11	3			2			8	4					
Nov 5	A	Dumbarton	0-1	1		6		5		7	14	9	10	11	3			2			8	4					
12	H	Stenhousemuir	0-2	1	2	6	12	5		7		9	10	11	3		8			14		4					
22	A	Greenock Morton	1-1	1		6	4	5		7	12	9	10¹	11	3		8	2						14			
26	H	Meadowbank Thistle	2-3	1		6	4	5		7	12	9¹	10¹	11	3		8	2						14			
Dec 3	A	Queen of the South	1-0	1		6	4¹	5		7	14	9	10	11	3		12	2			8						
24	H	Brechin City	2-0			6	4			7		9	10	11¹	3		8¹	2			14			1	5		
31	A	Berwick Rangers	0-1			6	4			7		9	10	11	3		8	2			14			1	5		
Jan 14	H	East Fife	3-0				4	5		7³		9	10	11	3		8	2					6	1			
17	A	Clyde	0-2			8	4	5		7		9	10	11	3			2		12			6	1			
21	A	Dumbarton	2-2			8¹	4	5		7		9	10	11	3		14	2		12¹			6	1			
Feb 4	A	Stenhousemuir	2-0			6	4	5		7¹	14¹		10	11	3		8	2				9	12	1			
11	H	Greenock Morton	0-3			6	4	5		7	14		10	11	3			2				9	8	1		12	
25	A	Queen of the South	1-1	1		6	4	5		7¹		9	10	11	3			2		14			8				
Mar 4	A	Brechin City	1-2	1		6	4	5		7		9¹	10	11	3		8	2		14							
8	A	Meadowbank Thistle	3-0	1		6	4			7¹		9	10¹	11	3		8			14		12			2	5¹	
11	A	Berwick Rangers	2-2	1		6	4			7		9	10	11¹	2		8			14¹				3		5	12
18	H	Stenhousemuir	3-1	1		6		5		7		9²	10	11¹	3			2								4	8
25	A	Greenock Morton	†2-2	1		6		5		7		9¹	10	11	3			2		7				14		4	8
Apr 1	A	Queen of the South	3-1	1		6	10	5		7		9¹		11¹	3¹			2		14						4	8
8	H	Meadowbank Thistle	2-1	1		6		5		7		9¹	10	11	3¹			2		14						4	8
15	H	Brechin City	2-0	1		6		5		7		9²	10	11	3			2								4	8
22	H	Berwick Rangers	0-0	1		6		5	12	7		9	10	11	3			2								4	8
29	A	East Fife	2-1	1		6		5¹	10	7		9		11	3			2								4	8
May 6	H	Clyde	2-0	1		6		5	10	7		9	12	11	3¹			2								4	8
13	A	Dumbarton	0-2	1		6		5	10	7		9	12	11	3			2						14		4	8
TOTAL FULL APPEARANCES				29	3	34	31	29	5	34	3	31	32	36	32	1	18	28	1	2	8	3	5	7	4	11	9
TOTAL SUB APPEARANCES							(1)	(1)		(1)	(9)	(3)	(2)			(2)	(3)	(5)	(2)	(1)	(10)	(2)	(1)	(3)		(2)	(1)
TOTAL GOALS SCORED						3	3	1		7	1	15	5	8	4			1		1	2						1

Small bold figures denote goalscorers. † denotes opponent's own goal.

FORTHBANK STADIUM

CAPACITY: 3,808, Seated 2,508, Standing 1,300
PITCH DIMENSIONS: 110 yds x 74 yds
FACILITIES FOR DISABLED SUPPORTERS: Disabled access, toilets and spaces for 36.

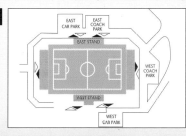

HOW TO GET THERE

Forthbank Stadium can be reached by the following routes.
TRAINS: The nearest station is Stirling Railway Station, which is approximately 2 miles from the ground. A bus service from Goosecroft Road travels to the stadium (buses run every 25 minutes from 1.50 p.m. – 2.40 p.m. and returns to town at 4.50 p.m.).
BUSES: To Goosecroft Bus Station, Stirling, and bus to stadium from Goosecroft Road (outside Bus Station) every 25 minutes from 1.50 p.m. – 2.40 p.m. and return to town at 4.50 p.m.
CARS: Follow signs for A91 St Andrews/Alloa. Car Parking is available in the club car park. Home support in West Car Park and visiting support in East Car Park.

STRANRAER

Stair Park, London Road,
Stranraer, DG9 8BS

CHAIRMAN
R. A. Graham Rodgers

VICE-CHAIRMAN
James Hannah

COMMITTEE
Andrew Hannah (Treasurer)
James Robertson
George F. Compton
Robert J. Clanachan
Thomas Rice
James Bark
Leo R. Sprott
Alexander McKie
Nigel C. Redhead
Thomas L. Sutherland

SECRETARY
R. A. Graham Rodgers

MANAGER
Alex McAnespie

COACH
Derek McHarg

PHYSIOTHERAPIST
Thomas McMillen

GROUNDSMAN
Patrick Dowey

KIT MAN
William Milliken, M.B.E.

COMMERCIAL MANAGER
Thomas L. Sutherland
(01776) 707070

TELEPHONES
Ground (01776) 703271
Sec. Home/Ticket Office/
Information Service/Fax
(01776) 702194

CLUB SHOP
Situated at Ground
2.30 p.m. – 3.00 p.m. and
half-time on matchdays

TEAM CAPTAIN
Nigel Howard

SHIRT SPONSOR
Stena Sealink

LIST OF PLAYERS 1995-96

SURNAME	FIRST NAME	MIDDLE NAME	DATE OF BIRTH	PLACE OF BIRTH	DATE OF SIGNING	HEIGHT FT INS	WEIGHT ST LBS	PREVIOUS CLUB
Callaghan	Thomas		28/08/69	Glasgow	03/12/94	5 10.0	11 4	Stirling Albion
Cran	Stephen		01/05/77	Irvine	08/09/95	5 9.0	10 11	Maybole
Duffy	Bernard	John	28/07/61	Kilmarnock	22/06/88	5 10.5	11 7	Annbank United
Duncan	Graham		02/02/69	Glasgow	30/06/89	5 11.0	11 6	Dumbarton
Ferguson	William		30/08/67	Glasgow	15/01/93	5 11.0	11 0	Albion Rovers
Fulton	Bryan		18/11/76	Irvine	01/08/95	5 8.0	9 7	Bonnyton B.C.
Gallagher	Anthony		16/03/63	Bellshill	31/03/88	6 1.0	12 3	Albion Rovers
Grant	Alexander		27/02/62	Glasgow	20/07/90	6 1.0	12 12	Partick Thistle
Henderson	Darren		12/10/66	Kilmarnock	15/07/93	5 11.0	11 0	Queen of the South
Howard	Nigel		06/10/70	Morecambe	27/06/94	6 0.0	13 8	Ayr United
Hughes	James	Francis	07/05/65	Kilwinning	29/03/91	5 10.0	11 5	Ayr United
McAulay	Ian		06/06/74	Glasgow	21/08/95	5 4.0	10 0	Tower Hearts
McCaffrey	John	Brendan	17/10/72	Glasgow	11/03/94	6 1.0	12 0	Albion Rovers
McGowan	Neil	William	15/04/77	Glasgow	01/08/95	5 10.0	10 12	Bonnyton Thistle
McGuire	Douglas	John	06/09/67	Bathgate	31/03/95	5 8.0	11 4	Queen of the South
McLean	Paul		25/07/64	Johnstone	24/10/92	5 10.0	12 0	Ayr United
Millar	Graham		12/03/65	Bellshill	25/03/93	5 8.0	11 0	Albion Rovers
Reilly	Robert	Piper	23/09/59	Kilmarnock	25/08/95	5 10.0	11 1	Stirling Albion
Robertson	John		28/03/76	Irvine	19/09/94	6 0.0	11 0	Unattached
Ross	Stephen		27/01/65	Glasgow	22/09/92	5 9.0	10 10	Clyde
Sloan	Thomas		24/08/64	Irvine	19/07/91	5 9.5	10 10	Kilmarnock
Walker	Thomas		23/12/64	Glasgow	26/02/94	5 7.5	10 10	Dumbarton

MILESTONES

YEAR OF FORMATION: 1870
MOST LEAGUE POINTS IN A SEASON: 56 (Second Division – 1993/94)
MOST LEAGUE GOALS SCORED BY A PLAYER IN A SEASON: D. Frye (Season 1977/78)
NO. OF GOALS SCORED: 27
RECORD ATTENDANCE: 6,500 (-v- Rangers – 24.1.1948)
RECORD VICTORY: 7-0 (-v- Brechin City – Division 2, 6.2.1965)
RECORD DEFEAT: 1-11 (-v- Queen of the South – Scottish Cup, 16.1.1932)

SEASON TICKET INFORMATION

Seated
Adult £95
Juvenile/OAP...£55
Standing
Adult £80
Juvenile/OAP...£45

LEAGUE ADMISSION PRICES

Seated
Adult..£7.50
Juvenile/OAP...£4.50
Standing
Adult £6
Juvenile/OAP £3

CLUB FACTFILE 1994/95
RESULTS .. APPEARANCES .. SCORERS

The BLUES

Small bold figures denote goalscorers. Goal markers shown in brackets, e.g. 9[1].

Date	Venue	Opponents	Result	Ross S.	Treanor M.	Hughes J.	Millar G.	Brannigan K.	McCaffrey J.	Reilly R.	Cody S.	Walker T.	Duncan G.	Henderson C.	Ferguson W.	Gallagher A.	McLean P.	Grant A.	Sloan T.	Howard N.	McCann J.	Farrell ?.	McAuley I.	Callaghan T.	Duffy B.	Robertson J.	Fulton B.	McGuire D.
Aug 13	A	Clydebank	0-2	1	2	3	4	5	6	7	8	9	10	11	12	14												
20	A	Dundee	1-3	1	2	3	6	5	4		10	9[1]	8	11	12			7	14									
27	H	Ayr United	2-1	1		3[1]	2	5	4[1]		6	8	9	11	12	10			14	7								
Sep 3	A	Hamilton Academical	0-1	1	10	3	2	5	4		6	8			11	12	9	14		7								
10	H	Raith Rovers	0-0	1	4	3	2		5		10	8	9	11				6	12	7	14							
24	A	Dunfermline Athletic	0-1	1		3	2		6		10	14	9	11				5	12	8	7		4					
Oct 1	H	Airdrieonians	0-1	1		3	2	5	4		10				11			6	9	8	7			14				
8	H	St. Mirren	1-1	1		3	2	5	4		10	11[1]	9					6	12	8	7			14				
15	A	St. Johnstone	0-3	1		3	2	5	4	7		8	9	11				6	12				10					
22	A	Clydebank	0-1	1		3			5	6	12	10	9	14	11			8	7				4	2				
29	A	Ayr United	1-2	1		3	2	5			12		9	6	11				10	8	7[1]			4				
Nov 12	A	Raith Rovers	2-4	1		3	2	5			14	9[1]	6		12[1]				10	8	7	4		11				
19	H	Hamilton Academical	2-0	1		3	2[1]	5[1]			14	10	9	11		12				7	6		4		8			
23	H	Dundee	0-2	1		3	2	5				10	9	11		12	14	6		7			4		8			
29	H	Dunfermline Athletic	0-0	1		3	2	5				11	10	9		12	14	6		7			4		8			
Dec 3	A	Airdrieonians	1-8	1		3	2	5				11	10	9			14	6[1]	7	12			4		8			
10	H	St. Johnstone	2-2	1		3	2	5			10		9	11		12		6	8	7[1]	4			14[1]		1		
26	A	St. Mirren	0-1	1		3	2	5			14		9	11		12		6	10	8	7			4				
31	A	Clydebank	3-2	1		3	2	5			10		9	11[1]		12[1]	14	4	8[1]	7	6							
Jan 2	H	Ayr United	2-0	1		3		5			10	14	9	11		12		4[1]	8[1]	7	6			2				
7	A	Dundee	0-2	1		3		5			10	12	9	11			14	4	8	7	2			6				
14	A	Hamilton Academical	0-1	1		3		5			2	11	9			12			8	7	4	6		10				
24	H	Raith Rovers	†2-4	1		3	2	5	14	11	10		9					4[1]	12	7	6			8				
Feb 4	H	Airdrieonians	1-4	1		3	2				14	10	7					6	11	8	12[1]	5		4	9	13		
14	A	Dunfermline Athletic	1-3	1		3		5	14	2		11	9					4	8	7[1]	6			10				
25	A	St. Johnstone	0-3	1		7		5	14	12		9	3					4	11	8	7	6		10				
Mar 11	H	St. Mirren	1-3	1		3	2	5				10	9	11[1]				7	8	12	4			6				
18	A	Raith Rovers	1-1	1			2	3			11[1]	10	9	6				5	8	7	4			12				
25	H	Hamilton Academical	0-5	1			2	5		3	10	8	9	11				6	7		4					12	14	
Apr 1	A	Airdrieonians	0-2				4	5		3	8	10		11					7	9	6				1	2		12
8	H	Dunfermline Athletic	0-1				4	5		3	7	10		11					8	9	6	14			1	2		12
15	A	St. Mirren	0-2	1		3	2	5			12	9	6	11				10	8	7	4				1			14
22	H	St. Johnstone	2-6	1		3	14	5	6			9	2	11[?]					12	8	4			10	1			7
29	A	Clydebank	0-1				2	3		5	4	14	6	11					8	9	7			10	1			12
May 6	A	Ayr United	0-3			3	2	5	4		8	10	6	11	9				12	7				14	1			
13	H	Dundee	0-5				2		6			9		11	12	5	3		8	7	4				1			14
TOTAL FULL APPEARANCES				28	4	33	28	31	14	16	16	28	30	22	1	23	14	21	29	16	15	1	1	14	8	2	1	
TOTAL SUB APPEARANCES							(1)		(3)	(9)		(3)	(1)		(13)	(1)	(12)	(5)	(3)	(1)	(1)		(3)	(2)	(1)	(1)	(1)	(5)
TOTAL GOALS SCORED						1	1	1	1	1		3		4	2	3		2	4		1			1				

Small bold figures denote goalscorers. † denotes opponent's own goal

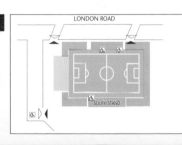

LONDON ROAD
SOUTH STAND

STAIR PARK

CAPACITY: 6,100; Seated 1,800, Standing 4,300
PITCH DIMENSIONS: 110 yds x 70 yds
FACILITIES FOR DISABLED SUPPORTERS: By prior arrangement with Club Secretary.

HOW TO GET THERE

Stair Park can be reached by the following routes.
TRAINS: There is a regular service of trains from Ayr and the station is only 1 mile from the ground.
BUSES: Two services pass the park. These are the buses from Glenluce to Portroadie and the Dumfries-Stranraer service.
CARS: Car parking is available in the club car park at the ground, where there is space for approximately 50 vehicles and also in the side streets around the park. Signs for away supporters will be displayed and parking situated at Stranraer Academy, McMasters Road.

Forfar Focus

Scottish League newcomers, Caledonian Thistle and Ross County, were the centre of attraction as the 1994/95 League season opened on 13th August, 1994. Nine months later, the focus of attention had switched from the Highlands to the county of Angus, as Forfar Athletic and Montrose deservedly earned promotion from the Bell's League Third Division.

Indeed, Forfar proved to be worthy champions. Their manager, Tommy Campbell, skilfully under-played the achievements of his side throughout the campaign until they had finally clinched their place in this season's Second Division. But those achievements were considerable, 80 points accumulated from their 36 League match programme, fully 13 points ahead of second place Montrose, as well as having the talented David Bingham, who deservedly won the Third Division's Players' Player of the Year award.

That all added up to a championship won in style... and that style continued in their celebrations, for after the Station Park side clinched the title by defeating Ross County 1-0 in Dingwall, their players celebrated in

triple fashion. It all began when they joined with their fans in celebrations minutes after the final whistle and this was followed up as they travelled south in what proved to be a long but enjoyable bus journey back to Forfar as they partied firstly at Aviemore and then in Perth.

Looking back over the campaign, manager, Tommy Campbell, commented, "This was a real team effort."

Forfar somehow, conveyed a feeling throughout the season that they were on target to achieve their ambition of promotion. That was not the case, however, with Montrose, who steered a much more eventful path towards their ultimate goal.

How many clubs dispense with their manager as they enter the final phase of the season? Montrose did, shocking football by dismissing John Holt at such a crucial stage. His assistant, Andy Dornan, was handed the onerous role of caretaker manager and, to his credit, steered the club to success.

Even though many observers felt it had been an unwise decision to part with the extremely able Holt, who had done well throughout the long winter months, Dornan turned out to be a

calming influence at a troubled time. It was no surprise therefore, that his reward was to be confirmed as manager on a permanent basis. Dornan deflected much of the praise however, by declaring, "The players must take great credit for achieving this outcome."

The Gable Endies also enjoyed the remarkable scoring partnership of Alan Kennedy and Colin McGlashan who, between them, scored 36 League goals during the long and eventful campaign.

Those aforementioned newcomers, Ross County and Caledonian Thistle, did nonetheless, make their mark in decisive fashion during their first season as members of The Scottish Football League.

Ross County, in addition to nearly gaining promotion under manager Bobby Wilson at their first attempt, attracted a total of over 28,000 supporters to their 18 home League games, averaging over 1,500 spectators per match, thus making them the best attended side in the division.

Caledonian Thistle were not far behind, with almost 23,000 fans attending matches at Telford Street Park to watch the newly merged club

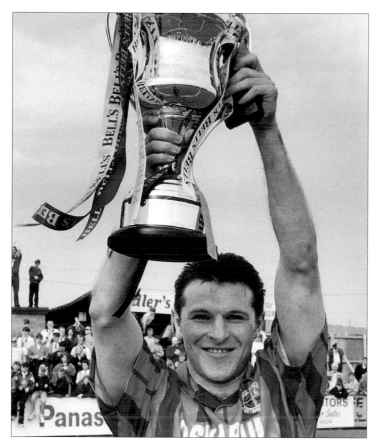

Neil Irvine (Forfar) with the championship trophy.

play its first season in the Scottish League. However, the Inverness club were not allowed as settled a start as Ross County during their first season. Many off-the-field anxieties regarding the merger affected the club, and these were not resolved until virtually the end of the season. In addition, manager Sergei Baltacha resigned and left the club when the season was completed in order that he could follow other business ventures and has been replaced by Steve Paterson, who has led Huntly to various Highland League successes in recent seasons.

While Forfar stamped their authority on the Third Division, it was not until almost the last ball was kicked that Montrose knew that they had clinched the second promotion spot as competition was fierce, with several clubs challenging for promotion throughout the season.

East Stirlingshire and their manager, Billy Little, were left deeply disappointed that a succession of injuries should kill off their challenge. With striker Michael Geraghty providing the impetus, the Firs

Park side had long threatened to claim the second promotion place, before, in the final few weeks of the season, the loss of three injured strikers proved too much of a burden for them.

Alloa also, seemed close to attaining their ambition to win promotion and mounted a worthwhile challenge until faltering in the last few weeks of the season. The price of failure even in this basement division is high however, and the Wasps' vastly experienced manager, Billy Lamont, who had found success

elsewhere during his career, paid the penalty and was dismissed when it became apparent that the Recreation Park club would not secure one of the two promotion places.

That dismissal highlighted the increasing demands now placed on managers, with a number of clubs making changes at managerial level as they sought success in the future. That most famous amateur club, Queen's Park, had seen the waygoing of their coach, Eddie Hunter, who had been at the club as player and coach for all of his adult life. He was ultimately replaced by Hugh McCann, who had previously managed Alloa and had also been assistant manager at Heart of Midlothian.

Former Stirling Albion manager, John Brogan, moved to Arbroath when they were second bottom of the table and immediately lifted their fortunes with a series of wins. Cowdenbeath parted company with manager Pat Dolan and like Alloa, appointed from within, by upgrading their youth team coach, Tom Steven. Even bottom club Albion Rovers looked to change their fortunes and the former Berwick Rangers manager, Jimmy Crease, was tempted back to the game to take on what must rate as one of the hardest jobs in football.

The new Third Division proved to be extremely competitive and exciting and this was reflected by the encouraging number of spectators attending matches during the course of the season and it is hoped that this trend will continue during what once again, is likely to be a season full of intrigue and drama.

BILL MARWICK
(Freelance)

Happy Montrose players celebrate promotion.

ALBION ROVERS

Cliftonhill Stadium, Main Street,
Coatbridge, ML5 9XX

CHAIRMAN
David T. Shanks, B.Sc.

DIRECTORS
Robin W. Marwick, J.P., R.I.B.A.
David Forrester, C.A.
Jack McGoogan, LL.B., D.M.S., N.P.
Andrew W. Beattie
James A. Munro
Hugh S. Munro, B.Sc., A.R.I.C.S.
James B. Greenhalgh, C.A.
Laurence G. Cameron, J.P.

SECRETARY
David Forrester, C.A.

MANAGER
James Crease

PLAYER COACH
Joe McBride

CLUB DOCTOR
Dr. Alisdair Purdie, M.B., Ch.B.

PHYSIOTHERAPISTS
Michael McBride B.Sc., M.C.S.P.
Walter Cannon

CHIEF SCOUT
Robert Watt

GROUNDSMAN
Hugh McBride

COMMERCIAL MANAGER
David T. Shanks B.Sc.
Bus. (01236) 427479
Home (01236) 475179

COMMERCIAL EXECUTIVE
Morris Kaplan

TELEPHONES
Ground (01236) 432350
Sec. Home (01236) 421892
Sec. Bus. (01236) 433438

CLUB SHOP
Cliftonhill Stadium, Main Street,
Coatbridge, ML5 3RB. Open one
hour prior to kick-off at first team
home matches.

OFFICIAL SUPPORTERS CLUB
Andy Morrison, 98 Dundyvan Road,
Coatbridge. (01236) 402336

TEAM CAPTAIN
Barry Strain

SHIRT SPONSOR
John C. Dalziel (Airdrie) Limited

LIST OF PLAYERS 1995-96

SURNAME	FIRST NAME	MIDDLE NAME	DATE OF BIRTH	PLACE OF BIRTH	DATE OF SIGNING	HEIGHT FT INS	WEIGHT ST LBS	PREVIOUS CLUB
Collins	Lee		03/02/74	Bellshill	25/11/93	5 7.0	11 0	Possil United
Crawford	Paul	Ian	27/04/72	Glasgow	19/06/95	5 9.0	10 10	Giffnock North
Deeley	Brian		10/11/72	Alexandria	14/07/94	6 1.0	12 0	Kilpatrick Juveniles
Docherty	Anthony	Joseph	24/01/71	East Kilbride	14/06/94	5 8.0	10 8	East Stirlingshire
Duncan	Mark		08/01/72	Glasgow	19/06/95	5 7.0	10 7	Giffnock North
Gallagher	John		02/06/69	Glasgow	29/11/91	5 9.0	10 10	Arbroath
McBride	Joseph		17/08/60	Glasgow	25/03/94	5 8.5	11 2	East Fife
McDonald	David		21/01/69	Glasgow	11/03/94	5 8.0	11 3	Fort William
McEwan	Alexander	Ian	15/05/70	Glasgow	24/02/95	5 10.0	12 7	Club Roma
Miller	David	John	25/11/75	Baillieston	14/07/94	5 10.0	10 6	Clyde B.C.
Moonie	David		09/10/72	Durban	05/08/95	5 11.0	11 1	Queen's Park
Osborne	Marc	Leslie	05/08/72	Broxburn	12/09/95	6 3.0	11 10	Berwick Rangers
Parry	Kenneth		21/12/75	Lanark	14/07/94	5 8.0	10 10	Clyde B.C.
Philliben	Robert	Devine	19/03/68	Stirling	14/07/94	5 8.0	10 12	Forfar Athletic
Quinn	Kenneth		19/12/71	Glasgow	14/07/94	5 9.0	9 12	Clyde
Russell	Robert		11/02/57	Glasgow	12/09/95	5 8.5	10 3	Cumbernauld United
Ryan	Martin		16/03/73	Glasgow	14/06/94	6 1.0	12 6	Kilpatrick Juveniles
Scott	Martin		27/04/71	Bellshill	31/07/92	5 10.0	10 0	Clyde
Seggie	David		13/11/74	Bellshill	13/07/92	5 7.0	9 7	Monklands Juveniles
Shanks	Craig		16/04/76	Coatbridge	05/08/95	6 2.0	11 8	Queen's Park
Strain	Barry		04/08/71	Glasgow	05/08/95	5 11.0	12 7	Clyde
Thompson	David	Reid	28/05/62	Glasgow	25/03/94	6 0.0	12 12	Clyde
Wight	John	Campbell	11/12/73	Alexandria	09/08/94	6 0.0	11 0	Kilpatrick Juveniles
Young	Gordon		01/05/72	Glasgow	14/07/94	6 1.0	12 8	Kilpatrick Juveniles

MILESTONES

YEAR OF FORMATION: 1882
MOST CAPPED PLAYER: John White
NO. OF CAPS: 1
MOST LEAGUE POINTS IN A SEASON: 54 (Division 2 – Season 1929/30)
MOST LEAGUE GOALS SCORED BY A PLAYER IN A SEASON: John Renwick (Season 1932/33)
NO. OF GOALS SCORED: 41
RECORD ATTENDANCE: 27,381 (-v- Rangers 8.2.1936)
RECORD VICTORY: 12-0 (-v- Airdriehill – Scottish Cup 3.9.1887)
RECORD DEFEAT: 1-11 (-v- Partick Thistle – League Cup, 11.8.1993)

SEASON TICKET INFORMATION

Seated
Adult £75
Juvenile/OAP £45
Standing
Enclosure Adult £60
Juvenile/OAP £40

LEAGUE ADMISSION PRICES

Seated
Adult £6
Juvenile/OAP £4
Standing
Adult £5
Juvenile/OAP £3

The WEE ROVERS

Small bold figures denote goalscorers. † denotes opponent's own goal.

Date	Venue	Opponents	Result	Davidson A.	McDonald D.	Beattie J.	Conn S.	Malone P	Collins L.	McBride W.	Docherty A.	Thompson D.	Quinn K.	Gallagher J.	Seggie D.	Wight J.	McBride J.	Philliben R.	Riley D	Scott M.	Tonna D.	Young G.	Deeley B.	Parry K	Kelly J.	Ryan M.	Miller D.	Kerr J.	Shah S	Dolan W.	Miller S.	McEwan A	Brown M	Arthur R.	Wilcox D.
Aug 13	H	Alloa	0-4	1	2	3	4	5	6	7	8	9	10	11	12	13	14																		
20	H	Montrose	2-4	1	5	3	4				8		11	10	6	12¹	14			2		7	9¹												
27	A	Queen's Park	1-2	1		3	10	4	6		8			11¹						2	7		5		9	14									
Sep 3	H	Caledonian Thistle	0-1	1	4		5	6	8		7		12	11	2					9		10				3									
10	A	East Stirlingshire	0-4				8	7		12	1	11	2		9		10	6	3	4	5	14													
24	H	Cowdenbeath	2-4	1	7		3¹	8	7			10¹	14	11		9		6		5			4												
Oct 1	H	Forfar Athletic	1-1	1		3		8	7		10		11	14		9				6¹		2	5		4										
8	H	Arbroath	1-2	1		3¹		8	7		10		11			9	12	6		2	5		4												
15	A	Ross County	0-3	1	4				7		14	10	6	11		12		8	9	3		2	5												
22	A	Alloa	0-1	1				8		7	14	10	12	6		11		9		4	3	2	5												
29	H	Queen's Park	3-2	1					7		6	10		11²		9				3		2	5		4¹	8									
Nov 5	A	Montrose	1-4	1				12	7		6	10		11¹		9	14	3		2	5		4		8										
12	H	East Stirlingshire	0-2	1				8	7		10			11		9		3		2	5		4	6											
19	A	Caledonian Thistle	1-2	1				8	7	14	10			9		11¹	12	3		2	5		4	6											
26	A	Cowdenbeath	2-2	1	14			8				3		9		11¹	10¹			7	5		4	6	2										
Dec 3	H	Forfar Athletic	0-1	1	4			12				3	13	9		11	10	6		2	5			8	7										
24	A	Arbroath	1-0	1	2			6	10			3		9		11				5¹		4	8	7											
31	H	Ross County	0-1		2			6	11			3		1	9	12	10	14		5		4	8	7											
Jan 2	A	Queen's Park	0-0		2			6				3	12	1	9	11	10			5			4		7	8									
14	H	Alloa	0-1					6	7			3		1	9	11	12			5			4	8	2	10									
Feb 11	H	Caledonian Thistle	1-2	1	4				7	14		3	11	8¹		6	9							2	10	5									
18	H	Cowdenbeath	2-0	1	4				7			3	11	8		9¹	12				6		5¹	2	10										
25	H	Forfar Athletic	0-4	1	4				7	14		3	11	8		9	12				6		5	2	10										
Mar 4	A	Arbroath	0-2	1	4	6		12	10	7		3	13	8		9	11			5				14	2										
7	A	East Stirlingshire	0-3		4		10		7			3		1	8	6	9			5				14	11	2									
22	H	Montrose	1-4	1	4	5		12	7			3	11	8		9					6				2	10¹									
29	A	Ross County	1-4		4				7			3	11¹	1	8	6	9			12	14		5		2	10									
Apr 1	A	Forfar Athletic	0-3			6		14	7			3	11	1	8	9					5				2	10									4
5	H	East Stirlingshire	3-1					11	7			3		1	8	9²	10¹	6		5				2	12										4
8	A	Cowdenbeath	0-2					11	7			3		1	8	9	10	6		5				2											4
11	H	Caledonian Thistle	2-0			11				7¹	12	3		1	8	9¹	10	6		5				2											4
15	A	Arbroath	0-3			11				7		3	12	1	8	9	10	6		5				2											4
22	H	Ross County	1-2		2			11		7	10	3		1	8	12	9			6				5											4¹
29	A	Alloa	0-5		2	14		10	7		12	3	11	1	8	9		6		5															4
May 6	H	Queen's Park	0-2		2			7		12	3	11	1	8	9		6		5		14									10				4
13	A	Montrose	1-4		2			7			3	11	1	8	9		6		5											10¹				4
TOTAL FULL APPEARANCES				21	18	10	7	4	16	22	7	18	7	26	12	15	31	4	6	33	1	12	20	3	14	29		12	9	16	1	10	1	2	9
TOTAL SUB APPEARANCES					(1)	(1)		(1)	(4)	(3)	(2)	(4)		(7)	(3)	(4)		(1)	(1)			(7)	(2)	(1)		(2)		(1)		(2)				
TOTAL GOALS SCORED						2					1	1		2		5				7		2	1		2		1				2			1

CLIFTONHILL STADIUM

CAPACITY: 1,238; Seated 538, Standing 700

PITCH DIMENSIONS: 100 yds x 70 yds

FACILITIES FOR DISABLED SUPPORTERS: Access from East Stewart Street with toilet facilities and space for wheelchairs, cars etc. Advanced contact with club advised – this area is uncovered.

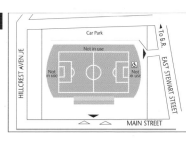

HOW TO GET THERE

The following routes can be used to reach Cliftonhill Stadium:

BUSES: The ground is conveniently situated on the main Glasgow-Airdrie bus route and there is a stop near the ground. Local buses serving most areas of Coatbridge and Airdrie pass by the stadium every few minutes

TRAINS: The nearest railway station is Coatdyke on the Glasgow-Airdrie line and the ground is a ten minute walk from there. The frequency is 15 minutes.

CARS: A large car park is situated behind the ground with access off Albion Street, and vehicles may also be parked in Hillcrest Avenue, Albion Street and East Stewart Street, which are all adjacent to the ground.

ALLOA

LIST OF PLAYERS 1995-96

SURNAME	FIRST NAME	MIDDLE NAME	DATE OF BIRTH	PLACE OF BIRTH	DATE OF SIGNING	HEIGHT FT INS	WEIGHT ST LBS	PREVIOUS CLUB
Balfour	Robert		26/12/69	Bellshill	10/08/95	5 11.0	11 0	Bathgate Thistle
Bennett	John	Neil	22/08/71	Falkirk	09/08/91	5 7.0	10 0	St. Johnstone
Cadden	Stephen	Joseph	26/11/68	Baillieston	04/03/94	6 0.0	11 6	Albion Rovers
Conway	Vincent	Matthew	25/02/75	Bellshill	16/09/94	5 11.0	12 6	Stirling Albion
Cully	David		16/02/73	Stirling	03/10/94	5 10.0	10 0	Bo'ness United
Diver	Daniel		15/11/66	Paisley	31/03/94	6 2.0	12 8	Arbroath
Duffy	Barry		11/09/78	Dunfermline	17/08/95	5 10.0	11 0	Valleyfield
Gibson	Scott		26/10/77	Glasgow	17/08/95	5 11.0	11 7	Bothkennar
Gilmour	James		17/12/61	Bellshill	08/09/95	5 6.0	9 4	Bo'ness United
Graham	Paul	Scott	17/05/70	Motherwell	08/06/94	6 2.0	12 4	Greenock Morton
Hannah	Kenneth		30/03/76	Bangour	03/10/94	5 7.0	10 7	Blackburn United
Kirkham	David	Gordon	20/10/73	Falkirk	17/03/95	6 1.0	11 0	I.C.I. Juveniles
Johnston	Neil	James	31/08/76	Dunfermline	09/09/95	5 11.0	10 8	Steelend Vics U'18s
Lawrie	Douglas	Gibb	11/06/66	Falkirk	04/03/94	5 10.0	11 1	Stirling Albion
Little	Thomas	Francis	13/02/78	Glasgow	20/07/95	5 4.0	9 8	Kilsyth Rangers U'18s
Livingstone	Gary		07/01/78	Falkirk	17/08/95	5 11.0	12 8	Bothkennar
Masterson	Brian		21/04/78	Stirling	17/08/95	5 11.0	12 0	Unattached
McAnenay	Michael	Samuel P.	16/09/66	Glasgow	09/10/93	5 10.0	10 7	Dumbarton
McCormack	John	Thomas	22/07/65	Stirling	26/11/93	5 9.0	10 0	Stirling Albion
McCulloch	Keith	George	27/05/67	Edinburgh	28/08/87	5 10.0	12 0	Cowdenbeath
McKenzie	Christopher		02/01/68	Bridge of Allan	10/07/95	5 5.0	9 8	Camelon Juniors
Moffat	Barrie		27/12/72	Bangour	09/10/90	5 8.0	11 0	Gairdock Colts U'18
Morrison	Stephen		15/08/61	St. Andrews	20/07/95	6 0.0	13 3	Larne
Nelson	Mark		09/08/69	Bellshill	01/03/94	5 11.0	11 0	Dumbarton
Newbigging	William	Matthew	07/09/68	Blairhall	18/08/90	5 10.0	13 0	Hill of Beath
Rixon	Steven		27/08/72	Hayes	30/03/95	6 0.0	12 4	Musselburgh Athletic
Smith	Gary	Colin	03/11/71	Falkirk	28/03/95	6 2.0	12 5	Camelon Juniors
Whyte	Mark		28/02/74	Edinburgh	03/10/94	5 11.0	11 0	Bo'ness United
Wilson	Robert		07/07/79	Alexandria	17/08/95	5 7.0	10 7	Alloa United U'16s
Wylie	Roderick		31/01/69	Glasgow	03/02/95	5 11.0	13 0	Cumbernauld Juniors

MILESTONES

YEAR OF FORMATION: 1883
MOST CAPPED PLAYER: Jock Hepburn
NO. OF CAPS: 1
MOST LEAGUE POINTS IN A SEASON: 60 (Division 2 – Season 1921/22)
MOST LEAGUE GOALS SCORED BY A PLAYER IN A SEASON: William Crilley (Season 1921/22)
NO. OF GOALS SCORED: 49
RECORD ATTENDANCE: 13,000 (-v- Dunfermline Athletic – 26.2.1939)
RECORD VICTORY: 9-2 (-v- Forfar Athletic – Division 2, 18.3.1933)
RECORD DEFEAT: 0-10 (-v- Dundee – Division 2 and Third Lanark – League Cup)

SEASON TICKET INFORMATION

Seated
Adult £90
Juvenile/OAP.....................................£50
Standing
Adult £75
Juvenile/OAP.....................................£36

LEAGUE ADMISSION PRICES

Seated
Adult £6
Juvenile/OAP..................................£3.50
Standing
Adult £5
Juvenile/OAP..................................£2.50

The WASPS

Player columns (left to right): Butter J., McMillan T., Kemp B., Campbell C., McCulloch K., Newbigging W., Nelson M., McCormack J., McCormick S., Bennett N., Morrison S., McNiven J., Moffat B., Lamont P., Diver D., McAtenay M., McAvoy N., Kelly S., Graham P., Lawrie D., Cadden S., Willock A., Hannah K., Wylie R., Whyte M., Conway V., Kirkham D., Cully D., Bell C., Rixon S.

Date	Venue	Opponents	Result	Appearances / Scorers
Aug 13	A	Albion Rovers	4-0	1 2 3· 4 5[1] 6 7[1] 8 9[1] 10 11 12 14[1]
20	A	Forfar Athletic	2-3	1 3 4 12[1] 5[1] 10 6 9 8 11 2 14 7
27	H	East Stirlingshire	1-3	1 3 4 5 6[1] 8 2 10 11 14 7 9 12
Sep 3	H	Ross County	3-3	1 12 5 6 4 2 3 8 11 9 7[3] 10 14
10	H	Arbroath	3-1	1 3 5 4 2 6 8 9 11[1] 12 7[2] 10 14
24	H	Caledonian Thistle	1-1	1 3 5 4 7 2 8 10[1] 14 9 12 11 6
Oct 1	A	Cowdenbeath	†3-1	1 3 5 4 10 2 9[1] 11 7[1] 14 6 8
8	H	Montrose	1-1	1 3 5 4 10 2 9 11[1] 7 6 8
15	A	Queen's Park	1-0	1 3 5 4 10 2 9[1] 11 12 7 6 8 14
22	A	Albion Rovers	1-0	1 3 5 4 6 2 11 9 12[1] 10 7 8 14
29	A	East Stirlingshire	2-1	1 3[1] 5 4 12 2 11 9[1] 10 7 6 8 14
Nov 5	H	Forfar Athletic	0-1	1 3 5 4 2 11 9 7 10 12 6 8 14
12	H	Arbroath	0-0	1 3 5 4 7 2 10 11 9 12 6 8 14
19	H	Ross County	1-1	1 3 5 4 8 2 10 9 11 12 7 14 6[1]
26	A	Caledonian Thistle	2-2	1 14 5 4 2 11 9[1] 12 10 7[1] 6 8 3
Dec 3	H	Cowdenbeath	1-0	1 4 6 2 3 9 11 12 7 10[1] 5 8 14
24	A	Montrose	2-1	1 6 4 3 11 9[1] 10[1] 5 8 7 2
31	H	Queen's Park	2-3	1 3 5 4 14 9[1] 10[1] 7 6 8 11 2
Jan 14	H	Albion Rovers	1-0	1 3 5[1] 6 4 14 10 11 9 7 8 12 2
24	H	Forfar Athletic	0-2	1 3 5 4 14 2 10 9 11 8 7 6 12
Feb 4	H	Arbroath	3-2	1 3 5 4 2 10 9 11 12[3] 14 8 6 7
7	H	East Stirlingshire	0-1	1 3 5 4 2 10 9 12 11 8 6 7
11	A	Ross County	0-6	1 10 5 4 12 2 3 9 11 7 6 8 14
18	H	Caledonian Thistle	1-0	1 12 5 4 2 10 11[1] 9 8 3 6 7 14
25	A	Cowdenbeath	3-1	1 12 5 14 4 3[1] 10[1] 11 9[1] 8 2 6 7
Mar 11	A	Queen's Park	1-2	1 5 10 4 3 9[1] 12 8 11 2 6 7 14
18	A	Arbroath	1-2	1 5 14 4 8 9 10[1] 12 2 6 11 7 3
25	H	Ross County	1-1	1 4[1] 12 2 3 9 11 7 10 5 6 8
28	H	Montrose	0-1	1 5 4 2 3 11 12 7 6 8 14 10 9
Apr 1	H	Cowdenbeath	2-1	1 5[1] 4 2 3 9 7 6 8[1] 12 11 14 10
8	A	Caledonian Thistle	1-0	1 4 14 3 7 5 8 2 6[1] 9 11 12 10
15	A	Montrose	0-0	1 5 4 2 11 10 14 7 6 8 12 3 9
22	A	Queen's Park	0-1	1 5 4 2 10 12 6 7 11 3 8 9
29	H	Albion Rovers	5-0	1 4 5 11 10[4] 12 6 8 2 7 3[1] 14 9
May 6	A	East Stirlingshire	1-1	1 4 2 11 10 7[1] 8 6 12 3 5 9
13	A	Forfar Athletic	0-2	1 4 14 2 11 10 7 8 6 12 3 5 9

		TOTAL FULL APPEARANCES		36 1 20 3 28 29 17 34 2 28 5 1 28 21 19 17 6 21 22 3 13 11 10 6 3 1 5 6
		TOTAL SUB APPEARANCES		(4) (1) (8) (2) (1) (3) (5) (8) (4) (2) (1) (1) (2) (9) (2) (4) (1) (4)
		TOTAL GOALS SCORED		1 5 2 1 1 1 13 5 7 7 2 1 1 1 1

Small bold figures denote goalscorers.   † denotes opponent's own goal.

RECREATION PARK

CAPACITY: 4,111; Seated 424, Standing 3,687
PITCH DIMENSIONS: 110 yds x 75 yds
FACILITIES FOR DISABLED SUPPORTERS: Accommodation for wheelchairs and invalid carriages in front of Stand. Disabled toilets are also available.

CLACKMANNAN ROAD

HILTON ROAD

HOW TO GET THERE

Recreation Park can be reached by the following routes.
TRAINS: The nearest railway station is Stirling, which is seven miles away. Fans would have to connect with an inter-linking bus service to reach the ground from here.
BUSES: There are three main services which stop outside the ground. These are the Dunfermline-Stirling, Stirling-Clackmannan and Falkirk-Alloa buses.
CARS: Car Parking is available in the car park adjacent to the ground and this can hold 175 vehicles.

ARBROATH

LIST OF PLAYERS 1995-96

SURNAME	FIRST NAME	MIDDLE NAME	DATE OF BIRTH	PLACE OF BIRTH	DATE OF SIGNING	HEIGHT FT INS	WEIGHT ST LBS	PREVIOUS CLUB
Balfour	Garry	Shaw	30/09/78	Dundee	31/08/95	5 8.0	11 0	Forfar Albion
Bertie	Lee	Darren	02/11/77	Dundee	18/07/95	6 0.0	11 0	Broughty Athletic JFC
Clark	Patrick	John	13/03/74	Hamilton	29/07/95	5 11.0	11 1	Hamilton Academical
Crawford	Jonathen		14/10/69	Johnstone	31/03/95	6 1.0	12 7	Arthurlie Juniors
Downie	Ian		16/11/72	Dunfermline	10/06/94	5 6.5	9 9	Forfar Athletic
Dunn	Gordon		21/01/62	Dundee	07/10/94	5 9.0	11 8	Forfar West End
Elder	Stuart	Richard	25/07/66	Rinteln	05/08/94	6 1.0	13 0	Meadowbank Thistle
Elliot	David	Euan	23/12/74	Dundee	30/03/94	5 9.5	10 3	Arbroath Sporting Club
Florence	Steven		28/10/71	Dundee	20/05/88	5 6.0	11 5	Arbroath Lads Club
Fowler	John	James	30/01/65	Glasgow	11/07/94	5 7.0	11 12	Greenock Morton
Gardner	Robert	Lee	11/07/70	Ayr	22/10/94	5 5.0	9 5	Meadowbank Thistle
Hinchcliffe	Craig	Peter	05/05/72	Glasgow	04/08/95	5 11.0	13 0	Elgin City
Kennedy	Allan		11/03/64	Arbroath	04/08/95	5 9.0	10 0	Montrose
Kerr	James		17/01/59	Hamilton	21/02/95	5 11.0	11 7	Albion Rovers
Knox	Glenn	Stephen	01/12/76	Dundee	28/03/95	5 10.0	10 9	Broughty Athletic
Lindsay	John		17/03/73	Dundee	21/09/94	5 7.5	10 7	Dundee United
McAulay	John		28/04/72	Glasgow	04/07/95	5 9.0	11 7	Clyde
McCormick	Stephen		19/03/65	Seafield	04/08/95	5 11.0	12 10	Forfar Athletic
McLean	Charles	Crossan N.	08/11/73	Glasgow	16/08/95	5 10.0	10 8	Hamilton Academical
McMillan	Thomas		08/08/72	Falkirk	21/10/94	5 10.5	11 13	Dundee United
Middleton	Alan		22/01/72	Armadale	06/09/94	5 8.0	11 7	Livingston United
Murray	Malcolm		26/07/64	Buckie	02/08/94	5 11.0	11 4	Meadowbank Thistle
Peters	Scott		09/12/72	Dundee	06/06/95	5 11.0	11 7	Forfar West End
Pew	David John		28/08/71	Glasgow	04/02/95	5 10.0	10 5	Stirling Albion
Porteous	Ian		21/11/64	Glasgow	21/02/95	5 7.0	10 6	Elgin City
Scott	Barry		02/03/75	Edinburgh	08/10/94	5 8.0	11 2	Glenrothes Juniors
Sexton	Brian		23/08/75	Glasgow	09/08/95	5 11.0	11 2	Greenock Morton
Smith	Craig	Duncan A.	07/09/76	Dundee	04/02/95	5 10.0	11 1	Arbroath Sporting Club
Thomson	John		28/06/78	Dundee	14/07/95	5 10.0	11 7	Dundee Violet
Ward	John		25/11/77	Dundee	02/06/95	6 4.0	12 10	Duncraig U'18s

Gayfield Park,
Arbroath, DD11 1QB

PRESIDENT
John D. Christison

VICE-PRESIDENT
Charles Kinnear

COMMITTEE
R. Alan Ripley (Treasurer)
Duncan Ferguson
Ian S. C. Wyllie
William J. Thomson
George Johnson
David G. Hodgens
Alexander C. Watt

SECRETARY
Charles Kinnear

MANAGER
John Brogan

ASSISTANT MANAGER
James Kerr

YOUTH COACH
John Martin

CLUB DOCTORS
Dr. William Smith
Dr. Bird

PHYSIOTHERAPIST
William Shearer

CHIEF SCOUTS
John Martin
Tom Fairweather

GROUNDSMAN
William Nicoll

COMMERCIAL MANAGER
Alexander C. Watt
(01241) 876116
Mobile 0831 408642

TELEPHONES
Ground/Fax/Ticket Office/Club Shop
(01241) 872157
Sec. Home (01241) 875677
Sec. Bus. (01382) 313452

CLUB SHOP
Gayfield Park, Arbroath, DD11 1QB.
Open on matchdays
Premier Sports, West Port, Arbroath,
DD11 1RF. Open Mon. to Sat.

TEAM CAPTAIN
John Fowler

SHIRT SPONSOR
Perimax Diana

MILESTONES

YEAR OF FORMATION: 1878
MOST CAPPED PLAYER: Ned Doig
NO. OF CAPS: 2
MOST LEAGUE POINTS IN A SEASON: 57 (Division 2 – Season 1966/67)
MOST LEAGUE GOALS SCORED BY A PLAYER IN A SEASON: David Easson (Season 1958/59)
NO. OF GOALS SCORED: 45
RECORD ATTENDANCE: 13,510 (-v- Rangers – Scottish Cup 23.2.1952)
RECORD VICTORY: 36-0 (-v- Bon Accord – Scottish Cup. 12.9.1885)
RECORD DEFEAT: 1-9 (-v- Celtic, League Cup, 25.8.1993)

SEASON TICKET INFORMATION

Seated
Adult £90
Juvenile/OAP...£50
Standing
Adult £80
Juvenile/OAP...£50

LEAGUE ADMISSION PRICES

Seated
Adult £6
Juvenile/OAP £4
Standing
Adult £5
Juvenile/OAP/Unemployed (with UB40)......£3

S·F·L

The RED LICHTIES

Player columns (left to right): Jackson D., Mitchell B., Dickson A., Elder S., Farnan C., Murray W., Downie I., Reilly J., Brock J., Tosh S., McGovern J., McKinnon C., Elliot D., Middleton A., Shanks C., Craik S., Duncan R., Spittal I., McGregor S., Florence S., Lindsay J., Dunn G., McMillan T., Bernie C., Scot B., Gardner R..., Heggie A., Hendry M., Ward J., Martin M., Pew D., Kerr J., Porteous I., Martin E., Crawford J.

Date	Venue	Opponents	Result	Jackson D.	Mitchell B.	Dickson A.	Elder S.	Farnan C.	Murray W.	Downie I.	Reilly J.	Brock J.	Tosh S.	McGovern J.	McKinnon C.	Elliot D.	Middleton A.	Shanks C.	Craik S.	Duncan R.	Spittal I.	McGregor S.	Florence S.	Lindsay J.	Dunn G.	McMillan T.	Bernie C.	Scot B.	Gardner R.	Heggie A.	Hendry M.	Ward J.	Martin M.	Pew D.	Kerr J.	Porteous I.	Martin E.	Crawford J.
Aug 13	A	Caledonian Thistle	2-5	1	2	3	4	5^1	6	7		8^1	9	10	11	12	14																					
20	A	Cowdenbeath	2-6	1	3	2	4	5	6	7		9^1	12	10^1	11	8	14																					
27	H	Forfar Athletic	0-1				5	2	6			9	12	10	8		7	3	4	11																		
Sep 3	H	Queen's Park	1-1				8	2	6	7		9	10^1	12			3	4	11	1	5																	
10	A	Alloa	1-3				8	2	4	7^1		9	10	14			3	6	11	1	5	12																
24	A	Ross County	†4-1	1			12	7	4			9	10^3				3	6	14		5	11	2	8														
Oct 1	H	Montrose	0-3	1			14	8	4	12		10					9	3	6	11	5		2	7														
8	A	Albion Rovers	2-1				11	8	6			10		14				4	12^1	5		3^1	7	1	2	9												
15	H	East Stirlingshire	0-1				11	6	4	12						8	10		5		3	7	1	2	14	9												
22	H	Caledonian Thistle	1-2				11^1		4			7			12	6	8	14	5		3	1	2		9	10												
29	A	Forfar Athletic	0-3				9	14	4	12		7				11	6	8	5		3	1	2		10													
Nov 5	A	Cowdenbeath	0-3				8	4	6			7							5		3	1	2	12	10	9	11											
12	H	Alloa	0-0	13			6		8			7		14					5		3	1	2	9	11	10		4										
19	A	Queen's Park	4-0				6	11	8^2			9							5		3	1	2	14^2	7	10		4										
26	H	Ross County	0-1				6	11	8			10		9					5		3	1	2	14	7	12		4										
Dec 3	A	Montrose	1-3				6	12	8			10		11	3		14^1		5			1	2	9	7			4										
24	H	Albion Rovers	0-1					8	6	11		10		7	3		9		4			1	2	12	5													
31	A	East Stirlingshire	0-1					8	5	11		9		7	3	14	10		6			1	2		12			4										
Jan 14	A	Caledonian Thistle	1-1				4	8	6^1			9	10			7	11		5		12	1	2	14				3										
21	H	Cowdenbeath	0-3				4	7	6			9		12	14	8	11		5		10	1	2					3										
28	H	Forfar Athletic	1-1				6	7	4			9	11			3	8^1	14	5			1	2		10													
Feb 4	A	Alloa	2-3	1			10	7	4	14		12^1	11			8			5				2		6					3	9^1							
15	H	Queen's Park	3-1				11		14			12				7		4	5		3		1		2	10^1				9	6	8^2						
18	A	Ross County	1-0				4		14			12			7		5				3		1	2	11	10^1				9	6	8						
25	H	Montrose	4-1				4					7^1			12	14	5				3		1	2	11^2	10^1				9	6	8						
Mar 4	A	Albion Rovers	2-0				4					7			12	3	5				14	1	2		11^1	10				9^1	6	8						
11	H	East Stirlingshire	5-2				4					7^3			12	3	5				14	1	2^1		11^1	10				9	6	8						
18	H	Alloa	2-1				4					7^1				3	5					1	2		11	10				9	6	8^1						
25	A	Queen's Park	3-2				14	4	2			7^1			12	3	5								11	10^1				9^1	6	8	1					
Apr 1	A	Montrose	0-5	1			14	4	3			7					5				2		11							9	6	8	10					
8	H	Ross County	0-1	1			12	4				7					5				10		2		11					9	6	8	3					
15	A	Albion Rovers	3-0					12				7					5	3	4^1	1	2^1		14	10						9^1	6	8	11					
22	A	East Stirlingshire	2-0					4				7					5	3	11	1	2		14	10						9^1		8^1	6					
29	H	Caledonian Thistle	2-0				14	4							12		5	3	11	1	2		7	10^2						9		8	6					
May 6	A	Forfar Athletic	1-4				14	4							12		5	3^1	11	1	2		7	10						9		8	6					
13	A	Cowdenbeath	1-1					4^1				7			11		5	3	12	1	2		14	10						9		8	6					
TOTAL FULL APPEARANCES				8	2	2	18	31	24	6	3	29	3	1	9	16	22	10	25	1	18	10	25	27	1	15	22	3	1	5	3	15	10	14	1	7		
TOTAL SUB APPEARANCES				(1)			(7)	(3)		(6)		(3)	(2)	(1)	(2)	(10)	(4)	(1)	(5)		(1)		(4)		(1)	(8)	(1)	(1)									
TOTAL GOALS SCORED					1	2	3	1	2	1	11			1	2		2	1		2		6	6			5	4										

Small bold figures denote goalscorers.   † denotes opponent's own goal.

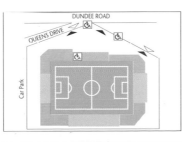

GAYFIELD PARK

CAPACITY: 6,488; Seated 715, Standing 5,773

PITCH DIMENSIONS: 115 yds x 71 yds

FACILITIES FOR DISABLED SUPPORTERS: Enclosure at West end of Stand with wide steps to take a wheelchair. Toilet facilities are also available.

HOW TO GET THERE

The following routes may be used to reach Gayfield Park:

BUSES: Arbroath is on the main route from both Glasgow and Edinburgh to Aberdeen. Buses from these three cities, plus Stirling, Dundee and Perth all stop at Arbroath Bus Station at hourly intervals. There is also a local service between Dundee-Arbroath and Montrose and this service is half hourly until 7.00 p.m. Between 7.00 p.m. and 10.45 p.m. the service is hourly. The bus station is 10 minutes walk from the ground.

TRAINS: Arbroath is on the Inter-City 125 route from London to Aberdeen and there are frequent local services between Arbroath and Edinburgh. Trains also travel north from Glasgow, Stirling and Perth. The station is a 15 minute walk from the ground.

CARS: There is free parking for 500 cars just next to the ground in Queen's Drive.

BRECHIN CITY

Glebe Park, Trinity Road,
Brechin, Angus, DD9 6BJ

CHAIRMAN
Hugh A. Campbell Adamson

VICE-CHAIRMAN
David H. Birse

HONORARY PRESIDENT
Ricardo Gallaccio

DIRECTORS
I. Michael Holland (Joint Treasurer)
Martin Smith (Joint Treasurer)
David H. Will
George C. Johnston
Kenneth W. Ferguson

SECRETARY
Kenneth W. Ferguson

MATCH SECRETARY
George C. Johnston

MANAGER
John Young

ASSISTANT MANAGER
Cammy Evans

CLUB DOCTOR
Dr. A. McInnes

PHYSIOTHERAPIST
Tom Gilmartin

CHIEF SCOUT
George Smith

GROUNDSMAN
Alex Laing

TELEPHONES
Ground (01356) 622856
Sec. Home (01356) 625691
Sec. Bus. (01356) 625285
Sec. Bus. Fax (01356) 625524
Sec. Home Fax (01356) 625691

CLUB SHOP
Glebe Park, Brechin, Angus, DD9 6BJ
Open during home matchdays

OFFICIAL SUPPORTERS CLUB
c/o Glebe Park, Brechin,
Angus, DD9 6BJ

TEAM CAPTAIN
Harry Cairney

SHIRT SPONSOR
Ferguson Oliver

LIST OF PLAYERS 1995-96

SURNAME	FIRST NAME	MIDDLE NAME	DATE OF BIRTH	PLACE OF BIRTH	DATE OF SIGNING	HEIGHT FT INS	WEIGHT ST LBS	PREVIOUS CLUB
Allan	Raymond	George K.	05/03/55	Cowdenbeath	24/07/95	6 0.0	11 7	Raith Rovers
Baillie	Richard	Ketchen	06/06/68	Dunfermline	24/11/89	5 5.5	10 0	Cowdenbeath
Balfour	Derek	Alun	16/02/72	Arbroath	15/03/94	6 0.0	12 2	Arbroath Sporting Club
Black	Roddy		22/02/78	Dundee	10/09/95	5 9.0	10 8	Carnoustie Panmure
Brand	Ralph		17/07/70	Dundee	10/08/91	5 9.0	10 3	Lochee United
Brown	Robert		11/11/59	Lincoln	10/01/85	5 10.0	11 4	Dundee North End
Buick	Garry	Robert	12/01/75	Arbroath	25/11/94	5 5.5	10 4	Keith
Cairney	Henry		01/09/61	Holytown	12/02/92	5 7.0	10 8	Stenhousemuir
Cargill	Harry		17/01/77	Arbroath	31/08/95	5 10.0	11 0	Arbroath Sporting Club
Christie	Graeme		01/01/71	Dundee	04/08/93	6 1.0	11 0	Carnoustie Panmure
Conway	Francis	Joseph	29/12/69	Dundee	25/11/89	5 11.0	11 4	Lochee Harp
Farnan	Craig		07/04/71	Dundee	07/06/95	5 10.0	13 3	Arbroath
Ferguson	Scott		04/11/77	Broxburn	08/08/95	5 8.0	10 7	"X" Form
Feroz	Craig		24/10/77	Aberdeen	28/01/95	5 8.0	10 7	Culter Juniors
Garden	Stuart	Robertson	10/02/72	Dundee	01/09/95	5 11.5	12 3	Dundee United
Graham	James	Ross	03/06/71	Baillieston	05/06/95	6 1.0	12 0	Lochee United
Marr	Sinclair	McLeod	21/11/72	Edinburgh	24/09/94	5 8.0	10 10	St. Andrews United
McKellar	James	Robert	29/12/76	Bellshill	26/07/94	5 6.0	10 4	Arbroath Lads Club
McNeill	William	John	12/03/67	Toronto	05/03/93	5 9.0	11 0	Meadowbank Thistle
Mearns	Gary		16/12/71	Dundee	28/01/95	5 8.0	10 2	Forfar Athletic
Mitchell	Brian	Charles	29/02/68	Arbroath	06/10/94	5 8.0	13 0	Arbroath
Petrie	Paul	Alexander B.	19/08/76	Salisbury, Rhod.	28/01/95	5 6.0	10 4	Lochee Harp
Reid	Scott	Lawrence	06/05/78	Dundee	10/09/95	5 10.0	10 8	Forfar Albion
Reid	Stephen	Richard	11/12/75	Auckland	23/05/95	5 7.0	10 4	Queensferry Albert
Ross	Alexander	Robert	01/08/63	Bellshill	26/08/95	6 0.0	11 8	Forfar Athletic
Scott	Walter	Douglas	01/01/64	Dundee	25/05/94	5 9.0	10 7	Dundee
Smith	Greig	Robert	26/03/76	Aberdeen	21/12/94	5 9.0	10 12	Culter Juniors
Smith	Raymond		01/04/72	Airdrie	10/09/94	5 8.0	12 0	Forfar Athletic
Smollet	Ronnie	David	28/11/75	Kirkcaldy	15/09/94	5 8.0	10 8	Hall Russell United
Vannett	Richard	Alexander	20/01/73	Dundee	03/09/93	5 8.0	10 12	Kinnoull

MILESTONES

YEAR OF FORMATION: 1906
MOST LEAGUE POINTS IN A SEASON: 55 (Second Division – Season 1982/83)
MOST LEAGUE GOALS SCORED BY A PLAYER IN A SEASON: W. McIntosh (Season 1959/60)
NO. OF GOALS SCORED: 26
RECORD ATTENDANCE: 8,122 (-v- Aberdeen – 3.2.1973)
RECORD VICTORY: 12-1 (-v- Thornhill – Scottish Cup 28.1.1926)
RECORD DEFEAT: 0-10 (-v- Airdrieonians, Albion Rovers and Cowdenbeath – Division 2, 1937/38))

SEASON TICKET INFORMATION

Seated
Adult £100
Parent/Juvenile (Under 12) £110
OAP £55
Standing or Seated Enclosure
Adult £90
Parent/Juvenile (Under 12) £100
Juvenile...£45

LEAGUE ADMISSION PRICES

Seated
Adult £7
Juvenile/OAP.......................................£4.50
Enclosure
Adult £5
Juvenile/OAP.......................................£2.50
Standing
Adult £5
Juvenile/OAP.......................................£2.50

CLUB FACTFILE 1994/95
RESULTS .. APPEARANCES .. SCORERS

The CITY

Date	Venue	Opponents	Result	Balfour D.	Cairney H.	Christie C.	Conway F.	Nicolson K.	Scott W.D.	Kemlo S.	Redford I.	McNeil W	Millar M.	Vannett R.	McKellar J.	Bell S.	Brown R.	Brand R.	Marr S.	Smith R.	Mitchell B.	Feroz Z.	Lawrie D.	Price G.	Buck J.	Mearns G.	Baillie R.	Ferguson S.
Aug 13	H	Meadowbank Thistle	*1-5	1	2	3	4	5	6	7	8	9	10^{1}	11	12	14												
20	H	Berwick Rangers	1-2	1	4	3	2	5	6	11		9^{1}	10	8		7												
27	A	East Fife	1-1	1	4	8	2	5	6			11	10^{1}	7	12		3	9										
Sep 3	H	Stenhousemuir	1-1	1	4	3	2	5	6			9	10	8^{1}	7	12				11								
10	A	Greenock Morton	0-2	1	4	3	2	5	6			9	10	8	7	12					11							
24	A	Queen of the South	2-0	1	4		2	5	6			8	10		7	12	3			11	9^{2}							
Oct 1	H	Dumbarton	1-2	1	4		2	5	6			8	10		7	3	12			11	9^{1}							
8	H	Stirling Albion	1-2	1	4		2	5	6			11	10		7	3	12^{1}			9	8							
15	A	Clyde	0-4	1	4		2	5	6	8		11		7		3	9			10	12							
22	A	Meadowbank Thistle	0-1		4		2		6	3		11			7	14	5	10		9	8		1					
29	H	East Fife	2-0		4		2		6	3		7					5		11	10^{1}	8		1	9^{1}				
Nov 5	A	Berwick Rangers	1-2	1	4		2			3		6	12	7			5	14	11	10^{1}	8			9				
12	H	Greenock Morton	1-3				4		6	3		8	2	7			5	12	11	10^{1}			1	9				
19	A	Stenhousemuir	0-2			5			6	3		8		14		4	7		11	10	2		1	9				
26	H	Queen of the South	0-1			4			6			8	14	7			5	12	11	10	3		1	9		2		
Dec 3	A	Dumbarton	0-6		4	5			6			8					3	12	11	10	2		1	9		7		
24	A	Stirling Albion	0-2		4	5				3		11	6			2		10	12		8		1	9		7		
31	H	Clyde	0-2		4	5				3		11	6	14		2		10			8		1	9		7		
Jan 2	A	East Fife	0-4	13	4	5						14	6	7			3		11	10	8		1	9		2		
14	H	Meadowbank Thistle	3-1	1	4	5			6			11	8	7^{1}			3	10			2			9^{2}				
21	H	Berwick Rangers	1-0	1	4	5			6			11	8	7			3	10^{1}			2			9				
Feb 4	A	Greenock Morton	0-1	1	4	5			6			11	8	7			3	10		9	2							
14	H	Stenhousemuir	0-2	1	5				6			11	2	12	7	3	14		10	4				9	8			
18	A	Queen of the South	1-0	1	4	5			6			11	8	7	14	3		10			2			9^{1}				
25	H	Dumbarton	0-0	1	4	5			6	3		11	8	7				10			2			9				
Mar 4	H	Stirling Albion	2-1	1	4	3	5		6			11			7	14		10^{1}			2			9^{1}		8		
11	A	Clyde	0-1	1	4	3	5		6			11	14		7			10	12		2			9		8		
18	H	Greenock Morton	1-1	1	4	3	5		6			8			7			10^{1}	11		2			9		14		
25	A	Stenhousemuir	0-3	1	4		5					6		7	8			10	11	12	2			9		14	3	
Apr 1	A	Dumbarton	1-4	1	5		4					7	6	12^{1}				10	11		2			9		8	3	
8	H	Queen of the South	0-2	1	4	3	5					7	6	12				10	11		2			9		8		
15	A	Stirling Albion	0-2	1	4	3	5					12	11	7				9	10		2					8	6	
22	H	Clyde	0-0	1	5		4					10	11	7				9	14		2					8	6	3
29	A	Meadowbank Thistle	1-2	1	4	3	5		6			10^{1}			7				11		2			9		8		
May 6	H	East Fife	1-1	1	4		5		6			10	8	7		3		12	11		2			9^{1}				
13	A	Berwick Rangers	0-2	1	4	3	5		6			12	8					10	7		2			9			14	11
TOTAL FULL APPEARANCES				27	32	15	33	9	27	11	1	31	8	24	20	6	21	17	14	22	27		9	23	5	8	4	2
TOTAL SUB APPEARANCES					(1)							(3)		(3)	(7)	(7)		(7)	(2)	(3)		(1)			(2)	(1)	
TOTAL GOALS SCORED												2	1	1	2			4		6			6				

Small bold figures denote goalscorers.   † denotes opponent's own goal.   *The goals scored in this game were expunged from the records

GLEBE PARK

CAPACITY: 3,960; Seated 1,519, Standing 2,441
PITCH DIMENSIONS: 110 yds x 67 yds
FACILITIES FOR DISABLED SUPPORTERS: Section of Terracing designated for disabled supporters.

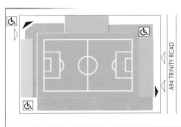

A94 TRINITY ROAD

HOW TO GET THERE

The following routes may be used to reach Glebe Park:

TRAINS: The nearest railway station is Montrose, which is eight miles away. There is a regular Inter-City service from all parts of the country and fans alighting at Montrose can then catch a connecting bus service to Brechin.

BUSES: Brechin bus station is only a few hundred yards from the ground and buses on the Aberdeen-Dundee and Montrose-Edzell routes stop here.

CARS: Car parking is available in the Brechin City car park, which is capable of holding 50 vehicles. There are also a number of side streets which may be used for this purpose.

CALEDONIAN THISTLE

Telford Street Park,
Telford Street,
Inverness, IV3 5LU

PRESIDENT
Dugald M. McGilvray

VICE-PRESIDENT
Norman H. Miller

HON LIFE PRESIDENT
John S. McDonald

DIRECTORS
Alister I. MacKenzie, John Price
Craig R. MacLean
David MacDonald, Ian Gordon
Kenneth A. Thomson
Roy MacLennan, Douglas Riach

SECRETARY
James Falconer

MANAGER
Steven W. Paterson

ASSISTANT MANAGER
Alec Caldwell

COACHES
David Milroy, Alex Young
Mike Fridge

YOUTH COACHES
John Beaton
Jackie Sutherland

CLUB DOCTOR
Dr. John N. MacAskill

PHYSIOTHERAPIST
Ian Manning

GROUNDSMAN
John Shaw

KIT MAN
Tommy Cumming

COMMERCIAL MANAGER
Charles Christie
(01463) 243526

TELEPHONES
Ground (01463) 230274
Sec. Home (01463) 792358
Sec. Bus. (01463) 724253

CLUB SHOP
Situated at the Ground

TEAM CAPTAIN
Michael Noble

SHIRT SPONSOR
Scottish Citylink Coaches

LIST OF PLAYERS 1995-96

SURNAME	FIRST NAME	MIDDLE NAME	DATE OF BIRTH	PLACE OF BIRTH	DATE OF SIGNING	HEIGHT FT INS	WEIGHT ST LBS	PREVIOUS CLUB
Bennett	Graeme	Peter	07/05/65	Inverness	08/08/94	5 10.0	12 7	Clachnacuddin
Benson	Robert		09/04/68	Inverness	03/08/95	5 9.0	12 5	Clachnacuddin
Brennan	David		02/01/71	Bellshill	08/08/94	5 9.0	11 6	Caledonian
Buchanan	David	John	07/04/60	Cardiff	17/03/95	5 10.0	11 7	Unattached
Calder	James	Evan	29/07/60	Grantown-On-Spey	29/06/94	5 11.0	13 4	Inverness Thistle
Christie	Charles		30/03/66	Inverness	05/08/94	5 8.5	11 2	Caledonian
Gray	Robin	Carr	03/04/65	Inverness	29/06/94	6 0.0	12 7	Caledonian
Green	Douglas	Alexander	03/01/73	Elgin	19/06/95	6 0.0	12 0	New Elgin Juniors
Hastings	Richard	Corey	18/05/77	Prince George, B.C.	19/07/95	6 0.0	11 8	"S" Form
Hercher	Alan	Alexander	11/08/65	Dingwall	29/06/94	6 1.0	14 3	Caledonian
Lisle	Martin	Andrew	09/01/63	Inverness	29/06/94	5 10.0	13 0	Caledonian
MacArthur	Iain		18/10/67	Elgin	10/08/95	5 11.0	12 10	Elgin City
MacDonald	Donald		29/08/66	Inverness	08/08/94	5 9.0	11 0	Caledonian
McKenzie	Paul		04/10/69	Aberdeen	08/08/94	5 9.0	11 8	Burnley
MacMillan	Norman	John	09/12/74	Portree	19/08/94	6 1.0	12 2	Nairn County
McAllister	Mark		13/02/71	Inverness	20/10/94	6 0.0	12 0	Caledonian
McCraw	Bruce	William	19/09/72	Keith	27/10/94	5 10.0	10 0	Unattached
McGinlay	David		09/02/69	Fort William	01/08/95	6 0.0	11 10	Huntly
McRitchie	Mark	Daniel	07/07/70	Clydebank	08/08/94	6 2.0	12 7	Caledonian
Mitchell	Colin		24/03/71	Glasgow	29/06/94	5 8.0	10 0	Caledonian
Noble	Michael		18/05/66	Inverness	08/08/94	5 11.0	12 2	Caledonian
Ross	David	William	30/06/70	Inverness	23/06/95	6 2.0	12 7	Brora Rangers
Scott	John	Alan	09/03/75	Aberdeen	30/03/95	5 8.0	11 2	Liverpool
Stewart	Iain		23/10/69	Dundee	09/06/95	5 7.0	9 12	Lossiemouth

MILESTONES

YEAR OF FORMATION: 1994
MOST LEAGUE POINTS IN A SEASON: 45 (Third Division – Season 1994/95)
MOST LEAGUE GOALS SCORED BY A PLAYER IN A SEASON: Alan Hercher & Charlie Christie (Season 1994/95)
NO. OF GOALS SCORED: 6
RECORD ATTENDANCE: 3,062 (-v- Ross County – 6.5.1995)
RECORD VICTORY: 5-2 (-v- Arbroath – Third Division –13.8.1994)
RECORD DEFEAT: 0-4 (-v- Queen's Park – Third Division–20.8.1994)
(-v- Montrose – Third Division–14.2.1995)

SEASON TICKET INFORMATION

Seated
Adult £100
Juvenile/OAP...£60
Standing
Adult £80
Juvenile/OAP...£45

LEAGUE ADMISSION PRICES

Seated
Adult £6
Juvenile/OAP £4
Standing
Adult £5
Juvenile/OAP £3

Date	Venue	Opponents	Result	McRitchie M.	Brennan D.	McAllister M.	Hercher A.	Scott J.	Andrew M.	Lisle M.	McKenzie P.	Noble M.	Bennett G.	Robertson W.	Smart A.	MacDonald D.	Hastings R.	MacMillan I.	Christie C.	Mitchel C.	Ballactra S.	McCraw B.	MacDonald S.	Sinclair C.	Watt C.	Calder J.	Sweeney K	MacDonald J.	Buchanan	Sanderson A.	Urquhart V.	Holmes M.
Aug 13	H	Arbroath	5-2	1	2	3	4^3	5	6	7	8^1	9	10	11^1	12	14																
20	H	Queen's Park	0-4	1	2	3	4	5	6		8	9	10	11			7	12	14													
27	A	Ross County	††3-1	1	2	3	4	5	6		8	9	10	11^1			7	12														
Sep 3	A	Albion Rovers	1-0	1	2	3	4	5			8	9	10	11			7		12^1	6												
10	H	Forfar Athletic	3-1	1	2	3	14	5			8^1	9	6^2	11			7		4	10												
24	A	Alloa	1-1	1	2	3		5^1	6		8	9		11			7		4	10												
Oct 1	H	East Stirlingshire	3-3	1	2	3^1	14		6	4	8	9^1	5	11^1	7				10	12												
8	H	Cowdenbeath	0-3	1	2	3		5	6	12	8	9		11			7		4	10	14											
15	A	Montrose	1-3	1	2	3	12		6	7	8	9				5		11^1	10	4												
22	A	Arbroath	2-1	1	2	3		5	6	8			10					11	7	4	9^2											
29	H	Ross County	0-0	1	2	3		5	8			6		11				12	10	7	4	9	14									
Nov 5	A	Queen's Park	2-0	1	2	3			6	12	8^1		5	10	11^1	14		9		7	4											
12	A	Forfar Athletic	1-2	1	2	3^1			5	8	11	6	10		9					7	4	14										
19	H	Albion Rovers	2-1	1	2	3			5	8	9	6	10					11	12^2	7	4	14										
26	H	Alloa	2-2	1	12	3				6^1	8	14	4					9	10^1	7		11	2	5								
Dec 3	A	East Stirlingshire	0-2	1	2	3			5	8	6		12					9	10	7	4	11										
26	A	Cowdenbeath	1-1	1		3	4		5^1	12	9	8		11					10	7	6		2		14							
Jan 2	A	Ross County	1-3	1		2	3	4	5^1		9	8		11			14		10	7	6											
14	H	Arbroath	1-1		2^1	3	4			14	9			11			7		10		6	12		5	8	1						
21	A	Queen's Park	1-4		2	3		8		12	7			11			6	14	10				5		1	4	9^1					
Feb 4	H	Forfar Athletic	1-1		5	3		4^1	6	8				11					10	7	14	2			1		9					
11	A	Albion Rovers	2-1			3		4		8^1				11			5	9^1	10	7	14	2	6		1							
14	H	Montrose	0-4			3	12	4		8				11			5	9	10	7	14	2	6		1							
18	A	Alloa	0-1			12	4	6	8	14				11			3	9	10	7		5		1	2							
25	H	East Stirlingshire	3-3			3		4		8	11^1			14			6	9	10^2	7		5		1	2							
Mar 4	H	Cowdenbeath	3-1	1	2	3^1	12	4		8	11							9^1	10	7^1		5				6	14					
11	A	Montrose	1-0	1	2	3		4		8	11			14^1				9	10	7		5				6						
18	A	Forfar Athletic	1-4	1	2	3	12	4^1		8				11				9	10	7		5				6	14					
Apr 1	A	East Stirlingshire	0-1	1	2	3	12	4		8		5		14			6	11	10	7												9
8	H	Alloa	0-1	1		3	12	10	6	8		5		11				9		7		2								4	14	
11	H	Albion Rovers	0-2	1		3	4	8				5						11	10	7	14	2			12					6	9	
15	A	Cowdenbeath	3-1	1		3		4^1	10^1			5	8^1				6	9		7	11	2								12		
22	H	Montrose	0-3	1		3	4			8		5	9	12				10		7	11	2								6		
29	A	Arbroath	0-2	1		3	4			8			10	11				9		7		2	5							12	6	
May 6	H	Ross County	3-0	1	2	3	4^1			12			8	11				9^1	10^1	7	14	5						6				
13	H	Queen's Park	1-1	1	2	3	4^1			8			6	11				12	7	9	5									14	10
TOTAL FULL APPEARANCES				29	25	35	13	21	19	22	20	21	15	23	2	7	8	23	24	26	9	7	10	10	1	7	6	2	5	3	2	1
TOTAL SUB APPEARANCES				(1)			(7)	(2)		(6)	(2)		(1)	(4)	(2)	(1)	(3)	(4)	(2)	(2)		(8)	(1)		(1)		(1)		(1)	(4)	(1)	
TOTAL GOALS SCORED						1	3	6	4	3	1	4	1	3				5	6	1		2					1				

Small bold figures denote goalscorers. † denotes opponent's own goal.

TELFORD STREET PARK

CAPACITY: 5,498; Seated 498, Standing 5,000
PITCH DIMENSIONS: 110 yds x 70 yds
FACILITIES FOR DISABLED SUPPORTERS: By prior arrangement with Secretary.

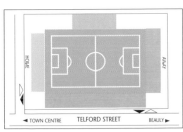

HOW TO GET THERE

The following routes may be used to reach Telford Street Park:
TRAINS: Nearest Railway Station is Inverness which is approximately one mile from ground.
BUSES: Local services available from Bus Station situated close to Inverness town centre.
CARS: The Ground is located to the West of Inverness on the old A9 Road. If approaching from North, South or East follow signs for town centre and Beauly. Car and bus parking is available within the Carsegate Industrial Estate area adjacent to the ground.

COWDENBEATH

Central Park, High Street,
Cowdenbeath, KY4 9QQ

CHAIRMAN
Gordon McDougall

VICE-CHAIRMAN
Eric Mitchell

DIRECTORS
Ian Fraser
Albert Tait
Paul McGlinchey

SECRETARY
Thomas Ogilvie

MANAGER
Thomas Steven

PLAYER COACH
Samuel Conn

RESERVE TEAM/
YOUTH TEAM COACH
William Aitchison

SPRINT COACH
Bert Oliver

CLUB DOCTOR
Dr. Robert Brownlee

PHYSIOTHERAPIST
Brian McNeill

GROUNDSMAN
Gordon McDougall

COMMERCIAL MANAGER
Joe McNamara
(01383) 610166

TELEPHONES
Ground/Ticket Office/
Information Service
(01383) 610166
Sec. Home (01383) 513013
Fax (01383) 512132

CLUB SHOP
Situated at Stadium

OFFICIAL SUPPORTERS CLUB
Central Park,
Cowdenbeath KY4 9QQ

TEAM CAPTAIN
Barry McMahon

SHIRT SPONSOR
Fountain Night Club

LIST OF PLAYERS 1995-96

SURNAME	FIRST NAME	MIDDLE NAME	DATE OF BIRTH	PLACE OF BIRTH	DATE OF SIGNING	HEIGHT FT INS	WEIGHT ST LBS	PREVIOUS CLUB
Adamson	Ross		16/08/76	Bellshill	17/08/95	5 9.5	11 1	Thorniewood United
Barclay	Alexander	Bruce	28/11/74	Edinburgh	02/09/95	5 7.0	10 0	Arnistone Rangers
Bowmaker	Kevin		03/04/75	Edinburgh	15/02/95	5 11.0	11 13	Musselburgh Athletic
Buckley	Graham		31/10/63	Edinburgh	31/07/95	5 7.0	10 0	Newtongrange Star JFC
Chappell	Stephen		20/08/65	Dunfermline	22/07/95	5 9.5	12 6	Oakley United JFC
Conn	Samuel	Craig	26/10/61	Lanark	29/10/94	5 11.0	12 0	Albion Rovers
Craib	Stephen	Thomas	14/01/72	Dundee	10/03/95	5 10.0	10 7	Arbroath
De Melo	Armando		08/09/72	Edinburgh	25/02/95	5 8.0	11 7	Gala Fairydean
Donachie	Andrew		06/10/76	Broxburn	09/09/95	5 10.0	12 3	Dalkeith Thistle
Fellenger	David		06/06/69	Edinburgh	17/10/94	5 8.0	11 4	Craigroyston
Godfrey	Ross		21/01/77	Edinburgh	17/08/95	5 11.0	10 12	Drum B.C.
Hamilton	Alistair	Strathern	12/11/75	Irvine	29/04/95	5 7.0	10 7	Musselburgh Athletic
Hancock	Brian		26/02/77	Edinburgh	17/08/95	5 9.0	10 11	Dalkeith Thistle
Humphreys	Martin	Jay	16/03/76	Dunfermline	24/02/95	6 0.0	12 11	Links United
Hutchison	Kevin		28/02/77	Glasgow	17/08/95	5 9.0	10 9	Thorniewood United
Lindsay	Anthony	Reid	29/12/72	Coatbridge	30/09/94	5 10.0	13 0	Ormiston Primrose
Malloy	Brian	John	04/05/67	Paisley	26/05/94	5 11.0	12 0	Bo'ness United
Maratea	Domenico		10/04/74	Brooklyn	23/03/95	5 9.0	12 4	Newtongrange Star
McMahon	Barry		08/04/71	Edinburgh	23/11/92	6 1.0	12 2	Kelty Hearts
Meldrum	Graham		27/02/73	Bangour	22/07/95	5 8.0	10 7	Bo'ness United
Petrie	Edward		15/06/73	Bathgate	13/07/92	5 10.0	12 7	Bathgate United U'21
Russell	Neil		29/05/71	Kirkcaldy	31/05/94	6 3.0	13 9	Forfar Athletic
Scott	David		18/04/63	Edinburgh	22/07/95	5 8.0	12 0	Whitburn JFC
Smith	Charles	Anthony	30/04/76	Glasgow	07/07/95	5 9.0	10 12	Queen's Park
Soutar	Graeme	Douglas	13/01/74	Inverness	09/08/94	5 7.0	11 0	Newtongrange Star
Steven	Shaun	Robert	28/08/65	Edinburgh	10/07/95	5 9.0	12 4	Bonnyrigg Rose J.F.C.
Stewart	William	Paul	16/04/77	Glasgow	28/08/95	5 10.0	10 0	Thorniewood United
Winter	Craig	John	30/06/76	Dunfermline	19/07/94	5 9.0	10 0	Raith Rovers
Wood	Garry		18/09/76	Edinburgh	23/02/95	5 11.0	12 7	Hutchison Vale B.C.
Yardley	Mark		14/09/69	Livingston	27/01/95	6 2.0	13 1	Rotherham United

MILESTONES

YEAR OF FORMATION: 1881
MOST CAPPED PLAYER: Jim Paterson
NO. OF CAPS: 3
MOST LEAGUE POINTS IN A SEASON: 60 (Division 2 – Season 1938/39)
MOST LEAGUE GOALS SCORED BY A PLAYER IN A SEASON: Willie Devlin (Season 1925/26)
NO. OF GOALS SCORED: 40
RECORD ATTENDANCE: 25,586 (-v- Rangers – 21.9.1949)
RECORD VICTORY: 12-0 (-v- Johnstone – Scottish Cup 21.1.1928)
RECORD DEFEAT: 1-11 (-v- Clyde – Division 2, 6.10.1951)

SEASON TICKET INFORMATION

Seated
Adult £80
Juvenile/OAP...£40
Standing
Adult £80
Juvenile/OAP...£40

LEAGUE ADMISSION PRICES

Seated
Adult £6
Juvenile/OAP £3
Standing
Adult £5
Juvenile/OAP £2.50

CLUB FACTFILE 1994/95
RESULTS .. APPEARANCES .. SCORERS

The BLUE BRAZIL

Note: In the appearance grid below, plain figures are shirt numbers worn; small superscript figures denote goals scored by that player. † denotes an opponent's own goal.

Date	Venue	Opponents	Result	Russell N.	Scott S.	Hamill A.	Malloy B.	Humphreys M.	Winter G.	Petrie E.	Black I.	Soutar G.	Thomson J.	Stout C.	Lynch J.	Carr R.	Tait C.	Yardley N.	McMahon B.	Davidson I.	Bowmaker K.	Callaghan N.	Murdoch S.	Hamilton F.	Barclay A.	Fellenger D.	Maloney J.	Conn S.	Wardell S.	Weatherson P.	Wood G.	Maratea J.	De Melo A.	Watson D.	Craib S.	Stewart W.
Aug 13	H	Ross County	0-2	1	2	3	4	5	6	7	8	9	10	11	12	14																				
20	H	Arbroath	6-2	1		3	4^1	5	7	2	8	10^1	12	11				6	9^4	14																
27	A	Montrose	0-2	1		3	4	5	12		8	10		11	14			7	9	6	2															
Sep 3	H	East Stirlingshire	1-1	1			4	5	6^1		8	12		11	14			7	9	2		3	10													
10	A	Queen's Park	3-0	1		14	4	5	6	2	8	11			12			7	9^3				10	3												
24	A	Albion Rovers	4-2	1		8	4^1	5	6	2	14	11						7	9^1	12			10^2	3												
Oct 1	H	Alloa	1-3	1			4		6	2	8	11			14			7	9^1	5			10	3	12											
8	A	Caledonian Thistle	3-0	1		14	4	5	6^1	2	8	11						7	9^2				10	3	12											
15	H	Forfar Athletic	1-0	1				5	14	7	2	8		11				9		4			10^1	3			6									
22	A	Ross County	0-4	1	12		4	5	6	2	8	11			14				9				10	3			7									
29	A	Montrose	1-1		2			5	4		8				12				9^1				10	3			6	1	7	11						
Nov 5	A	Arbroath	3-0	1	2	14		4			8				12			6	9^1				10	3			7		5^1	11^1						
12	H	Queen's Park	2-0	1	2		4	10			8				12			7	9^2	14				3			6		5	11						
19	A	East Stirlingshire	2-0	1	2		4		6		11^1				12			7	9	14				3			8		5	10^1						
26	H	Albion Rovers	2-2	1	2		4		14		8				12			7	9^2				10	3			6		5	11						
Dec 3	A	Alloa	0-1	1	2		4		12		8							6	9	14			10	3			7		5	11						
26	H	Caledonian Thistle	1-1	1	2			5	6		12							8	9	4			10^1	3			7			11						
31	A	Forfar Athletic	1-1	1	2		4				8							7	9^1				10	3			6		5	11	12					
Jan 2	A	Montrose	2-1	1	2		4				8	10						7	9^2	5				3	12	14			6	11						
14	H	Ross County	0-3				4	2			11	9											10	3			8	1	5		6	7	12			
21	A	Arbroath	3-0				4	14			8^1							9	5				10^1	3	12			1	11^1	6	7	2				
Feb 4	A	Queen's Park	0-1	1	2		4	14			8	12						9	5				10				6			11	3	7				
18	A	Albion Rovers	0-2	1	2		7				11				12			3	9	4			10				8		5	6	14					
25	H	Alloa	1-3	1			4	$2°$	7^1		10							8	9						11	6	5	12	3			14				
Mar 4	A	Caledonian Thistle	1-3	1			4		7						14			8	9	2			12	6			5	11	3			10^1	13			
11	H	Forfar Athletic	1-3	1			4		7		6							8	9^1	2			12					5	3		10		11			
18	H	Queen's Park	1-3	1				5	6		8							7	9	4			10		2		12	3		11^1	13					
22	H	East Stirlingshire	1-4	1				6	7		3							8	9						2	4	12^1		5		10	1	11			
25	H	East Stirlingshire	0-1	1				6			3							10	9	4					2		5		7	14	8	12		11		
Apr 1	A	Alloa	1-2	1				5			2	8	10						9	14					7		3^1		12	6	4	11				
8	A	Albion Rovers	2-0	1				5	4	6	2	8^1							9^1						7		11	14	3		10					
15	H	Caledonian Thistle	1-3	1				5	3	6	2	8							9^1						7		11			4	10	1				
22	H	Forfar Athletic	2-2	1				4	5	8	9^1	11			12				3						6	7	10^1	2					14			
29	A	Ross County	0-2	1				5	2	8	9	11			7				4						6		3	10	12							
May 6	H	Montrose	0-4	1				5	8		10	12						6	9						3		7		4	11		2			14	
13	H	Arbroath	1-1	1				5	7	2	11^1				14			9	6		3						4	10	12	8						
TOTAL FULL APPEARANCES				31	12	4	30	21	23	12	31	16	1	4	2			22	32	17	1	2	18	17		3	23	3	19	20	8	9	3	7	2	3
TOTAL SUB APPEARANCES					(2)	(2)		(1)	(5)		(2)	(3)	(1)		(14)	(2)				(5)				(2)		(1)	(4)	(1)			(3)	(7)		(1)	(2)	(2)	(2)
TOTAL GOALS SCORED							2		3		4	2							23							5		2	5		2				

Small bold figures denote goalscorers.   † denotes opponent's own goal.

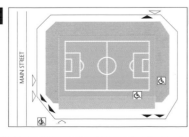

CENTRAL PARK

CAPACITY: 5,258; Seated 1,552, Standing 3,706
PITCH DIMENSIONS: 107 yds x 66 yds
FACILITIES FOR DISABLED SUPPORTERS: Direct access from car park into designated area within ground. Toilet and catering facilities also provided.

HOW TO GET THERE

You can get to Central Park by the following routes:

TRAINS: There is a regular service of trains from Edinburgh and Glasgow (via Edinburgh) which call at Cowdenbeath and the station is only 400 yards from the ground.

BUSES: A limited Edinburgh-Cowdenbeath service stops just outside the ground on matchdays and a frequent service of Dunfermline-Ballingry buses also stop outside the ground, as does the Edinburgh-Glenrothes service.

CARS: Car parking facilities are available in the public car park adjacent to the ground for 190 cars. There are also another 300 spaces at the Stenhouse Street car park, which is 200 yards from the ground.

EAST STIRLINGSHIRE

Firs Park, Firs Street,
Falkirk FK2 7AY

CHAIRMAN
William C. Whyte

VICE-CHAIRMAN
G. Marshall Paterson

DIRECTORS
William W. H. Lawless
Alexander S. H. Forsyth
Alexander C. Mitchell
G. Ross A. Strang
James Greenaway

SECRETARY
Mrs. Jaqui Wilson

MANAGER
William Little

ASSISTANT MANAGER/COACH
Lenny Reid

CLUB DOCTOR
Dr. Alan Buchan M.B., C.B.

PHYSIOTHERAPIST
Angus Williamson

COMMERCIAL MANAGER
Scott Bisio
Home (01324) 824870

TELEPHONES
Ground (01324) 623583
Sec. Home (01324) 713558
Fax (01324) 637862

CLUB SHOP
At ground. Open Mon-Fri
10 a.m.- 2 p.m. (except Thursday)
and on all home matchdays

TEAM CAPTAIN
Brian Ross

SHIRT SPONSOR
J. Kelly Watchmaker

LIST OF PLAYERS 1995-96

SURNAME	FIRST NAME	MIDDLE NAME	DATE OF BIRTH	PLACE OF BIRTH	DATE OF SIGNING	HEIGHT FT INS	WEIGHT ST LBS	PREVIOUS CLUB
Abercromby	Mark	Henry	14/07/74	Glasgow	08/11/94	5 10.0	10 7	Kitchee
Cameron	David		24/08/75	Bangor	01/09/95	6 0.0	11 8	Dunnipace Jnrs
Conroy	John	James	03/11/70	Glasgow	04/08/93	5 7.0	10 2	Alloa
Cuthbert	Lee	James	28/02/70	Edinburgh	03/08/94	5 8.0	11 0	Whitehill Welfare
Dodds	John	Charles	22/04/73	Salsbury	30/06/94	5 11.0	11 0	Dunipace Juniors
Dwyer	Peter		18/08/65	Glasgow	25/11/94	6 1.0	12 10	Dunipace Juniors
Geraghty	Michael	John	30/10/70	Glasgow	15/09/92	5 10.0	10 1	Stranraer
Hunter	Murray	Russell	08/01/71	Edinburgh	14/03/95	6 1.0	12 0	Whitehill Welfare
Lamont	Peter	Mitchell	24/11/66	Glasgow	03/08/95	6 1.0	12 2	Alloa
Lee	Iain	Caird C.	07/07/67	Hamilton	05/03/94	5 9.0	10 7	Cowdenbeath
Lee	Robert	Smith	19/05/66	Broxburn	14/01/94	5 10.0	11 0	Alloa
MacLean	Steven		01/09/73	Glasgow	03/08/95	5 11.0	12 10	Knightswood Juveniles
McBride	Martin	Joseph	22/03/71	Glasgow	11/08/95	5 9.0	10 7	Albion Rovers
McCallum	Mungo		28/10/65	Bellshill	12/11/93	5 10.0	11 7	Stirling Albion
McDougall	Gordon		17/02/71	Bellshill	16/07/93	6 2.0	12 3	Falkirk
McKenna	Thomas	Ronald	05/09/69	Bellshill	04/08/95	5 6.0	10 7	Great Harwood Town
Millar	Glen	Archibald	02/09/66	Falkirk	02/08/95	6 1.0	13 0	Queen's Park
Moffat	James		27/01/60	Dunfermline	21/07/94	6 0.0	12 0	Cowdenbeath
Neill	Alan	John	13/12/70	Baillieston	03/08/95	6 1.0	12 7	Clyde
Orr	James	Patrick	01/02/72	Blantyre	24/06/95	5 9.0	11 2	Queen's Park
Ross	Brian		15/08/67	Stirling	31/03/91	5 11.0	11 7	Ayr United
Scott	Colin	Andrew	30/11/66	Edinburgh	21/07/94	5 8.0	13 0	Cowdenbeath
Sneddon	Scott		07/12/71	Dechmont	08/11/94	6 2.0	11 4	Queen's Park
Stirling	David	Park	12/09/75	Bellshill	08/07/94	5 10.0	11 2	Partick Thistle
Watt	David		05/03/67	Edinburgh	19/07/94	5 7.0	11 6	Cowdenbeath

MILESTONES

YEAR OF FORMATION: 1881
MOST CAPPED PLAYER: Humphrey Jones
NO. OF CAPS: 5 (for Wales)
MOST LEAGUE POINTS IN A SEASON: 55 (Division 2 – Season 1931/32) (2 Points for a Win)
59 (Third Division – Season 1994/95) (3 Points for a Win)
MOST LEAGUE GOALS SCORED BY A PLAYER IN A SEASON: Malcolm Morrison (Season 1938/39)
NO. OF GOALS SCORED: 36
RECORD ATTENDANCE: 11,500 (-v- Hibernian – 10.2.1969)
RECORD VICTORY: 10-1 (-v- Stenhousemuir – Scottish Cup, 1.9.1888)
RECORD DEFEAT: 1-12 (-v- Dundee United – Division 2 – 13.4.1936)

SEASON TICKET INFORMATION

Seated
Adult £72
Juvenile/OAP...£36
Family Ticket...£100
Standing
Adult £60
Juvenile/OAP...£30
Family Ticket...£80

LEAGUE ADMISSION PRICES

Seated
Adult £7
Juvenile/OAP £4
Standing
Adult £6
Juvenile/OAP £3

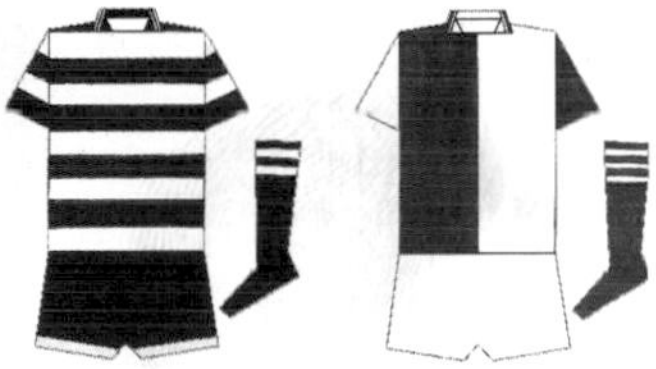

CLUB FACTFILE 1994/95

RESULTS . . APPEARANCES . . SCORERS

The SHIRE

Date	Venue	Opponents	Result	Moffat J.	Watt D.	Cuthbert L.	Russell G.	Yates E.	Lee R.	Lee I.	Millar G.	McCallum M	Scott C.	Geraghty M.	Dempsey S.	Stirling D.	Scott E.	Loney J.	Sneddon S.	Ross B.	Robertson A.	Conroy J.	McDougall C.	Abercromby M.	Dwyer P.	Hunter M.	McConville F.	Gilogley W.
Aug 13	A	Montrose	0-2	1	2	3	4	5	6	7	8	9	10	11	12	14												
20	H	Ross County	2-2	1	2		4	5	6	7	8	9^1	10^1	11			3	12										
27	A	Alloa	3-1	1	12		4		3	7	8^1	9	10	11^1		14		2^1	5	6								
Sep 3	A	Cowdenbeath	1-1	1	3		2	4		7	8	9^1	6	10		12		11	5		14							
10	H	Albion Rovers	4-0	1	2	3	4			7^2	8		6	10^2		9		11	5			14						
24	H	Forfar Athletic	3-1	1	4	11^1	2^1	6	3	7^1	8	12		10		9			5			14						
Oct 1	A	Caledonian Thistle	3-3		2	11	6	4	3	7^1	8	9	12	10		14			5^2				1					
8	H	Queen's Park	3-2			11	2	4	3^1	7	8	9^1	6	10^1					5			14	1					
15	A	Arbroath	1-0		2	12	11	4	3	7	8	9	6	10^1					5			14	1					
22	H	Montrose	1-2		2	11	6^1	4	3	7	8		12	10		9		14	5				1					
29	H	Alloa	1-2				2	4	3	7	8^1		6	10		9		12	5			11	1					
Nov 5	A	Ross County	4-1			12	2	4^1	3	7^1	8		6	10^1		9		14	5			11^1	1					
12	A	Albion Rovers	2-0			12	2	4	3^1	7	8^1			10		9			5	6		11	1	14				
19	H	Cowdenbeath	0-2		4		2		3	7	8			10		9			5	6		11	1	14				
26	A	Forfar Athletic	2-3		4		2		3	7^1	8			10				11	5	6			1	14	9^1			
Dec 3	H	Caledonian Thistle	2-0		4		2		3	7^1	8			10^1		12			5	6		11	1		9			
26	A	Queen's Park	3-2		4		2^1	5	3	7	8		11	10^2						6		14	1		9			
31	H	Arbroath	1-0		4		2		3	7	8		11	10^1					5	6		14	1		9			
Jan 21	H	Ross County	0-2		2		4		3	7	12	9	10	8					5	6		14	1		11			
Feb 7	A	Alloa	1-0		12		2		3	7	8	9	4	10				14	5	6			1		11^1			
18	H	Forfar Athletic	1-2		14		2		3	7	4	9^1		8				11	5	6			1		10			
25	A	Caledonian Thistle	3-3		4	12	2		3^1	7			10	8^1					5	6		14	1	9	11^1			
Mar 7	H	Albion Rovers	3-0		2	10			3	7^1	12		4	8^1					5	6			1	9	11^1			
11	A	Arbroath	2-5		2	10^1			3	7	4			8					5	6		12	1	9	11^1			
15	H	Montrose	1-0		2	10			3	7	14			9		4			5	6			1		11^1	8		
23	A	Cowdenbeath	4-1		2	10			3	7^1	14			9^2		4			5	6			1	12	11^1	8		
25	H	Cowdenbeath	1-0		2	10			3	7				9		4			5	6			1		11	8^1		
Apr 1	H	Caledonian Thistle	1-0		2	10			3	7	12			9^1		4			5	6			1	14	11	8		
5	A	Albion Rovers	1-3		2	10			3	7	12			9		4			5	6			1	14	11^1	8		
8	A	Forfar Athletic	0-1		2	10			3	7	4	9		8					5	6			1	12	11	14		
15	A	Queen's Park	0-1		2	10			3	7	4			9					5	6			1	8	11	12	14	
18	H	Queen's Park	3-2		2^1				3	7	4			9		10			5^1	6			1	8		11^1	12	
22	H	Arbroath	0-2		2	12			3	7	4			9					5	6			1	8	11	10	14	
29	A	Montrose	0-1		2				3	7	4			9		10			5	6			1	8	11		14	
May 6	H	Alloa	1-1		2	3				7	4			9		10			5	6			1	8	11^1		12	
13	A	Ross County	3-2			3			5	7^1	4		8	9^1		10				6			1	11		12^1		2
TOTAL FULL APPEARANCES				6	28	17	22	12	33	36	28	11	16	36		16	1	5	32	25		5	30	9	20	7		1
TOTAL SUB APPEARANCES					(3)	(5)					(6)	(1)	(2)		(1)	(5)		(5)			(1)	(9)		(7)		(3)	(5)	
TOTAL GOALS SCORED					1	2	3	1	3	10	3	4	1	16				1	3			1			9	3		

Small bold figures denote goalscorers. † denotes opponent's own goal.

FIRS PARK

CAPACITY: 1,880; Seated 297, Standing 1,583

PITCH DIMENSIONS: 106 yds x 73 yds

FACILITIES FOR DISABLED SUPPORTERS: By prior arrangement with Secretary.

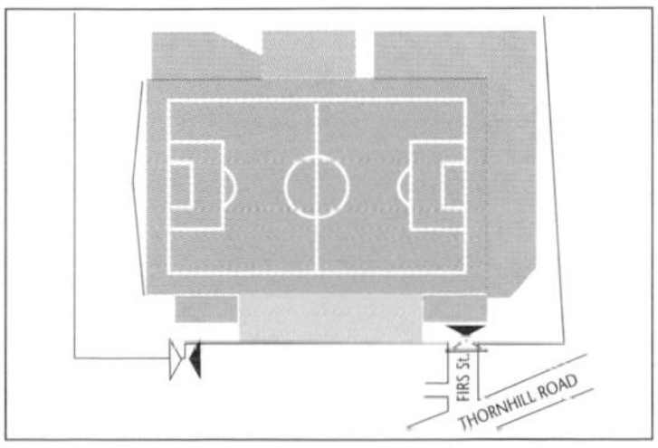
FIRS ST.
THORNHILL ROAD

HOW TO GET THERE

The following routes may be used to reach Firs Park:

TRAINS: Passengers should alight at Grahamston station and the ground is then ten minutes walk.

BUSES: All buses running from the city centre pass close by the ground. The Grangemouth via Burnbank Road and Tamfourhill via Kennard Street services both stop almost outside the ground.

CARS: Car parking is available in the adjacent side streets and in the car park adjacent to the Social Club. This can take 100 cars and there are also spaces available in the car park adjacent to the major stores around the ground.

LIVINGSTON

Meadowbank Stadium,
Edinburgh, EH7 6AE

ALL CORRESPONDENCE TO BE
ADDRESSED TO

Preston Farm, Preston Road,
Prestonpans, EH32 9LB

CHAIRMAN
William P. Hunter

VICE-CHAIRMAN
Hugh Cowan

DIRECTORS
John L. Bain, B.E.M.
Robert Clark (Treasurer)
James R. S. Renton

HONORARY PRESIDENT
John P. Blacklaw, C.Eng, M.I.E.E.

HONORARY VICE–PRESIDENT
Willaim L. Mill

SECRETARY
James R. S. Renton

MANAGER
James Leishman

RESERVE TEAM COACH
Michael Korotkich

CLUB DOCTOR
Malcolm Morrison

PHYSIOTHERAPIST
Arthur Duncan

COMMERCIAL DEPARTMENT
Ann Young (0131) 655 7757

TELEPHONES
Ground (0131) 661 5351
Sec. Home (01850) 706077
Sec. Bus. (01738) 474821
Fax (01875) 811130

OFFICIAL SUPPORTERS CLUB
Mrs B. Higgins, Almond Valley
Sports, Main Street, East Calder
(01506) 884848

TEAM CAPTAIN
Gordon McLeod

SHIRT SPONSOR
Mitsubishi Electric

SURNAME	FIRST NAME	MIDDLE NAME	DATE OF BIRTH	PLACE OF BIRTH	DATE OF SIGNING	HEIGHT FT INS	WEIGHT ST LBS	PREVIOUS CLUB
Alleyne	David	Richardo	15/02/72	Barbados	13/03/95	5 11.0	12 0	Lambada (Barbados)
Bailey	Lee		10/07/72	Edinburgh	04/08/92	5 6.0	10 0	Hibernian
Bowsher	Colin		11/06/73	Musselburgh	06/06/95	6 2.0	12 0	Easthouses B.C.
Brolly	Martin		17/08/77	Dechmont	04/09/95	5 9.0	11 0	Polbeth United
Callaghan	William	Thomas	23/03/67	Dunfermline	24/03/95	5 10.5	12 7	Cowdenbeath
Coulston	Douglas		12/08/71	Glasgow	14/10/94	5 10.0	11 0	Moray House College
Coyle	Malcolm	Arthur	19/03/74	Musselburgh	18/07/92	6 2.0	11 0	Hutchison Vale B.C.
Dallas	Andrew	Fraser	26/08/73	Edinburgh	16/08/94	5 10.0	10 12	Brechin City
Davidson	Graeme		18/01/68	Edinburgh	23/07/93	5 10.0	11 0	Berwick Rangers
Douglas	Robert	James	24/04/72	Lanark	26/10/93	6 3.0	14 12	Forth Wanderers
Duthie	Mark	James	19/08/72	Edinburgh	25/08/90	5 8.0	10 0	Edina Hibs
Ellison	Steven		03/03/70	Edinburgh	25/08/90	6 1.0	12 3	Lochend B.C.
Fulton	Alan		02/08/78	Dechmont	04/09/95	5 10.0	10 0	Murieston United
Graham	Thomas		12/05/68	Edinburgh	18/06/90	6 0.0	13 0	Cavalry Park B.C.
Harvey	Graham		23/04/61	Musselburgh	04/08/95	5 10.5	11 7	Instant Dict (Hong Kong)
Henderson	Robert		07/09/77	Uphall	04/09/95	5 8.0	10 7	Polbeth United
Higgins	Stephen	James	26/09/77	Dunfermline	08/06/95	5 8.0	11 0	"S" Form
Ingram	Nicholas	Charles	23/08/73	Edinburgh	08/11/93	5 8.5	10 9	Hibernian
Kennedy	David	Kerr	16/10/73	Stirling	07/08/95	6 1.0	12 7	Rosyth Recreation
Korotkich	Michael	James	26/05/63	Edinburgh	08/06/95	5 9.0	12 0	Dunbar
Laidlaw	Steven	James	17/06/73	Edinburgh	06/06/95	6 0.0	12 0	Easthouses B.C.
Lambie	Kenneth		18/05/79	Dechmont	04/09/95	5 7.0	10 0	Polbeth United
Martin	Craig	Richard S.	16/04/71	Haddington	16/08/94	6 0.0	11 10	Arbroath
McCartney	Craig		18/11/71	Edinburgh	22/11/94	5 9.0	11 0	Livingston Juniors
McLeod	Gordon	Thomas	02/09/67	Edinburgh	25/09/92	5 9.0	11 2	Dundee
McMartin	Grant	Thomas	31/12/70	Linlithgow	01/08/95	5 10.0	10 5	St. Johnstone
Sinclair	Christopher		11/11/70	Sheffield	07/10/94	5 9.0	10 10	Dunfermline Athletic
Smart	Craig	William	23/03/75	Dunfermline	01/08/95	6 0.0	10 3	Dunfermline Athletic
Sorbie	Stuart	Graham	07/09/63	Glasgow	08/08/94	5 9.5	10 5	Arbroath
Stoute	Horace	Antonio	29/05/71	Barbados	13/03/95	6 2.0	13 7	Lambada (Barbados)
Thomson	Mark		29/06/66	Johnstone	28/12/94	6 1.0	12 5	Spartans
Thorburn	Stuart	Halliday	03/05/68	Edinburgh	10/03/94	5 10.0	12 7	Whitehill Welfare
Wales	Gary		04/01/79	Inveralmond	04/09/95	5 10.0	10 0	Inveralmond
Walker	Stewart		22/06/79	Dechmont	04/09/95	5 9.0	9 7	Polbeth United
Wallace	Scott		19/12/78	Dechmont	04/09/95	5 7.0	9 7	Polbeth United
Weir	Mark		21/10/77	Motherwell	04/09/95	5 11.0	12 0	Polbeth United
Williamson	Robert		12/01/75	Edinburgh	22/11/94	5 8.0	10 11	Livingston Juniors
Williamson	Stewart		10/12/61	Lasswade	02/08/88	6 0.0	11 7	Cowdenbeath
Wood	Barry	Wilson	19/06/77	Edinburgh	08/06/95	5 7.0	11 0	"S" Form
Young	Jason	Anthony	01/03/72	Edinburgh	14/02/95	5 7.0	10 0	Wissen

MILESTONES

YEAR OF FORMATION: 1974 (From Seasons 1974/75 to 1994/95 known as Meadowbank Thistle F.C.)
MOST LEAGUE POINTS IN A SEASON: 55 (Second Division – Season 1986/87)
MOST LEAGUE GOALS SCORED BY A PLAYER IN A SEASON: John McGachie (Season 1986/87)
NO. OF GOALS SCORED: 21
RECORD ATTENDANCE: 2,818 (-v- Albion Rovers, 10.8.1974)
RECORD VICTORY: 6-0 (-v- Raith Rovers – Second Division, 9.11.1985)
RECORD DEFEAT: 0-8 (-v- Hamilton Academical – Division 2, 14.12.1974)

SEASON TICKET INFORMATION

Seated
Adult £100
Parent & Juvenile £140
Parent & 2 Juveniles £180
2 Parents & 2 Juveniles........................£250

LEAGUE ADMISSION PRICES

Seated
Adult £6
Juvenile/OAP £3
Parent & Juvenile £8

CLUB FACTFILE 1994/95
RESULTS .. APPEARANCES .. SCORERS

LIVVY'S LIONS

Players (left to right): Ellison S., Graham T., Fleming D., Wilson S., Williamson S., Hutchison M., Duthie M., McLeod G., Little L., Rutherford P., Bailey --, Thorburn S., Sorbie S., Coyle W., Price C., Davidson G., Ingram N., Martin C., Sinclair C., Dallas A., Douglas R., Coulston D., Samuel D., Thomson M., Harris C., Young J., Williamson R., McCarthey C., Alleyne D., Callaghan W., Strute H.

Date	Venue	Opponents	Result	Ell	Gra	Fle	Wil	WilS	Hut	Dut	McL	Lit	Rut	Bai	Tho	Sor	Coy	Pri	Dav	Ing	Mar	Sin	Dal	Dou	Cou	Sam	Tho	Har	You	WilR	McC	All	Cal	Str
Aug 13	A	*Brechin City	5-1	1	2	3	4	5	6	7	8	9	10^1	11^3	12	14^1																		
20	H	Greenock Morton	0-1	1	2	3	4	5		7		8	9	6	11		10	12	14															
27	H	Stenhousemuir	3-0	1	2	3	4	5	14	7	8	9^1	6	11^2			10	12																
Sep 3	A	Dumbarton	1-0	1	2	3	4^1	5		7	8	9	6	11			10	12																
10	H	Queen of the South	0-1	1	2	3	4	5		7	8	9		11	12	10			6	14														
24	H	Stirling Albion	1-2	1	2	3^1	4	5			8	9		11	6	10				7														
Oct 1	A	Clyde	1-2	1	2	3	4	5			8^1			11	6	10		9	7	12	14													
8	A	Berwick Rangers	1-2	1		4	12	5			6	9^1		10	7	8			2			3	11	14										
15	H	East Fife	0-1			4		7	5		2	6	9	12		8						3	11	10	1	14								
22	H	Brechin City	1-0			4		7	5^1		2	6	9	10		8	11					3	11		1	12								
29	A	Stenhousemuir	1-1			4		7	5	14	6	9^1		12		10			2			3	11	8	1									
Nov 5	A	Greenock Morton	0-4			4		8	5	14	6	9		12	7	10			2			3	11		1									
12	A	Queen of the South	0-0			4		8	5		7	6	9	10	11				2			3			1									
19	H	Dumbarton	0-0					8	5		7	6	9	10	11		12		2	14	3	4			1									
26	A	Stirling Albion	3-2			4		8	5			6	9	10		12^1	14		2			3	11		1		7^2							
Dec 3	H	Clyde	2-2			4		8	5			9^1		10^1		6			2			3	11		1		7							
10	H	Berwick Rangers	2-1	1		4		8	5^1	14		9		10	3	6	12		2			11^1					7							
31	A	East Fife	1-2	1		4		8		14	10			9	5	6^1			2			3	11				7							
Jan 10	A	Stenhousemuir	1-2	1		4		8		14	10	9		12	7^1	6			2			3	11					5						
14	A	Brechin City	1-3	1		4			7		10	14			12	6^1			2			3	11				8	5	9					
21	H	Greenock Morton	1-0	1				7	2		11	9		14		6^1			4			3					10	5	8					
Feb 4	H	Queen of the South	1-2	1		4			7		10	11		14	12	6			2			3					8	5	9^1					
11	A	Dumbarton	0-4	1	5						10			11	8	6	7		2			3		9			12	4		14				
25	A	Clyde	1-4	1				7	5		10			8	14	6			2			3					11	4	12	9^1				
Mar 4	A	Berwick Rangers	0-1	1	2			7	5		10			8	3	11						6					14	4	9	12				
8	H	Stirling Albion	0-3	1	2			7	5		10	8		12	3	14						6						4	9	11				
11	H	East Fife	1-3	1	2			8	5		10	9		11^1	3	7											6	4		12	14			
18	A	Queen of the South	3-2	1	5			6^1	2^1		10	9		7^1					3			11					12			4	8			
25	H	Dumbarton	1-0	1	5			6	2	11		9		7		12			3								8^1			4	10	14		
Apr 1	A	Clyde	0-1	1	5			6	2	11		9		7		12			3								8			4	10	14		
8	A	Stirling Albion	1-2	1	5			7	2			8		12		14			4		11						10			3	6	9^1		
15	H	Berwick Rangers	0-3	1	5			7			2	3	8	12					4		14						10			11	6	9		
22	A	East Fife	1-1	1	5			7			11	8		12	2	6^1			4		14						10			3		9		
29	A	Brechin City	2-1		5^1			7			11	10			2	6			4		12						8			3^1		9	1	
May 5	H	Stenhousemuir	1-0		5			10			8			7^1	2	6			4								11			3		9	1	
13	A	Greenock Morton	0-1		8						6	9		7	2	10			4		12						5		11	3		1	
TOTAL FULL APPEARANCES				25	32	7	32	28		2	13	31	27	4	24	17	26	1	2	26	16	13	6	8		9	10	5	10	9	5	5	3	
TOTAL SUB APPEARANCES					(1)		(1)	(5)		(1)				(10)	(5)	(6)	(7)	(1)		(1)		(2)	(1)	(4)	(1)		(2)	(2)		(1)	(4)	(1)		(2)
TOTAL GOALS SCORED					1		1	2	3			1	4			6	1	5					1						2		1	2	1		1

Small bold figures denote goalscorers. † denotes opponent's own goal. * Meadowbank Thistle were deducted 3 points for fielding an ineligible player in this match and the goals scored were expunged from the records

---

MEADOWBANK STADIUM

CAPACITY: 16,000(All Seated) (Only 7,500 Capacity Main Stand Used)
PLEASE NOTE THAT THE CLUB ARE SCHEDULED TO MOVE TO A NEWLY CONSTRUCTED STADIUM IN LIVINGSTON IN OCTOBER/NOVEMBER 1995 WITH AN INITIAL ALL SEATED CAPACITY FOR 4,000 SPECTATORS

PITCH DIMENSIONS: 105 yds x 72 yds

FACILITIES FOR DISABLED SUPPORTERS: By prior arrangement with Secretary. (Sponsored by British Telecom)

MARIONVILLE ROAD

LONDON ROAD

HOW TO GET THERE

Meadowbank Stadium can be reached by the following routes:
BUSES: A frequent service of buses pass close to the ground and the following can be boarded in Princes Street, St. Andrew Square or Leith Street : Eastern Scottish – C1, C5, C6, 34/35, 42/46, 104, 106, 107, 108, 112, 113, 124,125, 129, 130 and 137. Ian Glass – 7, 8 and 12. Lothian Region Transport – 4, 5,15, 26, 34/35, 42/46, 43, 44, 44A, 45, 51, 85 and 86. Lowland Scottish – 104,106, 124 and125.
TRAINS: Trains from all over the country can be taken into Edinburgh Waverly Station and from there supporters can take any of the above buses to the Stadium.
CARS: Meadowbank Stadium is located in London Road just 1 mile to the East of Princes St. and approx. 1/2 mile from Easter Rd. Car parking facilities are good, with accommodation for 600 spaces at Meadowbank Sports Centre. Visiting supporters' coaches are advised to park in Lower London Road to the immediate South West of the Stadium.

QUEEN'S PARK

Hampden Park, Letherby Drive,
Mount Florida, Glasgow, G42 9BA

PRESIDENT
Malcolm Mackay

COMMITTEE
W. Lindsay Ross, M.A., LL.B.
(Treasurer)
Martin B. Smith, LL.B., N.P.
Peter G. Buchanan, John Campbell
William Omand, Austin Reilly
James Nicholson, H. Gordon Wilson
A. Kenneth C. Harvey
Andrew McGlennan

SECRETARY
Alistair MacKay

COACH
Hugh McCann

ASSISTANT COACH
Andrew McGlennan

CLUB DOCTOR
Alan S. Hutchison

PHYSIOTHERAPIST
Robert C. Findlay

CHIEF SCOUT
William S. Burgess

STADIUM FOREMAN
Norman Henderson

KIT MANAGER
Sandy McNaughton

PAVILION ATTENDENT
Harry McGee

COMMERCIAL MANAGER
Ms. Carol J. Cairns
0141-649 9256

TELEPHONES
Ground 0141-632 1275
Fax 0141-636 1612

CLUB SHOP
Home matches only – Hampden Park
(Police Building at end of West Stand)
2.15 p.m. – 3.00 p.m. and 4.45 p.m.
– 5.00 p.m. on home matchdays

OFFICIAL SUPPORTERS CLUB
c/o Secretary, Keith McAllister,
58 Brunton Street,
Glasgow G44 3NQ

TEAM CAPTAIN
Graeme Elder

SHIRT SPONSOR
British Engine Insurance Ltd

LIST OF PLAYERS 1995-96

SURNAME	FIRST NAME	MIDDLE NAME	DATE OF BIRTH	PLACE OF BIRTH	DATE OF SIGNING	HEIGHT FT INS	WEIGHT ST LBS	PREVIOUS CLUB
Arbuckle	David		12/08/73	Bellshill	23/06/95	5 10.0	11 5	Gartferry Amateur
Brodie	David		04/01/71	Hardgate	22/09/93	5 10.0	11 11	Glenwood Amateurs
Bruce	Craig	David W.	20/11/73	Glasgow	23/06/95	6 2.0	12 9	Knightswood Juveniles
Bruce	Gordon		10/07/75	Edinburgh	23/06/95	5 11.0	11 12	Stoneyburn Juniors
Callan	Dominic		20/09/66	Glasgow	18/11/94	5 10.0	10 7	Vale of Leven
Caven	Ross		04/08/65	Glasgow	12/06/93	6 0.0	12 0	Possil Y.M.C.A.
Chalmers	James		03/02/70	Glasgow	31/07/95	6 0.0	11 4	Yoker Athletic
Connolly	Paul		15/08/76	Paisley	23/06/95	5 8.0	11 0	Queen's Park U'18s
Edgar	Scott		10/06/76	Glasgow	27/07/94	6 4.0	13 0	Milngavie Wanderers
Elder	Graeme		21/11/61	Glasgow	12/06/93	6 1.0	13 0	Drumchapel Y.M.C.A.
Ferguson	Paul		10/09/73	Glasgow	25/03/94	6 0.0	10 7	Wolves B.C.
Ferry	Daniel		31/01/77	Glasgow	23/06/95	5 7.0	11 4	Queen's Park U'18s
Fraser	Robert	Scott	02/10/67	Paisley	31/03/95	6 0.0	12 0	Renfrew Juniors
Graham	David		27/01/71	Bellshill	31/07/93	5 10.0	10 8	Queen's Park Youth
Kennedy	Kenneth	Leslie	11/03/77	Edinburgh	29/06/95	6 4.0	11 6	Bothkennar Y.M. U'18s
Kerr	Gary		24/02/74	Paisley	12/06/93	5 11.0	11 0	Hamilton Academical
MacLeod	Colin	Scott	09/09/75	Stirling	23/06/95	6 2.0	12 9	Forth Valley U'21s
Matchett	John		10/10/75	Glasgow	26/11/93	5 2.0	9 12	Clydebank B.C.
Maxwell	Ian		02/05/75	Glasgow	24/07/93	6 3.0	12 5	Unattached
McCusker	John		26/07/68	Bellshill	09/08/95	5 11.0	11 2	Dalziel H.S.F.P.
McGoldrick	Kevin		12/05/72	Glasgow	03/09/94	5 10.0	11 7	Campsie Black Watch
McGrath	Dennis	John M.	29/01/74	Stirling	23/06/95	6 2.0	11 12	Forth Valley U'21s
McInally	Anthony	Charles	24/02/68	Glasgow	12/07/95	5 8.0	11 0	Dalziel H.S.F.P.
McPhee	Brian		23/10/70	Glasgow	24/07/95	5 10.0	11 4	Rutherglen Amateurs
Orr	Garry		27/11/73	Glasgow	12/06/93	5 4.0	10 10	Dundee United
Porter	Craig		10/07/71	Bellshill	23/06/95	5 8.0	11 2	Airdrie Central Amateurs
Wilson	Derek	William	30/05/76	Bellshill	03/09/94	5 10.0	11 6	Airdrieonians

MILESTONES

YEAR OF FORMATION: 1867
MOST CAPPED PLAYER: Walter Arnott
NO. OF CAPS: 14
MOST LEAGUE POINTS IN A SEASON: 57 (Division 2 – Season 1922/23)
MOST LEAGUE GOALS SCORED BY A PLAYER IN A SEASON: William Martin (Season 1937/38)
NO. OF GOALS SCORED: 30
RECORD ATTENDANCE: 149,547 (Scotland v England – 17.4.1937)
RECORD VICTORY: 16-0 (-v- St. Peters – Scottish Cup 29.8.1885)
RECORD DEFEAT: 0-9 (-v- Motherwell – Division 1, 29.4.1930)

SEASON TICKET INFORMATION

Seated
Centre/West Stand   Adult £60
                     Juvenile/OAP £30

LEAGUE ADMISSION PRICES

Seated
Adult £4
Juvenile/OAP £2

CLUB FACTFILE 1994/95
RESULTS .. APPEARANCES .. SCORERS

The SPIDERS

Small bold figures denote goalscorers. † denotes opponent's own goal.

Date	Venue	Opponents	Result	Mochrie D.	Kavanagh J.	Stevenson C.	Kerr G.	Maxwell I.	Orr G.	Brodie D.	Fitzpatrick S.	Edgar S.	Rodden J.	Graham D.	Bradley R.	McPhee E.	Orr J.	McCormick S.	Elder C.	Lynch M.	Caven R.	McGoldrick K.	Chalmers J.	Callan D.	Ferguson P.	Matchett J.	Campbell S.	Smith C.	McFarane R.	Wilson C.	Fraser R.
Aug 13	H	Forfar Athletic	1-2	1	2	3	4	5	6¹	7	8	9	10	11	12	14															
20	A	Caledonian Thistle	4-0	1		3	4	5²	6¹		7	9	10	8¹	11	12		2													
27	H	Albion Rovers	2-1	1		3	4	5	6	7	8		11¹	10¹				2	9												
Sep 3	H	Arbroath	1-1	1		3	7	5	6¹		8	14	10	9				2	11	4	12										
10	H	Cowdenbeath	0-3	1		3	8	5	6	7		14	10	11	12			2	9	4											
24	A	Montrose	1-1	1		3	4	5	6	7	8			10¹				2	9	11											
Oct 1	H	Ross County	3-1	1		3	4	5	6¹	7	8¹	12	11	10				2	9¹		14										
8	A	East Stirlingshire	2-3	1		3	4	5¹	7	6		12	11	10¹				2	9		8										
15	H	Alloa	0-1	1	2			5	8	9	6	3	11	4	10					7	14										
22	A	Forfar Athletic	0-2	1				5	12	2		9	3	8	10	4				6	7	11									
29	A	Albion Rovers	2-3					5	14¹	2		10	3	8	9	4				6	7	11¹	1								
Nov 5	H	Caledonian Thistle	0-2			3		5		14	10			9		2	7	4	6	8	11	1	12								
12	A	Cowdenbeath	0-2			3		5		7				12		2	9	4	8	10	11	1	6								
19	H	Arbroath	0-4			3		5		7	14			9		2	12	4	8	10	11	1	6								
26	H	Montrose	1-1	13			4	3		6	8		10	9		2	14	5		7¹	11	1	12								
Dec 3	A	Ross County	0-2				4	3		6	8		10	9		2	14	5		7	11	1									
26	H	East Stirlingshire	2-3				14	3	7	11		12	9	6	4	2		5		8	10⁴	1									
31	A	Alloa	3-2				4	3¹	7		11¹		6		14	2		5		10	9	1	8¹								
Jan 2	H	Albion Rovers	0-0				4	3	6	12		10	9			11	2	5		8		1	7								
14	A	Forfar Athletic	0-3				4	5	7		12		14	9	2			10		1	8	3	6	11							
21	H	Caledonian Thistle	4-1				4	5¹	9¹			14¹	6	12¹	2			10	11	1	7	3		8							
Feb 4	H	Cowdenbeath	1-0				4	5	7			14	6	12	2			10¹	9	1	8	3		11							
15	A	Arbroath	1-3				4	5	11¹		12	8	9		2	14		10		1	7	3	6								
18	A	Montrose	2-2				12	5	9		11	6¹	14		2			8	10	1	7¹	3			4						
25	H	Ross County	1-2				4	5	9		8	14	12		2	11¹		10		1	7	3	6								
Mar 11	H	Alloa	2-1				3	5	9		6		11¹		2	10¹	4	8		1	7							7			
18	A	Cowdenbeath	3-1				11	6	7		3		10¹	4	9²	5		8	14	1				12	2						
25	H	Arbroath	2-3				11	6	7		3		10¹	4	9¹	5		8	14	1				12	2						
Apr 1	A	Ross County	0-1				4	6	7		14	3	10		5			9	1	2	11			12	8						
11	H	Montrose	1-0	1			8¹	6	9		12	3	10	4		5					14	11			2	7					
15	H	East Stirlingshire	†1-0	1			8	6	9		12	3	10	4		5					14	11			2	7					
18	A	East Stirlingshire	2-3	1			11	6¹	7		3	10		4	9¹	5		14						2	8						
22	A	Alloa	1-0	1			11¹	6	7			10		4	9	5			14	12				3	2	8					
29	H	Forfar Athletic	0-2	1			11	6	7			10		4	9	5			14	12				3	2	8					
May 6	A	Albion Rovers	2-0				5	10¹			3		14¹	4	9			8	11	1	12	6			2	7					
13	A	Caledonian Thistle	1-1					10			3		12	4	9¹			8	11	1	7	6	5		14	2					
TOTAL FULL APPEARANCES				15	9	1	27	34	28	8	15	8	10	29	4	22	34	18	19	6	22	16	21	12	10	7	1	2	1	10	7
TOTAL SUB APPEARANCES				(1)			(2)		(3)			(7)	(7)		(3)	(11)		(4)		(1)	(3)	(5)		(3)	(3)		(3)			(1)	
TOTAL GOALS SCORED							2	6	7	1	1	1	2	3			7		8		2	3	2							

HAMPDEN PARK

CAPACITY: 38,113 (All Seated)
PITCH DIMENSIONS: 115 yds x 75 yds
FACILITIES FOR DISABLED SUPPORTERS: Capacity 222 – Wheelchair 54, Ambulant Seated 48, Ambulant Standing 120.

HOW TO GET THERE

The following routes may be used to reach Hampden Park:

TRAINS: There are two stations within five minutes walk of the ground. Mount Florida Station, on the Cathcart Circle and King's Park Station. A 15 minute service runs from Glasgow Central.

BUSES: Services to approach Mount Florida end of Stadium: From City Centre: 5, 5A, 5B, M5, M14, 31, 37, 66, 66A, 66B, 66C; From Govan Cross; 34; From Drumchapel: 96, 97, Circular Service: 89, 90; G.C.T. Service: 1; Services to approach King's Park end of Stadium; From City Centre: 12, 12A, 74; Circular Service: 89, 90; G.C.T. Service: 19.

CARS: Car parking facilities are available in the car park at the front of the Stadium, which is capable of holding 1,200 vehicles. Side streets can also be used on major occasions.

ROSS COUNTY

Victoria Park, Jubilee Road,
Dingwall, Ross-shire, IV15 9QW

CHAIRMAN
Hector MacLennan

VICE-CHAIRMAN
Donald MacBean

DIRECTORS
Kenneth D. Cameron
Douglas K. Harper
Roy J. MacGregor, Ian Dingwall
Gordon M. R. Macrae, David R. Roan
Alistair Mackintosh

SECRETARY
Donald MacBean

OFFICE SECRETARY
Mrs. Cathy Caird

MANAGER
Robert Wilson

ASSISTANT MANAGER
Graham MacKenzie

RESERVE COACH
Donald Stuart

YOUTH COACH
Tommy Regan

CLUB DOCTOR
Dr. Gordon Bruce

PHYSIOTHERAPISTS
Chick Ogilvie & Dougie Sim

S.F.A. COMMUNITY COACH
Ross Jack

**GROUND CONVENOR AND
SAFETY OFFICER**
Douglas Harper

GROUNDSMAN
Dougie MacDonald

KIT MAN
David Hamilton

COMMERCIAL MANAGER
Brian Campbell
(01349) 862253

TELEPHONES
Ground/Ticket Office (01349) 862253
Fax (01349) 866277

CLUB SHOP
Situated at Ground

OFFICIAL SUPPORTERS CLUB
George Shiels, 4 Tulloch Place,
Dingwall (01349) 865135

TEAM CAPTAIN
Cameron Robertson

SHIRT SPONSOR
MacGregor Group

LIST OF PLAYERS 1995-96

SURNAME	FIRST NAME	MIDDLE NAME	DATE OF BIRTH	PLACE OF BIRTH	DATE OF SIGNING	HEIGHT FT INS	WEIGHT ST LBS	PREVIOUS CLUB
Bellshaw	Johnston	Cunningham	06/12/63	Dingwall	18/11/94	6 1.0	13 4	Inverness Caledonian
Campbell	Gary		14/10/70	Inverness	08/08/94	5 9.0	10 6	Invergordon
Connelly	Gordon	Paul	20/09/67	Stirling	12/08/94	5 7.0	11 2	Dunfermline Athletic
Crainie	Daniel		24/05/62	Kilsyth	17/08/95	5 8.0	10 11	Ballymena United
Ferries	Keith		16/08/65	Inverness	08/08/94	5 8.0	10 10	Elgin City
Furphy	William		07/05/66	London	23/09/94	5 11.0	11 7	Elgin City
Grant	Brian		13/12/68	Inverness	08/08/94	5 10.0	11 0	Brechin City
Herd	William	David	03/09/65	Buckhaven	08/08/94	5 11.0	12 0	Cowdenbeath
Hutchison	Stephen		18/09/70	Glasgow	08/08/94	5 11.5	12 10	Falkirk
Mackay	David		17/09/75	Dingwall	16/09/94	5 11.0	12 1	Ross County B.C.
MacLeod	Alexander	James	01/02/68	Inverness	08/08/94	6 0.0	12 0	Dingwall Thistle
MacLeod	Andrew	Donald	14/08/69	Glasgow	08/08/94	5 8.0	10 2	Fortuna Sittard
MacMillan	Donald		12/12/73	Helmsdale	12/08/94	5 11.5	12 4	Brora Rangers
MacPherson	Jamie		10/12/70	Sydney	08/08/94	6 0.0	11 6	Inverness Clachnacuddin
McFee	Russell		11/02/71	Arbroath	28/10/94	5 10.0	10 8	Invergordon
Milne	Colin	Richard	23/10/74	Aberdeen	02/08/95	6 1.0	12 0	Montrose
Reid	Craig		16/02/74	Aberdeen	08/08/94	5 10.0	10 12	Unattached
Robertson	Cameron	John	03/02/61	Luton	08/08/94	5 11.0	12 0	Invergordon
Somerville	Christopher Ian		08/12/67	Larne	08/08/94	5 5.0	10 0	Brora Rangers
Watt	William	George	08/10/76	Inverness	01/08/95	6 0.0	10 7	Unattached
Williamson	Robert		25/04/69	Inverness	08/08/94	5 10.0	11 4	Inverness Clachnacuddin

MILESTONES

YEAR OF FORMATION: 1929
MOST LEAGUE POINTS IN A SEASON: 60 (Third Division – Season 1994/95) (3 Points for a Win)
MOST LEAGUE GOALS SCORED BY A PLAYER IN A SEASON: Brian Grant
NO. OF GOALS SCORED: 12 (Season 1994/95)
RECORD ATTENDANCE: 8,000 (-v- Rangers – Scottish Cup 28.2.66)
RECORD VICTORY: 11-0 (-v- St. Cuthbert Wanderers – Scottish Cup 1994)
RECORD DEFEAT: 1-10 (-v- Inverness Thistle – Highland League)

SEASON TICKET INFORMATION

Seated
Adult £83
Juvenile/OAP.......................................£50
Standing
Adult £68
Juvenile/OAP.......................................£34

LEAGUE ADMISSION PRICES

Seated
Adult £6
Juvenile/OAP.......................................£3.50
Standing
Adult £5
Juvenile/OAP.......................................£2.50

S·F·L

The COUNTY

Date	Venue	Opponents	Result	Hutchison S.	Somerville C.	Campbell C.	Williamson R.	Macleod Alexander	Macleod Andrew	Ferries K.	Grant B.	MacPherson	Herd W.	Wilson B.	Connelly G.	Robertson C.	Duff A.	Reid C.	MacMillan C.	Furphy W.	Mackay D.	McFee R.	Belshaw J.	Stewart R.
Aug 13	A	Cowdenbeath	2-0	1	2	3	4	5	6	7	8	9[1]	10[1]	11	12	14								
20	A	East Stirlingshire	2-2	1	2	3	4	5	6	7	8	9[1]	10	11[1]	12		14							
27	H	Caledonian Thistle	1-3	1	2	3	4	5	6[1]	7	8	9	10	11	12									
Sep 3	H	Alloa	3-3	1	2		4[1]	5		7	8[1]	9[1]	6		10	11	12	3						
10	A	Montrose	2-0		2	6	4	5		7	8		10		11[1]		9[1]	3	1					
24	H	Arbroath	1-4	1	2	6	4			11	7	14	10[1]		5		9	3		8				
Oct 1	A	Queen's Park	1-3	1	2	6	4	5		7	12	8	9[1]		11		14	3	13	10				
8	A	Forfar Athletic	0-1		2	6	4	5		10	7	8			11		9	3	1	12	15			
15	H	Albion Rovers	3-0		2	3	4[2]	5		11	8				10[1]		9	7	1	6	14			
22	H	Cowdenbeath	4-0		2	3	4	5		11[2]	8[2]				10		9	7	1	6	12	14		
29	A	Caledonian Thistle	0-0		2	3	4			11	8				10	5	9	7	1	6	12	14		
Nov 5	A	East Stirlingshire	1-4			3	4			11[1]	8	14			10	5	9	7	1	6		2		
12	H	Montrose	0-1				4		9	7	8		11		10			3	1	6	2	14		5
19	A	Alloa	1-1	1	2		4		9	7	8		12		10			3		6	11[1]	14		5
26	A	Arbroath	1-0	1	2		4		9	7	8		12		10		14	3		6	11			5[1]
Dec 3	H	Queen's Park	†2-0	1	2		4		9	7	8		6		10[1]		14	3		11	12			5
31	A	Albion Rovers	1-0	1	2		4[1]			7	8	9	6		10	12	14	3		11				5
Jan 2	H	Caledonian Thistle	3-1	1	2		4			7	8[2]	9[1]	11		10			3		6				5
11	H	Forfar Athletic	2-1	1	2		4		14	7	8	9[1]	11		10[1]			3		6				5
14	A	Cowdenbeath	3-0	1	2		4		14	11	7[2]	8[1]	9		10			3		6	12			5
21	A	East Stirlingshire	2-0	1	2		4[1]		9	7	8		11		10		14	3		6	12			5
Feb 4	A	Montrose	1-1	1			4		14	7	8[1]	9	11		10			3		6	2			5
11	H	Alloa	6-0	1	2		4		11[2]	7	8[2]	9			10[1]		14[1]	3		6	12			5
18	H	Arbroath	0-1	1	2		4		11	7	8	14	9		10			3		6				5
25	A	Queen's Park	2-1	1	2		4[1]		11	7	8[1]	9			10		14	3		6				5
Mar 4	A	Forfar Athletic	2-4	1	2		4		11[1]	7	8[1]	9			10			3		6				5
25	A	Alloa	†1-1	1			4		11	7	8	9			10	12	14	3		6	2			5
29	H	Albion Rovers	4-1	1			4	12		7[1]	8		11		10[1]		9[1]	3		6[1]	2		5	14
Apr 1	H	Queen's Park	1-0	1			4	3	14	7	8		11		10		9[1]	2		6	12			5
8	A	Arbroath	1-0	1			4	12	11	7	14	8			10		9[1]	3		6				5
15	H	Forfar Athletic	0-1	1	2		4		11	7	14	8			10		9	3		6				5
19	H	Montrose	0-3	1	2		4	3	11	7	8	12	9		10		14			6				5
22	A	Albion Rovers	2-1	1	2		4[1]	3	11[1]	7	8	9			10		14	12		6				5
29	H	Cowdenbeath	2-0	1			4		11[1]	7	8[1]	9			10		14	2		6				5
May 6	A	Caledonian Thistle	0-3	1			4	3	11	7	8	12	9		10		14	2		6				5
13	H	East Stirlingshire	2-3	1	2		4	10[1]			8	9[1]			11	12		3	13	6	7			5
TOTAL FULL APPEARANCES				29	28	11	35	15	27	30	32	13	28	3	28	6	11	31	7	28	9	1		24
TOTAL SUB APPEARANCES							(3)	(3)	(2)	(3)	(3)	(2)		(3)	(3)	(15)	(1)	(2)		(7)	(7)		(1)
TOTAL GOALS SCORED							7	1	9	3	12	8	1	1	6	1	5				1	1		1

Small bold figures denote goalscorers.   † denotes opponent's own goal.

VICTORIA PARK

CAPACITY: 6,500; Seated 1,500, Standing 5,000

PITCH DIMENSIONS: 110 yds x 75 yds

FACILITIES FOR DISABLED SUPPORTERS: Areas in Main Stand and terracing. Toilet facilities are also available.

JUBILEE PARK ROAD

HOW TO GET THERE

The following routes may be used to reach Victoria Park:

TRAINS: The nearest mainline station is Inverness and fans travelling from the South should alight and board a train that takes them direct to Dingwall Station.

BUSES: Regular buses on a daily basis from Glasgow, Edinburgh and Perth.

CARS: The major trunk roads, A9 and A96, connect Dingwall with the North, the South and the East.

Scottish Football League – Final Tables 1994/95

PREMIER DIVISION CHAMPIONSHIP

	P	W	L	D	F	A	Pts
Rangers	36	20	7	9	60	35	69
Motherwell	36	14	10	12	50	50	54
Hibernian	36	12	7	17	49	37	53
Celtic	36	11	7	18	39	33	51
Falkirk	36	12	12	12	48	47	48
Heart of Midlothian	36	12	17	7	44	51	43
Kilmarnock	36	11	15	10	40	48	43
Partick Thistle	36	10	13	13	40	50	43
** Aberdeen	36	10	15	11	43	46	41
Dundee United	36	9	18	9	40	56	36

FIRST DIVISION CHAMPIONSHIP

	P	W	L	D	F	A	Pts
Raith Rovers	36	19	5	12	54	32	69
** Dunfermline Athletic	36	18	4	14	63	32	68
Dundee	36	20	8	8	65	36	68
Airdrieonians	36	17	9	10	50	33	61
St. Johnstone	36	14	8	14	59	39	56
Hamilton Academical	36	14	15	7	42	48	49
St. Mirren	36	8	16	12	34	50	36
Clydebank	36	8	17	11	33	47	35
Ayr United	36	6	19	11	31	58	29
Stranraer	36	4	27	5	25	81	17

** In the Premier Division Play-off matches Aberdeen F.C. defeated Dunfermline Athletic F.C. by 6 goals to 2 on aggregate.

SECOND DIVISION CHAMPIONSHIP

	P	W	L	D	F	A	Pts
Greenock Morton	36	18	8	10	55	33	64
Dumbarton	36	17	10	9	57	35	60
Stirling Albion	36	17	12	7	54	43	58
Stenhousemuir	36	14	8	14	46	39	56
Berwick Rangers	36	15	11	10	52	46	55
Clyde	36	14	12	10	53	48	52
Queen of the South	36	11	14	11	46	51	44
East Fife	36	11	15	10	48	56	43
* Meadowbank Thistle	36	11	20	5	32	54	35
^ Brechin City	36	6	24	6	22	60	24

* 3 points deducted for fielding an ineligible player in the match Brechin City v. Meadowbank Thistle on 13th August, 1994 and the goals scored in this match were expunged from the records.

^ In the match Brechin City v. Meadowbank Thistle on 13th August, 1994 the goals scored in this match were expunged from the records.

THIRD DIVISION CHAMPIONSHIP

	P	W	L	D	F	A	Pts
Forfar Athletic	36	25	6	5	67	33	80
Montrose	36	20	9	7	69	32	67
Ross County	36	18	12	6	59	44	60
East Stirlingshire	36	18	13	5	61	50	59
Alloa	36	15	12	9	50	45	54
Caledonian Thistle	36	12	15	9	48	61	45
Arbroath	36	13	18	5	51	62	44
Queen's Park	36	12	18	6	46	57	42
Cowdenbeath	36	11	18	7	48	60	40
Albion Rovers	36	5	28	3	27	82	18

PREMIER RESERVE LEAGUE

	P	W	L	D	F	A	Pts
Celtic	36	21	5	10	76	28	73
Motherwell	36	16	8	12	56	42	60
Dundee United	36	18	13	5	55	53	59
Partick Thistle	36	15	12	9	59	49	54
Heart of Midlothian	36	13	12	11	43	47	50
Hibernian	36	11	14	11	39	49	44
Aberdeen	36	10	14	12	39	44	42
Rangers	36	10	16	10	40	49	40
Kilmarnock	36	11	20	5	45	63	38
Falkirk	36	9	20	7	46	74	34

RESERVE LEAGUE EAST

	P	W	L	D	F	A	Pts
Raith Rovers	24	18	5	1	62	29	55
St. Johnstone	24	17	4	3	63	25	54
Dunfermline Athletic	24	14	8	2	52	40	44
Dundee	24	13	9	2	52	33	41
Hibernian	24	10	7	7	40	32	37
Meadowbank Thistle	24	11	9	4	46	51	37
Arbroath	24	11	12	1	48	43	34
Alloa	24	10	10	4	42	49	34
Cowdenbeath	24	6	11	7	30	38	25
East Fife	24	6	12	6	36	61	24
Brechin City	24	5	13	6	29	46	21
Montrose	24	5	15	4	24	50	19
Forfar Athletic	24	5	16	3	29	56	18

RESERVE LEAGUE WEST

	P	W	L	D	F	A	Pts
Rangers	28	20	3	5	66	25	65
St. Mirren	28	18	4	6	66	29	60
Clydebank	28	17	6	5	50	34	56
Hamilton Academical	28	15	11	2	52	34	47
Airdrieonians	28	13	9	6	43	48	45
Stirling Albion	28	13	11	4	46	37	43
Stranraer	28	11	12	5	43	46	38
Clyde	28	11	13	4	51	38	37
Queen's Park	28	10	12	6	36	44	36
Queen of the South	28	9	14	5	33	43	32
Ayr United	28	8	13	7	34	45	31
Dumbarton	28	9	15	4	45	59	31
Greenock Morton	28	7	12	9	31	42	30
Albion Rovers	28	6	18	4	33	70	22
Stenhousemuir	28	4	18	6	22	57	18

YOUTH DIVISION

	P	W	L	D	F	A	Pts
Celtic	24	19	4	1	80	23	58
Aberdeen	24	17	3	4	72	25	55
Rangers	24	15	2	7	82	20	52
Dundee United	24	16	4	4	70	17	52
St. Johnstone	24	12	4	8	49	22	44
Heart of Midlothian	24	11	11	2	71	26	35
Dundee	24	10	10	4	56	46	34
Partick Thistle	24	7	9	8	36	40	29
Cowdenbeath	24	8	11	5	33	69	29
Greenock Morton	24	5	15	4	30	54	19
Queen of the South	24	5	17	2	24	65	17
Berwick Rangers	24	3	16	5	24	88	14
Alloa	24	0	22	2	10	142	2

Bell's League Championship Play-off Matches

FIRST LEG
Sunday, 21st May, 1995

ABERDEEN 3
D. Shearer (2), S. Glass

DUNFERMLINE ATHLETIC 1
C. Robertson

Aberdeen: T. Snelders, S. McKimmie, S. Wright, B. Grant, B. Irvine, G. Smith, P. Hetherston, D. Shearer, J. Miller, S. Thomson, S. Glass
Substitutes not used: J. Inglis R. McKinnon, M. Watt (Goalkeeper)

Dunfermline Athletic: G. Van De Kamp, J. McNamara, D. Fleming, N. McCathie, A. Tod, P. Smith, I. Den Bieman, C. Robertson, A. Moore (G. Shaw), S. Petrie, M. McCulloch (A. Hawkins)
Substitute not used: I. Westwater (Goalkeeper)

SECOND LEG
Thursday, 25th May, 1995

DUNFERMLINE ATHLETIC 1 ABERDEEN 3
P. Smith   J. Miller, W. Dodds, S. Glass

Dunfermline Athletic: G. Van De Kamp, J. McNamara, D. Fleming (A. Hawkins), N. McCathie, A. Tod, P. Smith, I. Den Bieman, C. Robertson, A. Moore, S. Petrie, M. McCulloch (G. Shaw)
Substitute not used: I. Westwater (Goalkeeper)

Aberdeen: T. Snelders, S. McKimmie, S. Wright, B. Grant, B. Irvine (J. Inglis), G. Smith, P. Hetherston, D. Shearer, J. Miller (P. Kane), W. Dodds, S. Glass
Substitute not used: M. Watt (Goalkeeper)

Aberdeen won 6-2 on aggregate and retained their place in the Premier Division for Season 1995/96

Reserve League Cup - Season 1994/95

PRELIMINARY ROUND
8th September 1994
RAITH ROVERS 4   ALLOA 2

FIRST ROUND
15th August 1994
CLYDEBANK 0   GREENOCK MORTON 1 (AET)
ST. JOHNSTONE 2   CLYDE 0
18th August 1994
HAMILTON ACADEMICAL 2   AYR UNITED 3
4th September 1994
STRANRAER 1   ARBROATH 4
15th September 1994
RAITH ROVERS 1   DUNFERMLINE ATHLETIC 2
19th September 1994
BRECHIN CITY 3   COWDENBEATH 1
21st September 1994
FORFAR ATHLETIC 0   MEADOWBANK THISTLE 1
ST. MIRREN 3   MONTROSE 0 (AET)
22nd September 1994
STIRLING ALBION 1   ALBION ROVERS 5
28th September 1994
AIRDRIEONIANS 3   STENHOUSEMUIR 2
QUEEN OF THE SOUTH 4   EAST FIFE 1
29th September 1994
DUNDEE 1   QUEEN'S PARK 3
(AET–1-1 After 90 minutes)

SECOND ROUND
19th October 1994
ARBROATH 2   ST. JOHNSTONE 0
QUEEN'S PARK 0   GREENOCK MORTON 6
24th October 1994
ALBION ROVERS 3   AYR UNITED 4
(AET–3-3 After 90 minutes)
BRECHIN CITY 1   ST. MIRREN 4
26th October 1994
DUNFERMLINE ATHLETIC 2   AIRDRIEONIANS 1
QUEEN OF THE SOUTH 2   MEADOWBANK THISTLE 1

THIRD ROUND
12th November 1994
ABERDEEN 4   DUNDEE UNITED 1
21st November 1994
HIBERNIAN 1   AYR UNITED 0

KILMARNOCK 1   PARTICK THISTLE 2
QUEEN OF THE SOUTH 0   ST. MIRREN 3
22nd November 1994
ARBROATH 0   MOTHERWELL 4
1st December 1994
FALKIRK 1   HEART OF MIDLOTHIAN 0
6th December 1994
GREENOCK MORTON 3   DUNFERMLINE ATHLETIC 2
(AET–1-1 After 90 minutes)
17th December 1994
CELTIC 1   RANGERS 0

FOURTH ROUND
11th January 1995
PARTICK THISTLE 0   ABERDEEN 3
24th January 1995
CELTIC 3   ST. MIRREN 0
HIBERNIAN 0   FALKIRK 1
30th March 1995
GREENOCK MORTON 1   MOTHERWELL 2
(AET–1-1 After 90 minutes)

SEMI–FINALS
6th March 1995
FALKIRK 1   CELTIC 4
25th April 1995
ABERDEEN 1   MOTHERWELL 1
(AET–1-1 After 90 minutes)
Aberdeen won 5-4 on Kicks from the Penalty Mark

FINAL
Tuesday, 9th May, 1995
Pittodrie Stadium, Aberdeen
ABERDEEN 0   CELTIC 2

Aberdeen: M. Watt, G. McCulloch, C. Woodthorpe, K. Gilbert, J. Inglis (M. Kpedekpo), C. Ireland, R. Bell, D. Wyness (M. Buchan), S. Thomson, W. Dodds, D. Winnie
Substitute not used: D. Stillie (Goalkeeper)

Celtic: G. Marshall, M. McNally, B. Smith, M. Mackay, J. Slavin, G. Carberry, P. Byrne (G. White), S. Gray, J. O'Neill, C. Nicholas, J. McQuilken
Substitutes not used: A. Paterson, S. Kerr (Goalkeeper)

Scorers: Celtic: G. White, C. Nicholas (Pen)
Referee: A. C. Gemmill (Linlithgow) **Attendance:** 1,697

Scottish League Champions since inception

SEASON	DIVISION ONE	POINTS	DIVISION TWO	POINTS
1890/91	Dumbarton/Rangers	29	(No Competition)	
1891/92	Dumbarton	37	(No Competition)	
1892/93	Celtic	29	(No Competition)	
1893/94	Celtic	29	Hibernian	29
1894/95	Heart of Midlothian	31	Hibernian	30
1895/96	Celtic	30	Abercorn	27
1896/97	Heart of Midlothian	28	Partick Thistle	31
1897/98	Celtic	33	Kilmarnock	29
1898/99	Rangers	36	Kilmarnock	32
1899-1900	Rangers	32	Partick Thistle	29
1900/01	Rangers	35	St. Bernards	25
1901/02	Rangers	28	Port Glasgow	32
1902/03	Hibernian	37	Airdrieonians	35
1903/04	Third Lanark	43	Hamilton Academical	37
1904/05	Celtic (after play-off)	41	Clyde	32
1905/06	Celtic	49	Leith Athletic	34
1906/07	Celtic	55	St. Bernards	32
1907/08	Celtic	55	Raith Rovers	30
1908/09	Celtic	51	Abercorn	31
1909/10	Celtic	54	Leith Athletic	33
1910/11	Rangers	52	Dumbarton	31
1911/12	Rangers	51	Ayr United	35
1912/13	Rangers	53	Ayr United	34
1913/14	Celtic	65	Cowdenbeath	31
1914/15	Celtic	65	Cowdenbeath	37
1915/16	Celtic	67	(No Competition)	
1916/17	Celtic	64	(No Competition)	
1917/18	Rangers	56	(No Competition)	
1918/19	Celtic	58	(No Competition)	
1919/20	Rangers	71	(No Competition)	
1920/21	Rangers	76	(No Competition)	
1921/22	Celtic	67	Alloa	60
1922/23	Rangers	55	Queen's Park	57
1923/24	Rangers	59	St. Johnstone	56
1924/25	Rangers	60	Dundee United	50
1925/26	Celtic	58	Dunfermline Athletic	59
1926/27	Rangers	56	Bo'ness	56
1927/28	Rangers	60	Ayr United	54
1928/29	Rangers	67	Dundee United	51
1929/30	Rangers	60	Leith Athletic*	57
1930/31	Rangers	60	Third Lanark	61
1931/32	Motherwell	66	East Stirlingshire*	55
1932/33	Rangers	62	Hibernian	54
1933/34	Rangers	66	Albion Rovers	45
1934/35	Rangers	55	Third Lanark	52
1935/36	Celtic	66	Falkirk	59
1936/37	Rangers	61	Ayr United	54
1937/38	Celtic	61	Raith Rovers	59
1938/39	Rangers	59	Cowdenbeath	60
1939/40	(No Competition)		(No Competition)	
1940/41	(No Competition)		(No Competition)	
1941/42	(No Competition)		(No Competition)	
1942/43	(No Competition)		(No Competition)	
1943/44	(No Competition)		(No Competition)	
1944/45	(No Competition)		(No Competition)	

SEASON	DIVISION ONE	POINTS	DIVISION TWO	POINTS
1945/46	(No Competition)		(No Competition)	
1946/47	Rangers	46	Dundee	45
1947/48	Hibernian	48	East Fife	53
1948/49	Rangers	46	Raith Rovers*	42
1949/50	Rangers	50	Morton	47
1950/51	Hibernian	48	Queen of the South*	45
1951/52	Hibernian	45	Clyde	44
1952/53	Rangers*	43	Stirling Albion	44
1953/54	Celtic	43	Motherwell	45
1954/55	Aberdeen	49	Airdrieonians	46
1955/56	Rangers	52	Queen's Park	54
1956/57	Rangers	55	Clyde	64
1957/58	Heart of Midlothian	62	Stirling Albion	55
1958/59	Rangers	50	Ayr United	60
1959/60	Heart of Midlothian	54	St. Johnstone	53
1960/61	Rangers	51	Stirling Albion	55
1961/62	Dundee	54	Clyde	54
1962/63	Rangers	57	St. Johnstone	55
1963/64	Rangers	55	Morton	67
1964/65	Kilmarnock*	50	Stirling Albion	59
1965/66	Celtic	57	Ayr United	53
1966/67	Celtic	58	Morton	69
1967/68	Celtic	63	St. Mirren	62
1968/69	Celtic	54	Motherwell	64
1969/70	Celtic	57	Falkirk	56
1970/71	Celtic	56	Partick Thistle	56
1971/72	Celtic	60	Dumbarton¥	52
1972/73	Celtic	57	Clyde	56
1973/74	Celtic	53	Airdrieonians	60
1974/75	Rangers	56	Falkirk	54

SEASON	PREMIER DIVISION	POINTS	FIRST DIVISION	POINTS	SECOND DIVISION	POINTS	THIRD DIVISION	POINTS
1975/76	Rangers	54	Partick Thistle	41	Clydebank¥	40		
1976/77	Celtic	55	St. Mirren	62	Stirling Albion	55		
1977/78	Rangers	55	Morton¥	58	Clyde¥	53		
1978/79	Celtic	48	Dundee	55	Berwick Rangers	54		
1979/80	Aberdeen	48	Heart of Midlothian	53	Falkirk	50		
1980/81	Celtic	56	Hibernian	57	Queen's Park	50		
1981/82	Celtic	55	Motherwell	61	Clyde	59		
1982/83	Dundee United	56	St. Johnstone	55	Brechin City	55		
1983/84	Aberdeen	57	Morton	54	Forfar Athletic	63		
1984/85	Aberdeen	59	Motherwell	50	Montrose	53		
1985/86•	Celtic¥	50	Hamilton Academical	56	Dunfermline Athletic	57		
1986/87•	Rangers	69	Morton	57	Meadowbank Thistle	55		
1987/88•	Celtic	72	Hamilton Academical	56	Ayr United	61		
1988/89§	Rangers	56	Dunfermline Athletic	54	Albion Rovers	50		
1989/90§	Rangers	51	St. Johnstone	58	Brechin City	49		
1990/91§	Rangers	55	Falkirk	54	Stirling Albion	54		
1991/92§	Rangers	72	Dundee	58	Dumbarton	52		
1992/93	Rangers	73	Raith Rovers	65	Clyde	54		
1993/94	Rangers	58	Falkirk	66	Stranraer	56		
1994/95†	Rangers	69	Raith Rovers	69	Greenock Morton	64	Forfar Athletic	80

* *Champions on goal average.* • *Competition known as Fine Fare League.* † *Competition known as Bell's League Championship.*
¥ *Champions on goal difference.* § *Competition known as B & Q League.*

Fife Doubles

Raith Rovers became the first club from outwith Scotland's top division to win the League Cup since their Kingdom neighbours, East Fife, achieved this magnificent feat away back in season 1947-48.

By another incredible coincidence, Raith Rovers, like East Fife, went on to win their championship later the same season to ensure promotion to Scotland's elite division.

Back in 1947 when East Fife defeated Falkirk 4-1, after the first match had ended in a no score draw, the League Cup was just simply referred to as the League Cup. Sponsorship in those early post war years had not even been considered and indeed, the ball used the length and breadth of the country was still brown leather with lace!

However, since those days of cotton shirts, long baggy shorts and toe-capped boots, the game as we now know it, has changed out of all recognition and The League Cup competition is now generously sponsored and has been for several years, firstly by Bell's for a couple of years and later followed by Skol for a lengthy ten year period which helped popularise the tournament once again.

Last season witnessed Coca-Cola take over sponsorship of this famous old competition, as they had already done in England, and Raith Rovers' memorable and indeed first victory in this competition came about in Coca-Cola's inaugural season of sponsorship.

However, we are slightly ahead of ourselves. The Coca-Cola Cup is more than just a chance for clubs to win the first trophy of the season as well as gaining an automatic passport into Europe. It is also an opportunity for the so called smaller clubs to get in among the big-time players and endeavour to make a name for themselves.

First though, they have to take on their fellow peers in the First Round and so it was on Tuesday, 9th August, that East Fife defeated Forfar Athletic, Caledonian Thistle (in what was their first official competitive outing as a Scottish League club) accounted for East Stirlingshire, Meadowbank Thistle won at Stenhousemuir and Montrose won through on penalties at Berwick to get the competition well and truly underway. The Road to Ibrox had begun.

The bigger names entered the fray the following midweek, but it took until the Third Round for the first major

shock to take place and what a shock it turned out to be!

Although St. Johnstone overcame a two goal deficit to defeat Heart of Midlothian 4-2 at Tynecastle and Airdrieonians knocked out neighbours, Motherwell, at Fir Park after extra-time, the real upset of the competition came at Ibrox. Rangers 1 Falkirk 2 was the result that made everyone sit up and take notice with Falkirk striker, Richard Cadette, completely silencing the Rangers fans in the 40,697 crowd with a well taken double. Even a goal from Brian Laudrup couldn't prevent the Brockville club and its fans enjoying a great night.

Although Raith Rovers had taken care of Ross County up in Dingwall by the emphatic margin of five goals to nil and had then beaten Premier outfit, Kilmarnock, 3-2 at Stark's Park, thanks to a Colin Cameron hat-trick, no-one at that stage had taken too much notice of their progress. Indeed, even after Jimmy Nicholl's side defeated St. Johnstone 3-1 in Perth to join Celtic, Aberdeen and Airdrieonians in the Semi-Final draw, cup fever had yet to hit Kirkcaldy.

Celtic had made solid if unspectacular progress to reach the last

four, firstly by accounting for Ayr United down at Somerset Park, thanks to an early strike by Peter Grant, defeating Dundee 2-1 up at Dens Park and then beating Dundee United 1-0 at their adopted home, Hampden Park, with a spectacular strike late on in the game by John Collins.

Aberdeen at the same time, were also beginning to fancy themselves, as they attempted to bring the League Cup trophy back to Pittodrie for the first time in five years.

Early indications were that they would struggle to emulate their 1989 achievement and it was only a late goal from Duncan Shearer that saved their blushes against Stranraer in the Second Round at Pittodrie.

However, they then moved up a gear and disposed of Partick Thistle by five goals to nil at Firhill and then comfortably beat Rangers' conquerors, Falkirk, 4-1 at Brockville.

Meanwhile, Airdrieonians arrived at the Semi-Final stage the nerve racking way by recording a penalty shoot-out victory at Cappielow against Greenock Morton, an extra-time derby win at Fir Park and then a superb 2-1 win at Easter Road against Hibernian, who of course, had been beaten finalists the previous season.

At long last, the Kirkcaldy public woke up to what was happening with their unfashionable side and in as dramatic a Semi-Final that you could hope to see, Jimmy Nicholl's men defeated Airdrieonians in the first ever Semi-Final to be staged at McDiarmid Park, Perth, following a dramatic penalty shoot-out.

A goal from Raith's Ally Graham was cancelled out by the Diamonds' English striker, Steve Cooper, and with the tie evenly poised, Rovers' goalkeeper, Scott Thomson, was sent off for handling the ball just outside the penalty box. Teenager, Brian Potter, with one first team match to his credit, was thrust into the heat of the action and eventually proved to be the hero of the hour. With Davie Kirkwood being substituted to allow Raith a specialist goalkeeper, the Raith Rovers defence, superbly marshalled by Dave Narey, held out and the match moved into the penalty shoot-out. How young Potter rose to the occasion, saving Alan Lawrence's kick to take Raith through to their first Final since 1948.

The following evening, Celtic and

The Coca-Cola Cup

Aberdeen also had to go to extra-time at Ibrox. With both teams allowing the occasion to get the better of them, there were very few chances at either end, however, Brian O'Neil's header at least prevented the tension of a penalty shoot-out to take Celtic a stage closer to winning their first League Cup since season 1982/83.

With Celtic playing their home games at Hampden while Celtic Park was being rebuilt, the League Management Committee decided that the Final would be played at Ibrox. In what proved to be a thrilling affair and a great advert for Scottish football, Stevie Crawford opened the scoring early in the first half

before Andy Walker levelled the score for Celtic before half-time. In a dramatic finale to the regulation 90 minutes, a Charlie Nicholas strike looked certain to secure Celtic's first major domestic trophy since 1989, scoring with seven minutes remaining. However, Raith staged one final push and veteran skipper, Gordon Dalziel, headed an equalising goal two minutes from time to send the match into extra-time.

The 30 minutes of overtime brought no further goals and so the Final moved into a penalty shoot-out. What a dramatic and tension filled occasion it proved to be and as had happened in the Semi-Final, Raith had to thank their goalkeeper again. This time, however, it was Scott Thomson who became the hero of Kirkcaldy when he dived low to his right to knock away the spot kick of an anguished Celtic skipper Paul McStay. Raith Rovers had won 6-5 on penalties in a result that will certainly go down in Scottish football folklore.

11,000 Raith Rovers fans celebrated as skipper, Gordon Dalziel, received the trophy from Coca-Cola President, Penny Hughes. The Cup was Kirkcaldy bound and they haven't stopped celebrating in the streets of Raith since!

**BILL McFARLANE
(Sunday Post)**

Coca-Cola Final – Gordon Dalziel's equaliser

FIRST ROUND

Tuesday, 9th August, 1994

EAST FIFE 1   **FORFAR ATHLETIC 0**
G. Allan

East Fife: E. Wilson, G. Bell, A. Williamson, D. Barron, A. Sneddon, R. Hildersley, J. Cusick (G. Allan), D. Hope, R. Scott (A. Irvine), P. Hunter, R. Gibb

Substitute used: R. Charles (Goalkeeper)

Forfar Athletic: G. Arthur, P. McLaren, I. McPhee, R. Mann, E. Archibald, A. McKillop, H. O'Neill, N. Irvine, G. Lees, D. Bingham, I. Heddle

Substitutes not used: S. Kopel, R. Smith, C. Stephen (Goalkeeper)

EAST STIRLINGSHIRE 0   **CALEDONIAN THISTLE 2**
W. Robertson, I. Lee (o.g.)

East Stirlingshire: J. Moffat, D. Watt, L. Cuthbert, G. Russell, D. Yates, R. Lee, I. Lee, G. Millar, M. McCallum, C. Scott (D. Stirling), M. Geraghty

Substitutes not used: S. Dempsey, P. Imrie (Goalkeeper),

Caledonian Thistle: M. McRitchie, D. Brennan, M. McAllister, A. Hercher, J. Scott, M. Andrew, D. MacDonald, P. McKenzie (A. Smart), M. Noble, G. Bennett, W. Robertson

Substitute not used: M. Lisle, J. Calder (Goalkeeper)

STENHOUSEMUIR 0   **MEADOWBANK THISTLE 4**
M. Hutchison, G. McLeod, I. Little, L. Bailey

Stenhousemuir: M. Harkness, N. Aitken, E. Hallford, J. Clarke (G. Hutchison), G. McGeachie, M. Christie, T. Steel, L. Haddow, M. Mathieson, J. Sludden (J. Henderson), A. Sprott

Substitute not used: C. Wilson (Goalkeeper)

Meadowbank Thistle: S. Ellison, T. Graham, D. Fleming, S. Wilson, S. Williamson, M. Hutchison, M. Duthie, G. McLeod, I. Little, P. Rutherford (G. Price), L. Bailey (S. Thorburn)

Substitute not used: R. Douglas (Goalkeeper)

BERWICK RANGERS 0   **MONTROSE 0**
(AET–Montrose Won 3-2 on Kicks from the Penalty Mark)
Berwick Rangers: N. Young, D. Bell, A. Banks, C. Valentine, A. Cole (G. Fraser), M. Wilson, P. Forrester, M. Neil, W. Hawke, W. Irvine, K. Kane

Substitutes not used: T. King, M. Osborne (Goalkeeper)

Montrose: D. Larter, I. Robertson, K. Tindal, M. Craib, D. Grant, M. Haro, M. Garden, L. Stephen, C. McGlashan, A. Kennedy, P. Masson

Substitutes not used: C. Cooper, C. Milne

Wednesday, 10th August, 1994

ROSS COUNTY 3   **QUEEN'S PARK 2**
B. Grant (2), J. MacPherson   I. Maxwell, G. Orr

Ross County: S. Hutchison, C. Somerville, G. Campbell, R. Williamson, Alexander MacLeod, Andrew MacLeod, K. Ferries, B. Grant, J. MacPherson, W. Herd, B. Wilson (C. Robertson)

Substitutes not used: C. Reid, D. MacMillan (Goalkeeper)

Queen's Park: D. Moonie, S. Fitzpatrick, J. Kavanagh, G. Kerr, I. Maxwell, G. Orr, S. Campbell (R. Bradley), D. Graham, D. Brodie, S. McCormick (S. Edgar), J. Rodden

Substitute not used: M. McFadyen (Goalkeeper)

ARBROATH 1   **ALLOA 1**
(AET–1-1 After 90 Minutes)
J. Reilly   S. Morrison
Arbroath Won 5-4 on Kicks from the Penalty Mark
Arbroath: D. Jackson, B. Mitchell, C. McKinnon, M. Murray, S. Elder, J. McGovern, I. Downie, J. Reilly (D. Elliot), J. Brock, S. Tosh, S. Finlay

Substitutes not used: S. McGregor, R. Duncan (Goalkeeper)

Alloa: J. Butter, J. McNiven (M. Nelson), B. Kemp, C. Campbell, K. McCulloch, J. McCormack, S. Morrison, S. Cadden, S. McCormick, N. Bennett, A. Willock (N. McAvoy)

Substitute not used: P. Graham (Goalkeeper)

QUEEN OF THE SOUTH 2   **ALBION ROVERS 0**
T. Bryce, J. McLaren

Queen of the South: D. Purdie, K. Hetherington, G. Rowe (P. Sermanni), D. McKeown, D. Mills, D. Kennedy, D. McGuire, T. Bryce, J. McLaren, A. McFarlane, S. Mallan

Substitutes not used: G. Cochrane, R. McColm (Goalkeeper)

Albion Rovers: A. Davidson, D. Riley, S. Conn, D. McDonald, P. Malone, L. Collins, D. Walker (M. McBride), A. Docherty, D. Thompson, K. Quinn, J. Gallagher

Substitutes not used: J. McBride, J. Wight (Goalkeeper)

STRANRAER 2   **COWDENBEATH 2**
(AET–2-2 After 90 Minutes)
S. Cody, W. Ferguson   I. Black, G. Soutar
Stranraer Won 4-2 on Kicks from the Penalty Mark
Stranraer: S. Ross, G. Millar, J. Hughes, S. Cody, K. Brannigan, N. Howard (P. McLean), R. Reilly, A. Grant, T. Walker (W. Ferguson), G. Duncan, D. Henderson

Substitute not used: B. Duffy (Goalkeeper)

Cowdenbeath: N. Russell, S. Scott, A. Hamill, B. Malloy, M. Humphreys I. Davidson, R. Carr (C. Winter), I. Black, G. Soutar (J. Lynch), J. Thomson, D. Stout

SECOND ROUND

Tuesday, 16th August, 1994

MOTHERWELL 3   **CLYDEBANK 1**
A. Burns, T. Coyne, S. Kirk   J. Grady
Motherwell: S. Woods, J. Philliben, R. McKinnon, W. Davies (I. Ritchie) A. McLeish, B. Martin, P. Lambert, A. Burns, T. Coyne, P. O'Donnell, D. Arnott (S. Kirk)

Substitute not used: R. Allan (Goalkeeper)

Clydebank: G. Matthews, A. Lansdowne (S. Kerrigan), G. Bowman, S. Murdoch, S. Sweeney, T. Currie, D. Cooper, C. Harris, K. Eadie (C. Sutherland), J. Grady, S. Jack

Substitute not used: A. Monaghan (Goalkeeper)

DUMBARTON 0   **HEART OF MIDLOTHIAN 4**
A. Johnston (2), J. Robertson , J. Millar

Dumbarton: I. MacFarlane, J. Marsland, J. Boyd, M. Melvin, P. Martin, M. MacLeod, M. Mooney, J. Meechan, C. Gibson, M. McGarvey, H. Ward (C. Campbell)

Substitutes not used: S. Gow, P. Dennison (Goalkeeper)

Heart of Midlothian: J. N. Walker, S. Frail, T. McKinlay (S. Leitch), C. Levein, G. Mackay (J. Weir), A. McLaren, J. Colquhoun, A. Johnston, J. Robertson, M. Johnston, J. Millar

Substitute not used: H. Smith (Goalkeeper)

GREENOCK MORTON 1   **AIRDRIEONIANS 1**
(AET–1-1 After 90 Minutes)
D. Lilley   Andrew Smith
Airdrieonians Won 5-3 on Kicks from the Penalty Mark
Greenock Morton: D. Wylie, D. Collins, M. Pickering (J. Anderson), J. Hunter, S. McCahill, D. Johnstone, D. Lilley, J. Fowler, R. Alexander, S. McArthur, P. Cormack

Substitute not used: P. Blair

Airdrieonians: J. Martin, A. Stewart, Anthony Smith, J. Sandison, T. McIntyre, G. Hay (J. Boyle), P. Harvey (I. Ferguson), M. Wilson, Andrew Smith, K. Black, A. Lawrence

Substitute not used: W. McCulloch (Goalkeeper)

FALKIRK 1   **MONTROSE 1**
(AET–1-1 After 90 Minutes)
R. Cadette   A. Kennedy
Falkirk Won 5-4 on Kicks from the Penalty Mark
Falkirk: A. Parks, G. Hamilton, D. Weir (K. James), N. Oliver, J. McLaughlin, S. MacKenzie, E. May, S. Fulton, R. Cadette, I. McCall, F. Johnston (C. McDonald)

Montrose: D. Larter, I. Robertson, K. Tindal, M. Craib, D. Grant, M. Haro, M. Garden (C. Cooper), L. Stephen, C. McGlashan, A. Kennedy, P. Masson

Substitute not used: D. Taylor

PARTICK THISTLE 5   **BRECHIN CITY 0**
W. Jamieson, A. Taylor
J. Charnley (3)

Partick Thistle: C. Nelson, D. Byrne, R. Law, W. Jamieson, G. Tierney, D. McWilliams (I. Cameron), A. Taylor, T. Smith, R. Grant, I. English, J. Charnley

Substitutes not used: A. Gibson, K. Budinauckas (Goalkeeper)

Brechin City: D. Balfour, F. Conway, G. Christie, H. Cairney, K. Nicolson, D. Scott, S. Bell, R. Vannett, W. McNeill (J. McKellar), M. Millar, S. Kemlo

Substitutes not used: R. Brown, D. Lawrie (Goalkeeper)

AYR UNITED 0   **CELTIC 1**
P. Grant

Ayr United: C. Duncan, H. Burns, D. McVicar, G. Paterson, F. Rolling, J. Sharples, J. Traynor (V. Moore), N. McKilligan, S. McGivern, I. Gilzean (T. Woods), C. Connie

Substitute not used: S. McIntosh (Goalkeeper)

Celtic: G. Marshall, L. Martin, T. Boyd, M. McNally, A. Mowbray, P. Grant, M. Galloway, P. McStay, W. Falconer, A. Walker (S. Donnelly), J. Collins

Substitutes not used: B. O'Neil, P. Bonner (Goalkeeper)

ST. MIRREN 0   **DUNDEE UNITED 1** (AET)
D. Ristic

St. Mirren: A. Combe, M. Hick (R. Gillies), S. Watson, B. McLaughlin, S. Taylor, P. McIntyre, K. Gillies (B. Hetherston), A. Bone, B. Lavety, J. Gardner, D. Elliot

Substitute not used: C. Money (Goalkeeper)

Dundee United: H. Jorgensen, J. McInally (D. Craig), G. Bollan, D. Hannah, G. Petric, B. Welsh, D. Bowman, M. Perry, D. Ristic, C. Brewster, J. Nixon (P. Connolly)

Substitute not used: S. Garden (Goalkeeper)

Wednesday, 17th August, 1994

QUEEN OF THE SOUTH 0   **HIBERNIAN 3**
S. Tweed, G. Evans, M. O'Neill

Queen of the South: D. Purdie, K. Hetherington, D. McKeown, B. McKeown (M. Adams), D. Mills, A. McFarlane, D. McGuire, D. Kennedy, J. McLaren (P. Scrmanni), T. Bryce, S. Mallan

Substitute not used: R. McColm (Goalkeeper)

Hibernian: J. Leighton, W. Miller, G. Mitchell, W. Findlay, S. Tweed, G. Hunter (D. Beaumont), K. McAllister, B. Hamilton, G. Evans, D. Jackson, M. O'Neill (K. Harper)

Substitute not used: C. Reid (Goalkeeper)

ABERDEEN 1   **STRANRAER 0**
D. Shearer

Aberdeen: T. Snelders, S. McKimmie, D. Winnie, B. Grant, B. Irvine, S. Wright, E. Jess (J. Miller), D. Shearer (S. Booth), P. Kane, W. Dodds, H. Robertson

Substitute not used: D. Stillie (Goalkeeper)

Stranraer: S. Ross, M. Treanor, J. Hughes, J. McCaffrey (W. Ferguson), K. Brannigan, G. Millar, P. McLean, G. Duncan (C. Brown), T. Walker, S. Cody, D. Henderson

Substitute not used: B. Duffy (Goalkeeper)

DUNDEE 3   **CALEDONIAN THISTLE 0**
G. Shaw, P. Tosh (2)

Dundee: M. Pageaud, J. McQuillan, S. Pittman, G. McKeown, N. Blake, A. Dinnie, G. Shaw, I. Anderson (P. Tosh), C. Duffy, G. Britton (R. Farningham), N. McCann

Substitute not used: B. Thompson (Goalkeeper)

Caledonian Thistle: M. McRitchie, D. Brennan, M. McAllister, A. Hercher, J. Scott, M. Andrew, A. Smart, P. McKenzie (D. MacDonald), M. Noble, G. Bennett, W. Robertson

Substitutes not used: S. Baltacha, J. Calder (Goalkeeper)

DUNFERMLINE ATHLETIC 4   **MEADOWBANK THISTLE 1**
I. Den Bieman, N. McCathie   S. Sorbie
S. Petrie, K. Ward

Dunfermline Athletic: I. Westwater, I. Den Bieman, M. Bowes, N. McCathie, N. Cooper, P. Smith, J. McNamara, C. Robertson, A. Tod (D. Laing), S. Petrie, A. Moore (K. Ward)

Substitute not used: G. Smith (Goalkeeper)

Meadowbank Thistle: S. Ellison, T. Graham, D. Fleming, S. Wilson, S. Williamson, M. Hutchison (S. Thorburn), M. Duthie, G. McLeod, I. Little (M. Coyle), S. Sorbie, L. Bailey

Substitute not used: R. Douglas (Goalkeeper)

ARBROATH 1   **RANGERS 6**
C. McKinnon   S. McCall, D. Ferguson (3)
M. Hateley (2)

Arbroath: D. Jackson, B. Mitchell, J. Rae, C. Farnan, S. Elder, M. Murray, I. Downie (S. Finlay), C. McKinnon, J. Reilly (J. Brock), S. Tosh, J. McGovern

Substitute not used: R. Duncan (Goalkeeper)

Rangers: A. Maxwell, S. McCall, J. Brown, R. Gough, B. Boli, D. McPherson, C. Moore, I. Ferguson, D. Ferguson, M. Hateley, I. Durrant (N. Murray)

Substitutes not used: S. Pressley, W. Thomson (Goalkeeper)

ROSS COUNTY 0   **RAITH ROVERS 5**
G. Dalziel, A. Graham (3),
C. Cameron

Ross County: S. Hutchison, C. Somerville, G. Campbell, R. Williamson, Alexander MacLeod, Andrew MacLeod, K. Ferries, B. Grant (A. Duff), J. MacPherson, W. Herd, B. Wilson

Substitutes not used: C. Reid, D. MacMillan (Goalkeeper)

Raith Rovers: S. Thomson, J. Rowbotham, D. Kirkwood (J. Broddle), R. Coyle, R. Raeside, D. Sinclair, D. Lennon, G. Dalziel, A. Graham, C. Cameron (S. Crawford), J. Dair

Substitute not used: B. Potter (Goalkeeper)

KILMARNOCK 4   **EAST FIFE 1**
J. Henry, S. Maskrey (2)   D. Hope
G. McCluskey

Kilmarnock: R. Geddes, A. MacPherson, T. Black, R. Montgomerie, M. Reilly, A. Millen, A. Mitchell, J. Henry, S. Maskrey, G. McCluskey (R. Williamson), R. Connor (S. McSkimming)

Substitute not used: C. Meldrum (Goalkeeper)

East Fife: E. Wilson, G. Bell, A. Williamson, D. Barron, A. Sneddon, R. Hildersley (J. Cusick), G. Allan, D. Hope, R. Scott (A. Irvine), P. Hunter, R. Gibb

Substitute not used: R. Charles (Goalkeeper)

STIRLING ALBION 0   **ST. JOHNSTONE 2**
G. O'Boyle, P. Scott

Stirling Albion: M. McGeown, J. Hamilton, P. Armstrong, C. Mitchell, R. McQuilter, T. Tait, W. Reid (I. McInnes), P. Roberts, W. Watters, C. Taggart, J. McLeod

Substitutes not used: J. Gibson, M. Monaghan (Goalkeeper)

St. Johnstone: A. Rhodes, G. McGinnis, C. Miller, T. Turner, J. Inglis, K. McGowne (P. Scott), J. O'Neil, P. Ramsey, P. Davenport, G. O'Boyle, D. Irons

Substitutes not used: J. Davies, J. Donegan (Goalkeeper)

HAMILTON ACADEMICAL 5   **CLYDE 0**
S. McEntegart, C. Baptie,
J. Sherry, D. Campbell, C. McLean

Hamilton Academical: A. Ferguson, P. McKenzie, S. McInulty, S. McEntegart, C. Baptie, M. McIntosh, J. McQuade, J. Sherry, P. Chalmers (C. McLean), P. Duffield, D. Lorimer (D. Campbell)

Substitute not used: D. Cormack (Goalkeeper)

Clyde: L. Fridge, M. Clark (M. O'Neill), A. Neill (A. Frater), K. Knox, J. Thomson, B. Strain, G. Watson, A. Wright, I. McConnell, J. McAulay, G. Parks

Substitute not used: J. Hillcoat (Goalkeeper)

THIRD ROUND

Tuesday, 30th August, 1994

PARTICK THISTLE 0   ABERDEEN 5
D. Shearer (3), P. Kane, W. Dodds

Partick Thistle: C. Nelson, D. Byrne, R. Law, W. Jamieson,
G. Tierney, D. McWilliams, A. Taylor, I. Cameron, R. Grant
(T. Smith), I. English, J. Charnley

Substitutes not used: A. Gibson, A. Murdoch (Goalkeeper)

Aberdeen: T. Snelders, S. McKimmie, C. Woodthorpe, B. Grant,
B. Irvine (D. Winnie), S. Wright, E. Jess, D. Shearer, P. Kane,
W. Dodds, R. McKinnon (S. Booth)

Substitute not used: M. Watt (Goalkeeper)

HIBERNIAN 2   DUNFERMLINE ATHLETIC 0
M. O'Neill (2)

Hibernian: J. Leighton, D. Beaumont, J. Tortolano, W. Findlay
(D. Farrell), S. Tweed, G. Hunter (K. Harper), K. McAllister,
B. Hamilton, G. Evans, D. Jackson, M. O'Neill

Substitute not used: C. Reid (Goalkeeper)

Dunfermline Athletic: J. Will, I. Den Bieman, M. Bowes,
N. McCathie, N. Cooper, P. Smith, K. Ward, C. Robertson,
H. French, S. Petrie, A. Tod (D. Laing)

Substitute not used: C. Smart

Wednesday, 31st August, 1994

HEART OF MIDLOTHIAN 2   ST. JOHNSTONE 4
J. Colquhoun, G. Locke   C. Miller, J. O' Neil,
                              G. O'Boyle, D. Irons

Heart of Midlothian: J. N. Walker, S. Frail, J. Weir, C. Levein, N. Berry,
A. McLaren, J. Colquhoun, G. Locke, J. Robertson, A. Johnston
(T. Harrison), (W. Foster), J. Millar

Substitute not used: H. Smith (Goalkeeper)

St. Johnstone: A. Rhodes, P. Cherry, C. Miller, P. Ramsey, G. McGinnis
P. Deas (A. Preston), J. O'Neil, J. Davies, P. Davenport, G. O'Boyle,
D. Irons

Substitutes not used: G. McMartin, J. Donegan (Goalkeeper)

RANGERS 1   FALKIRK 2
B. Laudrup   R. Cadette (2)

Rangers: A. Goram, S. McCall, D. Robertson, R. Gough,
D. McPherson (D. Ferguson), C. Moore, I. Durrant, I. Ferguson,
G. Durie, M. Hateley, B. Laudrup

Substitutes not used: S. Pressley, A. Maxwell (Goalkeeper)

Falkirk: A. Parks, D. Weir, J. McGowan, N. Oliver, J. McLaughlin,
S. MacKenzie, E. May, S. Fulton, R. Cadette, N. Henderson
(C. Cramb), C. McDonald

Substitutes not used: J. McStay, W. Lamont (Goalkeeper)

RAITH ROVERS 3   KILMARNOCK 2
C. Cameron, (3)   R. Montgomerie, R. Williamson

Raith Rovers: S. Thomson, S. McAnespie, J. Broddle, J. Rowbotham,
D. Narey, D. Sinclair, D. Lennon, G. Dalziel (S. Crawford),
A. Graham, C. Cameron, I. Redford (R. Coyle)

Substitute not used: B. Potter (Goalkeeper)

Kilmarnock: R. Geddes, A. MacPherson, T. Black, R. Montgomerie,
M. Reilly, A. Millen, A. Mitchell, C. Napier (R. Williamson), T. Brown,
R. Connor, S. Maskrey

Substitutes not used: S. Hamilton, C. Meldrum (Goalkeeper)

MOTHERWELL 1   AIRDRIEONIANS 2
(AET–1-1After 90 Minutes)
C. McCart   J. Boyle (2)

Motherwell: S. Woods, R. Shannon, J. Philliben, J. Dolan (W. Davies),
B. Martin, C. McCart, P. Lambert, A. Burns (S. Kirk), T. Coyne,
P. O'Donnell, A. Roddie

Substitute not used: R. Allan (Goalkeeper)

Airdrieonians: J. Martin, J. Boyle, A. Stewart, J. Sandison, T. McIntyre,
K. Black, A. Lawrence (J. McIntyre), P. Harvey, Andrew Smith
(I. Ferguson), M. Wilson, P. Jack

Substitute not used: W. McCulloch (Goalkeeper)

HAMILTON ACADEMICAL 2   DUNDEE UNITED 2
(AET–1-1After 90 Minutes)
A. Cleland (o.g.), P. Duffield   D. Hannah(2)
Dundee United Won 5-3 on Kicks from the Penalty Mark

Hamilton Academical: A. Ferguson, P. McKenzie, S. McInulty,
S. McEntegart, C. Baptie, M. McIntosh, C. McLean (J. McQuade),
J. Sherry, P. Chalmers (P. Hartley), P. Duffield, D. Nicholls

Substitute not used: D. Cormack (Goalkeeper)

Dundee United: A. Main, A. Cleland, J. McInally, D. Hannah, G. Petric,
C. Dailly, D. Bowman, W. McKinlay, D. Ristic (C. Myers), C. Brewster
(J. Nixon), A. McLaren

Substitute not used: H. Jorgensen (Goalkeeper)

DUNDEE 1   CELTIC 2
R. Farningham   A. Walker, J. Collins

Dundee: M. Pageaud, J. McQuillan, J. Duffy, C. Duffy, N. Blake (P. Tosh)
R. Farningham, G. Shaw, D. Vrto, M. Wieghorst (M. Teasdale),
G. Britton, N. McCann

Substitute not used: B. Thompson (Goalkeeper)

Celtic: G. Marshall, P. Grant, T. Boyd, M. McNally, A. Mowbray,
P. McGinlay, M. Galloway, P. McStay, S. Donnelly (C. Nicholas),
A. Walker, J. Collins

Substitutes not used: B. O'Neil, P. Bonner (Goalkeeper)

FOURTH ROUND

Tuesday, 20th September, 1994

ST. JOHNSTONE 1   RAITH ROVERS 3
J. O'Neil   S. Dennis, A. Graham, D. Lennon

St. Johnstone: A. Rhodes, P. Cherry, C. Miller, P. Ramsey (A. Preston),
G. McGinnis, K. McGowne, J. O'Neil, T. Turner (G. McMartin),
P. Davenport, G. O'Boyle, D. Irons

Substitute not used: J. Donegan (Goalkeeper)

Raith Rovers: S. Thomson, S. McAnespie, J. Broddle, J. Rowbotham,
S. Dennis, D. Sinclair, J. Nicholl, S. Crawford (J. Dair), A. Graham,
C. Cameron, D. Lennon

Substitutes not used: I. Redford, B. Potter (Goalkeeper)

Wednesday, 21st September, 1994

CELTIC 1   DUNDEE UNITED 0
J. Collins

Celtic: G. Marshall, M. Galloway, T. Boyd, M. McNally, A. Mowbray,
P. Grant, P. McGinlay, P. McStay (B. O'Neil), S. Donnelly
(C. Nicholas), A. Walker, J. Collins

Substitute not used: P. Bonner (Goalkeeper)

Dundee United: A. Main, A. Cleland, M. Malpas, D. Hannah, G. Petric,
B. Welsh, J. McInally (C. Myers), W. McKinlay, D. Ristic, P. Connolly
(C. Brewster), J. Nixon

Substitute not used: H. Jorgensen (Goalkeeper)

FALKIRK 1   ABERDEEN 4
C. McDonald   S. Booth (3), B. Rice (o.g.)

Falkirk: A. Parks, J. McGowan, T. McQueen, J. Clark, J. McLaughlin,
S. MacKenzie, E. May, N. Henderson (F. McAvennie), R. Cadette,
B. Rice, C. McDonald

Substitutes not used: K. James, W. Lamont (Goalkeeper)

Aberdeen: M. Watt, S. McKimmie, C. Woodthorpe, B. Grant,
D. Winnie, S. Wright, E. Jess, G. Smith, S. Booth, W. Dodds
(J. Miller), R. McKinnon

Substitutes not used: P. Hetherston, D. Stillie (Goalkeeper)

HIBERNIAN 1   AIRDRIEONIANS 2
G. Evans   Andrew Smith, A. Lawrence

Hibernian: J. Leighton, W. Miller, D. Farrell, C. Jackson (K. Harper),
S. Tweed, G. Hunter, K. McAllister, B. Hamilton, G. Evans,
D. Jackson, M. O'Neill

Substitutes not used: D. Beaumont, C. Reid (Goalkeeper)

Airdrieonians: J. Martin, J. Boyle, P. Jack, J. Sandison, T. McIntyre,
A. Stewart, P. Harvey (G. Hay), M. Wilson, Andrew Smith, K. Black,
A. Lawrence (J. McIntyre)

Substitute not used: W. McCulloch (Goalkeeper)

SEMI–FINALS

Tuesday, 25th October, 1994

McDiarmid Park, Perth

AIRDRIEONIANS 1 **RAITH ROVERS 1**
(AET – 1-1 After 90 Minutes)
S. Cooper   A. Graham
Raith Rovers Won 5-4 on Kicks from the Penalty Mark

Airdrieonians: J. Martin, A. Stewart, P. Jack, J. Sandison, G. Hay, K. Black, J. Boyle, M. Wilson (T. McIntyre), S. Cooper, P. Harvey (Andrew Smith), A. Lawrence

Substitute not used: W. McCulloch (Goalkeeper)

Raith Rovers: S. Thomson, S. McAnespie, J. Broddle (J. Rowbotham), D. Sinclair, D. Dennis, D. Narey, D. Lennon, G. Dalziel (S. Crawford), A. Graham, C. Cameron, D. Kirkwood (B. Potter (Goalkeeper))

Wednesday, 26th October, 1994

Ibrox Stadium, Glasgow

CELTIC 1 **ABERDEEN 0** (AET)
B. O'Neil

Celtic: G. Marshall, B. Smith, T. Boyd, M. McNally, B. O'Neil, P. Grant, P. Byrne (P. McGinlay), P. McStay, S. Donnelly, A. Walker (C. Nicholas), J. Collins

Substitute not used: P. Bonner (Goalkeeper)

Aberdeen: T. Snelders, S. McKimmie, C. Woodthorpe, B. Grant, D. Winnie, S. Wright, G. Smith, P. Kane (H. Robertson), S. Booth, W. Dodds, R. McKinnon (P. Hetherston)

Substitute not used: M. Watt (Goalkeeper)

FINAL

Sunday, 27th November, 1994

IBROX STADIUM, GLASGOW

RAITH ROVERS 2 **CELTIC 2**

(AET–2-2 After 90 Minutes)
Raith Rovers Won 6-5 on Kicks from the Penalty Mark

Raith Rovers: S. Thomson, S. McAnespie, J. Broddle (J. Rowbotham), D. Narey, S. Dennis, D. Sinclair, S. Crawford, G. Dalziel (I. Redford), A. Graham, C. Cameron, J. Dair
Substitute not used: B. Potter (Goalkeeper)

Celtic: G. Marshall, M. Galloway, T. Boyd, M. McNally, A. Mowbray, B. O'Neil, S. Donnelly (W. Falconer), P. McStay, C. Nicholas (P. Byrne), A. Walker, J. Collins
Substitute not used: P. Bonner (Goalkeeper)

Scorers: Raith Rovers: S. Crawford, G. Dalziel
Celtic: C. Nicholas, A. Walker

Referee: J. McCluskey (Stewarton)

Attendance: 45,384

COCA–COLA CUP – SEASON 1994/95

ROUND BY ROUND GOALS ANALYSIS

	No. of Goals Scored	Ties Played	Average Per Game
First Round	20	8	2.5
Second Round	55	16	3.4
Third Round	31	8	3.9
Fourth Round	13	4	3.3
Semi-Finals	3	2	1.5
Final	4	1	4
Total No. of Goals Scored:		126	
Ties Played		39	
Average Goals per Game:		3.2	

SEASON 1946/47

5th April, 1947 at Hampden Park;
Attendance 82,584;
Referee: Mr R. Calder (Rutherglen)

RANGERS 4   **ABERDEEN 0**
Gillick, Williamson, Duncanson (2)

SEASON 1947/48

25th October, 1947 at Hampden Park;
Attendance 52,781; Referee: Mr P. Craigmyle (Aberdeen)

EAST FIFE 0   **FALKIRK 0**
After Extra Time

REPLAY
1st November, 1947 at Hampden Park;
Attendance 30,664; Referee: Mr. P. Craigmyle (Aberdeen)

EAST FIFE 4   **FALKIRK 1**
Duncan (3), Adams   Aikman

SEASON 1948/49

12th March, 1949 at Hampden Park; Attendance 53,359;
Referee: Mr W. G. Livingstone (Glasgow)

RANGERS 2   **RAITH ROVERS 0**
Gillick, Paton

SEASON 1949/50

29th October, 1949 at Hampden Park;
Attendance 38,897; Referee: Mr W. Webb (Glasgow)

EAST FIFE 3   **DUNFERMLINE ATHLETIC 0**
Fleming, Duncan, Morris

SEASON 1950/51

28th October, 1950 at Hampden Park;
Attendance 63,074; Referee: Mr J. A. Mowat (Glasgow)

MOTHERWELL 3   **HIBERNIAN 0**
Kelly, Forrest, Watters

SEASON 1951/52

27th October, 1951 at Hampden Park;
Attendance 91,075; Referee: Mr J. A. Mowat (Glasgow)

DUNDEE 3   **RANGERS 2**
Flavell, Pattillo, Boyd   Findlay, Thornton

SEASON 1952/53

25th October, 1952 at Hampden Park;
Attendance 51,830; Referee: Mr J. A. Mowat (Glasgow)

DUNDEE 2   **KILMARNOCK 0**
Flavell (2)

SEASON 1953/54

24th October, 1953 at Hampden Park;
Attendance 88,529; Referee: Mr J. S. Cox (Rutherglen)

EAST FIFE 3   **PARTICK THISTLE 2**
Gardiner, Fleming, Christie   Walker, McKenzie

SEASON 1954/55

23rd October, 1954 at Hampden Park;
Attendance 55,640; Referee: Mr J. A. Mowat (Glasgow)

HEART OF MIDLOTHIAN 4   **MOTHERWELL 2**
Bauld (3), Wardhaugh   Redpath (pen), Bain

SEASON 1955/56

22nd October, 1955 at Hampden Park;
Attendance 44,103; Referee: Mr H. Phillips (Wishaw)

ABERDEEN 2   **ST. MIRREN 1**
Mallan (og), Leggat   Holmes

SEASON 1956/57

27th October, 1956 at Hampden Park;
Attendance 58,973; Referee: Mr J. A. Mowat (Glasgow)

CELTIC 0   **PARTICK THISTLE 0**

REPLAY
31st October, 1956 at Hampden Park;
Attendance 31,126; Referee: Mr J. A. Mowat (Glasgow)

CELTIC 3   **PARTICK THISTLE 0**
McPhail (2), Collins

SEASON 1957/58

19th October, 1957 at Hampden Park;
Attendance 82,293; Referee: Mr J. A. Mowat (Glasgow)

CELTIC 7   **RANGERS 1**
Mochan (2), McPhail (3),   Simpson
Wilson, Fernie (pen)

SEASON 1958/59

25th October, 1958 at Hampden Park;
Attendance 59,960; Referee: Mr R. H. Davidson (Airdrie)

HEART OF MIDLOTHIAN 5   **PARTICK THISTLE 1**
Murray (2), Bauld (2), Hamilton   Smith

SEASON 1959/60

24th October, 1959 at Hampden Park;
Attendance 57,974; Referee: Mr R. H. Davidson (Airdrie)

HEART OF MIDLOTHIAN 2   **THIRD LANARK 1**
Hamilton, Young   Gray

SEASON 1960/61

29th October, 1960 at Hampden Park;
Attendance 82,063; Referee: Mr T. Wharton (Glasgow)

RANGERS 2   **KILMARNOCK 0**
Brand, Scott

SEASON 1961/62

28th October, 1961 at Hampden Park;
Attendance 88,635; Referee: Mr R. H. Davidson (Airdrie)

RANGERS 1   **HEART OF MIDLOTHIAN 1**
Millar   Cumming (pen)

REPLAY
18th December, 1961 at Hampden Park;
Attendance 47,552; Referee: Mr R. H. Davidson (Airdrie)

RANGERS 3   **HEART OF MIDLOTHIAN 1**
Millar, Brand, McMillan   Davidson

SEASON 1962/63

27th October, 1962 at Hampden Park;
Attendance 51,280; Referee: Mr T. Wharton (Glasgow)

HEART OF MIDLOTHIAN 1   **KILMARNOCK 0**
Davidson

SEASON 1963/64

26th October, 1963 at Hampden Park;
Attendance 105,907; Referee: Mr H. Phillips (Wishaw)

RANGERS 5 **MORTON 0**
Forrest (4), Willoughby

SEASON 1964/65

24th October, 1964 at Hampden Park;
Attendance 91,000; Referee: Mr H. Phillips (Wishaw)

RANGERS 2 **CELTIC 1**
Forrest (2) Johnstone

SEASON 1965/66

23rd October, 1965 at Hampden Park;
Attendance 107,609; Referee: Mr H. Phillips (Wishaw)

CELTIC 2 **RANGERS 1**
Hughes (2 (2 pen)) Young (o.g.)

SEASON 1966/67

29th October, 1966 at Hampden Park;
Attendance 94,532; Referee: Mr T. Wharton (Glasgow)

CELTIC 1 **RANGERS 0**
Lennox

SEASON 1967/68

28th October, 1967 at Hampden Park;
Attendance 66,660; Referee: Mr R. H. Davidson (Airdrie)

CELTIC 5 **DUNDEE 3**
Chalmers (2), Hughes, G. McLean (2), J. McLean
Wallace, Lennox

SEASON 1968/69

5th April, 1969 at Hampden Park;
Attendance 74,000; Referee: Mr W. M. M. Syme (Airdrie)

CELTIC 6 **HIBERNIAN 2**
Lennox (3), Wallace, Auld, Craig O'Rourke, Stevenson

SEASON 1969/70

25th October, 1969 at Hampden Park;
Attendance 73,067; Referee: Mr J. W. Paterson (Bothwell)

CELTIC 1 **ST. JOHNSTONE 0**
Auld

SEASON 1970/71

24th October, 1970 at Hampden Park;
Attendance 106,263; Referee: Mr T. Wharton (Glasgow)

RANGERS 1 **CELTIC 0**
Johnstone

SEASON 1971/72

23rd October, 1971 at Hampden Park;
Attendance 62,740; Referee: Mr W. J. Mullan (Dalkeith)

PARTICK THISTLE 4 **CELTIC 1**
Rae, Lawrie, McQuade, Bone Dalglish

SEASON 1972/73

9th December, 1972 at Hampden Park;
Attendance 71,696; Referee: Mr A. MacKenzie (Larbert)

HIBERNIAN 2 **CELTIC 1**
Stanton, O'Rourke Dalglish

SEASON 1973/74

15th December, 1973 at Hampden Park;
Attendance 27,974; Referee: Mr R. H. Davidson (Airdrie)

DUNDEE 1 **CELTIC 0**
Wallace

SEASON 1974/75

26th October, 1974 at Hampden Park;
Attendance 53,848; Referee: Mr J. R. P. Gordon (Newport on Tay)

CELTIC 6 **HIBERNIAN 3**
Johnstone, Deans (3), Wilson, Murray Harper (3)

SEASON 1975/76

25th October, 1975 at Hampden Park;
Attendance 58,806; Referee: Mr W. Anderson (East Kilbride)

RANGERS 1 **CELTIC 0**
MacDonald

SEASON 1976/77

6th November, 1976 at Hampden Park;
Attendance 69,268; Referee: Mr J. W. Paterson (Bothwell)

ABERDEEN 2 **CELTIC 1**
Jarvie, Robb Dalglish (pen.)
After extra-time

SEASON 1977/78

18th March, 1978 at Hampden Park;
Attendance 60,168; Referee: Mr D. F. T. Syme (Rutherglen)

RANGERS 2 **CELTIC 1**
Cooper, Smith Edvaldsson
After extra-time

SEASON 1978/79

31st March, 1979 at Hampden Park;
Attendance 54,000; Referee: Mr I. M. D. Foote (Glasgow)

RANGERS 2 **ABERDEEN 1**
McMaster (o.g.), Jackson Davidson

SEASON 1979/80 –
BELL'S LEAGUE CUP

8th December, 1979 at Hampden Park;
Attendance 27,299; Referee: Mr B. R. McGinlay (Balfron)

DUNDEE UNITED 0 **ABERDEEN 0**
After extra-time

REPLAY

12th December, 1979 at Dens Park;
Attendance 28,984; Referee: Mr B. R. McGinlay (Balfron)

DUNDEE UNITED 3 **ABERDEEN 0**
Pettigrew (2), Sturrock

SEASON 1980/81 –
BELL'S LEAGUE CUP

6th December, 1980 at Dens Park;
Attendance 24,466; Referee: Mr R. B. Valentine (Dundee)

DUNDEE UNITED 3 **DUNDEE 0**
Dodds, Sturrock (2)

SEASON 1981/82

28th November, 1981 at Hampden Park;
Attendance 53,795;
Referee: Mr E. H. Pringle (Edinburgh)

RANGERS 2   **DUNDEE UNITED 1**
Cooper, Redford   Milne

SEASON 1982/83

4th December, 1982 at Hampden Park;
Attendance 55,372; Referee: Mr K. J. Hope (Clarkston)

CELTIC 2   **RANGERS 1**
Nicholas, MacLeod   Bett

SEASON 1983/84

25th March, 1984 at Hampden Park;
Attendance 66,369; Referee: Mr R. B. Valentine (Dundee)

RANGERS 3   **CELTIC 2**
McCoist 3 (2 pen)   McClair, Reid (pen)

SEASON 1984/85 – SKOL CUP

28th October, 1984 at Hampden Park;
Attendance 44,698; Referee: Mr B. R. McGinlay (Balfron)

RANGERS 1   **DUNDEE UNITED 0**
Ferguson

SEASON 1985/86 – SKOL CUP

27th October, 1985 at Hampden Park;
Attendance 40,065; Referee: Mr R. B. Valentine (Dundee)

ABERDEEN 3   **HIBERNIAN 0**
Black (2), Stark

SEASON 1986/87 – SKOL CUP

26th October, 1986 at Hampden Park;
Attendance 74,219; Referee: Mr D. F. T. Syme (Rutherglen)

RANGERS 2   **CELTIC 1**
Durrant, Cooper (pen)   McClair

SEASON 1987/88 – SKOL CUP

25th October, 1987 at Hampden Park;
Attendance 71,961; Referee: Mr R. B. Valentine (Dundee)

RANGERS 3   **ABERDEEN 3**
Cooper, Durrant, Fleck   Bett, Falconer, Hewitt
After extra-time
Rangers won 5-3 on Kicks from the Penalty Mark

SEASON 1988/89 – SKOL CUP

23rd October, 1988 at Hampden Park;
Attendance 72,122; Referee: Mr G. B. Smith (Edinburgh)

RANGERS 3   **ABERDEEN 2**
McCoist (2), I. Ferguson   Dodds (2)

SEASON 1989/90 – SKOL CUP

22nd October, 1989 at Hampden Park;
Attendance 61,190; Referee: Mr G. B. Smith (Edinburgh)

ABERDEEN 2   **RANGERS 1**
Mason (2)   Walters (pen)
After extra-time – 1-1 after 90 minutes

SEASON 1990/91 – SKOL CUP

28th October, 1990 at Hampden Park;
Attendance 62,817; Referee: Mr J. McCluskey (Stewarton)

RANGERS 2   **CELTIC 1**
Walters, Gough   Elliott

SEASON 1991/92 – SKOL CUP

27th October, 1991 at Hampden Park;
Attendance 40,377; Referee: Mr B. R. McGinlay (Balfron)

HIBERNIAN 2   **DUNFERMLINE ATHLETIC 0**
McIntyre (pen), Wright

SEASON 1992/93 – SKOL CUP

25th October, 1992 at Hampden Park;
Attendance 45,298; Referee: Mr D. D. Hope (Erskine)

RANGERS 2   **ABERDEEN 1**
McCall, Smith (o.g.)   Shearer
After extra-time – 1-1 after 90 minutes

SEASON 1993/94

24th October, 1993 at Celtic Park;
Attendance 47,632; Referee: Mr J. McCluskey (Stewarton)

RANGERS 2   **HIBERNIAN 1**
Durrant, McCoist   McPherson (O.G.)

SEASON 1994/95 – COCA-COLA CUP

27th November, 1994 at Ibrox Stadium;
Attendance 45,384; Referee: Mr J. McCluskey (Stewarton)

RAITH ROVERS 2   **CELTIC 2**
S. Crawford, G. Dalziel   C. Nicholas, A. Walker
After extra-time – 2-2 after 90 minutes
Raith Rovers won 6-5 on Kicks from the Penalty Mark

WINNERS AT A GLANCE

RANGERS	19
CELTIC	9
ABERDEEN	4
HEART OF MIDLOTHIAN	4
DUNDEE	3
EAST FIFE	3
DUNDEE UNITED	2
HIBERNIAN	2
MOTHERWELL	1
PARTICK THISTLE	1
RAITH ROVERS	1

APPEARANCES IN FINALS
(Figures do not include replays)

RANGERS	25	KILMARNOCK	3
CELTIC	21	DUNFERMLINE ATHLETIC	2
ABERDEEN	10	MOTHERWELL	2
HIBERNIAN	7	RAITH ROVERS	2
DUNDEE	5	FALKIRK	1
HEART OF MIDLOTHIAN	5	GREENOCK MORTON	1
DUNDEE UNITED	4	ST. JOHNSTONE	1
PARTICK THISTLE	4	ST. MIRREN	1
EAST FIFE	3	THIRD LANARK	1

Player of the Year Awards

Scottish Professional Footballers' Association

1977/78
Premier Division — Derek Johnstone *(Rangers)*
First Division — Billy Pirie *(Dundee)*
Second Division — Dave Smith *(Berwick Rangers)*
Young Player of the Year — Graeme Payne *(Dundee United)*

1978/79
Premier Division — Paul Hegarty *(Dundee United)*
First Division — Brian McLaughlin *(Ayr United)*
Second Division — Michael Leonard *(Dunfermline Athletic)*
Young Player of the Year — Raymond Stewart *(Dundee United)*

1979/80
Premier Division — Davie Provan *(Celtic)*
First Division — Sandy Clark *(Airdrieonians)*
Second Division — Paul Leetion *(Falkirk)*
Young Player of the Year — John MacDonald *(Rangers)*

1980/81
Premier Division — Mark McGhee *(Aberdeen)*
First Division — Eric Sinclair *(Dundee)*
Second Division — Jimmy Robertson *(Queen of the South)*
Young Player of the Year — Charlie Nicholas *(Celtic)*

1981/82
Premier Division — Sandy Clark *(Airdrieonians)*
First Division — Brian McLaughlin *(Motherwell)*
Second Division — Pat Nevin *(Clyde)*
Young Player of the Year — Frank McAvennie *(St. Mirren)*

1982/83
Premier Division — Charlie Nicholas *(Celtic)*
First Division — Gerry McCabe *(Clydebank)*
Second Division — John Colquhoun *(Stirling Albion)*
Young Player of the Year — Paul McStay *(Celtic)*

1983/84
Premier Division — Willie Miller *(Aberdeen)*
First Division — Gerry McCabe *(Clydebank)*
Second Division — Jim Liddle *(Forfar Athletic)*
Young Player of the Year — John Robertson *(Heart of Midlothian)*

1984/85
Premier Division — Jim Duffy *(Morton)*
First Division — Gerry McCabe *(Clydebank)*
Second Division — Bernie Slaven *(Albion Rovers)*
Young Player of the Year — Craig Levein *(Heart of Midlothian)*

1985/86
Premier Division — Richard Gough *(Dundee United)*
First Division — John Brogan *(Hamilton Academical)*
Second Division — Mark Smith *(Queen's Park)*
Young Player of the Year — Craig Levein *(Heart of Midlothian)*

1986/87
Premier Division — Brian McClair *(Celtic)*
First Division — Jim Holmes *(Morton)*
Second Division — John Sludden *(Ayr United)*
Young Player of the Year — Robert Fleck *(Rangers)*

1987/88
Premier Division — Paul McStay *(Celtic)*
First Division — Alex Taylor *(Hamilton Academical)*
Second Division — Henry Templeton *(Ayr United)*
Young Player of the Year — John Collins *(Hibernian)*

1988/89
Premier Division — Theo Snelders *(Aberdeen)*
First Division — Ross Jack *(Dunfermline Athletic)*
Second Division — Paul Hunter *(East Fife)*
Young Player of the Year — Billy McKinlay *(Dundee United)*

1989/90
Premier Division — Jim Bett *(Aberdeen)*
First Division — Ken Eadie *(Clydebank)*
Second Division — Willie Watters *(Kilmarnock)*
Young Player of the Year — Scott Crabbe *(Heart of Midlothian)*

1990/91
Premier Division — Paul Elliott *(Celtic)*
First Division — Simon Stainrod *(Falkirk)*
Second Division — Kevin Todd *(Berwick Rangers)*
Young Player of the Year — Eoin Jess *(Aberdeen)*

1991/92
Premier Division — Alistair McCoist *(Rangers)*
First Division — Gordon Dalziel *(Raith Rovers)*
Second Division — Andrew Thomson *(Queen of the South)*
Young Player of the Year — Philip O'Donnell *(Motherwell)*

1992/93
Premier Division — Andy Goram *(Rangers)*
First Division — Gordon Dalziel *(Raith Rovers)*
Second Division — Alexander Ross *(Brechin City)*
Young Player of the Year — Eoin Jess *(Aberdeen)*

1993/94
Premier Division — Mark Hateley *(Rangers)*
First Division — Richard Cadette *(Falkirk)*
Second Division — Andrew Thomson *(Queen of the South)*
Young Player of the Year — Philip O'Donnell *(Motherwell)*

1994/95
Premier Division — Brian Laudrup *(Rangers)*
First Division — Stephen Crawford *(Raith Rovers)*
Second Division — Derek McInnes *(Greenock Morton)*
Third Division — David Bingham *(Forfar Athletic)*
Young Player of the Year — Charlie Miller *(Rangers)*

The Scottish Football Writers' Association

1965	Billy McNeill *(Celtic)*
1966	John Greig *(Rangers)*
1967	Ronnie Simpson *(Celtic)*
1968	Gordon Wallace *(Raith Rovers)*
1969	Bobby Murdoch *(Celtic)*
1970	Pat Stanton *(Hibernian)*
1971	Martin Buchan *(Aberdeen)*
1972	Dave Smith *(Rangers)*
1973	George Connelly *(Celtic)*
1974	World Cup Squad
1975	Sandy Jardine *(Rangers)*
1976	John Greig *(Rangers)*
1977	Danny McGrain *(Celtic)*
1978	Derek Johnstone *(Rangers)*
1979	Andy Ritchie *(Morton)*
1980	Gordon Strachan *(Aberdeen)*
1981	Alan Rough *(Partick Thistle)*
1982	Paul Sturrock *(Dundee United)*
1983	Charlie Nicholas *(Celtic)*
1984	Willie Miller *(Aberdeen)*
1985	Hamish McAlpine *(Dundee United)*
1986	Sandy Jardine *(Heart of Midlothian)*
1987	Brian McClair *(Celtic)*
1988	Paul McStay *(Celtic)*
1989	Richard Gough *(Rangers)*
1990	Alex McLeish *(Aberdeen)*
1991	Maurice Malpas *(Dundee United)*
1992	Alistair McCoist *(Rangers)*
1993	Andy Goram *(Rangers)*
1994	Mark Hateley *(Rangers)*
1995	Brian Laudrup *(Rangers)*

TENNENTS SCOTTISH CUP WINNERS 1995

Waiting Over

The Tennents Scottish Cup fairly went "pop" when it splashed off on 10th December, 1994 last season. It was a case of Wet Wet Wet alright as three ties were rained off before they started.... and a fourth was called to a soggy halt at half-time.

Dumbarton and Stirling Albion were the wet weather victims, with the game standing at 1-1 when referee Doug Smith called a halt, possibly concerned for the non-swimmers. The tie was eventually played a week later... and ended up 3-3 before Stirling went on to win the replay 3-0.

Caledonian Thistle's first Scottish Cup excursion as a League club was brief - beaten 2-1 at home by Queen of the South, whilst Adrian Sprott, famous for his goal for Hamilton Accies back in 1987 which knocked out Rangers at Ibrox, was on the mark for Stenhousemuir in the local derby with East Stirlingshire.

The Second Round on 7th January, 1995 produced the first hat-tricks of the competition - for East Fife's Steve Hutcheon against Gala Fairydean in his side's 6-2 victory and Rob Matthew of Burntisland Shipyard, when his side won by the same score against St. Cuthberts.

The big-time clubs hit the Cup trail on 28th January... or some of them did at any rate. In view of various demands, ties were played over a ten day period and at the end of it all, only two of the Premier elite fell. Partick Thistle going down 2-1 away against ambitious Dundee, while the lights went out on Falkirk for a second time - the first game had to be abandoned due to floodlight failure - when Motherwell's Alex Burns fired in a double at Brockville.

Kilmarnock, Heart of Midlothian and Dundee United needed replays to get their names in the bag for the Fourth Round, with Killie also requiring extra time at Greenock to see off a battling Greenock Morton side 2-1 after a goalless first game.

Ace of Hearts, John Robertson, came up with the goal that earned his team a replay against Clydebank in a 1-1 draw and also scored in the 2-1 victory in the second match, while after a hesitant goalless home performance against Clyde, holders Dundee United swept to a 5-1 replay victory.

Hibernian were 2-0 winners over Montrose at Links Park, an Eoin Jess goal edged Aberdeen through at home against Stranraer and Celtic's Pierre van Hooijdonk was on target in the 2-0 home win over a gutsy St. Mirren side.

Favourites Rangers, eased through against old jinx team Hamilton - with a bit of help from their "Foreign Legion". Their goals in the 3-1 win came from Englishman Trevor Steven, Frenchman Basile Boli and Danish superstar Brian Laudrup.

However, although the Third Round results had been fairly predictable, the Fourth Round of competition was the one that produced two shock results and really brought the tournament to life. On the Saturday, 18th February, out went Aberdeen in what proved to be the major upset of the tournament, beaten 2-0 by Stenhousemuir, who were singing (whether it was raining or not) when farmer Tommy Steel banged in a devastating double.

In the all Premier Division tie, Hibernian were 2-0 victors over rivals Motherwell in a tousy match at Easter Road, where six players were booked and Brian Martin of Motherwell was ordered off.

Meanwhile, Celtic coasted to a comfortable 3-0 victory over Meadowbank Thistle, with their recent Dutch signing, Pierre van Hooijdonk, notching a double, while holders, Dundee United, overcame a potentially difficult trip to the Highlands by defeating Huntly by three goals to one.

Kilmarnock, who had reached the Semi-Final the previous season, stayed on course to repeat that feat by easily dispensing with East Fife, recording a 4-0 victory at Rugby Park.

The draw had provided two extremely intriguing all First Division clashes, with Airdrieonians defeating promotion rivals, Dunfermline Athletic, 2-0 at Broadwood Stadium, while Coca-Cola Cup holders, Raith Rovers, recovered from a 1-0 half-time deficit, to record a 2-1 victory over Dundee at Dens Park.

In the live BSkyB match that was seen throughout the length and breadth of the United Kingdom on the Monday evening, the second shock occurred as Rangers went out, beaten 4-2 in Edinburgh by a jubilant Hearts side in a see-saw match that had thrills and spills aplenty and what was regarded as the game of the competition... with John Robertson again contributing a vital goal, and two of the others coming from ex-Ibrox men Colin Miller and Dave McPherson.

The Quarter Final draw resulted in four very interesting ties and with Raith Rovers and Airdrieonians being paired together in a domestic cup tournament for the third time in the season, it guaranteed that at least one club from outwith the Premier Division would feature in the Semi-Finals.

Celtic played their tie on a Friday night, once again, for the benefit of live television, and in another cup tie that was affected by floodlight failure, after a lengthy delay, the match was settled when John Collins scored the only goal of the game from the penalty spot against Kilmarnock after Celtic's tricky little winger, Brian McLaughlin, had been adjudged to have been tripped inside the penalty box.

Heart of Midlothian were on their Sunday best, again for live television, when two goals from John Millar eased them through against holders Dundee United after Brazilian, Sergio, had given the Tannadice club an early lead.

Sandwiched in between on Saturday, 11th March were the other two ties... with the Diamonds from Airdrie magnificently sweeping aside the more fancied Coca-Cola Cup holders, Raith Rovers, with a 4-1 victory which included two superb goals from Paul Harvey, while at Ochilview, Hibernian gave shock troops Stenhousemuir no

Paul McStay - family celebration

time to conjure up another upset as two goal Kevin Harper led them to a convincing 4-0 win.

The draw resulted in East meeting West in both Semi-Final ties, Hibernian being drawn against Celtic at Ibrox, again on a televised Friday night and Heart of Midlothian travelling to Hampden to take on Airdrieonians the following day.

Veteran goalkeeper, Jim Leighton, must thrive on Friday night shoot-outs. He was in stunning form against Celtic with a series of saves that included a late penalty stop from Andy Walker that kept the score level, but even Leighton couldn't stop Celtic in the replay as the Bhoys cruised to a 3-1 win, thanks to goals from Willie Falconer, John Collins and Phil O'Donnell with Keith Wright netting for the Hibees.

First Division Airdrieonians, ended the other Edinburgh challenge thanks to a Steve Cooper goal, thereby ending any

possibility of the first all Edinburgh Scottish Cup Final since the Tynecastle club defeated their arch rivals 3-1 at Logie Green nearly 100 years ago.

So it was a Premier versus First Division showdown at Hampden on 27th May for the 1995 Tennents Scottish Cup Final, and while the Parkhead faithful were confident, at the same time were fearful, in view of what had happened in The Coca-Cola Cup Final earlier in the season when Raith Rovers had shocked the Glasgow giants (and indeed football), by beating them in a penalty shoot-out.

However, with one mighty leap... and a flashing downward header early in the first half... one million pound Dutch giant, Pierre van Hooijdonk, ended the years of waiting for Celtic, and repaid his transfer fee all in one go. Tosh McKinlay, recruited earlier from Heart of Midlothian, made his contribution too, sending in the cross that helped bring the Cup to Parkhead for the 30th time.

Finally, after a long six year famine without a trophy, the loyal Celtic following cheered as Paul McStay collected his first piece of silverware as captain of the club from the Duchess of Kent and ensured that European football would return to Celtic Park this season. It had been a long wait, but all Celtic fans will be hoping that this Tennents Scottish Cup victory will be the catalyst for bigger and indeed better times ahead.

DIXON BLACKSTOCK
(Scottish Sunday Express)

Pierre van Hooijdonk leaps to conquer

FIRST ROUND

Saturday, 10th December, 1994

DUMBARTON 1   **STIRLING ALBION 1**
McKinnon   McInnes
(Abandoned at Half-time due to a Waterlogged Pitch)
Dumbarton: MacFarlane, Gow, Foster, Melvin, Fabiani, MacLeod, Mooney, King, McKinnon, McGarvey, Ward
Substitutes not used: Campbell, J. Meechan, Dennison (Goalkeeper)
Stirling Albion: McGeown, Paterson, Gibson, Mitchell, Watson, Tait, McInnes, Stewart, Watters, Taggart, McLeod
Substitutes not used: Armstrong, Farquhar, Monaghan (Goalkeeper)

Saturday, 17th December, 1994

STENHOUSEMUIR 3   **EAST STIRLINGSHIRE 0**
Mathieson, Sprott, Christie
Stenhousemuir: Harkness, McNiven, Donaldson, Armstrong, Godfrey, Christie, Steel, Fisher, Mathieson, Hutchison, Sprott
Substitutes not used: McGeachie, Clarke
East Stirlingshire: McDougall, Russell, R. Lee, Watt (Stirling), Millar, Ross, I. Lee, Scott, Dwyer, Geraghty, Conroy
Substitute not used: Abercromby

CALEDONIAN THISTLE 1   **QUEEN OF THE SOUTH 2**
McAllister   Bell, Bryce
Caledonian Thistle: McRitchie, Brennan, McAllister, Hercher, Andrew, Baltacha, S. MacDonald, Noble, MacMillan, Christie, Robertson
Substitutes not used: McKenzie, Mitchell, Calder (Goalkeeper)
Queen of the South: Purdie, B. McKeown, D. McKeown, C. Campbell, Hetherington, McFarlane, Bryce, Bell, McLaren (Brown), Kennedy, Jackson
Substitutes not used: Cook, McQueen (Goalkeeper)

DUMBARTON 3   **STIRLING ALBION 3**
Ward (2), McKinnon   Watters, Mitchell, Tait
Dumbarton: MacFarlane, Gow, Foster, Melvin, Fabiani, MacLeod (J. Meechan), Mooney (Campbell), King, McKinnon, McGarvey, Ward
Substitute not used: Dennison (Goalkeeper)

Stirling Albion: Monaghan, Paterson, Gibson, Mitchell, Watson, Tait, McInnes, Stewart (Armstrong), Watters (Farquhar), Taggart, McLeod
Substitute not used: Kerr (Goalkeeper)

Monday, 26th December, 1994

ALBION ROVERS 2   **MONTROSE 5**
J. McBride, Docherty   MacRonald (2), Milne, Kennedy, McGlashan
Albion Rovers: Davidson, McDonald, Gallagher, Kerr, Ryan, Collins, Dolan, Shah (Docherty), J. McBride, M. McBride (Quinn), Scott
Substitute not used: Wight (Goalkeeper)
Montrose: Larter, Robertson, Tindal, Garden, Masson, Haro, Cooper (Milne), Stephen, McGlashan, Kennedy, MacRonald
Substitute not used: Brown

FIRST ROUND REPLAY

Monday, 19th December, 1994

STIRLING ALBION 3   **DUMBARTON 0**
Taggart (2), McInnes
Stirling Albion: Monaghan, Paterson (Kerr), Gibson, Mitchell, Watson, Tait, McInnes, Armstrong, Watters, Taggart, McLeod
Substitutes not used: Farquhar, McAneny (Goalkeeper)
Dumbarton: MacFarlane, Gow, Fabiani, Melvin, Marsland, Campbell, Mooney (Gibson), King, McKinnon, McGarvey, Ward
Substitute not used: J. Meechan, Dennison (Goalkeeper)

SECOND ROUND

Saturday, 7th January, 1995

BRECHIN CITY 2   **STIRLING ALBION 3**
McNeill, Brand   McInnes (2), Taggart
Brechin City: Balfour, Buick, Marr, Cairney, Conway, Vannett (Bell), McKellar, Mitchell, Price, R. Smith (Brand), McNeill
Stirling Albion: Monaghan, Paterson, Gibson, Mitchell, McQuilter, Kerr, McInnes, Armstrong, Watters (Drinkell), Taggart, McLeod
Substitutes not used: Watson, McAneny (Goalkeeper)

WHITEHILL WELFARE 0   **MONTROSE 0**
Whitehill Welfare: Elen, Richford, Gowrie, Hunter, Steel, Millar, O'Rourke, (R. Smith), Bird (Blackie), Sneddon, Purves, D. Smith
Substitute not used: Cantley (Goalkeeper)
Montrose: Larter, Robertson, Tindal, Stephen, Masson, Haro, Cooper, MacDonald (Milne), McGlashan, Kennedy, MacRonald
Substitutes not used: Brown, Massie (Goalkeeper)

FORFAR ATHLETIC 0   **MEADOWBANK THISTLE 1**
     Sinclair
Forfar Athletic: Arthur, Irvine, McPhee, Mann, Archibald, Glennie, Mearns (Hannigan), Heddle, Ross, McCormick, Bingham
Substitutes not used: McLaren, Stephen (Goalkeeper)
Meadowbank Thistle: Ellison, Davidson, Martin, Graham (Thorburn), Thomson, Sorbie, Samuel, Wilson, Little, McLeod, Bailey (Sinclair)
Substitute not used: Douglas (Goalkeeper)

BURNTISLAND SHIPYARD 6   **ST. CUTHBERT WANDERERS 2**
Matthew (3), Taylor, Paton,   Tweedie, Baker
Drummond
Burntisland Shipyard: Shanahan, Parnell, Taylor (Lewis), Lawrie, Bray, McIlvean, Matthew, Horsburgh (Murray), Campbell, Paton Drummond
Substitute not used: Kelly (Goalkeeper)
St. Cuthbert Wanderers: McHenry, Johnston, Kirkpatrick, Christie McCulloch, Crosbie (Murray), Niven, Durham (Maxwell), Tweedie, Simpson, Baker

GALA FAIRYDEAN 2   **EAST FIFE 6**
Cockburn, Hunter   Burns, Hutcheon (3), Allan, Donaghy
Gala Fairydean: Brown, Catterson, Henry, Potts (Dixon), Rae, Wilson (Campbell), Hunter, Sinclair, De Melo, Cockburn, Ritchie
Substitute not used: Fraser (Goalkeeper)
East Fife: Wilson, Sneddon (Gibb), Hildersley, Burns, Beaton, Cusick, Allan, Donaghy, Scott, Hutcheon (Hunter), Hope
Substitute not used: Robertson (Goalkeeper)

COVE RANGERS 2   **COWDENBEATH 1**
Caldwell (2)   Conn
Cove Rangers: MacLean, Morrison, Whyte, Morland, Paterson, Baxter, Megginson, Park (Walker), Caldwell, Lorimer, Beattie (Buchan)
Substitute not used: Charles (Goalkeeper)
Cowdenbeath: Russell, Scott (Barclay), Murdoch, Humphreys, Conn, Tait (Callaghan), Fellenger, Black, Yardley, Soutar (Maloney), Wardell

ALLOA 2   **ROSS COUNTY 3**
Lamont, Diver   Connelly (2), MacPherson
Alloa: Butter, Hannah (Willock), Bennett (McAnenay), Kemp, McCulloch, Lawrie, McAvoy, Cadden, Diver, Moffat, Lamont
Substitute not used: Graham (Goalkeeper)
Ross County: Hutchison, Somerville, Reid, Williamson, Bellshaw, Furphy, Ferries (Mackay), Grant, MacPherson (Duff), Connelly, Herd
Substitute not used: MacMillan (Goalkeeper)

QUEEN OF THE SOUTH 0   **CLYDE 2**
     Dickson, O'Neill
Queen of the South: McQueen, B. McKeown, D. McKeown, C. Campbell, Hetherington, Bell (McLaren), Kennedy (Jackson), Ramsay, D. Campbell, Bryce, Mallan
Substitute not used: Purdie (Goalkeeper)
Clyde: Fridge, O'Neill, Angus, McCarron (McAulay), Thomson, Brown, Dickson, Watson, McCluskey (McConnell), Neill, Parks
Substitute not used: Hillcoat (Goalkeeper)

KEITH 2   **HUNTLY 2**
Thomson, Rougvie (o.g.)   Whyte, Thomson
Keith: Thain (Marr), Thow, Tosh, Allan, Collie, Gibson, Maver, Thomson, Lavelle, Will, Wilson (McPherson)
Substitute not used: Leddie
Huntly: Gardiner, Murphy, Dunsire, Mone, Rougvie, De Barros, Gray, Stewart (Grant), Thomson (Yeats), Whyte, Lennox
Substitute not used: Inverarity (Goalkeeper)

BUCKIE THISTLE 1
Robertson

BERWICK RANGERS 4
Hawke, Graham, Valentine
Mann (o.g.)

Buckie Thistle: Innes, Girling, Bruce, Mathieson, Henderson, Mann, Gibson, Robertson, Begg (Galbraith), McPherson, Smith
Substitute not used: Bruce

Berwick Rangers: Osborne, Fraser, Valentine, Cole, Cowan, Irvine, Gallacher, Forrester (Kane), Hawke, Rutherford, Graham (Clegg)
Substitute not used: N. Young (Goalkeeper)

STENHOUSEMUIR 4
Fisher, Mathieson (2), Steel

ARBROATH 0

Stenhousemuir: Harkness, McNiven, Roseburgh (McGeachie), Armstrong, Godfrey, Christie, Steel, Fisher (Donaldson), Mathieson, Hutchison, Sprott

Arbroath: Dunn, McMillan (Shanks), Elder, Ward, Murray, Spittal, Elliot, Farnan, Gardner, Tosh (Craib), Downie
Substitute not used: Jackson (Goalkeeper)

Monday, 9th January, 1995

QUEEN'S PARK 2
G. Orr, Rodden

GREENOCK MORTON 2
Alexander, Anderson

Queen's Park: Chalmers, J. Orr (Campbell), Maxwell, Kerr, Elder, Graham, Callan, G. Orr, McPhee, Caven, Edgar (Rodden)
Substitute not used: Moonie (Goalkeeper)

Greenock Morton: Wylie, Collins, Cormack, Anderson, McCahill, Lindberg, McArthur, Mahood, Alexander, McInnes, Rajamaki
Substitutes not used: Blair, Fowler

SECOND ROUND REPLAYS
Saturday, 14th January, 1995

MONTROSE 5
Kennedy (2), Masson, McLashan, Stephen

WHITEHILL WELFARE 2
Millar, Steel

Montrose: Larter, Robertson, Tindal, Masson, Grant, Haro, MacDonald (Cooper), Stephen, McGlashan, Kennedy, MacRonald
Substitutes not used: Milne, Massie (Goalkeeper)

Whitehill Welfare: Elen, Purves, Gowrie, Hunter, Steel, Millar, O'Rourke (McCulloch), R. Smith, Sneddon, Brown, D. Smith (Bird)
Substitute not used: Cantley (Goalkeeper)

HUNTLY 3
Rougvie, Stewart, Whyte

KEITH 1
Lavelle

Huntly: Gardiner, Grant, Dunsire, Mone, Rougvie, De Barros, Gray, Stewart (Yeats), Thomson, Whyte (Copland), Lennon
Substitute not used: Inverarity (Goalkeeper)

Keith: Cathcart, Thow (Leddie), Tosh, Allan, Collie, Gibson, Maver, Thomson, Lavelle, Will, Wilson (McPherson)
Substitute not used: Marr (Goalkeeper)

Tuesday, 17th January, 1995

GREENOCK MORTON 2
Rajamaki, Lilley

QUEEN'S PARK 1 (AET)
(1-1 After 90 minutes)
Caven

Greenock Morton: Wylie, Collins, McArthur, Anderson, McCahill, Lindberg, Lilley, Mahood, Alexander, Blair (McPherson), Rajamaki
Substitute not used: Fowler

Queen's Park: Chalmers, J. Orr, Ferguson, Kerr, Maxwell, Matchett, Callan, Smith (Bradley), G. Orr, Caven, McGoldrick (Rodden)
Substitute not used: Moonie (Goalkeeper)

THIRD ROUND
Saturday, 28th January, 1995

MONTROSE 0

HIBERNIAN 2
McGinlay, D. Jackson

Montrose: Larter, Robertson, Tindal, Masson (Cooper), Grant, Haro, Garden (Stephen), Beedie, McGlashan, Kennedy, MacRonald
Substitute not used: Massie (Goalkeeper)

Hibernian: Leighton, W. Miller, Mitchell, McGinlay, Tweed, Farrell, McAllister (Findlay), Evans, Wright, D. Jackson, Tortolano
Substitutes not used: Weir, Reid (Goalkeeper)

COVE RANGERS 0

DUNFERMLINE ATHLETIC 4
Petrie (2), Smith, Hawkins

Cove Rangers: Charles, Morrison, Whyte, Walker, Paterson, Buchan, Megginson (Gibson), Park, Caldwell (Leslie), Lorimer, Beattie
Substitute not used: MacLean (Goalkeeper)

Dunfermline Athletic: Van De Kamp, McNamara, Fleming, McCathie, Cooper, Smith, French, Robertson, Tod, Petrie, Hawkins (Ward)
Substitute not used: Paterson

RAITH ROVERS 1
Crawford

AYR UNITED 0

Raith Rovers: Thomson, McAnespie, Broddle, Coyle, Raeside, Sinclair, Nicholl, Dalziel, Crawford (Graham), Lennon, Wilson
Substitutes not used: Kirkwood, Allan (Goalkeeper)

Ayr United: Duncan, McKilligan, Connie, Sharples, Rolling, MacFarlane, Gribben (Bilsland), Moore, Gilzean, Jackson, Gorgues (Tannock)
Substitute not used: McIntosh (Goalkeeper)

DUNDEE UNITED 0

CLYDE 0

Dundee United: O'Hanlon, Perry, Malpas, Hannah, Petric, Welsh, Bowman, McKinlay, Nixon, Brewster, Dailly
Substitutes not used: Ferreri, Crabbe, Jorgensen (Goalkeeper)

Clyde: Fridge, O'Neill, Angus, Nisbit, Knox, Brown, Dickson, Watson, McCluskey (MacKenzie), Neill, Parks
Substitutes not used: McCarron, Hillcoat (Goalkeeper)

HUNTLY 7
Stewart (3), Whyte, Lawrie (o.g.),
Thomson, De Barros

BURNTISLAND SHIPYARD 0

Huntly: Gardiner, Yeats, Dunsire (Copland), Mone, Grant, De Barros, Gray, Stewart, Thomson, Whyte , Lennox (Robertson)
Substitute not used: Inverarity (Goalkeeper)

Burntisland Shipyard: Shanahan (Kelly), Parnell, Taylor, Lawrie, (Lewis), Bray, McIlvean, Matthew, Horsburgh, Campbell, Paton (Murray), Drummond

CELTIC 2
Falconer, Van Hooijdonk

ST. MIRREN 0

Celtic: Bonner, Boyd, Gray, O'Neill, McNally, Grant, McLaughlin, O'Donnell, Van Hooijdonk (Walker), Falconer, Collins
Substitutes not used: McKinlay, Marshall (Goalkeeper)

St. Mirren: Money, Dawson, McIntyre, McWhirter, McLaughlin, Fullarton, Dick, Bone (Inglis), Lavety, R. Gillies (Hewitt), Elliot
Substitute not used: Combe (Goalkeeper)

ABERDEEN 1
Jess

STRANRAER 0

Aberdeen: Snelders, Wright, Glass, Kane, Inglis, G. Smith, Jess, Shearer (Thomson), Miller, Dodds, Grant
Substitutes not used: Irvine, Watt (Goalkeeper)

Stranraer: Ross, McLean, Hughes, Gallagher, Howard, Millar, Sloan, Walker, Duncan, Callaghan (Cody), Reilly
Substitutes not used: McCaffrey, Duffy (Goalkeeper)

KILMARNOCK 0

GREENOCK MORTON 0

Kilmarnock: Lekovic, MacPherson, Black, Montgomerie, Anderson, Reilly, Mitchell (Maskrey), Henry, Brown, Connor, McKee (Williamson)
Substitute not used: Geddes (Goalkeeper)

Greenock Morton: Wylie, Collins, McArthur, Anderson, McCahill, Lindberg, Lilley, Blair (Fowler), Alexander, McInnes, Rajamaki
Substitute not used: McPherson

Sunday, 29th January, 1995

DUNDEE 2
Shaw, Hamilton

PARTICK THISTLE 1
Craig

Dundee: Pageaud, McQuillan, C. Duffy, Wieghorst (Ritchie), J. Duffy, Bain, Shaw, Vrto, Hamilton, Britton, McCann
Substitutes not used: Tosh, Mathers (Goalkeeper)

Partick Thistle: Walker, Dinnie, Pittman, Watson, Welsh, Turner, McDonald (Gibson), Craig, Foster, McWilliams, Taylor
Substitutes not used: Milne, Cairns (Goalkeeper)

Tuesday, 31st January, 1995

FALKIRK 0   MOTHERWELL 0
(Abandoned after 52 Minutes Due to Floodlight Failure)

Falkirk: Parks, Hamilton, McQueen, Oliver, Weir, McGowan, May, Henderson, McDonald, Fulton, MacKenzie

Substitutes not used: Rice, James, Lamont (Goalkeeper)

Motherwell: Woods, Shannon, McKinnon, Krivokapic, Martin, McCart, Lambert, Dolan, Coyne, Arnott, S. McMillan

Substitutes not used: McGrillen, Philliben, Howie (Goalkeeper)

ST. JOHNSTONE 1   STENHOUSEMUIR 1
McNiven (o.g.)   Sprott

St. Johnstone: Main, Cherry, Preston, Irons, Weir, McGowne, O'Neil, Curran, Twaddle (Davenport), O'Boyle, Deas

Substitutes not used: McMartin, Robertson (Goalkeeper)

Stenhousemuir: Harkness, McNiven, Donaldson, Armstrong, McGeachie, Christie, Steel, Fisher, Mathieson, Hutchison, Sprott

Substitutes not used: Godfrey, Clarke

Wednesday, 1st February, 1995

CLYDEBANK 1   HEART OF MIDLOTHIAN 1
Eadie   Robertson

Clydebank: Matthews, McStay, Crawford, Murdoch, Sweeney, Currie, Cooper, Lansdowne, Eadie, Flannigan, Jack

Substitutes not used: Walker, Grady, Monaghan (Goalkeeper)

Heart of Midlothian: Nelson, Frail, C. Miller, Levein, Mackay, McPherson, Hamilton, Bett (Colquhoun), Thomas (Jamieson), Robertson, Hagen

Substitute not used: Smith (Goalkeeper)

STIRLING ALBION 1   AIRDRIEONIANS 2
McQuilter   Andrew Smith (2)

Stirling Albion: Monaghan, Paterson, Gibson, Mitchell, McQuilter, Kerr (Drinkell), McInnes, Tait, Watters, Taggart, McLeod

Substitutes not used: Watson, McGeown (Goalkeeper)

Airdrieonians: Martin, Stewart, Anthony Smith, Sandison, Hay, Black, Boyle, Lawrence, Cooper (J. McIntyre), Harvey (Wilson), Andrew Smith

Substitute not used: McCulloch (Goalkeeper)

EAST FIFE 1   ROSS COUNTY 0
Allan

East Fife: Robertson, Bell, Hamill, Sneddon, Cusick, Donaghy, Allan, Hildersley, Scott, Hunter (Hutcheon), Hope

Substitutes not used: Gibb, Wilson (Goalkeeper)

Ross County: Hutchison, Somerville, Reid, Williamson, Bellshaw, Furphy, Ferries, Grant, Herd, Connelly, Andrew MacLeod (MacPherson)

Substitutes not used: Mackay, MacMillan (Goalkeeper)

Monday, 6th February, 1995

HAMILTON ACADEMICAL 1   RANGERS 3
Lorimer   Steven, Boli, Laudrup

Hamilton Academical: Ferguson, Renicks, Hillcoat, McEntegart, McCall, McIntosh, G. Clark, McStay (Lorimer), Chalmers, Duffield, McQuade (Baptie)

Substitute not used: Cormack (Goalkeeper)

Rangers: Maxwell, Moore, D. Robertson, Gough, Boli, McCall, Steven, Miller, Durie (Brown), Hateley, Laudrup

Substitutes not used: Durrant, Scott (Goalkeeper)

MEADOWBANK THISTLE 1   BERWICK RANGERS 1
Cowan (o.g.)   Fraser

Meadowbank Thistle: Ellison, Davidson, Martin, Williamson, Thomson, Sorbie (Little), Wilson, Bailey, Harris, McLeod, Sinclair (Samuel)

Substitute not used: Douglas (Goalkeeper)

Berwick Rangers: Osborne, Greenwood, Banks, Valentine, Cowan, Fraser, Forrester (Kane), Neil, Hawke, Irvine, Graham

Substitutes not used: Clegg, N. Young (Goalkeeper)

FALKIRK 0   MOTHERWELL 2
          Burns (2)

Falkirk: Parks, Weir, McQueen (James), Oliver, McLaughlin, Rice, May, McGowan, McDonald (Henderson), Fulton, MacKenzie

Substitute not used: Lamont (Goalkeeper)

Motherwell: Woods, Philliben, McKinnon, Krivokapic (S. McMillan), Martin, McCart, Lambert, Dolan, Burns, McGrillen (Roddie), Davies

Substitute not used: Howie (Goalkeeper)

THIRD ROUND REPLAYS

Tuesday, 31st January, 1995

GREENOCK MORTON 1   KILMARNOCK 2 (AET)
Anderson   (1-1 After 90 minutes)
          Maskrey (2)

Greenock Morton: Wylie, Collins, McArthur, Anderson, McCahill, Lindberg, Lilley (Fowler), Mahood, Alexander (McPherson) McInnes, Rajamaki

Kilmarnock: Lekovic, MacPherson, Black, Montgomerie, Whitworth, Anderson (Maskrey), Mitchell, Henry, Brown, Reilly, Williamson (Napier)

Substitute not used: Geddes (Goalkeeper)

Tuesday, 7th February, 1995

HEART OF MIDLOTHIAN 2   CLYDEBANK 1
Robertson, Thomas   Eadie

Heart of Midlothian: Nelson, Frail, Berry, Levein, Bett, McPherson, Colquhoun (Mackay), Hamilton, Thomas (C. Miller), Robertson, Hagen

Substitute not used: Smith (Goalkeeper)

Clydebank: Matthews, McStay, Crawford (Bowman), Murdoch, Sweeney, Currie, Cooper, Lansdowne, Eadie, Flannigan (Grady), Jack

Substitute not used: Monaghan (Goalkeeper)

BERWICK RANGERS 3   MEADOWBANK THISTLE 3
(AET–2-2 After 90 minutes)
Meadowbank Thistle Won 7-6 on Kicks from the Penalty Mark
Irvine, Neil, Clegg   Graham, Bailey, Wilson

Berwick Rangers: Osborne, Greenwood, Banks, Valentine, Cowan (Clegg), Fraser, Forrester (Graham), Neil, Hawke, Irvine, Kane

Substitute not used: N. Young (Goalkeeper)

Meadowbank Thistle: Ellison, Davidson, Martin, Williamson, Graham, Samuel, Wilson, Little, Harris (Bailey), McLeod, Sinclair (Sorbie)

Substitute not used: Douglas (Goalkeeper)

CLYDE 1   DUNDEE UNITED 5
Angus   McKinlay, Craig, Hannah
          Bowman, Nixon

Clyde: Fridge, O'Neill, Angus, Nisbet (Neill), Thomson, Brown, Dickson, Watson, Parks, Knox, MacKenzie (Prunty)

Substitute not used: Hillcoat (Goalkeeper)

Dundee United: O'Hanlon, McInally (Welsh), Malpas, Hannah, Petric, Dailly, Bowman, McKinlay (Nixon), Brewster, Ristic, Craig

Substitute not used: Jorgensen (Goalkeeper)

STENHOUSEMUIR 4   ST. JOHNSTONE 0
Sprott (2), Clarke, Donaldson

Stenhousemuir: Harkness, McNiven, Donaldson, Armstrong, McGeachie, Christie, Steel (Clarke), Fisher, Mathieson, Hutchison (Roseburgh), Sprott

St. Johnstone: Main, Cherry, Preston (O'Boyle), Irons, Weir, McGowne, O'Neil, Curran, Wright, Twaddle (English), Farquhar

Substitute not used: Robertson (Goalkeeper)

FOURTH ROUND

Saturday, 18th February, 1995

HIBERNIAN 2   MOTHERWELL 0
Harper, McGinlay

Hibernian: Leighton, W. Miller, Mitchell, McGinlay, Tweed, Hunter (Tortolano), Weir, Harper, Wright, D. Jackson (McGraw), C. Jackson

Substitute not used: Reid (Goalkeeper)

Motherwell: Woods, Shannon, McKinnon, Krivokapic, Martin, Philliben, Lambert (McGrillen), Dolan (Kirk), Burns, Arnott, Davies

Substitute not used: Howie (Goalkeeper)

HUNTLY 1   DUNDEE UNITED 3
Stewart   Brewster, Malpas, Hannah

Huntly: Gardiner, Murphy, Dunsire, Mone, Rougvie, De Barros, Gray (Copland), Stewart, Thomson, Whyte (Yeats), Lennox

Substitute not used: Inverarity (Goalkeeper)

Dundee United: O'Hanlon, McInally, Malpas, Hannah, Petric, Welsh, Bowman, McKinlay, Gomes (Nixon), Brewster (Ristic), Dailly

Substitute not used: Garden (Goalkeeper)

AIRDRIEONIANS 2   DUNFERMLINE ATHLETIC 0
Cooper, Andrew Smith

Airdrieonians: Martin, Stewart, Jack, Sandison, T. McIntyre, Black, Boyle, Davies, Cooper, Harvey (Andrew Smith), Lawrence

Substitutes not used: J. McIntyre, McCulloch (Goalkeeper)

Dunfermline Athletic: Van De Kamp, Den Bieman, Fleming, McCathie, Paterson, Smith, French, Robertson, Tod (Moore), Petrie, Ward

Substitutes not used: Cooper, Westwater (Goalkeeper)

STENHOUSEMUIR 2 **ABERDEEN 0**
Steel (2)

Stenhousemuir: Harkness, Clarke, Donaldson, Armstrong, McGeachie, Christie, Steel, Fisher, Mathieson, Hutchison, Sprott
Substitutes not used: Roseburgh, Godfrey
Aberdeen: Snelders, Wright, Glass, Kane, Inglis (Irvine), G. Smith, Jess, Shearer, Miller (Hetherston), Dodds, McKinnon
Substitute not used: Wall (Goalkeeper)

CELTIC 3 **MEADOWBANK THISTLE 0**
Van Hooijdonk (2), Falconer

Celtic: Marshall, McNally, McKinlay, O'Neil, Mowbray, Grant, McLaughlin (Walker), O'Donnell (Craig), Van Hooijdonk, Falconer, Collins
Substitute not used: Bonner (Goalkeeper)
Meadowbank Thistle: Ellison, Davidson, Martin, Graham, Williamson, Sorbie, Wilson, Bailey (Thorburn), Harris (Little), McLeod, Samuel
Substitute not used: Douglas (Goalkeeper)

DUNDEE 1 **RAITH ROVERS 2**
Shaw Graham, Rowbotham

Dundee: Pageaud, Farningham, C. Duffy (Hamilton), J. Duffy, Blake (Tosh), Bain, Shaw, Vrto, Wieghorst, Britton, McCann
Substitute not used: Mathers (Goalkeeper)
Raith Rovers: Thomson, McAnespie, Broddle (Rowbotham), Coyle, Dennis, Raeside (Wilson), Sinclair, Cameron, Graham, Lennon, Crawford
Substitute not used: Allan (Goalkeeper)

KILMARNOCK 4 **EAST FIFE 0**
Maskrey (2), Reilly, Black

Kilmarnock: Lekovic, MacPherson (McKee), Black, Reilly, Whitworth, Anderson, Mitchell, Henry, Brown, Connor, Maskrey
Substitutes not used: Roberts, Geddes (Goalkeeper)
East Fife: Robertson, Bell, Hamill, Burns, Sneddon, Gibb, Allan, Archibald, Andrew, Hunter, Hope (Hutcheon)
Substitutes not used: Irvine, Wilson (Goalkeeper)

Monday, 20th February, 1995

HEART OF MIDLOTHIAN 4 **RANGERS 2**
C. Miller, McPherson, Laudrup, Durie
Robertson, Thomas

Heart of Midlothian: Nelson, Frail, C. Miller, (Colquhoun), Levein, Bett, McPherson, Hamilton, Mackay, Robertson (Thomas), J. Millar, Hagen
Substitute not used: Smith (Goalkeeper)
Rangers: Maxwell, Moore, D. Robertson (Durrant), Gough, McLaren, Cleland (Brown), Steven, McCall, Miller, Durie, Laudrup
Substitute not used: Thomson (Goalkeeper)

FIFTH ROUND

Friday, 10th March, 1995

CELTIC 1 **KILMARNOCK 0**
Collins

Celtic: Bonner, Boyd, McKinlay, O'Neil, Mowbray, O'Donnell (Grant), McLaughlin, McStay, Van Hooijdonk, Falconer, Collins
Substitutes not used: Walker, Marshall (Goalkeeper)
Kilmarnock: Lekovic, MacPherson, Black, Reilly, Whitworth, Anderson, Mitchell, Henry, McKee (Skilling), Connor (McCarrison), Maskrey
Substitute not used: Geddes (Goalkeeper)

Saturday, 11th March, 1995

RAITH ROVERS 1 **AIRDRIEONIANS 4**
Cameron Harvey (2), Davies, Black

Raith Rovers: Thomson, McAnespie, Rowbotham, Cameron, Dennis, Sinclair, Wilson (Dalziel), Crawford, Graham, Lennon (Broddle), Dair
Substitute not used: Allan (Goalkeeper)
Airdrieonians: Martin, Stewart, Jack, Sandison, Hay, Black, Boyle, Davies, Cooper, Harvey (Lawrence), Andrew Smith
Substitutes not used: Anthony Smith, McCulloch (Goalkeeper)

STENHOUSEMUIR 0 **HIBERNIAN 4**
Harper (2), Tortolano, O'Neill

Stenhousemuir: Harkness, Clarke (Roseburgh), Donaldson, Armstrong, McGeachie (McNiven), Christie, Steel, Fisher, Mathieson, Hutchison, Sprott
Hibernian: Leighton, W. Miller, Mitchell, Farrell, Tweed, Hunter, Harper, Tortolano, Wright, D. Jackson, O'Neill
Substitutes not used: Weir, McGraw, Reid (Goalkeeper)

Sunday, 12th March, 1995

HEART OF MIDLOTHIAN 2 **DUNDEE UNITED 1**
J. Millar (2) Gomes

Heart of Midlothian: Nelson, Frail, J. Millar, Berry, Jamieson, McPherson, Colquhoun (Thomas), Hamilton, Robertson, Mackay, Hagen (Leitch)
Substitute not used: Smith (Goalkeeper)
Dundee United: O'Hanlon, McInally, Malpas, Hannah (Brewster), Petric, Welsh, Bowman, McKinlay, Gomes, Crabbe (Nixon), Dailly
Substitute not used: Jorgensen (Goalkeeper)

SEMI-FINALS
Friday, 7th April, 1995
IBROX STADIUM, GLASGOW

CELTIC 0 **HIBERNIAN 0**

Celtic: Bonner, Boyd, McKinlay, Vata, O'Neil, Grant, McLaughlin, McStay, Van Hooijdonk (Falconer), Walker, Collins
Substitutes not used: O'Donnell, Marshall (Goalkeeper)
Hibernian: Leighton, W. Miller, Mitchell, McGinlay, Tweed, Millen, Harper (McGraw), Farrell, Wright, D. Jackson, O'Neill
Substitutes not used: Tortolano, Reid (Goalkeeper)

Saturday, 8th April, 1995
HAMPDEN PARK, GLASGOW

AIRDRIEONIANS 1 **HEART OF MIDLOTHIAN 0**
Cooper

Airdrieonians: Martin, Stewart, Jack, Sandison, Andrew Smith (Hay), Black, Boyle, Davies, Cooper, Harvey (Anthony Smith), Lawrence
Substitute not used: McCulloch (Goalkeeper)
Heart of Midlothian: Nelson, Mackay, C. Miller, Levein, Jamieson (Thomas), McPherson, Hamilton (Colquhoun), Bett, Robertson, J. Millar, Hagen
Substitute not used: Smith (Goalkeeper)

SEMI-FINAL REPLAY
Tuesday, 11th April, 1995
IBROX STADIUM, GLASGOW

CELTIC 3 **HIBERNIAN 1**
Falconer, Collins, O'Donnell Wright

Celtic: Bonner, Boyd, McKinlay, Vata, O'Neil, Grant (O'Donnell), McLaughlin, McStay, Falconer, Walker (Donnelly), Collins
Substitute not used: Marshall (Goalkeeper)
Hibernian: Leighton, Miller, Mitchell, McGinlay, Tweed, Millen, Harper (Tortolano), McGraw (Evans), Wright, D. Jackson, O'Neill
Substitute not used: Reid (Goalkeeper)

FINAL
Saturday, 27th May, 1995
HAMPDEN PARK, GLASGOW

CELTIC 1 AIRDRIEONIANS 0

Celtic: Bonner, Boyd, McKinlay, Vata, McNally, Grant, McLaughlin, McStay, Van Hooijdonk (Falconer), Donnelly (O'Donnell), Collins
Substitute not used: Marshall (Goalkeeper)
Airdrieonians: Martin, Stewart, Jack, Sandison, Hay (J. McIntyre), Black, Boyle, Andrew Smith, Cooper, Harvey (Anthony Smith), Lawrence
Substitute not used: McCulloch (Goalkeeper)

Scorer: Van Hooijdonk
Referee: L. W. Mottram (Forth)
Attendance: 38,672

SEASON 1919/20

17th April, 1920 at Hampden Park; Attendance 95,000;
Referee: Mr W. Bell (Hamilton)

KILMARNOCK 3	ALBION ROVERS 2
Culley, Shortt, J. Smith	Watson, Hillhouse

SEASON 1920/21

16th April, 1921 at Celtic Park; Attendance 28,294;
Referee: Mr H. Humphreys (Greenock)

PARTICK THISTLE 1	RANGERS 0
Blair	

SEASON 1921/22

15th April, 1922 at Hampden Park; Attendance 75,000
Referee: Mr T. Dougray (Bellshill)

MORTON 1	RANGERS 0
Gourlay	

SEASON 1922/23

31th March, 1923 at Hampden Park;
Attendance 80,100; Referee: Mr T. Dougray (Bellshill)

CELTIC 1	HIBERNIAN 0
Cassidy	

SEASON 1923/24

19th April, 1924 at Ibrox Stadium; Attendance 59,218;
Referee: Mr T. Dougray (Bellshill)

AIRDRIEONIANS 2	HIBERNIAN 0
Russell (2)	

SEASON 1924/25

11th April, 1925 at Hampden Park;
Attendance 75,137; Referee: Mr T. Dougray (Bellshill)

CELTIC 2	DUNDEE 1
Gallacher, McGrory	McLean

SEASON 1925/26

10th April, 1926 at Hampden Park; Attendance 98,620;
Referee: Mr P. Craigmyle (Aberdeen)

ST. MIRREN 2	CELTIC 0
McCrae, Howieson	

SEASON 1926/27

16th April, 1927 at Hampden Park; Attendance 79,500;
Referee: Mr T. Dougray (Bellshill)

CELTIC 3	EAST FIFE 1
Robertson (o.g.), McLean, Connolly	Wood

SEASON 1927/28

14th April, 1928 at Hampden Park; Attendance 118,115;
Referee: Mr W. Bell (Motherwell)

RANGERS 4	CELTIC 0
Meiklejohn (pen), McPhail, Archibald (2)	

SEASON 1928/29

6th April, 1929 at Hampden Park; Attendance 114,708;
Referee: Mr T. Dougray (Bellshill)

KILMARNOCK 2	RANGERS 0
Aitken, Williamson	

SEASON 1929/30

12th April, 1930 at Hampden Park; Attendance 107,475;
Referee: Mr W. Bell (Motherwell)

RANGERS 0	PARTICK THISTLE 0

REPLAY
16th April, 1930 at Hampden Park; Attendance 90,000;
Referee: Mr W. Bell (Motherwell)

RANGERS 2	PARTICK THISTLE 1
Marshall, Craig	Torbet

SEASON 1930/31

11th April, 1931 at Hampden Park; Attendance 104,803;
Referee: Mr P. Craigmyle (Aberdeen)

CELTIC 2	MOTHERWELL 2
McGrory, Craig (o.g.)	Stevenson, McMenemy

REPLAY
15th April, 1931 at Hampden Park; Attendance 98,579;
Referee: Mr P. Craigmyle (Aberdeen)

CELTIC 4	MOTHERWELL 2
R. Thomson (2), McGrory (2)	Murdoch, Stevenson

SEASON 1931/32

16th April, 1932 at Hampden Park; Attendance 111,982;
Referee: Mr P. Craigmyle (Aberdeen)

RANGERS 1	KILMARNOCK 1
McPhail	Maxwell

REPLAY
20th April, 1932 at Hampden Park; Attendance 110,695;
Referee: Mr P. Craigmyle (Aberdeen)

RANGERS 3	KILMARNOCK 0
Fleming, McPhail, English	

SEASON 1932/33

15th April, 1933 at Hampden Park; Attendance 102,339;
Referee: Mr T. Dougray (Bellshill)

CELTIC 1	MOTHERWELL 0
McGrory	

SEASON 1933/34

21st April, 1934 at Hampden Park; Attendance 113,430;
Referee: Mr M. C. Hutton (Glasgow)

RANGERS 5	ST. MIRREN 0
Nicholson (2), McPhail, Main, Smith	

SEASON 1934/35

20th April, 1935 at Hampden Park; Attendance 87,286;
Referee: Mr H. Watson (Glasgow)

RANGERS 2	HAMILTON ACADEMICAL 1
Smith (2)	Harrison

SEASON 1935/36

18th April 1936 at Hampden Park; Attendance 88,859;
Referee: Mr J. M. Martin (Ladybank)

RANGERS 1	THIRD LANARK 0
McPhail	

SEASON 1936/37

24th April, 1937 at Hampden Park; Attendance 147,365;
Referee: Mr M. C. Hutton (Glasgow)

CELTIC 2	ABERDEEN 1
Crum, Buchan	Armstrong

SEASON 1937/38

23rd April, 1938 at Hampden Park; Attendance 80,091;
Referee: Mr H. Watson (Glasgow)

EAST FIFE 1	KILMARNOCK 1
McLeod	McAvoy

REPLAY
27th April, 1938 at Hampden Park, Attendance 92,716;
Referee: Mr H. Watson (Glasgow)

EAST FIFE 4
McKerrell (2), McLeod, Miller
After extra-time

KILMARNOCK 2
Thomson (pen), McGrogan

SEASON 1938/39
22nd April, 1939 at Hampden Park; Attendance 94,770;
Referee: Mr W. Webb (Glasgow)

CLYDE 4
Wallace, Martin (2), Noble

MOTHERWELL 0

SEASON 1946/47
19th April, 1947 at Hampden Park; Attendance 82,140;
Referee: Mr R. Calder (Glasgow)

ABERDEEN 2
Hamilton, Williams

HIBERNIAN 1
Cuthbertson

SEASON 1947/48
17th April, 1948 at Hampden Park; Attendance 129,176;
Referee: Mr J. M. Martin (Blairgowrie)

RANGERS 1
Gillick
After extra-time

MORTON 1
Whyte

REPLAY
21st April, 1948 at Hampden Park; Attendance 131,975;
Referee: Mr J. M. Martin (Blairgowrie)

RANGERS 1
Williamson
After extra-time

MORTON 0

SEASON 1948/49
23rd April, 1949 at Hampden Park; Attendance 108,435;
Referee: Mr R. G. Benzie (Irvine)

RANGERS 4
Young (2 (2 pens)),
Williamson, Duncanson

CLYDE 1
Galletly

SEASON 1949/50
22nd April, 1950 at Hampden Park; Attendance 118,262
Referee: Mr J. A. Mowat (Burnside)

RANGERS 3
Findlay, Thornton (2)

EAST FIFE 0

SEASON 1950/51
21st April, 1951 at Hampden Park; Attendance 131,943
Referee: Mr J. A. Mowat (Burnside)

CELTIC 1
McPhail

MOTHERWELL 0

SEASON 1951/52
19th April, 1952 at Hampden Park; Attendance 136,304;
Referee: Mr J. A. Mowat (Burnside)

MOTHERWELL 4
Watson, Redpath, Humphries, Kelly

DUNDEE 0

SEASON 1952/53
25th April, 1953 at Hampden Park; Attendance 129,861;
Referee: Mr J. A. Mowat (Burnside)

RANGERS 1
Prentice

ABERDEEN 1
Yorston

REPLAY
29th April, 1953 at Hampden Park; Attendance 112,619;
Referee: Mr J. A. Mowat (Burnside)

RANGERS 1
Simpson

ABERDEEN 0

SEASON 1953/54
24th April, 1954 at Hampden Park; Attendance 129,926;
Referee: Mr C. E. Faultless (Giffnock)

CELTIC 2
Young (o.g.), Fallon

ABERDEEN 1
Buckley

SEASON 1954/55
23rd April, 1955 at Hampden Park; Attendance 106,111;
Referee: Mr C. E. Faultless (Giffnock)

CLYDE 1
Robertson

CELTIC 1
Walsh

REPLAY
27th April, 1955 at Hampden Park; Attendance 68,735;
Referee: Mr C. E. Faultless (Giffnock)

CLYDE 1
Ring

CELTIC 0

SEASON 1955/56
21st April, 1956 at Hampden Park; Attendance 133,399;
Referee: Mr R. H. Davidson (Airdrie)

HEART OF MIDLOTHIAN 3
Crawford (2), Conn

CELTIC 1
Haughney

SEASON 1956/57
20th April, 1957 at Hampden Park; Attendance 81,057;
Referee: Mr J. A. Mowat (Burnside)

FALKIRK 1
Prentice (pen)

KILMARNOCK 1
Curlett

REPLAY
24th April, 1957 at Hampden Park; Attendance 79,785;
Referee: Mr J. A. Mowat (Burnside)

FALKIRK 2
Merchant, Moran
After extra-time

KILMARNOCK 1
Curlett

SEASON 1957/58
26th April, 1958 at Hampden Park; Attendance 95,123;
Referee: Mr J. A. Mowat (Burnside)

CLYDE 1
Coyle

HIBERNIAN 0

SEASON 1958/59
25th April 1959 at Hampden Park; Attendance 108,951;
Referee: Mr J. A. Mowat (Burnside)

ST. MIRREN 3
Bryceland, Miller, Baker

ABERDEEN 1
Baird

SEASON 1959/60
23rd April, 1960 at Hampden Park; Attendance 108,017;
Referee: Mr R. H. Davidson (Airdrie)

RANGERS 2
Millar (2)

KILMARNOCK 0

SEASON 1960/61
22nd April, 1961 at Hampden Park; Attendance 113,618;
Referee: Mr H. Phillips (Wishaw)

DUNFERMLINE ATHLETIC 0

CELTIC 0

REPLAY
26th April, 1961 at Hampden Park; Attendance 87,866;
Referee: Mr H. Phillips (Wishaw)

DUNFERMLINE ATHLETIC 2
Thomson, Dickson

CELTIC 0

SEASON 1961/62

21st April, 1962 at Hampden Park; Attendance 126,930;
Referee: Mr T. Wharton (Clarkston)

RANGERS 2   **ST. MIRREN 0**
Brand, Wilson

SEASON 1962/63

4th May, 1963 at Hampden Park; Attendance 129,527;
Referee: Mr T. Wharton (Clarkston)

RANGERS 1   **CELTIC 1**
Brand   Murdoch

REPLAY
15th May, 1963 at Hampden Park; Attendance 120,263;
Referee: Mr T. Wharton (Clarkston)

RANGERS 3   **CELTIC 0**
Brand (2), Wilson

SEASON 1963/64

25th April, 1964 at Hampden Park; Attendance 120,982
Referee: Mr H. Phillips (Wishaw)

RANGERS 3   **DUNDEE 1**
Millar (2), Brand   Cameron

SEASON 1964/65

24th April, 1965 at Hampden Park; Attendance 108,800;
Referee: Mr H. Phillips (Wishaw)

CELTIC 3 DUNFERMLINE ATHLETIC 2
Auld (2), McNeill   Melrose, McLaughlin

SEASON 1965/66

23rd April, 1966 at Hampden Park; Attendance 126,559;
Referee: Mr T. Wharton (Clarkston)

RANGERS 0   **CELTIC 0**

REPLAY
27th April, 1966 at Hampden Park; Attendance 96,862;
Referee: Mr T. Wharton (Clarkston)

RANGERS 1   **CELTIC 0**
Johansen

SEASON 1966/67

29th April, 1967 at Hampden Park; Attendance 127,117;
Referee: Mr W. M. M. Syme (Glasgow)

CELTIC 2   **ABERDEEN 0**
Wallace (2)

SEASON 1967/68

27th April, 1968 at Hampden Park; Attendance 56,365;
Referee: Mr W. Anderson (East Kilbride)

DUNFERMLINE ATHLETIC 3   **HEART OF MIDLOTHIAN 1**
Gardner (2), Lister (pen)   Lunn (o.g.)

SEASON 1968/69

26th April, 1969 at Hampden Park; Attendance 132,870;
Referee: Mr J. Callaghan (Glasgow)

CELTIC 4   **RANGERS 0**
McNeill, Lennox, Connelly, Chalmers

SEASON 1969/70

11th April, 1970 at Hampden Park; Attendance 108,434;
Referee: Mr R. H. Davidson (Airdrie)

ABERDEEN 3   **CELTIC 1**
Harper (pen), McKay (2)   Lennox

SEASON 1970/71

8th May, 1971 at Hampden Park; Attendance 120,092;
Referee: Mr T. Wharton (Glasgow)

CELTIC 1   **RANGERS 1**
Lennox   D. Johnstone

REPLAY
12th May, 1971 at Hampden Park; Attendance 103,332;
Referee: Mr T. Wharton (Glasgow)

CELTIC 2   **RANGERS 1**
Macari, Hood (pen)   Callaghan (o.g.)

SEASON 1971/72

6th May, 1972 at Hampden Park; Attendance 106,102;
Referee: Mr A. MacKenzie (Larbert)

CELTIC 6   **HIBERNIAN 1**
McNeill, Deans (3), Macari (2)   Gordon

SEASON 1972/73

5th May, 1973 at Hampden Park; Attendance 122,714;
Referee: Mr J. R. P. Gordon (Newport-on-Tay)

RANGERS 3   **CELTIC 2**
Parlane, Conn, Forsyth   Dalglish, Connelly (pen)

SEASON 1973/74

4th May, 1974 at Hampden Park; Attendance 75,959;
Referee: Mr W. S. Black (Glasgow)

CELTIC 3   **DUNDEE UNITED 0**
Hood, Murray, Deans

SEASON 1974/75

3rd May, 1975 at Hampden Park; Attendance 75,457;
Referee: Mr I. M. D. Foote (Glasgow)

CELTIC 3   **AIRDRIEONIANS 1**
Wilson (2), McCluskey (pen)   McCann

SEASON 1975/76

1st May 1976 at Hampden Park; Attendance 85,354;
Referee: Mr R. H. Davidson (Airdrie)

RANGERS 3   **HEART OF MIDLOTHIAN 1**
Johnstone (2), MacDonald   Shaw

SEASON 1976/77

7th May, 1977 at Hampden Park; Attendance 54,252;
Referee: Mr R. B. Valentine (Dundee)

CELTIC 1   **RANGERS 0**
Lynch (pen)

SEASON 1977/78

6th May, 1978 at Hampden Park; Attendance 61,563;
Referee: Mr B. R. McGinlay (Glasgow)

RANGERS 2   **ABERDEEN 1**
MacDonald, Johnstone   Ritchie

SEASON 1978/79

12th May, 1979 at Hampden Park; Attendance 50,610;
Referee: Mr B. R. McGinlay (Glasgow)

RANGERS 0   **HIBERNIAN 0**

REPLAY

16th May, 1979 at Hampden Park; Attendance 33,504;
Referee: Mr B. R. McGinlay (Glasgow)

RANGERS 0   **HIBERNIAN 0**
After extra–time

SECOND REPLAY

28th May, 1979 at Hampden Park; Attendance 30,602;
Referee: Mr I. M. D. Foote (Glasgow)

RANGERS 3   **HIBERNIAN 2**
Johnstone (2), Duncan (o.g.)   Higgins, MacLeod (pen)
After extra–time

SEASON 1979/80

10th May, 1980 at Hampden Park; Attendance 70,303;
Referee: Mr G. B. Smith (Edinburgh)

CELTIC 1   **RANGERS 0**
McCluskey
After extra–time

SEASON 1980/81

9th May, 1981 at Hampden Park; Attendance 53,000;
Referee: Mr I. M. D. Foote (Glasgow)

RANGERS 0   **DUNDEE UNITED 0**
After extra–time

REPLAY

12th May, 1981 at Hampden Park; Attendance 43,099;
Referee: Mr I. M. D. Foote (Glasgow)

RANGERS 4   **DUNDEE UNITED 1**
Cooper, Russell, MacDonald (2) Dodds

SEASON 1981/82

22nd May, 1982 at Hampden Park; Attendance 53,788;
Referee: Mr B. R. McGinlay (Balfron)

ABERDEEN 4   **RANGERS 1**
McLeish, McGhee, Strachan, Cooper   MacDonald
After extra–time – 1-1 after 90 minutes

SEASON 1982/83

21st May, 1983 at Hampden Park; Attendance 62,979;
Referee: Mr D. F. T. Syme (Rutherglen)

ABERDEEN 1   **RANGERS 0**
Black
After extra–time

SEASON 1983/84

19th May 1984 at Hampden Park; Attendance 58,900;
Referee: Mr R. B. Valentine (Dundee)

ABERDEEN 2   **CELTIC 1**
Black, McGhee   P. McStay
After extra–time – 1-1 after 90 minutes

SEASON 1984/85

18th May, 1985 at Hampden Park; Attendance 60,346;
Referee: Mr B. R. McGinlay (Balfron)

CELTIC 2   **DUNDEE UNITED 1**
Provan, McGarvey   Beedie

SEASON 1985/86

10th May, 1986 at Hampden Park; Attendance 62,841;
Referee: Mr H. Alexander (Irvine)

ABERDEEN 3   **HEART OF MIDLOTHIAN 0**
Hewitt (2), Stark

SEASON 1986/87

16th May, 1987 at Hampden Park; Attendance 51,782;
Referee: Mr K. J. Hope (Clarkston)

ST. MIRREN 1   **DUNDEE UNITED 0**
Ferguson
After extra–time

SEASON 1987/88

14th May, 1988 at Hampden Park; Attendance 74,000;
Referee: Mr G. B. Smith (Edinburgh)

CELTIC 2   **DUNDEE UNITED 1**
McAvennie (2)   Gallacher

SEASON 1988/89

20th May, 1989 at Hampden Park; Attendance 72,069;
Referee: Mr R. B. Valentine (Dundee)

CELTIC 1   **RANGERS 0**
Miller

SEASON 1989/90

12th May, 1990 at Hampden Park; Attendance 60,493;
Referee: Mr G. B. Smith (Edinburgh)

ABERDEEN 0   **CELTIC 0**
After extra–time. Aberdeen won 9–8 on Kicks from the Penalty Mark

SEASON 1990/91

18th May, 1991 at Hampden Park; Attendance 57,319;
Referee: Mr D. F. T. Syme (Rutherglen)

MOTHERWELL 4   **DUNDEE UNITED 3**
Ferguson, O'Donnell, Angus, Kirk   Bowman, O'Neil, Jackson
After extra–time - 3-3 after 90 minutes

SEASON 1991/92

9th May 1992 at Hampden Park; Attendance 44,045;
Referee: Mr D. D. Hope (Erskine)

RANGERS 2   **AIRDRIEONIANS 1**
Hateley, McCoist   Smith

SEASON 1992/93

29th May, 1993 at Celtic Park; Attendance 50,715;
Referee: Mr J. McCluskey (Stewarton)

RANGERS 2   **ABERDEEN 1**
Murray, Hateley   Richardson

SEASON 1993/94

21st May, 1994 at Hampden Park; Attendance 37,709;
Referee: Mr D. D. Hope (Erskine)

DUNDEE UNITED 1   **RANGERS 0**
Brewster

SEASON 1994/95

27th May, 1995 at Hampden Park; Attendance 38,672;
Referee: Mr L. W. Mottram (Forth)

CELTIC 1   **AIRDRIEONIANS 0**
Van Hooijdonk

B&Q
The B&Q Cup

Better Late...

A Cup success story of the Nineties reached a milestone on Sunday, 6th November, 1994 as a partnership between The Scottish Football League and the DIY giants B&Q came to an end at McDiarmid Park, Perth.

After an exhilarating five year run, the sponsors regrettably called a halt to a competition which had given clubs from outwith the Premier arena, a platform in the first half of the season. Back in 1990, the Scottish League celebrated its Centenary with a cup tourney for First and Second Division clubs and the enthusiasm generated by the one-off knock-out competition led to an annual event, and cup glory for four different clubs.

Dundee led the way with a win in the Centenary celebrations and Hamilton Academical wrote their way into the record books with two back-to-back B&Q Cup wins.

Falkirk were next to go into Scottish football folklore as the only club to complete a promotion and B&Q Cup double in season 1993-94 and Airdrieonians wrapped up the sponsor's Scottish involvement by laying hands on their first major

trophy for 70 years.

The 3-2 win over Dundee at Perth was a just reward for Alex MacDonald and his Airdrie side whose cup campaigning last season was nothing short of phenomenal!

The homeless Diamonds, operating from Broadwood only on home match days, somehow carved out a cup formula from humble training headquarters at Strathclyde Park. Their efforts earned them a total of 14 cup games in three competitions and two Cup Final experiences.

The 1994 competition broke with tradition by spreading the opening round over a Friday, Saturday and Sunday in September and The B&Q Cup had the curious distinction for being the only Scottish competition starting off at Hampden and finish with a Final in the East.

The 14 First Round ties brought a total of 44 goals with Clydebank's James Grady collecting the first hat-trick bonus in Bankies 5-0 win over Queen's Park at Hampden. Dundee duplicated the nap hand at Dens against Arbroath with striker Gerry Britton writing his name into the

competition's record books as the first player to score four in a tie.

The most prominent victims at the first stage were Jimmy Bone's St. Mirren, cup finalists of the previous season. Saints lost out in a penalty shoot-out with First Division new boys Stranraer at Stair Park.

Ross County were the first Highland club to take to The B&Q Cup stage but fell at the first hurdle to East Fife at Methil.

The Second Round deadlines were claimed by Airdrie and Raith Rovers who were paired at Broadwood just days after being drawn for a Coca-Cola Cup Semi-Final shoot-out at Perth. The Diamonds kept up their relentless cup march with a penalty shoot-out win over Rovers and the true irony was to follow as the situation was reversed in The Coca-Cola Cup re-run.

Hamilton Accies dream of a hat-trick of Cup wins ended with a 4-2 defeat at Dunfermline and strongly fancied St. Johnstone suffered a Second Round shock with a 4-3 defeat in extra-time at Cappielow. Adding to the Perth misery was the fact that Saints George O'Boyle became the

B&Q Final – Heading for victory

first player in the competition to score a hat-trick and end on the losing side.

In the Fife derby at Bayview, Cowdenbeath's Mark Yardley posted the fourth hat-trick of the tourney as the "Blue Brazil" torpedoed East Fife 3-0, whilst in the first ever B&Q Cup game to be staged in the Highlands, Caley Thistle lost out in a penalty shoot-out with Dundee.

The eight Second Round ties pulled in over 12,000 fans with an average of over four goals a game. The Quarter Final stage brought near neighbours Cowdenbeath and Dunfermline together at Central Park and nearly 4,000 fans saw the Pars cruise into the last four with a 3-1 win.

Airdrie dismissed Ayr United at Broadwood to reach their second Semi-Final of the season and Dundee and Clydebank made it a First Division foursome with wins over Greenock Morton and Montrose respectively.

The Semi-Final clash between Airdrie and Clydebank threw up a bizarre statistic for both clubs. The draw gave the Diamonds their eighth home B&Q Cup game in a row, while the Bankies almost in disbelief were handed their eighth successive away tie! Goals by Jimmy Boyle, Sandy Stewart and English striker Steve Cooper eased Airdrie into the Final with the late Davie Cooper scoring for Bankies.

A record pre-Final crowd of 7,154 took their places at East End Park for the clash between Dunfermline and Dundee. Goals from Kevin Bain and Neil McCann earned Jim Duffy and his

men their second Cup Final appearance in four years but the red card figure for the competition moved to six as home skipper Norrie McCathie and Dundee's George Shaw were dismissed.

For the third time, East was pitted against West in the Final and McDiarmid Park became the third venue in The B&Q Cup series. Fir Park had hosted the event on three occasions with St. Mirren Park also sharing the honour.

An all ticket crowd of 8,844 set up a carnival atmosphere to welcome the sides. With the curtain to be rung down on the B&Q link and some doubt about the future of the competition, the sides amply demonstrated the value of the event with the most exciting Final in the series.

A superb strike by Paul Harvey, later crowned Man of the Match, opened Airdrie's account but by the interval, Dundee had levelled through an own goal from Graham Hay.

Jimmy Boyle restored the Diamonds' advantage from the penalty spot but Gerry Britton hammered in the 100th goal of the tourney to send the tie into overtime. With a penalty shoot-out looming (an ominous prospect for Airdrie after losing to Raith Rovers in The Coca-Cola Cup Semi-Final weeks earlier), super substitute Andy Smith settled the issue.

The success in the Perth late-late show handed Alex MacDonald his first trophy as a manager and added another club to the Roll of Honour in Scotland's third domestic cup tournament.

The title of the event is now in the history books along with others such as the Drybrough, Texaco and Skol but while a fresh benefactor is still over the horizon, thirty clubs are again rarin' to go!

**FRASER ELDER
(Sunday Mail)**

B&Q Final – Paul Harvey scores Airdrie's first goal

FIRST ROUND
Friday, 16th September, 1994

QUEEN'S PARK 0   **CLYDEBANK 5**
K. Eadie, J. Grady (3), D. Cooper

Queen's Park: D. Moonie, J. Orr, J. Kavanagh, G. Kerr, I. Maxwell, G. Orr, S. Fitzpatrick, M. Lynch, S. McCormick (S. Edgar), B. McPhee, D. Graham (D. Wilson)

Substitute not used: M. McFadyen (Goalkeeper)

Clydebank: G. Matthews, A. Lansdowne, D. Crawford, S. Murdoch, S. Sweeney, T. Currie, J. Walker (P. Agnew), S. Jack, K. Eadie, J. Grady (S. Kerrigan), D. Cooper

Substitute not used: A. Monaghan (Goalkeeper)

Saturday, 17th September, 1994

EAST FIFE 2   **ROSS COUNTY 1**
R. Scott, P. Hunter   Andrew MacLeod

East Fife: E. Wilson, G. Bell (A. Irvine), A. Sneddon, W. Burns, D. Beaton, C. Dow, G. Allan, R. Hildersley (J. Cusick), R. Scott, P. Hunter, R. Gibb

Substitute not used: R. Charles (Goalkeeper)

Ross County: D. MacMillan, C. Somerville, C. Reid, R. Williamson, W. Herd, G. Campbell, K. Ferries, B. Grant, A. Duff, J. MacPherson, Andrew MacLeod

Substitutes not used: D. Mackay, Alexander MacLeod, S. Hutchison (Goalkeeper)

HAMILTON ACADEMICAL 2   **STENHOUSEMUIR 0**
P. Duffield (2)

Hamilton Academical: D. Cormack, P. McKenzie, S. McInulty, S. McEntegart, C. Baptie, D. Nicholls, J. McQuade (P. Hartley), J. Sherry, D. Campbell, P. Duffield, D. Lorimer

Substitutes not used: D. McGill, D. Murphy (Goalkeeper)

Stenhousemuir: M. Harkness, J. Clarke, D. Roseburgh (E. Hallford), G. Armstrong, P. Godfrey, M. Christie, T. Steel, J. Fisher, J. Irvine (J. Sludden), G. Hutchison, A. Sprott

Substitute not used: C. Wilson (Goalkeeper)

BRECHIN CITY 0   **DUNFERMLINE ATHLETIC 2**
N. McCathie, S. Petrie

Brechin City: D. Balfour, F. Conway, R. Brown, H. Cairney, K. Nicolson, D. Scott, S. Bell, W. McNeill, R. Smith (C. Feroz), M. Millar, G. Christie

Substitutes not used: J. McKellar, R. Smollet (Goalkeeper)

Dunfermline Athletic: J. McQueen, M. Bowes, R. Sharp, N. McCathie, A. Tod, P. Smith, I. Den Bieman, C. Robertson, H. French (D. Laing), S. Petrie, K. Ward (C. Sinclair)

Substitute not used: J. Will (Goalkeeper)

STRANRAER 1   **ST. MIRREN 1** (A.E.T.)
                       (0-0 After 90 Minutes)
W. Ferguson   S. Watson
Stranraer Won 5-4 on Kicks from the Penalty Mark

Stranraer: S. Ross, G. Millar, J. Hughes, J. McCann (A. Grant), J. McCaffrey, A. Gallagher, T. Sloan, P. McLean (W. Ferguson), G. Duncan, S. Cody, D. Henderson

Substitute not used: B. Duffy (Goalkeeper)

St. Mirren: C. Money, R. Dawson, S. Watson, B. McLaughlin, P. McIntyre, J. Dick, K. Gillies (R. Gillies), M. Baker, B. Lavety, J. Gardner (J. Fullarton), D. Elliot

Substitute not used: A. Combe (Goalkeeper)

MEADOWBANK THISTLE 1   **MONTROSE 2**
(AET.-1-1 After 90 Minutes)
T. Graham   C. McGlashan, C. Cooper

Meadowbank Thistle: S. Ellison, T. Graham, D. Fleming, S. Wilson, S. Williamson, C. Martin (M. Duthie), G. Davidson (G. Price), G. McLeod, I. Little, S. Sorbie, L. Bailey

Substitute not used: R. Douglas (Goalkeeper)

Montrose: D. Larter, I. Robertson, M. Craib (M. Garden), S. Beedie, D. Grant, M. Haro, I. MacDonald, L. Stephen (C. Cooper), C. McGlashan, C. Milne, P. Masson

Substitutes not used: J. Rae, R. Duncan (Goalkeeper)

DUNDEE 5   **ARBROATH 0**
G. Shaw, G. Britton (4)

Dundee: M. Pageaud, J. McQuillan, M. Hutchison, M. Teasdale, N. Blake, J. Duffy, G. Shaw, R. Farningham, T. Pomb, G. Britton (J. Hamilton), I. Anderson (D. Vrto)

Substitute not used: B. Thompson (Goalkeeper)

Arbroath: D. Jackson, B. Mitchell, A. Middleton, M. Murray, I. Spittal, D. Shanks, J. McGovern, S. Elder, S. McGregor, J. Tosh, I. Downie (S. Finlay)

Substitutes not used: J. Rae, R. Duncan (Goalkeeper)

STIRLING ALBION 4   **ALBION ROVERS 0**
I. McInnes, W. Watters
C. Taggart (2)

Stirling Albion: M. McGeown, A. Paterson, J. Gibson, C. Mitchell (R. Kerr), R. McQuilter, T. Tait, I. McInnes, A. Farquhar, W. Watters, C. Taggart, J. McLeod

Substitutes not used: K. Drinkell, M. Monaghan (Goalkeeper)

Albion Rovers: A. Davidson, R. Philliben, K. Parry, D. McDonald, S. Conn, J. Kelly, M. Scott, A. Docherty (D. Seggie), G. Young, K. Quinn (M. McBride), B. Deeley

Substitute not used: J. Wight (Goalkeeper)

COWDENBEATH 2   **CLYDE 1**
G. Tait, G. Soutar   A. MacKenzie

Cowdenbeath: N. Russell, E. Petrie, S. Murdoch, B. Malloy, M. Humphreys, C. Winter, G. Tait, A. Hamill, M. Yardley, W. Callaghan, I. Black (G. Soutar)

Substitutes not used: B. McMahon, J. Maloney (Goalkeeper)

Clyde: J. Hillcoat, J. Prunty, G. McCheyne, K. Knox, J. Thomson, G. Watson (M. O'Neill), J. Dickson, J. McAulay, A. MacKenzie, J. McCarron, I. Nisbet

Substitutes not used: D. McGill, L. Fridge (Goalkeeper)

FORFAR ATHLETIC 0   **ALLOA 1**
                          B. Moffat

Forfar Athletic: G. Arthur, G. Mearns, I. McPhee, R. Mann, E. Archibald, A. McKillop (S. Kopel), H. O'Neill, N. Irvine (I. Heddle), S. McCormick, D. Bingham, G. Lees

Substitute not used: C. Stephen (Goalkeeper)

Alloa: P. Graham, J. McCormack, B. Kemp, M. Nelson, K. McCulloch, D. Lawrie, M. McAnenay, B. Moffat, D. Diver, N. Bennett, P. Lamont

Substitutes not used: S. Cadden, V. Conway, J. Butter (Goalkeeper)

DUMBARTON 2   **ST. JOHNSTONE 4**
C. Campbell (2)   P. Ramsey, P. Davenport,
                          G. O'Boyle (2)

Dumbarton: I. MacFarlane (P. Dennison), J. Marsland (G. Farrell), R. Fabiani, M. Melvin, J. Boyd, M. MacLeod, M. Mooney, J. Meechan (C. Campbell), C. Gibson, M. McGarvey, H. Ward

St. Johnstone: A. Rhodes, P. Cherry, C. Miller, P. Ramsey, J. Inglis, K. McGowne, J. O'Neil, D. Irons, P. Davenport, G. O'Boyle, C. Davidson

Substitutes not used: G. McGinnis, G. McMartin, J. Donegan (Goalkeeper)

QUEEN OF THE SOUTH 0   **RAITH ROVERS 2**
                          S. Crawford, C. Cameron

Queen of the South: D. Purdie, D. Kennedy, D. McKeown, B. McKeown, A. McFarlane, S. Ramsay, P. Sermanni, T. Bryce, J. McLaren (G. Cochrane), S. Leslie (D. McGuire), S. Mallan

Substitute not used: R. McColm (Goalkeeper)

Raith Rovers: S. Thomson, S. McAnespie, J. Rowbotham, D. Lennon, D. Narey, D. Sinclair, J. Nicholl, S. Crawford, A. Graham, C. Cameron, B. Wilson (J. Dair)

Substitutes not used: S. Dennis, B. Potter (Goalkeeper)

AIRDRIEONIANS 3   **BERWICK RANGERS 1**
J. Davies, Andrew Smith (2)   G. Fraser

Airdrieonians: J. Martin, J. Boyle, A. Stewart, J. Sandison, T. McIntyre, P. Jack, P. Harvey, J. Davies, Andrew Smith, K. Black (C. Honor), A. Lawrence

Substitutes not used: I. Ferguson, W. McCulloch (Goalkeeper)

Berwick Rangers: N. Young, C. Valentine, A. Banks, A. Cole, G. Fraser, M. Wilson (T. King), P. Forrester, M. Neil, W. Hawke, W. Irvine, J. Gallacher (T. Graham)

Substitute not used: M. Osborne (Goalkeeper)

Sunday, 18th September, 1994

EAST STIRLINGSHIRE 1   **AYR UNITED 1**
(AET.-1-1 After 90 Minutes)
D. Watt   H. Burns
Ayr United Won 4-2 on Kicks from the Penalty Mark

East Stirlingshire: J. Moffat, G. Russell, L. Cuthbert, D. Yates, S. Sneddon, D. Watt, I. Lee, G. Millar, M. Geraghty (J. Conroy), C. Scott, D. Stirling (M. McCallum)

Substitute not used: G. McDougall (Goalkeeper)

Ayr United: C. Duncan, H. Burns, C. Connie, G. Paterson, F. Rolling, D. George, R. Gorgues, V. Moore, S. McGivern, S. Stainrod, B. Bilsland (I. Gilzean)

Substitutes not used: J. Sharples, S. McIntosh (Goalkeeper)

SECOND ROUND
Tuesday, 27th September, 1994

AYR UNITED 4   **STRANRAER 2**
H. Burns, G. Paterson,   T. Walker, D. Henderson
D. George, J. Jackson

Ayr United: C. Duncan, H. Burns, C. Connie, G. Paterson, F. Rolling, D. George, J. Traynor, V. Moore, J. Jackson, S. Stainrod (I. Gilzean) (N. McKilligan), R. Gorgues

Substitute not used: S. McIntosh (Goalkeeper)

Stranraer: S. Ross, G. Millar, J. Hughes, P. McLean, A. Gallagher, J. McCaffrey, T. Sloan, T. Walker (A. Grant), G. Duncan, S. Cody (J. McCann), D. Henderson

Substitute not used: B. Duffy (Goalkeeper)

MONTROSE 3   **STIRLING ALBION 0**
C. McGlashan (2), L. Stephen

Montrose: D. Larter, I. Robertson, K. Tindal, P. Masson, D. Grant, M. Haro, C. Cooper (M. Brown), I. MacDonald, C. McGlashan, A. Kennedy (C. Milne), L. Stephen

Stirling Albion: M. McGeown, A. Paterson, J. Gibson, C. Mitchell, R. McQuilter, T. Tait, I. McInnes, A. Farquhar (P. Roberts), W. Watters, C. Taggart, J. McLeod

Substitutes not used: R. Stewart, A. McGuinness (Goalkeeper)

The B&Q Cup Competition – Season 1994/95

DUNFERMLINE ATHLETIC 4
C. Robertson, H. French
S. Petrie (2)

HAMILTON ACADEMICAL 2
M. McIntosh, P. Duffield

Dunfermline Athletic: I. Westwater, M. Bowes, J. McNamara, N. McCathie, A. Tod, P. Smith, I. Den Bieman, C. Robertson, H. French, S. Petrie, K. Ward

Substitutes not used: D. Laing, C. Sinclair, J. Will (Goalkeeper)

Hamilton Academical: D. Cormack, P. McKenzie, S. McInulty, S. McEntegart, C. Baptie, M. McIntosh, J. McQuade, J. Sherry (P. Clark), D. McGill, P. Duffield, D. Nicholls

Substitutes not used: D. Campbell, D. Murphy (Goalkeeper)

GREENOCK MORTON 4
(A.E.T.–3-3 After 90 Minutes)
D. Lilley (2), J. Fowler
R. Alexander

ST. JOHNSTONE 3
G. O'Boyle (3)

Greenock Morton: D. Wylie, D. Collins, M. Pickering, J. Anderson, P. Cormack, D. Johnstone, D. Lilley, J. Fowler, R. Alexander, A. Mahood, S. McArthur (L. Gibson)

Substitute not used: P. Flannery

St. Johnstone: A. Rhodes, P. Cherry (T. Turner), S. McAuley, G. McGinnis, J. Inglis, K. McGowne, J. O'Neil, G. McMartin (P. Ramsey), P. Davenport, G. O'Boyle, D. Irons

Substitute not used: J. Donegan (Goalkeeper)

EAST FIFE 0

COWDENBEATH 3
M. Yardley (3)

East Fife: E. Wilson, A. Sneddon, D. Hope, W. Burns, D. Beaton, R. Hildersley, G. Allan (C. Dow), A. Irvine, R. Scott, P. Hunter, R. Gibb

Substitute not used: J. Cusick, R. Charles (Goalkeeper)

Cowdenbeath: N. Russell, E. Petrie, S. Murdoch, B. Malloy, B. McMahon, C. Winter, G. Tait, A. Hamill (I. Black), M. Yardley, W. Callaghan, G. Soutar (M. Humphreys)

Substitute not used: J. Maloney (Goalkeeper)

ALLOA 1
M. McAnenay

CLYDEBANK 3
C. Harris, K. Eadie, J. Grady

Alloa: P. Graham, J. McCormack, B. Kemp (D. Diver), W. Newbigging, K. McCulloch, D. Lawrie, N. McAvoy (N. Bennett), M. Nelson, B. Moffat, M. McAnenay, P. Lamont

Substitute not used: J. Butter (Goalkeeper)

Clydebank: G. Matthews, A. Lansdowne, D. Crawford, S. Murdoch, T. Currie, C. Harris (J. Walker), D. Cooper, P. Agnew, K. Eadie (C. Flannigan), J. Grady, S. Jack

Substitute not used: A. Monaghan (Goalkeeper)

AIRDRIEONIANS 1
(AET–1-1 After 90 minutes)
A. Lawrence

RAITH ROVERS 1
G. Dalziel

Airdrieonians won 5-3 on Kicks from the Penalty Mark

Airdrieonians: J. Martin, A. Stewart, P. Jack (M. Wilson), J. Sandison, G. Hay, K. Black, J. Boyle, J. Davies, Andrew Smith, P. Harvey, A. Lawrence

Substitutes not used: J. McIntyre, W. McCulloch (Goalkeeper)

Raith Rovers: S. Thomson, S. McAnespie, I. Redford (J. Broddle), D. Lennon, S. Dennis, D. Narey, B. Wilson, G. Dalziel (D. Sinclair), S. Crawford, C. Cameron, J. Dair

Substitute not used: B. Potter (Goalkeeper)

Wednesday, 28th September, 1994

CALEDONIAN THISTLE 1
(AET 1-1 After 90 minutes)
D. MacDonald

DUNDEE 1
M. Wieghorst

Dundee won 4-3 on Kicks from the Penalty Mark

Caledonian Thistle: M. McRitchie, D. Brennan, M. McAllister, C. Sinclair, J. Scott (M. Lisle), M. Andrew, D. MacDonald (A. Smart), P. McKenzie, N. MacMillan, C. Christie, W. Robertson

Substitute not used: J. Calder (Goalkeeper)

Dundee: P. Mathers, R. Farningham, M. Hutchison, C. Duffy, N. Blake, J. Duffy, G. Shaw, M. Dailly (J. Hamilton), M. Wieghorst (M. Teasdale), G. Britton, K. Bain

Substitute not used: B. Thompson (Goalkeeper)

THIRD ROUND
Tuesday, 4th October, 1994

DUNDEE 2
M. Wieghorst, G. Britton

GREENOCK MORTON 1
J. Anderson

Dundee: M. Pageaud, J. McQuillan, K. Bain, R. Farningham, N. Blake, J. Duffy (M. Hutchison), G. Shaw, M. Wieghorst, P. Tosh, G. Britton, J. Hamilton

Substitutes not used: I. Anderson, P. Mathers (Goalkeeper)

Greenock Morton: D. Wylie, D. Collins, M. Pickering, J. Anderson, P. Cormack, D. Johnstone, M. McCann, J. Fowler (J. Hunter), R. Alexander (L. Gibson), A. Mahood, S. McArthur

COWDENBEATH 1
M. Yardley

DUNFERMLINE ATHLETIC 3
P. Smith, H. French, S. Petrie

Cowdenbeath: N. Russell, E. Petrie, S. Murdoch, B. Malloy, B. McMahon, C. Winter, J. Lynch (M. Humphreys), I. Black, M. Yardley, W. Callaghan, G. Soutar (A. Barclay)

Substitute not used: J. Maloney (Goalkeeper)

Dunfermline Athletic: I. Westwater, J. McNamara, A. Hawkins, N. McCathie, A. Tod, P. Smith, I. Den Bieman, C. Robertson, H. French, S. Petrie (D. Laing), K. Ward

Substitutes not used: M. Bowes, J. Will (Goalkeeper)

AIRDRIEONIANS 2
J. Davies, S. Cooper

AYR UNITED 0

Airdrieonians: J. Martin, A. Stewart, P. Jack, J. Sandison, I. McIntyre, K. Black, J. Boyle, J. Davies, S. Cooper, P. Harvey (C. Honor), A. Lawrence

Substitutes not used: Andrew Smith, W. McCulloch (Goalkeeper)

Ayr United: C. Duncan, K. Biggart, D. McVicar (B. Bilsland), J. Sharples, F. Rolling, N. McKilligan, H. Burns, V. Moore (C. Connie), G. Paterson, J. Jackson, R. Gorgues

Substitute not used: S. McIntosh (Goalkeeper)

Wednesday, 5th October, 1994

MONTROSE 1
(AET–0-0 After 90 minutes)
A. Kennedy

CLYDEBANK 2
D. Cooper, C. Flannigan

Montrose: D. Larter, I. Robertson, K. Tindal, P. Masson, J. Tosh, M. Haro, C. Cooper, (M. Brown), I. MacDonald, C. McGlashan, A. Kennedy, L. Stephen (C. MacRonald)

Clydebank: G. Matthews, A. Lansdowne, D. Crawford, S. Murdoch, T. Currie, G. Bowman, D. Cooper, J. Walker, K. Eadie, J. Grady (C. Flannigan), S. Jack (C. Harris)

Substitute not used: A. Monaghan (Goalkeeper)

SEMI-FINALS
Tuesday, 18th October, 1994

DUNFERMLINE ATHLETIC 1
A. Tod

DUNDEE 2
K. Bain, N. McCann

Dunfermline Athletic: I. Westwater, J. McNamara, M. Bowes, N. McCathie, A. Tod, P. Smith, I. Den Bieman (D. Laing), C. Robertson, H. French, S. Petrie, K. Ward (A. Hawkins)

Substitute not used: J. Will (Goalkeeper)

Dundee: M. Pageaud, J. McQuillan, K. Bain, R. Farningham, J. Duffy, M. Wieghorst, G. Shaw, D. Vrto, P. Tosh, G. Britton, N. McCann

Substitutes not used: N. Blake, I. Anderson, P. Mathers (Goalkeeper)

AIRDRIEONIANS 3
A. Stewart, J. Boyle, S. Cooper

CLYDEBANK 1
D. Cooper

Airdrieonians: J. Martin, A. Stewart, P. Jack, J. Sandison, G. Hay, K. Black, J. Boyle, J. Davies, S. Cooper, P. Harvey (M. Wilson), Andrew Smith (J. McIntyre)

Substitute not used: W. McCulloch (Goalkeeper)

Clydebank: G. Matthews, S. Jack, D. Crawford, S. Murdoch, S. Sweeney, G. Bowman (J. Grady), D. Cooper, J. Walker, K. Eadie, C. Flannigan, C. Harris (A. Lansdowne)

Substitute not used: A. Monaghan (Goalkeeper)

ROUND BY ROUND GOALS ANALYSIS

	No. of Goals Scored	Ties Played	Average Per Game
First Round	44	14	3.1
Second Round	33	8	4.1
Third Round	12	4	3
Semi-Finals	7	2	3.5
Final	5	1	5
Total No. of Goals Scored:		101	
Ties Played		29	
Average Goals per Game:		3.5	

1983/84

Premier Division
23 B. McClair (Celtic)
18 W. Irvine (Hibernian)
15 D. Dodds (Dundee United)
    J. Robertson (Heart of Midlothian)
13 M. McGhee (Aberdeen)
    G. Strachan (Aberdeen)
    W. McCall (Dundee)
    F. McDougall (St. Mirren)
12 J. Hewitt (Aberdeen)
    I. Ferguson (Dundee)
    F. McAvennie (St. Mirren)
    J. Scanlon (St. Mirren)

First Division
19 I. M. Campbell (Brechin City)
17 J. F. Frye (Clyde)
    J. McNeil (Morton)
16 D. Robertson (Morton)
    J. Kerr (Raith Rovers)
15 A. McInally (Ayr United)
    J. Coyle (Dumbarton)
13 K. Ashwood (Dumbarton)
    J. Bourke (Dumbarton)
    K. McDowall (Partick Thistle)

Second Division
22 J. Liddle (Forfar Athletic)
18 J. Harley (Arbroath)
17 A. Grant (Queen's Park)
16 G. Durie (East Fife)
14 G. Forrest (Stenhousemuir)
13 C. Gibson (East Stirlingshire)
    K. Macdonald (Forfar Athletic)
    G. Murray (Stenhousemuir)
12 J. Clark (Forfar Athletic)
    W. Irvine (Stirling Albion)

1984/85

Premier Division
22 F. McDougall (Aberdeen)
19 B. McClair (Celtic)
17 E. Black (Aberdeen)
16 F. McAvennie (St. Mirren)
15 W. Stark (Aberdeen)
    F. McGarvey (Celtic)
14 P. Sturrock (Dundee United)
    M. Johnston (Celtic)
12 A. McCoist (Rangers)
10 E. Bannon (Dundee United)

First Division
22 G. McCoy (Falkirk)
21 D. MacCabe (Airdrieonians)
19 J. F. Frye (Clyde)
17 J. Flood (Airdrieonians)
    K. Eadie (Brechin City)
14 K. Macdonald (Forfar Athletic)
    A. Sprott (Meadowbank Thistle)
12 G. Murray (East Fife)
    B. Millar (Kilmarnock)
    A. Logan (Partick Thistle)

Second Division
27 B. Slaven (Albion Rovers)
22 K. Wright (Raith Rovers)
21 W. Irvine (Stirling Albion)
19 P. Smith (Raith Rovers)
18 J. Nicholson (Queen's Park)
16 D. Lloyd (Alloa)
    K. Ward (Cowdenbeath)
15 J. Watson (Dunfermline Athletic)
12 I. Paterson (Cowdenbeath)
    S. Maskrey (East Stirlingshire)
    D. Somner (Montrose)

1985/86

Premier Division
24 A. McCoist (Rangers)
22 B. McClair (Celtic)
20 J. Robertson (Heart of Midlothian)
19 S. Cowan (Hibernian)
15 M. Johnston (Celtic)
14 F. McDougall (Aberdeen)
    R. Stephen (Dundee)
12 D. Dodds (Dundee United)
    A. Clark (Heart of Midlothian)
11 E. Bannon (Dundee United)
    J. Brown (Dundee)

First Division
23 J. Brogan (Hamilton Academical)
22 K. Eadie (Brechin City)
15 J. Gilmour (Falkirk)
14 S. Kirk (East Fife)
    I. Bryson (Kilmarnock)
    J. McNeil (Morton)
13 G. McCoy (Dumbarton)
12 J. F. Frye (Clyde)
11 J. Flood (Airdrieonians)
    M. Jamieson (Alloa)
    S. Sorbie (Alloa)
    J. McNaught (Hamilton Academical)
    S. McGivern (Kilmarnock)
    G. Smith (Partick Thistle)

Second Division
24 J. Watson (Dunfermline Athletic)
21 P. Smith (Raith Rovers)
    K. Wright (Raith Rovers)
17 D. Jackson (Meadowbank Thistle)
    A. Lawrence (Meadowbank Thistle)
    W. Irvine (Stirling Albion)
15 C. McGlashan (Cowdenbeath)
    I. M. Campbell (Dunfermline Athletic)
    T. Bryce (Queen of the South)
    S. Cochrane (Queen of the South)

1986/87

Premier Division
35 B. McClair (Celtic)
33 A. McCoist (Rangers)
23 M. Johnston (Celtic)
19 R. Fleck (Rangers)
16 J. Robertson (Heart of Midlothian)
    I. Ferguson (Dundee United)
15 A. McInally (Celtic)
13 J. Colquhoun (Heart of Midlothian)
12 G. Harvey (Dundee)
    W. Stark (Aberdeen)

First Division
23 R. Alexander (Morton)
21 G. McCoy (Dumbarton)
20 T. Bryce (Queen of the South)
18 D. Robertson (Morton)
17 O. Coyle (Dumbarton)
    K. Macdonald (Forfar Athletic)
15 B. McNaughton (East Fife)
13 D. MacCabe (Airdrieonians)
    J. Watson (Dunfermline Athletic)
12 C. Adam (Brechin City)
    J. Murphy (Clyde)
    S. Burgess (East Fife)

Second Division
26 J. Sludden (Ayr United)
25 W. Brown (St. Johnstone)
22 C. Harris (Raith Rovers)
21 J. McGachie (Meadowbank Thistle)
14 S. Sorbie (Alloa)
    J. Fotheringham (Arbroath)
    W. Blackie (Cowdenbeath)
    R. Grant (Cowdenbeath)
13 R. Caven (Queen's Park)
    K. Wright (Raith Rovers)
    B. Cleland (Stranraer)

1987/88

Premier Division
33 T. Coyne (Dundee)
31 A. McCoist (Rangers)
26 J. Robertson (Heart of Midlothian)
    A. Walker (Celtic)
15 J. Colquhoun (Heart of Midlothian)
    F. McAvennie (Celtic)
    K. Wright (Dundee)
13 C. Robertson (Dunfermline Athletic)
11 I. Ferguson (Dundee United)
10 J. Bett (Aberdeen)
    P. Chalmers (St. Mirren)
    I. Durrant (Rangers)
    P. Kane (Hibernian)

First Division
25 G. Dalziel (Raith Rovers)
20 D. MacCabe (Airdrieonians)
    K. Macdonald (Partick Thistle)
17 J. Hughes (Queen of the South)
    P. Hunter (East Fife)
16 C. Harkness (Kilmarnock)
    C. McGlashan (Clyde)
    D. Walker (Clyde)
15 C. Campbell (Airdrieonians)
14 O. Coyle (Dumbarton)
    C. Harris (Raith Rovers)
    J. McGachie (Meadowbank Thistle)

Second Division
31 J. Sludden (Ayr United)
23 J. Brogan (Stirling Albion)
    H. Templeton (Ayr United)
19 T. Walker (Ayr United)
17 P. O'Brien (Queen's Park)
16 W. Watters (St. Johnstone)
15 G. Buckley (Brechin City)
14 P. Rutherford (Alloa)
13 T. Coyle (St. Johnstone)
    C. Gibson (Stirling Albion)

1988/89

Premier Division
16 M. McGhee (Celtic)
    C. Nicholas (Aberdeen)
14 S. Kirk (Motherwell)
13 S. Archibald (Hibernian)
12 K. Drinkell (Rangers)
    F. McAvennie (Celtic)
11 P. Chalmers (St. Mirren)
10 M-M. Paatelainen (Dundee United)
9   T. Coyne (Dundee/Celtic)
    K. Gallacher (Dundee United)
    A. McCoist (Rangers)
    W. Stark (Celtic)

First Division
22 K. Macdonald (Airdrieonians)
21 K. Eadie (Clydebank)
19 G. McCoy (Partick Thistle)
18 R. Jack (Dunfermline Athletic)
17 H. Templeton (Ayr United)
16 T. Bryce (Clydebank)
    O. Coyle (Clydebank)
    C. McGlashan (Clyde)
15 J. Sludden (Ayr United)
14 C. Campbell (Airdrieonians)
    J. Watson (Dunfermline Athletic)

Second Division
23 C. Lytwyn (Alloa)
21 G. Murray (Montrose)
18 C. Gibson (Stirling Albion)
16 W. McNeill (East Stirlingshire)
15 C. Adam (Brechin City)
    J. Brogan (Stirling Albion)
    J. Chapman (Albion Rovers)
    A. Graham (Albion Rovers)
13 S. MacIver (Dumbarton)
11 J. Fotheringham (Arbroath)
    D. Lloyd (Stranraer)
    P. Teevan (Albion Rovers)

1989/90

Premier Division
17 J. Robertson (Heart of Midlothian)
16 R. Jack (Dunfermline Athletic)
15 M. Johnston (Rangers)
14 A. McCoist (Rangers)
13 W. Dodds (Dundee)
12 S. Crabbe (Heart of Midlothian)
    G. Torfason (St. Mirren)
11 N. Cusack (Motherwell)
    C. Nicholas (Aberdeen)
    K. Wright (Dundee)

First Division
27 O. Coyle (Airdrieonians/Clydebank)
21 K. Eadie (Clydebank)
20 G. Dalziel (Raith Rovers)
19 R. Grant (St. Johnstone)
18 C. Campbell (Partick Thistle)
17 D. McWilliams (Falkirk)
15 K. Macdonald (Raith Rovers/Airdrieonians)
13 A. Moore (St. Johnstone)
12 S. Maskrey (St. Johnstone)
11 R. Alexander (Morton)
    J. Charnley (Partick Thistle)
    C. McGlashan (Clyde)

Second Division
23 W. Watters (Kilmarnock)
20 C. Gibson (Dumbarton)
19 S. MacIver (Dumbarton)
16 J. Reid (Stirling Albion)
    A. Ross (Cowdenbeath)
    S. Sloan (Berwick Rangers)
15 D. Lloyd (Stirling Albion)
    S. McCormick (Stenhousemuir)
14 P. Hunter (East Fife)
    V. Moore (Stirling Albion)

1990/91

Premier Division
18 T. Coyne (Celtic)
14 D. Arnott (Motherwell)
    H. Gillhaus (Aberdeen)
13 E. Jess (Aberdeen)
12 D. Jackson (Dundee United)
    J. Robertson (Heart of Midlothian)
    M. Walters (Rangers)
11 M. Johnston (Rangers)
    A. McCoist (Rangers)
10 M. Hateley (Rangers)

First Division
29 K. Eadie (Clydebank)
25 G. Dalziel (Raith Rovers)
21 D. MacCabe (Morton)
20 O. Coyle (Airdrieonians)
18 K. Wright (Dundee)
16 S. Stainrod (Falkirk)
15 W. Dodds (Dundee)
    S. McGivern (Falkirk)
    D. Roseburgh (Meadowbank Thistle)
14 G. McCluskey (Hamilton Academical)
    P. Ritchie (Brechin City)
    R. Williamson (Kilmarnock)

Second Division
17 M. Hendry (Queen's Park)
    A. Speirs (Stenhousemuir)
16 A.Ross (Cowdenbeath/Berwick Rangers)
15 A. MacKenzie (Cowdenbeath)
14 C. Harkness (Stranraer)
    D. Lloyd (Stirling Albion)
    J. McQuade (Dumbarton)
    K. Todd (Berwick Rangers)
13 S. McCormick (Stenhousemuir)
    V. Moore (Stirling Albion)

1991/92

Premier Division
34 A. McCoist (Rangers)
21 M. Hateley (Rangers)
   C. Nicholas (Celtic)
18 P. Wright (St. Johnstone)
15 T. Coyne (Celtic)
   S. Crabbe (Heart of Midlothian)
   D. Ferguson (Dundee United)
14 G. Creaney (Celtic)
   J. Robertson (Heart of Midlothian)
12 E. Jess (Aberdeen)

First Division
26 G. Dalziel (Raith Rovers)
22 K. Eadie (Clydebank)
19 W. Dodds (Dundee)
18 A. Mathie (Morton)
   C. McGlashan (PartickThistle)
17 W. Watters (Stirling Albion)
14 G. Clark (Hamilton Academical)
   A. Graham (Ayr United)
13 T. Smith (Hamilton Academical)
12 C. Brewster (Raith Rovers)
   G. McCluskey (Hamilton Academical)

Second Division
26 A. Thomson (Queen of the South)
21 G. Buckley (Cowdenbeath)
   J Sludden (East Fife)
19 J Gilmour (Dumbarton)
18 D. Diver (East Stirlingshire)
   P. Lamont (Cowdenbeath)
17 S. McCormick (Queen's Park)
16 R. Scott (East Fife)
   D. Thompson (Clyde)
14 T. Sloan (Stranraer)

1992/93

Premier Division
34 A. McCoist (Rangers)
22 D. Shearer (Aberdeen)
19 M. Hateley (Rangers)
16 P. Connolly (Dundee United)
   W. Dodds (Dundee)
   M-M. Paatelainen (Aberdeen)
14 P. Wright (St. Johnstone)
13 S. Booth (Aberdeen)
   D. Jackson (Hibernian)
   A. Payton (Celtic)

First Division
32 G. Dalziel (Raith Rovers)
22 C. Brewster (Raith Rovers)
21 C. Flannigan (Clydebank)
20 K. Eadie (Clydebank)
18 B. Lavety (St. Mirren)
15 J. McQuade (Dumbarton)
13 A. Mathie (Morton)
12 H. French (Dunfermline Athletic)
   E. Gallagher (St. Mirren)
   J. Henry (Clydebank)
   M. Mooney (Dumbarton)

Second Division
26 M. Mathieson (Stenhousemuir)
23 A. Ross (Brechin City)
21 S. Petrie (Forfar Athletic)
   A. Thomson (Queen of the South)
19 B. Moffat (Alloa)
   T. Sloan (Stranraer)
   S. Sorbie (Arbroath)
16 F. McGarvey (Clyde)
   M. Scott (Albion Rovers)
   R. Scott (East Fife)

1993/94

Premier Division
22 M. Hateley (Rangers)
17 D. Shearer (Aberdeen)
16 C. Brewster (Dundee United)
   K. Wright (Hibernian)
14 A. Craig (Partick Thistle)
13 R. Grant (Partick Thistle)
12 T. Coyne (Motherwell)
   G. Durie (Rangers)
10 P. McGinlay (Celtic)
   J. Robertson (Heart of Midlothian)

First Division
19 P. Duffield (Hamilton Academical)
18 R. Cadette (Falkirk)
17 G. O'Boyle (Dunfermline Athletic)
15 H. French (Dunfermline Athletic)
13 C. Gibson (Dumbarton)
   W. Watters (Stirling Albion)
12 S. McGivern (Ayr United)
11 R. Alexander (Greenock Morton)
   K. Eadie (Clydebank)
   C. Flannagan (Clydebank)
   A. Tod (Dunfermline Athletic)

Second Division
29 A. Thomson (Queen of the South)
18 J. O'Neill (Queen's Park)
17 M. Scott (Albion Rovers)
16 D. Diver (2 for Alloa,10 for Arbroath, 4 for Stranraer)
   T. Sloan (Stranraer)
15 W. Irvine (Berwick Rangers)
14 M. Mathieson (Stenhousemuir)
13 D. Bingham (Forfar Athletic)
   J. Sludden (Stenhousemuir)
12 D. Grant (Montrose)
   W. Hawke (Berwick Rangers)
   I. Little (Meadowbank Thistle)
   M. McCallum (East Stirlingshire)

1994/95

Premier Division
16 T. Coyne (Motherwell)
15 W. Dodds (Aberdeen)
13 M. Hateley (Rangers)
10 D. Arnott (Motherwell)
   D. Jackson (Hibernian)
   B. Laudrup (Rangers)
   M. O'Neill (Hibernian)
   J. Robertson (Heart of Midlothian)
   K. Wright (Hibernian)
9 C. McDonald (Falkirk)

First Division
20 P. Duffield (Hamilton Academical)
19 G. O'Boyle (St. Johnstone)
16 G. Shaw (Dundee)
15 G. Dalziel (Raith Rovers)
14 S. Petrie (Dunfermline Athletic)
12 G. Britton (Dundee)
   H. French (Dunfermline Athletic)
   J. Hamilton (Dundee)
   Andrew Smith (Airdrieonians)
11 S. Cooper (Airdrieonians)
   S. Crawford (Raith Rovers)
   A. Lawrence (Airdrieonians)

Second Division
17 M. Mooney (Dumbarton)
16 W. Hawke (Berwick Rangers)
   D. Lilley (Greenock Morton)
15 W. Watters (Stirling Albion)
14 M. Rajamaki (Greenock Morton)
   R. Scott (East Fife)
12 H. Ward (Dumbarton)
11 W. Irvine (Berwick Rangers)
10 J. Dickson (Clyde)
   G. Hutchison (Stenhousemuir)

Third Division
23 M. Yardley (Cowdenbeath)
22 D. Bingham (Forfar Athletic)
19 C. McGlashan (Montrose)
17 A. Kennedy (Montrose)
16 M. Geraghty (East Stirlingshire)
13 R. Moffat (Alloa)
   A. Ross (Forfar Athletic)
12 B. Grant (Ross County)
11 S. Tosh (Arbroath)
10 I. Lee (East Stirlingshire)
   S. McCormick (Forfar Athletic)

Leading Goalscorers – Club By Club Since 1980/81

ABERDEEN

Season	Div	No. of Goals	Player
1980-81	P	13	M. McGhee
1981-82	P	11	J. Hewitt
1982-83	P	16	M. McGhee
1983-84	P	13	M. McGhee
			G. Strachan
1984-85	P	22	F. McDougall
1985-86	P	14	F. McDougall
1986-87	P	12	W. Stark
1987-88	P	10	J. Bett
1988-89	P	16	C. Nicholas
1989-90	P	11	C. Nicholas
1990-91	P	14	H. Gillhaus
1991-92	P	12	E. Jess
1992-93	P	22	D. Shearer
1993-94	P	17	D. Shearer
1994-95	P	15	W. Dodds

AIRDRIEONIANS

Season	Div	No. of Goals	Player
1980-81	P	10	A. Clark
1981-82	F	15	A. Clark
1982-83	F	12	B. Millar
1983-84	F	11	J. Flood
1984-85	F	21	D. MacCabe
1985-86	F	11	J. Flood
1986-87	F	13	D. MacCabe
1987-88	F	20	D. MacCabe
1988-89	F	22	K. Macdonald
1989-90	F	10	O. Coyle
1990-91	F	20	O. Coyle
1991-92	P	11	O. Coyle
1992-93	P	9	O. Coyle
1993-94	F	10	D. Kirkwood
1994-95	F	12	Andrew Smith

ALBION ROVERS

Season	Div	No. of Goals	Player
1980-81	S	12	I. Campbell
1981-82	S	16	S. Evans
1982-83	S	13	S. Evans
1983-84	S	11	T. McGurn
1984-85	S	27	B. Slaven
1985-86	S	6	S. Conn
			V. Kasule
			A. Rodgers
1986-87	S	11	C. Wilson
1987-88	S	10	A. Graham
1988-89	S	15	J. Chapman
			A. Graham
1989-90	S	10	M. McAnenay
1990-91	S	12	M. McAnenay
1991-92	S	11	G. McCoy
1992-93	S	16	M. Scott
1993-94	S	17	M. Scott
1994-95	T	7	M. Scott

ALLOA

Season	Div	No. of Goals	Player
1980-81	S	14	A. Holt
1981-82	S	14	S. Murray
1982-83	F	12	L. McComb
1983-84	F	10	D. Lloyd
1984-85	S	16	D. Lloyd
1985-86	F	11	M. Jamieson
			S. Sorbie
1986-87	S	14	S. Sorbie
1987-88	S	14	P. Rutherford
1988-89	S	23	C. Lytwyn
1989-90	F	9	P. Lamont
1990-91	S	11	J. Irvine
1991-92	S	12	M. Hendry
1992-93	S	19	B. Moffat
1993-94	T	7	W. Newbigging
1994-95	T	13	B. Moffat

ARBROATH

Season	Div	No. of Goals	Player
1980-81	S	15	J. Harley
1981-82	S	21	D. Robb
1982-83	S	15	W. Gavine
			W. Steele
1983-84	S	18	J. Harley
1984-85	S	6	R. Brown
1985-86	S	14	M. McWalter
1986-87	S	14	J. Fotheringham
1987-88	S	13	A. McKenna
1988-89	S	11	J. Fotheringham
1989-90	S	12	J. Marshall
1990-91	S	10	M. Bennett
			S. Sorbie
1991-92	S	12	S. Sorbie
1992-93	S	19	S. Sorbie
1993-94	S	10	D. Diver
1994-95	I	11	S. Tosh

AYR UNITED

Season	Div	No. of Goals	Player
1980-81	F	10	J. F. Frye
			E. Morris
1981-82	F	13	J. F. Frye
1982-83	F	7	J. F. Frye
			M. Larnach
			A. McInally
1983-84	F	15	A. McInally
1984-85	F	8	G. Collins
			J. McNiven
1985-86	F	6	D. Irons
1986-87	F	26	J. Sludden
1987-88	S	31	J. Sludden
1988-89	F	17	H. Templeton
1989-90	F	10	T. Bryce
1990-91	F	11	T. Bryce
1991-92	F	14	A. Graham
1992-93	F	9	A. Graham
1993-94	F	12	S. McGivern
1994-95	F	4	J. Jackson

BERWICK RANGERS

Season	Div	No. of Goals	Player
1980-81	F	8	E. Tait
1981-82	S	16	M. Lawson
1982-83	S	8	I. Cashmore
			S. Romaines
1983-84	S	9	P. Davidson
			A. O'Hara
1984-85	S	9	P. Davidson
1985-86	S	12	S. Sokoluk
1986-87	S	8	E. Tait
1987-88	S	3	M. Cameron
			H. Douglas
			T. Graham
			G. Leitch
			C. Lytwyn
			M. Thompson
1988-89	S	10	J. Hughes
1989-90	S	16	S. Sloan
1990-91	S	14	K. Todd
1991-92	S	12	S. Bickmore
1992-93	S	11	D. Scott
1993-94	S	15	W. Irvine
1994-95	S	16	W. Hawke

BRECHIN CITY

Season	Div	No. of Goals	Player
1980-81	S	11	I. M. Campbell
1981-82	S	16	I. M. Campbell
1982-83	S	23	I. M. Campbell
1983-84	F	19	I. M. Campbell
1984-85	F	17	K. Eadie
1985-86	F	22	K. Eadie
1986-87	F	12	C. Adam
1987-88	S	15	G. Buckley
1988-89	S	15	C. Adam
1989-90	S	12	G. Lees
1990-91	F	14	P. Ritchie
1991-92	S	12	P. Ritchie
1992-93	S	23	A. Ross
1993-94	F	10	M. Miller
1994-95	S	6	G. Price
			R. Smith

CALEDONIAN THISTLE

Season	Div	No. of Goals	Player
1994-95	T	6	C. Christie
			A. Hercher

CELTIC

Season	Div	No. of Goals	Player
1980-81	P	23	F. McGarvey
1981-82	P	21	G. McCluskey
1982-83	P	29	C. Nicholas
1983-84	P	23	B. McClair
1984-85	P	19	B. McClair
1985-86	P	22	B. McClair
1986-87	P	35	B. McClair
1987-88	P	26	A. Walker
1988-89	P	16	M. McGhee
1989-90	P	8	D. Dziekanowski
1990-91	P	18	T. Coyne
1991-92	P	21	C. Nicholas
1992-93	P	13	A. Payton
1993-94	P	10	P. McGinlay
1994-95	P	8	J. Collins

CLYDE

Season	Div	No. of Goals	Player
1980-81	S	19	D. Masterton
1981-82	S	23	D. Masterton
1982-83	F	14	D. Masterton
1983-84	F	17	J. F. Frye
1984-85	F	19	J. F. Frye
1985-86	F	12	J. F. Frye
1986-87	F	12	J. Murphy
1987-88	F	16	C. McGlashan / D. Walker
1988-89	F	16	C. McGlashan
1989-90	F	11	C. McGlashan
1990-91	F	8	S. Mallan
1991-92	S	16	D. Thompson
1992-93	S	16	F. McGarvey
1993-94	F	5	I. McConnell / G. Parks
1994-95	S	10	J. Dickson

CLYDEBANK

Season	Div	No. of Goals	Player
1980-81	F	18	B. Millar
1981-82	F	20	B. Millar
1982-83	F	21	R. Williamson
1983-84	F	10	T. Coyne
1984-85	F	11	M. Conroy
1985-86	P	7	M. Conroy / D. Lloyd
1986-87	P	9	M. Conroy / S. Gordon
1987-88	F	11	M. Conroy
1988-89	F	21	K. Eadie
1989-90	F	21	K. Eadie
1990-91	F	29	K. Eadie
1991-92	F	22	K. Eadie
1992-93	F	21	C. Flannigan
1993-94	F	11	K. Eadie / C. Flannigan
1994-95	F	9	K. Eadie

COWDENBEATH

Season	Div	No. of Goals	Player
1980-81	S	18	J. Liddle
1981-82	S	16	G. Forrest
1982-83	S	13	W. Gibson / C. McIntosh
1983-84	S	7	I. Paterson
1984-85	S	16	K. Ward
1985-86	S	15	C. McGlashan
1986-87	S	14	W. Blackie / R. Grant
1987-88	S	11	R. Grant
1988-89	S	8	A. McGonigal
1989-90	S	16	A. Ross
1990-91	S	15	A. MacKenzie
1991-92	S	26	G. Buckley
1992-93	F	9	W. Callaghan
1993-94	S	11	W. Callaghan
1994-95	T	23	M. Yardley

DUMBARTON

Season	Div	No. of Goals	Player
1980-81	F	14	B. Gallagher
1981-82	F	9	R. Blair
1982-83	F	10	R. Blair
1983-84	F	15	J. Coyle
1984-85	P	7	J. Coyle
1985-86	F	13	G. McCoy
1986-87	F	21	G. McCoy
1987-88	F	14	O. Coyle
1988-89	S	13	S. MacIver
1989-90	S	20	C. Gibson
1990-91	S	14	J. McQuade
1991-92	S	19	J. Gilmour
1992-93	F	15	J. McQuade
1993-94	F	13	C. Gibson
1994-95	S	17	M. Mooney

DUNDEE

Season	Div	No. of Goals	Player
1980-81	F	19	E. Sinclair
1981-82	P	12	I. Ferguson
1982-83	P	9	I. Ferguson
1983-84	P	13	W. McCall
1984-85	P	8	R. Stephen
1985-86	P	14	R. Stephen
1986-87	P	12	G. Harvey
1987-88	P	33	T. Coyne
1988-89	P	9	T. Coyne
1989-90	P	13	W. Dodds
1990-91	F	18	K. Wright
1991-92	F	19	W. Dodds
1992-93	P	16	W. Dodds
1993-94	P	6	D. Ristic
1994-95	F	16	G. Shaw

DUNDEE UNITED

Season	Div	No. of Goals	Player
1980-81	P	14	D. Dodds
1981-82	P	15	P. Sturrock
1982-83	P	22	D. Dodds
1983-84	P	15	D. Dodds
1984-85	P	14	P. Sturrock
1985-86	P	12	D. Dodds
1986-87	P	16	I. Ferguson
1987-88	P	11	I. Ferguson
1988-89	P	10	M-M. Paatelainen
1989-90	P	7	D. Jackson / M-M. Paatelainen
1990-91	P	12	D. Jackson
1991-92	P	17	D. Ferguson
1992-93	P	16	P. Connolly
1993-94	P	16	C. Brewster
1994-95	P	7	C. Brewster

DUNFERMLINE ATHLETIC

Season	Div	No. of Goals	Player
1980-81	F	20	A. McNaughton
1981-82	F	13	A. McNaughton
1982-83	F	8	R. Forrest / S. Morrison
1983-84	S	9	S. Morrison
1984-85	S	15	J. Watson
1985-86	S	24	J. Watson
1986-87	F	13	J. Watson
1987-88	P	13	C. Robertson
1988-89	F	18	R. Jack
1989-90	P	16	R. Jack
1990-91	P	8	R. Jack
1991-92	P	6	D. Moyes
1992-93	F	12	H. French
1993-94	F	17	G. O'Boyle
1994-95	F	14	S. Petrie

EAST FIFE

Season	Div	No. of Goals	Player
1980-81	S	10	R. Thomson
1981-82	S	16	G. Scott
1982-83	S	14	R. Thomson
1983-84	S	16	G. Durie
1984-85	F	12	G. Murray
1985-86	F	14	S. Kirk
1986-87	F	15	B. McNaughton
1987-88	F	17	P. Hunter
1988-89	S	9	P. Hunter
1989-90	S	14	P. Hunter
1990-91	S	10	W. Brown / R. Scott
1991-92	S	21	J. Sludden
1992-93	S	16	R. Scott
1993-94	S	10	R. Scott
1994-95	S	14	R. Scott

EAST STIRLINGSHIRE

Season	Div	No. of Goals	Player
1980-81	F	7	P. Lamont / D. McCaig
1981-82	F	4	J. Blair / R. Edgar / P. Lamont
1982-83	S	6	C. Gibson
1983-84	S	13	C. Gibson
1984-85	S	12	S. Maskrey
1985-86	S	12	S. Maskrey
1986-87	S	5	A. McGonigal / J. Paisley / D. Strange
1987-88	S	9	G. Murray
1988-89	S	16	W. McNeill
1989-90	S	4	W. McNeill / D. Wilcox / C. Wilson
1990-91	S	10	C. Lytwyn / Dk. Walker
1991-92	S	18	D. Diver
1992-93	S	9	P. Roberts
1993-94	S	12	M. McCallum
1994-95	T	16	M. Geraghty

FALKIRK

Season	Div	No. of Goals	Player
1980-81	F	5	C. Spence
1981-82	F	10	W. Herd
1982-83	F	8	P. Houston
1983-84	F	11	K. McAllister
1984-85	F	22	G. McCoy
1985-86	F	15	J. Gilmour
1986-87	P	6	K. Eadie
1987-88	P	9	C. Baptie
1988-89	F	12	A. Rae
1989-90	F	17	D. McWilliams
1990-91	F	16	S. Stainrod
1991-92	F	9	K. McAllister / E. May
1992-93	P	8	R. Cadette
1993-94	F	18	R. Cadette
1994-95	P	9	C. McDonald

FORFAR ATHLETIC

Season	Div	No. of Goals	Player
1980-81	S	13	N. J. Watt
1981-82	S	9	J. Clark / S. Hancock
1982-83	S	16	K. Macdonald
1983-84	S	22	J. Liddle
1984-85	F	14	K. Macdonald
1985-86	F	10	J. Clark
1986-87	F	17	K. Macdonald
1987-88	F	20	K. Macdonald
1988-89	F	12	K. Ward
1989-90	F	8	C. Brewster
1990-91	F	12	G. Whyte
1991-92	F	8	G. Winter
1992-93	S	21	S. Petrie
1993-94	S	13	D. Bingham
1994-95	T	22	D. Bingham

GREENOCK MORTON

Season	Div	No. of Goals	Player
1980-81	P	8	A. Ritchie
1981-82	P	6	A. Ritchie
1982-83	P	7	J. Rooney
1983-84	F	17	J. McNeil
1984-85	F	5	J. Gillespie
1985-86	F	14	J. McNeil
1986-87	F	23	R. Alexander
1987-88	P	8	Jim Boag
1988-89	F	11	R. Alexander
1989-90	F	11	R. Alexander
1990-91	F	21	D. MacCabe
1991-92	F	18	A. Mathie
1992-93	F	13	A. Mathie
1993-94	F	11	R. Alexander
1994-95	S	16	D. Lilley

HAMILTON ACADEMICAL

Season	Div	No. of Goals	Player
1980-81	F	13	J. Fairlie
1981-82	F	10	J. Fairlie
1982-83	F	15	J. Fairlie
1983-84	F	9	D. Somner
1984-85	F	8	J. Brogan / J. McGachie
1985-86	F	23	J. Brogan
1986-87	P	6	J. Brogan
1987-88	F	10	M. Caughey
1988-89	P	5	S. Gordon / C. Harris
1989-90	F	9	C. Harris
1990-91	F	14	G. McCluskey
1991-92	F	14	G. Clark
1992-93	F	11	P. McDonald
1993-94	F	19	P. Duffield
1994-95	F	20	P. Duffield

HEART OF MIDLOTHIAN

Season	Div	No. of Goals	Player
1980-81	P	4	W. Gibson / D. O'Connor
1981-82	F	16	W. Pettigrew
1982-83	F	21	J. Robertson
1983-84	F	14	J. Robertson
1984-85	P	8	A. Clark / J. Robertson
1985-86	P	20	J. Robertson
1986-87	P	16	J. Robertson
1987-88	P	26	J. Robertson
1988-89	P	5	J. Colquhoun / I. Ferguson
1989-90	P	17	J. Robertson
1990-91	P	12	J. Robertson
1991-92	P	15	S. Crabbe
1992-93	P	11	J. Robertson
1993-94	P	9	J. Robertson
1994-95	P	10	J. Robertson

HIBERNIAN

Season	Div	No. of Goals	Player
1980-81	F	15	A. MacLeod
1981-82	P	11	G. Rae
1982-83	P	6	G. Murray / G. Rae / R. Thomson
1983-84	P	18	W. Irvine
1984-85	P	8	G. Durie / P. Kane
1985-86	P	19	S. Cowan
1986-87	P	9	G. McCluskey
1987-88	P	10	P. Kane
1988-89	P	13	S. Archibald
1989-90	P	8	K. Houchen
1990-91	P	6	P. Wright
1991-92	P	11	M. Weir
1992-93	P	13	D. Jackson
1993-94	P	16	K. Wright
1994-95	P	10	D. Jackson / M. O'Neill / K. Wright

KILMARNOCK

Season	Div	No. of Goals	Player
1980-81	P	5	J. Bourke
1981-82	F	14	J. Bourke
1982-83	P	9	B. Gallagher
1983-84	F	11	R. Clark
			B. Gallagher
1984-85	F	12	B. Millar
1985-86	F	14	I. Bryson
1986-87	F	10	I. Bryson
1987-88	F	16	C. Harkness
1988-89	F	12	W. Watters
1989-90	S	23	W. Watters
1990-91	F	14	R. Williamson
1991-92	F	10	C. Campbell
			A. Mitchell
1992-93	F	11	G. McCluskey
1993-94	P	7	R. Williamson
1994-95	P	6	C. McKee

LIVINGSTON

FORMERLY MEADOWBANK THISTLE

Season	Div	No. of Goals	Player
1980-81	S	12	J. Jobson
1981-82	S	15	J. Jobson
1982-83	S	13	T. Hendrie
1983-84	F	10	C. Robertson
1984-85	F	14	A. Sprott
1985-86	S	17	D. Jackson
			A. Lawrence
1986-87	S	21	J. McGachie
1987-88	F	14	J. McGachie
1988-89	F	6	D. Roseburgh
1989-90	F	8	B. McNaughton
1990-91	F	15	D. Roseburgh
1991-92	F	8	D. Roseburgh
1992-93	F	9	P. Rutherford
1993-94	S	12	I. Little
1994-95	S	6	L. Bailey

MONTROSE

Season	Div	No. of Goals	Player
1980-81	S	12	G. Murray
			D. Robb
1981-82	S	9	I. Campbell
1982-83	S	12	E. Copland
1983-84	S	7	N. Burke
1984-85	S	12	D. Somner
1985-86	F	6	M. Allan
1986-87	F	10	I. Paterson
1987-88	S	11	H. Mackay
1988-89	S	21	G. S. Murray
1989-90	S	11	D. Powell
1990-91	S	11	G. Murray
1991-92	F	9	J. McGachie
1992-93	S	10	D. Grant
1993-94	S	12	D. Grant
1994-95	T	19	C. McGlashan

MOTHERWELL

Season	Div	No. of Goals	Player
1980-81	F	13	A. Kidd
1981-82	F	20	W. Irvine
1982-83	P	11	B. McClair
1983-84	P	7	J. Gahagan
1984-85	F	9	A. Harrow
			R. Stewart
1985-86	P	9	J. Reilly
1986-87	P	10	S. Kirk
			A. Walker
1987-88	P	9	S. Cowan
1988-89	P	14	S. Kirk
1989-90	P	11	N. Cusack
1990-91	P	14	D. Arnott
1991-92	P	8	D. Arnott
1992-93	P	10	S. Kirk
1993-94	P	12	T. Coyne
1994-95	P	16	T. Coyne

PARTICK THISTLE

Season	Div	No. of Goals	Player
1980-81	P	7	A. Higgins
			A. O'Hara
1981-82	P	9	M. Johnston
1982-83	F	22	M. Johnston
1983-84	F	13	K. McDowall
1984-85	F	12	A. Logan
1985-86	F	11	G. Smith
1986-87	F	10	C. West
1987-88	F	13	E. Gallagher
1988-89	F	19	G. McCoy
1989-90	F	18	C. Campbell
1990-91	F	13	D. Elliot
1991-92	F	10	C. McClashan
1992-93	P	12	G. Britton
1993-94	P	14	A. Craig
1994-95	P	7	W. Foster

QUEEN OF THE SOUTH

Season	Div	No. of Goals	Player
1980-81	S	19	J. Robertson
1981-82	F	12	G. Phillips
1982-83	S	22	R. Alexander
1983-84	S	9	J. Robertson
1984-85	S	9	G. Cloy
1985-86	S	15	T. Bryce
			S. Cochrane
1986-87	F	20	T. Bryce
1987-88	F	17	J. Hughes
1988-89	F	7	G. Fraser
1989-90	S	8	S. Gordon
1990-91	S	11	A. Thomson
1991-92	S	26	A. Thomson
1992-93	S	21	A. Thomson
1993-94	S	29	A. Thomson
1994-95	S	9	D. Campbell
			S. Mallan

QUEEN'S PARK

Season	Div	No. of Goals	Player
1980-81	S	17	G. McCoy
1981-82	F	10	C. Crawley
1982-83	F	10	J. Gilmour
1983-84	S	17	A. Grant
1984-85	S	18	J. Nicholson
1985-86	S	11	G. Fraser
1986-87	S	13	R. Caven
1987-88	S	17	P. O'Brien
1988-89	S	9	M. Hendry
1989-90	S	10	M. Hendry
1990-91	S	17	M. Hendry
1991-92	S	17	S. McCormick
1992-93	S	11	R. Caven
1993-94	S	18	J. O'Neill
1994-95	T	8	S. McCormick

RAITH ROVERS

Season	Div	No. of Goals	Player
1980-81	F	12	I. Ballantyne
1981-82	F	12	I. Ballantyne
1982-83	F	18	C. Harris
1983-84	F	16	J. Kerr
1984-85	S	22	K. Wright
1985-86	S	21	P. Smith
			K. Wright
1986-87	S	22	C. Harris
1987-88	F	25	G. Dalziel
1988-89	F	11	G. Dalziel
1989-90	F	20	G. Dalziel
1990-91	F	25	G. Dalziel
1991-92	F	26	G. Dalziel
1992-93	F	32	G. Dalziel
1993-94	F	8	G. Dalziel
1994-95	F	15	G. Dalziel

RANGERS

Season	Div	No. of Goals	Player
1980-81	P	12	C. McAdam
1981-82	P	14	J. MacDonald
1982-83	P	10	J. MacDonald
1983-84	P	9	A. Clark
			A. McCoist
1984-85	P	12	A. McCoist
1985-86	P	24	A. McCoist
1986-87	P	33	A. McCoist
1987-88	P	31	A. McCoist
1988-89	P	12	K. Drinkell
1989-90	P	15	M. Johnston
1990-91	P	12	M. Walters
1991-92	P	34	A. McCoist
1992-93	P	34	A. McCoist
1993-94	P	22	M. Hateley
1994-95	P	13	M. Hateley

ST. JOHNSTONE

Season	Div	No. of Goals	Player
1980-81	F	22	A. McCoist
1981-82	F	17	J. Morton
1982-83	F	26	J. Brogan
1983-84	P	9	J. Brogan
1984-85	F	9	J. Reid
1985-86	S	11	W. Brown
1986-87	S	25	W. Brown
1987-88	S	16	W. Watters
1988-89	F	12	S. Maskrey
1989-90	F	19	R. Grant
1990-91	P	9	H. Curran
1991-92	P	18	P. Wright
1992-93	P	14	P. Wright
1993-94	P	7	P. Wright
1994-95	F	19	G. O'Boyle

ST. MIRREN

Season	Div	No. of Goals	Player
1980-81	P	13	D. Somner
1981-82	P	13	F. McAvennie
1982-83	P	9	F. McAvennie
1983-84	P	13	F. McDougall
1984-85	P	16	F. McAvennie
1985-86	P	7	G. Speirs
1986-87	P	10	F. McGarvey
1987-88	P	10	P. Chalmers
1988-89	P	11	P. Chalmers
1989-90	P	12	G. Torfason
1990-91	P	4	P. Kinnaird
			K. McDowall
			G. Torfason
1991-92	P	8	G. Torfason
1992-93	F	18	B. Lavety
1993-94	F	10	B. Lavety
1994-95	F	7	B. Lavety

STENHOUSEMUIR

Season	Div	No. of Goals	Player
1980-81	S	20	S. Hancock
1981-82	S	8	B. Jenkins
1982-83	S	15	G. Murray
1983-84	S	14	G. Forrest
1984-85	S	6	H. Erwin
			A. McNaughton
1985-86	S	11	J. Sinnet
1986-87	S	5	A. Bateman
			P. Russell
1987-88	S	10	T. Condie
1988-89	S	9	C. Walker
1989-90	S	15	S. McCormick
1990-91	S	17	A. Speirs
1991-92	S	6	M. Mathieson
1992-93	S	26	M. Mathieson
1993-94	S	14	M. Mathieson
1994-95	S	10	G. Hutchison

ROSS COUNTY

Season	Div	No. of Goals	Player
1994-95	T	12	B. Grant

Darren Jackson (Hibernian)

STIRLING ALBION

Season	Div	No. of Goals	Player
1980-81	F	4	G. Armstrong
			W. B. Steele
1981-82	S	13	J. Colquhoun
1982-83	S	21	J. Colquhoun
1983-84	S	12	W. Irvine
1984-85	S	21	W. Irvine
1985-86	S	17	W. Irvine
1986-87	S	7	S. Gavin
			C. Gibson
1987-88	S	23	J. Brogan
1988-89	S	18	C. Gibson
1989-90	S	16	J. Reid
1990-91	S	14	D. Lloyd
1991-92	F	17	W. Watters
1992-93	F	11	W. Watters
1993-94	F	13	W. Watters
1994-95	S	15	W. Watters

STRANRAER

Season	Div	No. of Goals	Player
1980-81	S	7	H. Hay
1981-82	S	11	S. Sweeney
1982-83	S	12	S. Sweeney
1983-84	S	11	J. McGuire
1984-85	S	10	J. Sweeney
1985-86	S	8	J. McGuire
			S. Mauchlen
1986-87	S	13	B. Cleland
1987-88	S	8	B. Cleland
1988-89	S	11	D. Lloyd
1989-90	S	13	C. Harkness
1990-91	S	14	C. Harkness
1991-92	S	14	T. Sloan
1992-93	S	19	T. Sloan
1993-94	S	16	T. Sloan
1994-95	F	4	D. Henderson
			T. Sloan

The following section details the League Championship careers, appearances and goals of all players currently registered with each Premier Division club for season 1995/96 as at 14th September, 1995. It should be noted that all appearances include both full League appearances and substitute League appearances made by players. All club names shown in italics are for League appearances made when a player moved to a club on a Temporary Transfer basis with the player's registration subsequently reverting back to his original club.

SEASON	CLUB	LEAGUE APPEARANCES	GOALS
AITKEN, Robert Sime			
Born: Irvine 24/11/58			
1975-76	Celtic	12	–
1976-77	Celtic	33	5
1977-78	Celtic	33	2
1978-79	Celtic	36	5
1979-80	Celtic	35	3
1980-81	Celtic	33	4
1981-82	Celtic	33	3
1982-83	Celtic	33	6
1983-84	Celtic	31	5
1984-85	Celtic	33	3
1985-86	Celtic	36	–
1986-87	Celtic	42	1
1987-88	Celtic	43	1
1988-89	Celtic	32	–
1989-90	Celtic	18	2
1989-90	Newcastle United	22	1
1990-91	Newcastle United	32	–
1991-92	St. Mirren	34	1
1992-93	Aberdeen	26	2
1993-94	Aberdeen	1	–
1994-95	Aberdeen	2	–
ANDERSON, Derek Christopher			
Born: Paisley 15/05/72			
1991-92	Greenock Morton	–	–
1993-94	Kilmarnock	–	–
1994-95	Kilmarnock	20	–
ARNOTT, Douglas			
Born: Lanark 05/08/61			
1986-87	Motherwell	1	–
1987-88	Motherwell	2	–
1988-89	Motherwell	14	1
1989-90	Motherwell	30	5
1990-91	Motherwell	29	14
1991-92	Motherwell	26	8
1992-93	Motherwell	33	6
1993-94	Motherwell	29	8
1994-95	Motherwell	27	10
AYTON, Stuart			
Born: Glasgow 19/10/75			
1991-92	Rangers	–	–
1992-93	Rangers	–	–
1993-94	Rangers	–	–
1994-95	Partick Thistle	1	–
BERRY, Neil			
Born: Edinburgh 06/04/63			
1980-81	Bolton Wanderers	–	–
1981-82	Bolton Wanderers	3	–
1982-83	Bolton Wanderers	9	–
1983-84	Bolton Wanderers	14	–
1984-85	Bolton Wanderers	6	–
1984-85	Heart of Midlothian	3	–
1985-86	Heart of Midlothian	32	2
1986-87	Heart of Midlothian	30	3
1987-88	Heart of Midlothian	35	–
1988-89	Heart of Midlothian	32	1
1989-90	Heart of Midlothian	10	1
1990-91	Heart of Midlothian	19	1
1991-92	Heart of Midlothian	–	–
1992-93	Heart of Midlothian	17	1
1993-94	Heart of Midlothian	30	–
1994-95	Heart of Midlothian	29	–

SEASON	CLUB	LEAGUE APPEARANCES	GOALS
BLACK, Thomas			
Born: Lanark 11/10/62			
1980-81	Airdrieonians	–	–
1981-82	Airdrieonians	–	–
1982-83	Airdrieonians	5	–
1983-84	Airdrieonians	32	4
1984-85	Airdrieonians	37	1
1985-86	Airdrieonians	12	–
1986-87	Airdrieonians	24	1
1987-88	Airdrieonians	29	1
1988-89	Airdrieonians	37	4
1989-90	St. Mirren	31	1
1990-91	St. Mirren	34	2
1991-92	St. Mirren	9	1
1991-92	Kilmarnock	23	3
1992-93	Kilmarnock	10	1
1993-94	Kilmarnock	44	4
1994-95	Kilmarnock	32	5
BOLLAN, Gary			
Born: Dundee 24/03/73			
1987-88	Celtic	–	–
1988-89	Celtic	–	–
1989-90	Celtic	–	–
1990-91	Dundee United	2	–
1991-92	Dundee United	10	1
1992-93	Dundee United	15	3
1993-94	Dundee United	12	–
1994-95	Dundee United	7	–
1994-95	Rangers	6	–
BONNER, Patrick Joseph			
Born: Donegal 24/05/60			
1978-79	Celtic	2	–
1979-80	Celtic	–	–
1980-81	Celtic	36	–
1981-82	Celtic	36	–
1982-83	Celtic	36	–
1983-84	Celtic	33	–
1984-85	Celtic	34	–
1985-86	Celtic	30	–
1986-87	Celtic	43	–
1987-88	Celtic	32	–
1988-89	Celtic	26	–
1989-90	Celtic	36	–
1990-91	Celtic	36	–
1991-92	Celtic	19	–
1992-93	Celtic	33	–
1993-94	Celtic	31	–
1994-95	Celtic	20	–
BOOTH, Scott			
Born: Aberdeen 16/12/71			
1988-89	Aberdeen	–	–
1989-90	Aberdeen	2	–
1990-91	Aberdeen	19	6
1991-92	Aberdeen	33	5
1992-93	Aberdeen	29	13
1993-94	Aberdeen	25	4
1994-95	Aberdeen	12	6
BOYD, Thomas			
Born: Glasgow 24/11/65			
1983-84	Motherwell	13	–
1984-85	Motherwell	36	–
1985-86	Motherwell	31	–
1986-87	Motherwell	31	–
1987-88	Motherwell	42	2
1988-89	Motherwell	36	1
1989-90	Motherwell	33	1

SEASON	CLUB	LEAGUE APPEARANCES	GOALS
1990-91	Motherwell	30	2
1991-92	Chelsea	23	–
1991-92	Celtic	13	1
1992-93	Celtic	42	–
1993-94	Celtic	38	–
1994-95	Celtic	35	1
BRODDLE, Julian			
Born: Sheffield 01/11/64			
1981-82	Sheffield United	1	–
1982-83	Sheffield United	–	–
1983-84	Scunthorpe United	13	1
1984-85	Scunthorpe United	45	14
1985-86	Scunthorpe United	41	7
1986-87	Scunthorpe United	38	10
1987-88	Scunthorpe United	7	–
1987-88	Barnsley	19	1
1988-89	Barnsley	38	3
1989-90	Barnsley	20	–
1989-90	Plymouth Argyle	9	–
1990-91	Plymouth Argyle	–	–
1990-91	*Bradford City*	–	–
1990-91	St. Mirren	10	–
1991-92	St. Mirren	35	2
1992-93	St. Mirren	14	–
1992-93	*Scunthorpe United*	5	–
1992-93	Partick Thistle	6	–
1992-93	*Preston North End*	–	–
1993-94	Raith Rovers	18	–
1994-95	Raith Rovers	28	1
BROWN, John			
Born: Stirling 26/01/62			
1979-80	Hamilton Academical	19	–
1980-81	Hamilton Academical	38	6
1981-82	Hamilton Academical	28	5
1982-83	Hamilton Academical	9	–
1983-84	Hamilton Academical	39	–
1984-85	Dundee	34	7
1985-86	Dundee	29	11
1986-87	Dundee	31	10
1987-88	Dundee	20	3
1987-88	Rangers	9	2
1988-89	Rangers	29	1
1989-90	Rangers	27	1
1990-91	Rangers	27	1
1991-92	Rangers	25	4
1992-93	Rangers	39	4
1993-94	Rangers	24	–
1994-95	Rangers	13	1
BROWN, Thomas			
Born: Glasgow 01/04/68			
1991-92	Queen of the South	–	–
1993-94	Kilmarnock	31	5
1994-95	Kilmarnock	27	4
BURNS, Alexander			
Born: Bellshill 04/08/73			
1991-92	Motherwell	–	–
1992-93	Motherwell	–	–
1993-94	Motherwell	4	1
1994-95	Motherwell	14	3
CAIRNS, Mark Henry			
Born: Edinburgh 25/09/69			
1988-89	Heart of Midlothian	–	–
1988-89	*Berwick Rangers*	4	–
1989-90	Heart of Midlothian	–	–
1989-90	*East Stirlingshire*	6	–
1990-91	Heart of Midlothian	–	–
1994-95	Partick Thistle	1	–

SEASON	CLUB	LEAGUE APPEARANCES	GOALS
CAMERON, Colin			
Born: Kirkcaldy 23/10/72			
1990-91	Raith Rovers	–	–
1991-92	Sligo Rovers	–	–
1992-93	Raith Rovers	16	1
1993-94	Raith Rovers	42	6
1994-95	Raith Rovers	34	7
CAMERON, Ian			
Born: Glasgow 24/08/66			
1983-84	St. Mirren	8	
1984-85	St. Mirren	9	1
1985-86	St. Mirren	12	
1986-87	St. Mirren	31	6
1987-88	St. Mirren	41	8
1988-89	St. Mirren	26	2
1989-90	Aberdeen	11	
1990-91	Aberdeen	10	1
1991-92	Aberdeen	6	–
1992-93	Partick Thistle	41	5
1993-94	Partick Thistle	41	1
1994-95	Partick Thistle	34	3
CLARK, John			
Born: Edinburgh 22/09/64			
1981-82	Dundee United	–	–
1982-83	Dundee United	1	–
1983-84	Dundee United	9	1
1984-85	Dundee United	10	3
1985-86	Dundee United	11	1
1986-87	Dundee United	30	3
1987-88	Dundee United	28	3
1988-89	Dundee United	20	2
1989-90	Dundee United	29	1
1990-91	Dundee United	18	2
1991-92	Dundee United	35	1
1992-93	Dundee United	37	2
1993-94	Dundee United	14	–
1993-94	Stoke City	12	–
1994-95	Stoke City	5	–
1994-95	Falkirk	31	8
CLELAND, Alexander			
Born: Glasgow 10/12/70			
1987-88	Dundee United	1	–
1988-89	Dundee United	9	–
1989-90	Dundee United	15	–
1990-91	Dundee United	20	2
1991-92	Dundee United	31	4
1992-93	Dundee United	24	–
1993-94	Dundee United	33	1
1994-95	Dundee United	18	1
1994-95	Rangers	10	–
COLLINS, John Angus Paul			
Born: Galashiels 31/01/68			
1984-85	Hibernian	–	–
1985-86	Hibernian	19	–
1986-87	Hibernian	30	1
1987-88	Hibernian	44	6
1988-89	Hibernian	35	2
1989-90	Hibernian	35	6
1990-91	Celtic	35	1
1991-92	Celtic	38	11
1992-93	Celtic	43	8
1993-94	Celtic	38	8
1994-95	Celtic	34	8
COLQUHOUN, John Mark			
Born: Stirling 14/07/63			
1980-81	Stirling Albion	13	–
1981-82	Stirling Albion	37	13
1982-83	Stirling Albion	39	21
1983-84	Stirling Albion	15	11
1983-84	Celtic	12	2
1984-85	Celtic	20	2
1985-86	Heart of Midlothian	36	8
1986-87	Heart of Midlothian	43	13
1987-88	Heart of Midlothian	44	15
1988-89	Heart of Midlothian	36	5
1989-90	Heart of Midlothian	36	6
1990-91	Heart of Midlothian	36	7
1991-92	Millwall	27	3
1992-93	Sunderland	20	–
1993-94	Heart of Midlothian	41	6
1994-95	Heart of Midlothian	31	2
CONNOR, Robert			
Born: Kilmarnock 04/08/60			
1977-78	Ayr United	9	–
1978-79	Ayr United	29	–
1979-80	Ayr United	38	9
1980-81	Ayr United	39	8
1981-82	Ayr United	30	–
1982-83	Ayr United	39	4
1983-84	Ayr United	39	7
1984-85	Dundee	34	7
1985-86	Dundee	35	2
1986-87	Dundee	2	–
1986-87	Aberdeen	32	4
1987-88	Aberdeen	34	1
1988-89	Aberdeen	36	4
1989-90	Aberdeen	34	1
1990-91	Aberdeen	29	6
1991-92	Aberdeen	11	–
1992-93	Aberdeen	6	–
1993-94	Aberdeen	25	1
1994-95	Kilmarnock	28	–
COYLE, Ronald			
Born: Glasgow 04/08/64			
1983-84	Celtic	–	–
1984-85	Celtic	1	–
1985-86	Celtic	1	–
1986-87	Middlesbrough	3	–
1987-88	Rochdale	24	1
1987-88	Raith Rovers	16	3
1988-89	Raith Rovers	36	1
1989-90	Raith Rovers	28	2
1990-91	Raith Rovers	35	1
1991-92	Raith Rovers	29	–
1992-93	Raith Rovers	35	1
1993-94	Raith Rovers	41	1
1994-95	Raith Rovers	9	–
COYNE, Thomas			
Born: Glasgow 14/11/62			
1981-82	Clydebank	31	9
1982-83	Clydebank	38	18
1983-84	Clydebank	11	10
1983-84	Dundee United	18	3
1984-85	Dundee United	21	3
1985-86	Dundee United	13	2
1986-87	Dundee	20	9
1987-88	Dundee	43	33
1988-89	Dundee	26	9
1988-89	Celtic	7	–
1989-90	Celtic	23	7
1990-91	Celtic	26	18
1991-92	Celtic	39	15
1992-93	Celtic	10	3
1992-93	Tranmere Rovers	12	1
1993-94	Tranmere Rovers	–	–
1993-94	Motherwell	26	12
1994-95	Motherwell	31	16
CRAIG, Albert Hughes			
Born: Glasgow 03/01/62			
1981-82	Dumbarton	13	2
1982-83	Dumbarton	32	7
1983-84	Dumbarton	26	4
1984-85	Dumbarton	35	4
1985-86	Dumbarton	32	6
1986-87	Hamilton Academical	16	5
1986-87	Newcastle United	6	–
1987-88	Newcastle United	3	
1987-88	Hamilton Academical	6	1
1988-89	Newcastle United	1	–
1988-89	Northampton Town	2	1
1988-89	Dundee	6	2
1989-90	Dundee	20	2
CRAMB, Colin			
Born: Lanark 23/06/74			
1990-91	Hamilton Academical	3	2
1991-92	Hamilton Academical	12	1
1992-93	Hamilton Academical	33	7
1993-94	Southampton	1	–
1994-95	Southampton	–	–
1994-95	Falkirk	8	1
1994-95	Heart of Midlothian	6	1
CRAWFORD, Stephen			
Born: Dunfermline 09/01/74			
1992-93	Raith Rovers	20	3
1993-94	Raith Rovers	36	5
1994-95	Raith Rovers	32	11
CURRAN, Henry			
Born: Glasgow 09/10/66			
1984-85	Dumbarton	2	–
1985-86	Dumbarton	6	–
1986-87	Dumbarton	8	–
1986-87	Dundee United	3	–
1987-88	Dundee United	6	–
1988-89	Dundee United	6	–
1989-90	St. Johnstone	31	3
1990-91	St. Johnstone	35	9
1991-92	St. Johnstone	39	8
1992-93	St. Johnstone	34	8
1993-94	St. Johnstone	39	3
1994-95	St. Johnstone	26	4
DAIR, Jason			
Born: Dunfermline 15/06/74			
1991-92	Raith Rovers	4	–
1992-93	Raith Rovers	15	1
1993-94	Raith Rovers	38	6
1994-95	Raith Rovers	18	1
DAVIES, William McIntosh			
Born: Glasgow 31/05/64			
1980-81	Rangers	–	–
1981-82	Rangers	4	–
1982-83	Rangers	4	–
1983-84	Rangers	3	1
1984-85	Rangers	–	–
1985-86	Rangers	–	–
1987-88	St. Mirren	18	–
1988-89	St. Mirren	27	4
1989-90	St. Mirren	29	1
1990-91	St. Mirren	–	–
1990-91	Leicester City	6	–
1990-91	Dunfermline Athletic	26	–
1991-92	Dunfermline Athletic	33	–
1992-93	Dunfermline Athletic	41	10
1993-94	Dunfermline Athletic	4	–
1993-94	Motherwell	10	–
1994-95	Motherwell	31	4
DENNIS, Shaun			
Born: Kirkcaldy 20/12/69			
1988-89	Raith Rovers	10	–
1989-90	Raith Rovers	18	–
1990-91	Raith Rovers	35	1
1991-92	Raith Rovers	42	–
1992-93	Raith Rovers	31	1
1993-94	Raith Rovers	43	3
1994-95	Raith Rovers	26	1
DINNIE, Alan			
Born: Glasgow 14/05/63			
1987-88	Partick Thistle	37	1
1988-89	Partick Thistle	31	1
1989-90	Partick Thistle	14	2
1989-90	Dundee	22	–
1990-91	Dundee	25	3

SEASON	CLUB	LEAGUE APPEARANCES	GOALS
1991-92	Dundee	29	–
1992-93	Dundee	26	1
1993-94	Dundee	7	–
1994-95	Dundee	1	–
1994-95	Partick Thistle	25	2

DOCHERTY, Stephen
Born: Glasgow 18/02/76

SEASON	CLUB	LEAGUE APPEARANCES	GOALS
1992-93	Partick Thistle	1	–
1993-94	Partick Thistle	–	–
1994-95	Partick Thistle	1	–

DODS, Darren
Born: Edinburgh 07/06/75

SEASON	CLUB	LEAGUE APPEARANCES	GOALS
1992-93	Hibernian	–	–
1993-94	Hibernian	–	–
1994-95	Hibernian	1	–

DODDS, William
Born: New Cumnock 05/02/69

SEASON	CLUB	LEAGUE APPEARANCES	GOALS
1986-87	Chelsea	1	–
1987-88	Chelsea	–	–
1987-88	*Partick Thistle*	30	9
1988-89	Chelsea	2	–
1989-90	Dundee	30	13
1990-91	Dundee	37	15
1991-92	Dundee	42	19
1992-93	Dundee	41	16
1993-94	Dundee	24	6
1993-94	St. Johnstone	20	6
1994-95	Aberdeen	35	15

DOLAN, James
Born: Salsburgh 22/02/69

SEASON	CLUB	LEAGUE APPEARANCES	GOALS
1987-88	Motherwell	–	–
1988-89	Motherwell	5	–
1989-90	Motherwell	12	–
1990-91	Motherwell	8	1
1991-92	Motherwell	32	2
1992-93	Motherwell	25	2
1993-94	Motherwell	36	–
1994-95	Motherwell	31	–

DONALD, Graeme Still
Born: Stirling 14/04/74

SEASON	CLUB	LEAGUE APPEARANCES	GOALS
1991-92	Hibernian	5	3
1992-93	Hibernian	4	–
1993-94	Hibernian	6	–
1994-95	Hibernian	–	–

DONNELLY, Simon
Born: Glasgow 01/12/74

SEASON	CLUB	LEAGUE APPEARANCES	GOALS
1993-94	Celtic	12	5
1994-95	Celtic	17	–

DURIE, Gordon Scott
Born: Paisley 06/12/65

SEASON	CLUB	LEAGUE APPEARANCES	GOALS
1981-82	East Fife	13	1
1982-83	East Fife	25	2
1983-84	East Fife	34	16
1984-85	East Fife	9	7
1984-85	Hibernian	22	8
1985-86	Hibernian	25	6
1985-86	Chelsea	1	–
1986-87	Chelsea	25	5
1987-88	Chelsea	26	12
1988-89	Chelsea	32	17
1989-90	Chelsea	15	5
1990-91	Chelsea	24	12
1991-92	Tottenham Hotspur	31	7
1992-93	Tottenham Hotspur	17	3
1993-94	Tottenham Hotspur	10	1
1993-94	Rangers	24	12
1994-95	Rangers	20	6

DURRANT, Ian
Born: Glasgow 29/10/66

SEASON	CLUB	LEAGUE APPEARANCES	GOALS
1984-85	Rangers	5	–
1985-86	Rangers	30	2
1986-87	Rangers	39	4
1987-88	Rangers	40	10
1988-89	Rangers	8	2
1989-90	Rangers	–	–
1990-91	Rangers	4	1
1991-92	Rangers	13	–
1992-93	Rangers	30	3
1993-94	Rangers	23	–
1994-95	Rangers	26	4

ELLIOT, David
Born: Glasgow 13/11/69

SEASON	CLUB	LEAGUE APPEARANCES	GOALS
1987-88	Celtic	–	–
1988-89	Celtic	4	–
1989-90	Celtic	2	–
1990-91	Partick Thistle	37	13
1991-92	St. Mirren	28	1
1992-93	St. Mirren	40	5
1993-94	St. Mirren	36	8
1994-95	St. Mirren	28	3

EVANS, Gareth John
Born: Coventry 14/01/67

SEASON	CLUB	LEAGUE APPEARANCES	GOALS
1984-85	Coventry City	–	–
1985-86	Coventry City	6	–
1986-87	Coventry City	1	–
1986-87	Rotherham United	34	9
1987-88	Rotherham United	29	4
1987-88	Hibernian	12	2
1988-89	Hibernian	35	5
1989-90	Hibernian	28	3
1990-91	Hibernian	15	2
1990-91	*Northampton Town*	2	–
1990-91	*Stoke City*	5	1
1991-92	Hibernian	41	6
1992-93	Hibernian	39	6
1993-94	Hibernian	40	4
1994-95	Hibernian	24	–

FALCONER, William Henry
Born: Aberdeen 05/04/66

SEASON	CLUB	LEAGUE APPEARANCES	GOALS
1982-83	Aberdeen	1	–
1983-84	Aberdeen	8	1
1984-85	Aberdeen	16	4
1985-86	Aberdeen	8	–
1986-87	Aberdeen	8	–
1987-88	Aberdeen	36	8
1988-89	Watford	33	5
1989-90	Watford	30	3
1990-91	Watford	35	4
1991-92	Middlesbrough	25	5
1992-93	Middlesbrough	28	5
1993-94	Middlesbrough	–	–
1993-94	Celtic	14	1
1994-95	Celtic	26	4

FARRELL, David
Born: Glasgow 29/10/69

SEASON	CLUB	LEAGUE APPEARANCES	GOALS
1988-89	Hibernian	–	–
1989-90	Hibernian	–	–
1990-91	Hibernian	2	–
1991-92	Hibernian	6	–
1992-93	Hibernian	12	–
1993-94	Hibernian	35	2
1994-95	Hibernian	19	–

FERGUSON, Derek
Born: Glasgow 31/07/67

SEASON	CLUB	LEAGUE APPEARANCES	GOALS
1983-84	Rangers	1	–
1984-85	Rangers	8	–
1985-86	Rangers	19	–
1986-87	Rangers	30	1
1987-88	Rangers	32	4
1988-89	Rangers	16	2
1989-90	Rangers	5	–
1989-90	*Dundee*	4	–
1990-91	Heart of Midlothian	28	2
1991-92	Heart of Midlothian	38	1
1992-93	Heart of Midlothian	37	1
1993-94	Sunderland	41	–
1994-95	Sunderland	23	–

FERGUSON, Ian
Born: Glasgow 15/03/67

SEASON	CLUB	LEAGUE APPEARANCES	GOALS
1984-85	Clyde	2	–
1985-86	Clyde	19	4
1986-87	Clyde	5	–
1986-87	St. Mirren	35	4
1987-88	St. Mirren	22	6
1987-88	Rangers	8	1
1988-89	Rangers	30	6
1989-90	Rangers	24	–
1990-91	Rangers	11	1
1991-92	Rangers	16	1
1992-93	Rangers	30	4
1993-94	Rangers	35	5
1994-95	Rangers	16	1

FINDLAY, William McCall
Born: Kilmarnock 29/08/70

SEASON	CLUB	LEAGUE APPEARANCES	GOALS
1987-88	Hibernian	–	–
1988-89	Hibernian	3	1
1989-90	Hibernian	10	–
1990-91	Hibernian	26	2
1991-92	Hibernian	9	–
1992-93	Hibernian	7	–
1993-94	Hibernian	20	3
1994-95	Hibernian	18	1
1994-95	Kilmarnock	9	–

FOSTER, Wayne Paul
Born: Tyldesley 11/09/63

SEASON	CLUB	LEAGUE APPEARANCES	GOALS
1981-82	Bolton Wanderers	23	2
1982-83	Bolton Wanderers	24	4
1983-84	Bolton Wanderers	30	3
1984-85	Bolton Wanderers	28	4
1985-86	Preston North End	31	3
1986-87	Heart of Midlothian	31	4
1987-88	Heart of Midlothian	39	4
1988-89	Heart of Midlothian	9	1
1989-90	Heart of Midlothian	17	1
1990-91	Heart of Midlothian	28	1
1991-92	Heart of Midlothian	7	–
1992-93	Heart of Midlothian	11	–
1993-94	Heart of Midlothian	18	1
1994-95	Heart of Midlothian	–	–
1994-95	Partick Thistle	16	7

FRAIL, Stephen Charles
Born: Glasgow 10/08/69

SEASON	CLUB	LEAGUE APPEARANCES	GOALS
1985-86	Dundee	–	–
1986-87	Dundee	–	–
1987-88	Dundee	4	–
1988-89	Dundee	23	1
1989-90	Dundee	6	–
1990-91	Dundee	26	–
1991-92	Dundee	3	–
1992-93	Dundee	7	–
1993-94	Dundee	32	–
1993-94	Heart of Midlothian	9	2
1994-95	Heart of Midlothian	25	2

FRIDGE, Leslie Francis
Born: Inverness 27/08/68

SEASON	CLUB	LEAGUE APPEARANCES	GOALS
1985-86	Chelsea	1	–
1986-87	Chelsea	–	–
1986-87	St. Mirren	1	–
1987-88	St. Mirren	3	–
1987-88	*Arbroath*	3	–
1988-89	St. Mirren	15	–
1989-90	St. Mirren	8	–
1990-91	St. Mirren	10	–
1991-92	St. Mirren	17	–
1992-93	St. Mirren	18	–
1993-94	Clyde	42	–
1994-95	Clyde	26	–

FULTON, Stephen
Born: Greenock 10/08/70

SEASON	CLUB	APPEARANCES	GOALS
1986-87	Celtic	–	–
1987-88	Celtic	–	–
1988-89	Celtic	3	–
1989-90	Celtic	16	–
1990-91	Celtic	21	–
1991-92	Celtic	30	2
1992-93	Celtic	6	–
1993-94	Bolton Wanderers	4	–
1994-95	Falkirk	28	3

GALLOWAY, Michael
Born: Oswestry 30/05/65

SEASON	CLUB	APPEARANCES	GOALS
1983-84	Mansfield Town	17	–
1984-85	Mansfield Town	31	3
1985-86	Mansfield Town	6	–
1985-86	Halifax Town	19	–
1986-87	Halifax Town	43	3
1987-88	Halifax Town	17	2
1987-88	Heart of Midlothian	25	6
1988-89	Heart of Midlothian	31	2
1989-90	Celtic	33	2
1990-91	Celtic	6	1
1991-92	Celtic	34	2
1992-93	Celtic	30	3
1993-94	Celtic	22	–
1994-95	Celtic	11	–
1994-95	Leicester City	5	–

GASCOIGNE, Paul
Born: Gateshead 27/05/67

SEASON	CLUB	APPEARANCES	GOALS
1984-85	Newcastle United	2	–
1985-86	Newcastle United	31	9
1986-87	Newcastle United	24	5
1987-88	Newcastle United	35	7
1988-89	Tottenham Hotspur	32	6
1989-90	Tottenham Hotspur	34	6
1990-91	Tottenham Hotspur	26	7
1991-92	Tottenham Hotspur	–	–
1992-93	Lazio Societa Sportiva	22	4
1993-94	Lazio Societa Sportiva	17	2
1994-95	Lazio Societa Sportiva	2	–

GEDDES, Alexander Robert
Born: Inverness 12/08/60

SEASON	CLUB	APPEARANCES	GOALS
1977-78	Dundee	–	–
1978-79	Dundee	–	–
1979-80	Dundee	–	–
1980-81	Dundee	20	–
1981-82	Dundee	28	–
1982-83	Dundee	1	–
1983-84	Dundee	24	–
1984-85	Dundee	16	–
1985-86	Dundee	36	–
1986-87	Dundee	44	–
1987-88	Dundee	38	–
1988-89	Dundee	34	–
1989-90	Dundee	12	–
1990-91	Kilmarnock	38	–
1991-92	Kilmarnock	33	–
1992-93	Kilmarnock	44	–
1993-94	Kilmarnock	44	–
1994-95	Kilmarnock	12	–

GIBSON, Andrew
Born: Dechmont 02/02/69

SEASON	CLUB	APPEARANCES	GOALS
1987-88	Stirling Albion	5	–
1988-89	Stirling Albion	12	1
1988-89	Aberdeen	–	–
1989-90	Aberdeen	–	–
1990-91	Aberdeen	–	–
1991-92	Aberdeen	5	–
1992-93	Aberdeen	1	1
1993-94	Aberdeen	2	–

SEASON	CLUB	APPEARANCES	GOALS
1993-94	Partick Thistle	11	–
1994-95	Partick Thistle	11	1

GLASS, Stephen
Born: Dundee 23/05/76

SEASON	CLUB	APPEARANCES	GOALS
1994-95	Aberdeen	19	1

GORAM, Andrew Lewis
Born: Bury 13/04/64

SEASON	CLUB	APPEARANCES	GOALS
1981-82	Oldham Athletic	3	–
1982-83	Oldham Athletic	38	–
1983-84	Oldham Athletic	22	–
1984-85	Oldham Athletic	41	–
1985-86	Oldham Athletic	41	–
1986-87	Oldham Athletic	41	–
1987-88	Oldham Athletic	9	–
1987-88	Hibernian	33	1
1988-89	Hibernian	36	–
1989-90	Hibernian	34	–
1990-91	Hibernian	35	–
1991-92	Rangers	44	–
1992-93	Rangers	34	–
1993-94	Rangers	8	–
1994-95	Rangers	19	–

GOUGH, Charles Richard
Born: Stockholm 05/04/62

SEASON	CLUB	APPEARANCES	GOALS
1980-81	Dundee United	4	–
1981-82	Dundee United	30	1
1982-83	Dundee United	34	8
1983-84	Dundee United	33	3
1984-85	Dundee United	33	6
1985-86	Dundee United	31	5
1986-87	Tottenham Hotspur	40	2
1987-88	Tottenham Hotspur	9	–
1987-88	Rangers	31	5
1988-89	Rangers	35	4
1989-90	Rangers	26	–
1990-91	Rangers	26	–
1991-92	Rangers	33	2
1992-93	Rangers	25	2
1993-94	Rangers	37	3
1994-95	Rangers	25	1

GRAHAM, Alastair
Born: Glasgow 11/08/66

SEASON	CLUB	APPEARANCES	GOALS
1984-85	Clydebank	1	–
1985-86	Clydebank	2	–
1986-87	Clydebank	–	–
1987-88	Albion Rovers	28	10
1988-89	Albion Rovers	39	15
1989-90	Albion Rovers	31	7
1990-91	Ayr United	38	8
1991-92	Ayr United	40	14
1992-93	Ayr United	30	9
1992-93	Motherwell	4	1
1993-94	Motherwell	5	–
1993-93	Raith Rovers	36	5
1994-95	Raith Rovers	27	6

GRANT, Brian
Born: Bannockburn 19/06/64

SEASON	CLUB	APPEARANCES	GOALS
1981-82	Stirling Albion	1	–
1982-83	Stirling Albion	1	–
1983-84	Stirling Albion	24	3
1984-85	Aberdeen	–	–
1985-86	Aberdeen	–	–
1986-87	Aberdeen	15	4
1987-88	Aberdeen	7	1
1988-89	Aberdeen	26	1
1989-90	Aberdeen	31	6
1990-91	Aberdeen	32	3
1991-92	Aberdeen	33	6
1992-93	Aberdeen	29	3
1993-94	Aberdeen	30	2
1994-95	Aberdeen	32	2

GRANT, Peter
Born: Bellshill 30/08/65

SEASON	CLUB	APPEARANCES	GOALS
1982-83	Celtic	–	–
1983-84	Celtic	3	–
1984-85	Celtic	20	4
1985-86	Celtic	30	1
1986-87	Celtic	37	1
1987-88	Celtic	37	2
1988-89	Celtic	21	–
1989-90	Celtic	26	–
1990-91	Celtic	27	–
1991-92	Celtic	22	–
1992-93	Celtic	31	2
1993-94	Celtic	28	–
1994-95	Celtic	28	2

GRAY, Donal
Born: Newry, County Down 22/05/77

From Portadown

SEASON	CLUB	APPEARANCES	GOALS
1994-95	Partick Thistle	1	–

GRAY, Stuart
Born: Harrogate 18/12/73

SEASON	CLUB	APPEARANCES	GOALS
1992-93	Celtic	1	–
1993-94	Celtic	–	–
1994-95	Celtic	11	–

HAGEN, David
Born: Edinburgh 05/05/73

SEASON	CLUB	APPEARANCES	GOALS
1989-90	Rangers	–	–
1990-91	Rangers	–	–
1991-92	Rangers	–	–
1992-93	Rangers	8	2
1993-94	Rangers	6	1
1994-95	Rangers	2	–
1994-95	Heart of Midlothian	20	3

HAMILTON, Brian
Born: Paisley 05/08/67

SEASON	CLUB	APPEARANCES	GOALS
1985-86	St. Mirren	8	–
1986-87	St. Mirren	28	3
1987-88	St. Mirren	27	–
1988-89	St. Mirren	23	1
1989-90	Hibernian	28	1
1990-91	Hibernian	26	2
1991-92	Hibernian	40	3
1992-93	Hibernian	41	1
1993-94	Hibernian	42	2
1994-95	Hibernian	18	–
1994-95	Heart of Midlothian	13	2

HAMILTON, Graeme John
Born: Stirling 22/01/74

SEASON	CLUB	APPEARANCES	GOALS
1991-92	Falkirk	3	–
1992-93	Falkirk	–	–
1993-94	Falkirk	7	–
1994-95	Falkirk	3	–

HARPER, Kevin Patrick
Born: Oldham 15/01/76

SEASON	CLUB	APPEARANCES	GOALS
1992-93	Hibernian	–	–
1993-94	Hibernian	2	–
1994-95	Hibernian	23	5

HATELEY, Mark
Born: Wallasey 07/11/61

SEASON	CLUB	APPEARANCES	GOALS
1978-79	Coventry City	1	–
1979-80	Coventry City	4	–
1980-81	Coventry City	19	3
1981-82	Coventry City	34	13
1982-83	Coventry City	35	9
1983-84	Portsmouth	38	22
1984-85	AC Milan	21	7
1985-86	AC Milan	22	8

SEASON	CLUB	LEAGUE APPEARANCES	GOALS	SEASON	CLUB	LEAGUE APPEARANCES	GOALS	SEASON	CLUB	LEAGUE APPEARANCES	GOALS

SEASON	CLUB	LEAGUE APPEARANCES	GOALS
1986-87	AC Milan	23	2
From Monaco			
1990-91	Rangers	33	10
1991-92	Rangers	30	21
1992-93	Rangers	37	19
1993-94	Rangers	42	22
1994-95	Rangers	23	13

HAY, Christopher Drummond
Born: Glasgow 28/08/74

SEASON	CLUB	LEAGUE APPEARANCES	GOALS
1993-94	Celtic	2	–
1994-95	Celtic	5	–

HENDERSON, Nicholas Sinclair
Born: Edinburgh 08/02/69

SEASON	CLUB	LEAGUE APPEARANCES	GOALS
1990-91	Raith Rovers	1	–
1991-92	Raith Rovers	–	–
1992-93	Raith Rovers	–	–
1992-93	Cowdenbeath	32	5
1993-94	Cowdenbeath	22	9
1993-94	Falkirk	10	2
1994-95	Falkirk	21	5

HENDRY, John
Born: Glasgow 06/01/70

SEASON	CLUB	LEAGUE APPEARANCES	GOALS
1988-89	Dundee	2	–
1989-90	Dundee	–	–
1989-90	*Forfar Athletic*	10	6
1990-91	Tottenham Hotspur	4	2
1991-92	Tottenham Hotspur	5	1
1991-92	*Charlton Athletic*	5	1
1992-93	Tottenham Hotspur	5	2
1993-94	Tottenham Hotspur	3	1
1994-95	Tottenham Hotspur	–	–

HENRY, John
Born: Vale of Leven 31/12/71

SEASON	CLUB	LEAGUE APPEARANCES	GOALS
1990-91	Clydebank	3	1
1991-92	Clydebank	35	8
1992-93	Clydebank	32	12
1993-94	Clydebank	44	6
1994-95	Kilmarnock	30	4

HETHERSTON, Peter
Born: Bellshill 06/11/64

SEASON	CLUB	LEAGUE APPEARANCES	GOALS
1984-85	Falkirk	12	2
1985-86	Falkirk	22	2
1986-87	Falkirk	36	3
1987-88	Watford	5	–
1987-88	Sheffield United	11	–
1988-89	Falkirk	31	3
1989-90	Falkirk	22	2
1990-91	Falkirk	26	4
1991-92	Raith Rovers	31	1
1992-93	Raith Rovers	44	4
1993-94	Raith Rovers	33	5
1994-95	Aberdeen	22	–

HOWIE, Scott
Born: Glasgow 04/01/72

SEASON	CLUB	LEAGUE APPEARANCES	GOALS
1991-92	Clyde	15	–
1992-93	Clyde	39	–
1993-94	Clyde	1	–
1993-94	Norwich City	2	–
1994-95	Norwich City	–	–
1994-95	Motherwell	3	–

HUGHES, John
Born: Edinburgh 09/09/64

SEASON	CLUB	LEAGUE APPEARANCES	GOALS
1988-89	Berwick Rangers	27	10
1989-90	Berwick Rangers	14	4
1989-90	Swansea City	24	4
1990-91	Swansea City	–	–
1990-91	Falkirk	32	2
1991-92	Falkirk	38	2
1992-93	Falkirk	15	–

SEASON	CLUB	LEAGUE APPEARANCES	GOALS
1993-94	Falkirk	29	3
1994-95	Falkirk	20	–

HUNTER, Gordon
Born: Wallyford 03/05/67

SEASON	CLUB	LEAGUE APPEARANCES	GOALS
1983-84	Hibernian	1	–
1984-85	Hibernian	6	–
1985-86	Hibernian	25	–
1986-87	Hibernian	29	–
1987-88	Hibernian	35	–
1988-89	Hibernian	33	1
1989-90	Hibernian	34	–
1990-91	Hibernian	20	1
1991-92	Hibernian	37	2
1992-93	Hibernian	23	–
1993-94	Hibernian	29	1
1994-95	Hibernian	29	2

INGLIS, John
Born: Edinburgh 16/10/66

SEASON	CLUB	LEAGUE APPEARANCES	GOALS
1983-84	East Fife	4	1
1984-85	East Fife	9	–
1985-86	East Fife	30	–
1986-87	East Fife	13	–
1986-87	Brechin City	15	–
1987-88	Brechin City	26	3
1988-89	Brechin City	12	1
1988-89	Meadowbank Thistle	12	1
1989-90	Meadowbank Thistle	38	3
1990-91	St. Johnstone	31	1
1991-92	St. Johnstone	40	–
1992-93	St. Johnstone	39	–
1993-94	St. Johnstone	25	1
1994-95	St. Johnstone	5	–
1994-95	Aberdeen	17	1

IRVINE, Brian Alexander
Born: Bellshill 24/05/65

SEASON	CLUB	LEAGUE APPEARANCES	GOALS
1983-84	Falkirk	3	–
1984-85	Falkirk	35	–
1985-86	Aberdeen	1	–
1986-87	Aberdeen	20	1
1987-88	Aberdeen	16	1
1988-89	Aberdeen	27	2
1989-90	Aberdeen	31	1
1990-91	Aberdeen	29	2
1991-92	Aberdeen	41	4
1992-93	Aberdeen	39	5
1993-94	Aberdeen	42	7
1994-95	Aberdeen	17	1

JACKSON, Christopher
Born: Edinburgh 29/10/73

SEASON	CLUB	LEAGUE APPEARANCES	GOALS
1992-93	Hibernian	1	–
1993-94	Hibernian	12	–
1994-95	Hibernian	–	–

JACKSON, Darren
Born: Edinburgh 25/07/66

SEASON	CLUB	LEAGUE APPEARANCES	GOALS
1985-86	Meadowbank Thistle	39	17
1986-87	Meadowbank Thistle	9	5
1986-87	Newcastle United	23	3
1987-88	Newcastle United	31	2
1988-89	Newcastle United	15	2
1988-89	Dundee United	1	–
1989-90	Dundee United	25	7
1990-91	Dundee United	33	12
1991-92	Dundee United	28	11
1992-93	Hibernian	36	13
1993-94	Hibernian	39	7
1994-95	Hibernian	31	10

JAMES, Kevin Francis
Born: Edinburgh 03/12/75

SEASON	CLUB	LEAGUE APPEARANCES	GOALS
1993-94	Falkirk	–	–
1994-95	Falkirk	1	–

JAMIESON, William George
Born: Barnsley 27/04/63

SEASON	CLUB	LEAGUE APPEARANCES	GOALS
1980-81	Hibernian	28	12
1981-82	Hibernian	12	5
1982-83	Hibernian	19	2
1983-84	Hibernian	33	4
1984-85	Hibernian	25	2
1985-86	Hamilton Academical	39	2
1986-87	Hamilton Academical	15	–
1987-88	Hamilton Academical	41	4
1988-89	Hamilton Academical	34	1
1989-90	Dundee	14	–
1990-91	Dundee	38	2
1991-92	Dundee	38	4
1992-93	Partick Thistle	28	3
1993-94	Partick Thistle	43	1
1994-95	Partick Thistle	15	–
1994-95	Heart of Midlothian	15	3

JESS, Eoin
Born: Aberdeen 13/12/70

SEASON	CLUB	LEAGUE APPEARANCES	GOALS
1987-88	Aberdeen	–	–
1988-89	Aberdeen	2	–
1989-90	Aberdeen	11	3
1990-91	Aberdeen	27	13
1991-92	Aberdeen	39	12
1992-93	Aberdeen	31	12
1993-94	Aberdeen	41	6
1994-95	Aberdeen	25	1

JOHNSTON, Allan
Born: Glasgow 14/12/73

SEASON	CLUB	LEAGUE APPEARANCES	GOALS
1991-92	Heart of Midlothian	–	–
1992-93	Heart of Midlothian	2	1
1993-94	Heart of Midlothian	28	1
1994-95	Heart of Midlothian	21	1

JOHNSTON, Forbes Duthie Stephen
Born: Aberdeen 03/08/71

SEASON	CLUB	LEAGUE APPEARANCES	GOALS
1990-91	Falkirk	–	–
1991-92	Falkirk	12	–
1992-93	Falkirk	22	1
1993-94	Falkirk	15	1
1994-95	Falkirk	3	–

JOHNSTON, Maurice Thomas
Born: Glasgow 13/04/63

SEASON	CLUB	LEAGUE APPEARANCES	GOALS
1980-81	Partick Thistle	–	–
1981-82	Partick Thistle	32	9
1982-83	Partick Thistle	39	22
1983-84	Partick Thistle	14	10
1983-84	Watford	29	20
1984-85	Watford	9	3
1984-85	Celtic	27	14
1985-86	Celtic	32	15
1986-87	Celtic	40	23
1987-88	Nantes	32	13
1988-89	Nantes	34	9
1989-90	Rangers	36	15
1990-91	Rangers	29	11
1991-92	Rangers	11	5
1991-92	Everton	21	7
1992-93	Everton	13	3
1993-94	Everton	–	–
1993-94	Heart of Midlothian	31	4
1994-95	Heart of Midlothian	4	1
1994-95	Falkirk	10	1

KANE, Paul James
Born: Edinburgh 20/06/65

SEASON	CLUB	LEAGUE APPEARANCES	GOALS
1982-83	Hibernian	–	–
1983-84	Hibernian	13	1
1984-85	Hibernian	34	8
1985-86	Hibernian	32	5
1986-87	Hibernian	37	1
1987-88	Hibernian	44	10
1988-89	Hibernian	35	5
1989-90	Hibernian	31	3
1990-91	Hibernian	21	–
1990-91	Oldham Athletic	17	–
1991-92	Oldham Athletic	4	–
1991-92	Aberdeen	25	2

SEASON	CLUB	LEAGUE APPEARANCES	GOALS
1992-93	Aberdeen	27	4
1993-94	Aberdeen	39	3
1994-95	Aberdeen	27	2

KIDD, Walter Joseph
Born: Edinburgh 10/03/58

1977-78	Heart of Midlothian	23	–
1978-79	Heart of Midlothian	30	–
1979-80	Heart of Midlothian	34	2
1980-81	Heart of Midlothian	25	1
1981-82	Heart of Midlothian	30	–
1982-83	Heart of Midlothian	37	–
1983-84	Heart of Midlothian	31	1
1984-85	Heart of Midlothian	33	1
1985-86	Heart of Midlothian	28	–
1986-87	Heart of Midlothian	35	–
1987-88	Heart of Midlothian	18	–
1988-89	Heart of Midlothian	20	–
1989-90	Heart of Midlothian	17	1
1990-91	Heart of Midlothian	4	–
1991-92	Airdrieonians	32	–
1992-93	Airdrieonians	30	1
1994-95	Heart of Midlothian	1	–

KIRK, Stephen David
Born: Kirkcaldy 03/01/63

1979-80	East Fife	25	2
1980-81	Stoke City	–	–
1981-82	Stoke City	12	–
1982-83	Partick Thistle	–	–
1982-83	East Fife	25	8
1983-84	East Fife	33	5
1984-85	East Fife	38	8
1985-86	East Fife	39	14
1986-87	Motherwell	35	10
1987-88	Motherwell	38	4
1988-89	Motherwell	33	14
1989-90	Motherwell	34	8
1990-91	Motherwell	29	2
1991-92	Motherwell	38	6
1992-93	Motherwell	40	10
1993-94	Motherwell	36	7
1994-95	Motherwell	18	2
1994-95	Falkirk	11	5

KIRKWOOD, David Stewart
Born: St. Andrews 27/08/67

1983-84	East Fife	14	2
1984-85	East Fife	17	4
1985-86	East Fife	34	2
1986-87	East Fife	35	2
1987-88	Rangers	4	–
1988-89	Rangers	2	–
1989-90	Heart of Midlothian	19	–
1990-91	Heart of Midlothian	9	1
1991-92	Airdrieonians	36	9
1992-93	Airdrieonians	27	2
1993-94	Airdrieonians	29	10
1994-95	Raith Rovers	19	1

KPEDEKPO, Malcolm
Born: Aberdeen 27/08/76

1994-95	Aberdeen	1	–

KRIVOKAPIC, Miodrag
Born: Niksic Crna Gora 06/09/59

From Red Star Belgrade

1988-89	Dundee United	24	1
1989-90	Dundee United	26	–
1990-91	Dundee United	24	–
1991-92	Dundee United	–	–
1992-93	Dundee United	8	–
1993-94	Motherwell	42	1
1994-95	Motherwell	16	–

LAMBERT, Paul
Born: Glasgow 07/08/69

1985-86	St. Mirren	1	–
1986-87	St. Mirren	36	2
1987-88	St. Mirren	36	2
1988-89	St. Mirren	16	2

SEASON	CLUB	LEAGUE APPEARANCES	GOALS
1989-90	St. Mirren	25	3
1990-91	St. Mirren	31	2
1991-92	St. Mirren	40	2
1992-93	St. Mirren	39	1
1993-94	St. Mirren	3	–
1993-94	Motherwell	32	3
1994-95	Motherwell	36	1

LAUCHLAN, James Harley
Born: Glasgow 02/02/77

1993-94	Kilmarnock	1	–
1994-95	Kilmarnock	2	–

LAUDRUP, Brian
Born: Vienna 22/02/69
From Fiorentina

1994-95	Rangers	33	10

LAWRENCE, Alan
Born: Edinburgh 19/08/62

1984-85	Meadowbank Thistle	35	–
1985-86	Meadowbank Thistle	38	17
1986-87	Meadowbank Thistle	29	6
1986-87	Dundee	4	1
1987-88	Dundee	22	1
1988-89	Dundee	10	–
1988-89	Airdrieonians	7	2
1989-90	Airdrieonians	34	9
1990-91	Airdrieonians	38	13
1991-92	Airdrieonians	31	7
1992-93	Airdrieonians	35	2
1993-94	Airdrieonians	27	5
1994-95	Airdrieonians	32	11

LEIGHTON, James
Born: Johnstone 24/07/58

1978-79	Aberdeen	11	–
1979-80	Aberdeen	1	–
1980-81	Aberdeen	35	–
1981-82	Aberdeen	36	–
1982-83	Aberdeen	35	–
1983-84	Aberdeen	36	–
1984-85	Aberdeen	34	–
1985-86	Aberdeen	26	–
1986-87	Aberdeen	42	–
1987-88	Aberdeen	44	–
1988-89	Manchester United	38	–
1989-90	Manchester United	35	–
1990-91	Manchester United	–	–
1990-91	Arsenal	–	–
1991-92	Manchester United	–	–
1991-92	Reading	8	–
1991-92	Dundee	13	–
1992-93	Dundee	8	–
1993-94	Hibernian	44	–
1994-95	Hibernian	36	–

LEITCH, Donald Scott
Born: Motherwell 06/10/69

1987-88	Motherwell	–	–
1989-90	Dunfermline Athletic	–	–
1990-91	Dunfermline Athletic	14	3
1991-92	Dunfermline Athletic	33	4
1992-93	Dunfermline Athletic	42	9
1993-94	Heart of Midlothian	28	2
1994-95	Heart of Midlothian	21	–

LEKOVIC, Dragoje
Born: Sivac, Montenegro 21/11/67
From Buducnost Podgorica

1994-95	Kilmarnock	20	–

LENNON, Daniel Joseph
Born: Whitburn 06/04/69

1987-88	Hibernian	1	–
1988-89	Hibernian	1	–
1989-90	Hibernian	–	–
1990-91	Hibernian	6	–
1991-92	Hibernian	11	1
1992-93	Hibernian	13	–
1993-94	Hibernian	5	1

SEASON	CLUB	LEAGUE APPEARANCES	GOALS
1993-94	Raith Rovers	7	–
1994-95	Raith Rovers	20	–

LEVEIN, Craig William
Born: Dunfermline 22/10/64

1981-82	Cowdenbeath	15	–
1982-83	Cowdenbeath	30	–
1983-84	Cowdenbeath	15	–
1983-84	Heart of Midlothian	22	–
1984-85	Heart of Midlothian	36	1
1985-86	Heart of Midlothian	33	2
1986-87	Heart of Midlothian	12	–
1987-88	Heart of Midlothian	21	–
1988-89	Heart of Midlothian	9	–
1989-90	Heart of Midlothian	35	–
1990-91	Heart of Midlothian	33	4
1991-92	Heart of Midlothian	36	2
1992-93	Heart of Midlothian	37	3
1993-94	Heart of Midlothian	30	3
1994-95	Heart of Midlothian	24	–

LOCKE, Gary
Born: Edinburgh 16/06/75

1992-93	Heart of Midlothian	1	–
1993-94	Heart of Midlothian	33	–
1994-95	Heart of Midlothian	9	–

LOVE, Graeme
Born: Bathgate 07/12/73

1991-92	Hibernian	1	–
1992-93	Hibernian	1	–
1993-94	Hibernian	4	–
1994-95	Hibernian	12	–

MACKAY, Gary
Born: Edinburgh 23/01/64

1980-81	Heart of Midlothian	12	–
1981-82	Heart of Midlothian	17	2
1982-83	Heart of Midlothian	34	6
1983-84	Heart of Midlothian	31	4
1984-85	Heart of Midlothian	17	2
1985-86	Heart of Midlothian	32	4
1986-87	Heart of Midlothian	37	7
1987-88	Heart of Midlothian	41	5
1988-89	Heart of Midlothian	29	2
1989-90	Heart of Midlothian	33	1
1990-91	Heart of Midlothian	30	3
1991-92	Heart of Midlothian	43	1
1992-93	Heart of Midlothian	37	2
1993-94	Heart of Midlothian	36	1
1994-95	Heart of Midlothian	34	2

MACKAY, Malcolm George
Born: Bellshill 19/02/72

1989-90	Queen's Park	–	–
1990-91	Queen's Park	10	–
1991-92	Queen's Park	27	3
1992-93	Queen's Park	33	3
1993-94	Celtic	–	–
1994-95	Celtic	1	–

McKENZIE, Scott
Born: Glasgow 07/07/70

1990-91	Falkirk	–	–
1991-92	Falkirk	2	–
1992-93	Falkirk	3	–
1993-94	Falkirk	19	–
1994-95	Falkirk	36	1

MacPHERSON, Angus Ian
Born: Glasgow 11/10/68

1988-89	Rangers	–	–
1989-90	Rangers	–	–
1989-90	Exeter City	11	1
1990-91	Kilmarnock	11	–
1991-92	Kilmarnock	43	3
1992-93	Kilmarnock	40	5
1993-94	Kilmarnock	43	2
1994-95	Kilmarnock	33	1

MARSHALL, Gordon George Banks
Born: Edinburgh 19/04/64

SEASON	CLUB	APPEARANCES	GOALS
1980-81	Rangers	–	–
1981-82	Rangers	–	–
1982-83	Rangers	–	–
1982-83	East Stirlingshire	15	–
1982-83	East Fife	10	–
1983-84	East Fife	34	–
1984-85	East Fife	39	–
1985-86	East Fife	39	–
1986-87	East Fife	36	–
1986-87	Falkirk	10	–
1987-88	Falkirk	44	–
1988-89	Falkirk	39	–
1989-90	Falkirk	39	–
1990-91	Falkirk	–	–
1991-92	Celtic	25	–
1992-93	Celtic	11	–
1993-94	Celtic	1	–
1993-94	Stoke City	10	–
1994-95	Celtic	16	–

MARTIN, Brian
Born: Bellshill 24/02/63

SEASON	CLUB	APPEARANCES	GOALS
1980-81	Albion Rovers	10	–
1980-81	Stenhousemuir	2	–
1985-86	Falkirk	25	1
1986-87	Falkirk	34	1
1986-87	Hamilton Academical	7	–
1987-88	Hamilton Academical	23	–
1987-88	St. Mirren	12	1
1988-89	St. Mirren	34	2
1989-90	St. Mirren	35	2
1990-91	St. Mirren	31	2
1991-92	St. Mirren	17	2
1991-92	Motherwell	25	–
1992-93	Motherwell	44	3
1993-94	Motherwell	43	2
1994-95	Motherwell	32	2

MARTIN, Lee Andrew
Born: Hyde, Manchester 05/02/68

SEASON	CLUB	APPEARANCES	GOALS
1986-87	Manchester United	–	–
1987-88	Manchester United	1	–
1988-89	Manchester United	24	1
1989-90	Manchester United	32	–
1990-91	Manchester United	14	–
1991-92	Manchester United	1	–
1992-93	Manchester United	–	–
1993-94	Manchester United	1	–
1993-94	Celtic	15	–
1994-95	Celtic	4	–

MASKREY, Stephen William
Born: Edinburgh 16/08/62

SEASON	CLUB	APPEARANCES	GOALS
1984-85	East Stirlingshire	37	12
1985-86	East Stirlingshire	21	12
1985-86	Queen of the South	12	2
1986-87	Queen of the South	31	2
1987-88	St. Johnstone	33	5
1988-89	St. Johnstone	31	12
1989-90	St. Johnstone	29	11
1990-91	St. Johnstone	34	7
1991-92	St. Johnstone	24	2
1992-93	St. Johnstone	19	2
1993-94	St. Johnstone	4	–
1994-95	Kilmarnock	30	4

MAY, Edward
Born: Edinburgh 30/08/67

SEASON	CLUB	APPEARANCES	GOALS
1983-84	Dundee United	–	–
1984-85	Dundee United	–	–
1984-85	Hibernian	–	–

SEASON	CLUB	APPEARANCES	GOALS
1985-86	Hibernian	19	1
1986-87	Hibernian	30	5
1987-88	Hibernian	35	2
1988-89	Hibernian	25	2
1989-90	Brentford	30	8
1990-91	Brentford	17	2
1990-91	Falkirk	13	6
1991-92	Falkirk	36	9
1992-93	Falkirk	42	6
1993-94	Falkirk	38	9
1994-95	Falkirk	24	2
1994-95	Motherwell	10	2

McALLISTER Kevin
Born: Falkirk 08/11/62

SEASON	CLUB	APPEARANCES	GOALS
1983-84	Falkirk	35	11
1984-85	Falkirk	29	7
1985-86	Chelsea	20	–
1986-87	Chelsea	8	–
1987-88	Chelsea	5	–
1987-88	Falkirk	6	3
1988-89	Chelsea	36	6
1989-90	Chelsea	24	1
1990-91	Chelsea	13	1
1991-92	Falkirk	42	9
1992-93	Falkirk	41	3
1993-94	Hibernian	36	6
1994-95	Hibernian	23	1

McANESPIE, Stephen
Born: Kilmarnock 01/02/72

SEASON	CLUB	APPEARANCES	GOALS
1987-88	Aberdeen	–	–
1988-89	Aberdeen	–	–
1989-90	Aberdeen	–	–
1990-91	Aberdeen	–	–
1991-92	Aberdeen	–	–
1992-93	Aberdeen	–	–
From Vasterhaninge I. F.			
1993-94	Raith Rovers	3	–
1994-95	Raith Rovers	34	–

McCALL, Stuart
Born: Leeds 10/06/64

SEASON	CLUB	APPEARANCES	GOALS
1982-83	Bradford City	28	4
1983-84	Bradford City	46	5
1984-85	Bradford City	46	8
1985-86	Bradford City	38	4
1986-87	Bradford City	36	7
1987-88	Bradford City	44	9
1988-89	Everton	33	–
1989-90	Everton	37	3
1990-91	Everton	33	3
1991-92	Rangers	36	1
1992-93	Rangers	36	5
1993-94	Rangers	34	3
1994-95	Rangers	30	2

McCART, Christopher
Born: Motherwell 17/04/67

SEASON	CLUB	APPEARANCES	GOALS
1984-85	Motherwell	–	–
1985-86	Motherwell	13	–
1986-87	Motherwell	–	–
1987-88	Motherwell	1	–
1988-89	Motherwell	26	–
1989-90	Motherwell	34	1
1990-91	Motherwell	36	–
1991-92	Motherwell	22	2
1992-93	Motherwell	29	3
1993-94	Motherwell	36	–
1994-95	Motherwell	24	–

McCOIST, Alistair
Born: Bellshill 24/09/62

SEASON	CLUB	APPEARANCES	GOALS
1978-79	St. Johnstone	4	–
1979-80	St. Johnstone	15	–
1980-81	St. Johnstone	38	22
1981-82	Sunderland	28	2
1982-83	Sunderland	28	6
1983-84	Rangers	30	9

SEASON	CLUB	APPEARANCES	GOALS
1984-85	Rangers	25	12
1985-86	Rangers	33	24
1986-87	Rangers	44	33
1987-88	Rangers	40	31
1988-89	Rangers	19	9
1989-90	Rangers	34	14
1990-91	Rangers	26	11
1991-92	Rangers	38	34
1992-93	Rangers	34	34
1993-94	Rangers	21	7
1994-95	Rangers	9	1

McDONALD, Colin
Born: Edinburgh 10/04/74

SEASON	CLUB	APPEARANCES	GOALS
1990-91	Hibernian	–	–
1991-92	Hibernian	–	–
1992-93	Falkirk	–	–
1993-94	Falkirk	17	1
1994-95	Falkirk	31	9

McDONALD, Rodney
Born: London 20/03/67

SEASON	CLUB	APPEARANCES	GOALS
1990-91	Walsall	36	5
1991-92	Walsall	39	18
1992-93	Walsall	39	12
1993-94	Walsall	35	6
1994-95	Walsall	–	–
1994-95	Partick Thistle	25	5

McGINLAY, Patrick David
Born: Glasgow 30/05/67

SEASON	CLUB	APPEARANCES	GOALS
1985-86	Blackpool	–	–
1986-87	Blackpool	12	1
1987-88	Hibernian	–	–
1988-89	Hibernian	2	–
1989-90	Hibernian	28	3
1990-91	Hibernian	32	1
1991-92	Hibernian	43	9
1992-93	Hibernian	40	10
1993-94	Celtic	41	10
1994-95	Celtic	8	1
1994-95	Hibernian	24	7

McGINTY, Brian
Born: East Kilbride 10/12/76

SEASON	CLUB	APPEARANCES	GOALS
1993-94	Rangers	–	–
1994-95	Rangers	1	–

McGOWAN, Jamie
Born: Morecambe 05/12/70

SEASON	CLUB	APPEARANCES	GOALS
1992-93	Dundee	21	1
1993-94	Dundee	14	–
1993-94	Falkirk	9	2
1994-95	Falkirk	31	1

McGRAW, Mark Robertson
Born: Rutherglen 05/01/71

SEASON	CLUB	APPEARANCES	GOALS
1988-89	Morton	1	–
1989-90	Morton	11	3
1990-91	Hibernian	13	–
1991-92	Hibernian	24	1
1992-93	Hibernian	2	–
1993-94	Hibernian	2	–
1994-95	Hibernian	8	2

McGRILLEN Paul
Born: Glasgow 19/08/71

SEASON	CLUB	APPEARANCES	GOALS
1990-91	Motherwell	2	–
1991-92	Motherwell	16	–
1992-93	Motherwell	22	6
1993-94	Motherwell	40	5
1994-95	Motherwell	7	2
1994-95	Falkirk	6	1

McINALLY, James Edward
Born: Glasgow 19/02/64

SEASON	CLUB	APPEARANCES	GOALS
1982-83	Celtic	1	–

SEASON	CLUB	LEAGUE APPEARANCES	GOALS
1983-84	Celtic	–	–
1983-84	Dundee	11	2
1984-85	Nottingham Forest	24	–
1985-86	Nottingham Forest	12	–
1985-86	Coventry City	5	–
1986-87	Dundee United	32	1
1987-88	Dundee United	36	2
1988-89	Dundee United	29	1
1989-90	Dundee United	35	3
1990-91	Dundee United	33	1
1991-92	Dundee United	32	4
1992-93	Dundee United	32	–
1993-94	Dundee United	31	–
1994-95	Dundee United	25	–

McKEE, Colin
Born: Glasgow 22/08/73

SEASON	CLUB	LEAGUE APPEARANCES	GOALS
1991-92	Manchester United	–	–
1992-93	Manchester United	–	–
1992-93	Bury	2	–
1993-94	Manchester United	1	–
1994-95	Manchester United	–	–
1994-95	Kilmarnock	25	6

McKEE, Kevin George
Born: Edinburgh 10/06/66

SEASON	CLUB	LEAGUE APPEARANCES	GOALS
1981-82	Hibernian	–	–
1982-83	Hibernian	4	–
1983-84	Hibernian	16	–
1984-85	Hibernian	17	–
1985-86	Hibernian	2	–
1986-87	Hamilton Academical	29	4
1987-88	Hamilton Academical	40	–
1988-89	Hamilton Academical	36	–
1989-90	Hamilton Academical	39	1
1990-91	Hamilton Academical	38	–
1991-92	Hamilton Academical	34	1
1992-93	Hamilton Academical	20	1
1993-94	Partick Thistle	23	–
1994-95	Partick Thistle	17	–

McKIMMIE, Stewart
Born: Aberdeen 27/10/62

SEASON	CLUB	LEAGUE APPEARANCES	GOALS
1980-81	Dundee	17	–
1981-82	Dundee	16	–
1982-83	Dundee	31	–
1983-84	Dundee	16	–
1983-84	Aberdeen	18	1
1984-85	Aberdeen	34	3
1985-86	Aberdeen	34	3
1986-87	Aberdeen	37	–
1987-88	Aberdeen	42	–
1988-89	Aberdeen	35	–
1989-90	Aberdeen	33	–
1990-91	Aberdeen	26	1
1991-92	Aberdeen	39	–
1992-93	Aberdeen	14	–
1993-94	Aberdeen	40	–
1994-95	Aberdeen	34	1

McKINLAY, Thomas Valley
Born: Glasgow 03/12/64

SEASON	CLUB	LEAGUE APPEARANCES	GOALS
1981-82	Dundee	–	–
1982-83	Dundee	1	–
1983-84	Dundee	36	3
1984-85	Dundee	34	3
1985-86	Dundee	22	–
1986-87	Dundee	32	2
1987-88	Dundee	19	–
1988-89	Dundee	18	–
1988-89	Heart of Midlothian	17	1
1989-90	Heart of Midlothian	29	1
1990-91	Heart of Midlothian	33	2
1991-92	Heart of Midlothian	39	2
1992-93	Heart of Midlothian	34	–
1993-94	Heart of Midlothian	43	–
1994-95	Heart of Midlothian	11	–
1994-95	Celtic	17	–

McKINNON, Raymond
Born: Dundee 05/08/70

SEASON	CLUB	LEAGUE APPEARANCES	GOALS
1987-88	Dundee United	–	–

SEASON	CLUB	LEAGUE APPEARANCES	GOALS
1988-89	Dundee United	1	–
1989-90	Dundee United	10	–
1990-91	Dundee United	17	2
1991-92	Dundee United	25	4
1992-93	Nottingham Forest	6	1
1993-94	Nottingham Forest	–	–
1993-94	Aberdeen	5	–
1994-95	Aberdeen	20	–

McKINNON, Robert
Born: Glasgow 31/07/66

SEASON	CLUB	LEAGUE APPEARANCES	GOALS
1984-85	Newcastle United	–	–
1985-86	Newcastle United	1	–
1986-87	Hartlepool United	45	–
1987-88	Hartlepool United	42	2
1988-89	Hartlepool United	46	2
1989-90	Hartlepool United	46	1
1990-91	Hartlepool United	45	1
1990-91	Manchester United	–	–
1991-92	Hartlepool United	23	1
1991-92	Motherwell	16	1
1992-93	Motherwell	35	–
1993-94	Motherwell	42	4
1994-95	Motherwell	32	3

McKNIGHT Paul
Born: Belfast 08/02/77

SEASON	CLUB	LEAGUE APPEARANCES	GOALS
1993-94	Rangers	–	–
1994-95	Rangers	1	–

McLAREN, Alan James
Born: Edinburgh 04/01/71

SEASON	CLUB	LEAGUE APPEARANCES	GOALS
1987-88	Heart of Midlothian	1	–
1988-89	Heart of Midlothian	12	1
1989-90	Heart of Midlothian	27	1
1990-91	Heart of Midlothian	23	1
1991-92	Heart of Midlothian	38	1
1992-93	Heart of Midlothian	34	–
1993-94	Heart of Midlothian	37	1
1994-95	Heart of Midlothian	10	1
1994-95	Rangers	24	2

McLAUGHLIN, Brian
Born: Bellshill 14/05/74

SEASON	CLUB	LEAGUE APPEARANCES	GOALS
1992-93	Celtic	–	–
1993-94	Celtic	8	–
1994-95	Celtic	21	–

McLAUGHLIN, Joseph
Born: Greenock 02/06/60

SEASON	CLUB	LEAGUE APPEARANCES	GOALS
1977-78	Morton	–	–
1978-79	Morton	–	–
1979-80	Morton	30	2
1980-81	Morton	34	1
1981-82	Morton	36	–
1982-83	Morton	34	–
1983-84	Chelsea	41	–
1984-85	Chelsea	36	1
1985-86	Chelsea	40	1
1986-87	Chelsea	36	2
1987-88	Chelsea	36	1
1988-89	Chelsea	31	–
1989-90	Charlton Athletic	31	–
1990-91	Watford	24	1
1991-92	Watford	22	1
1992-93	Watford	–	–
1992-93	Falkirk	8	1
1993-94	Falkirk	37	2
1994-95	Falkirk	28	2

McLEISH, Alexander
Born: Glasgow 21/01/59

SEASON	CLUB	LEAGUE APPEARANCES	GOALS
1977-78	Aberdeen	1	–
1978-79	Aberdeen	19	1
1979-80	Aberdeen	35	2
1980-81	Aberdeen	32	3

SEASON	CLUB	LEAGUE APPEARANCES	GOALS
1981-82	Aberdeen	32	5
1982-83	Aberdeen	34	2
1983-84	Aberdeen	32	2
1984-85	Aberdeen	30	1
1985-86	Aberdeen	34	3
1986-87	Aberdeen	40	3
1987-88	Aberdeen	36	1
1988-89	Aberdeen	34	–
1989-90	Aberdeen	32	2
1990-91	Aberdeen	33	–
1991-92	Aberdeen	7	–
1992-93	Aberdeen	27	–
1993-94	Aberdeen	35	–
1994-95	Motherwell	2	–

MacLEOD, Murdo Davidson
Born: Glasgow 24/09/58

SEASON	CLUB	LEAGUE APPEARANCES	GOALS
1974-75	Dumbarton	–	–
1975-76	Dumbarton	7	–
1976-77	Dumbarton	27	7
1977-78	Dumbarton	39	1
1978-79	Dumbarton	14	1
1978-79	Celtic	23	3
1979-80	Celtic	36	7
1980-81	Celtic	18	8
1981-82	Celtic	36	10
1982-83	Celtic	35	11
1983-84	Celtic	34	7
1984-85	Celtic	31	3
1985-86	Celtic	30	3
1986-87	Celtic	38	4
From Borussia Dortmund			
1990-91	Hibernian	25	2
1991-92	Hibernian	22	–
1992-93	Hibernian	31	–
1993-94	Dumbarton	42	1
1994-95	Dumbarton	24	–

McMILLAN, Ian
Born: Broxburn 09/06/76

SEASON	CLUB	LEAGUE APPEARANCES	GOALS
1992-93	Raith Rovers	–	–
1993-94	Raith Rovers	–	–
1994-95	Raith Rovers	1	–

McMILLAN, Stephen
Born: Edinburgh 19/01/76

SEASON	CLUB	LEAGUE APPEARANCES	GOALS
1993-94	Motherwell	1	–
1994-95	Motherwell	3	–

McNALLY, Mark
Born: Motherwell 10/03/71

SEASON	CLUB	LEAGUE APPEARANCES	GOALS
1987-88	Celtic	–	–
1988-89	Celtic	–	–
1989-90	Celtic	–	–
1990-91	Celtic	19	–
1991-92	Celtic	25	1
1992-93	Celtic	27	–
1993-94	Celtic	32	2
1994-95	Celtic	20	–

McPHERSON David
Born: Paisley 28/01/64

SEASON	CLUB	LEAGUE APPEARANCES	GOALS
1980-81	Rangers	–	–
1981-82	Rangers	–	–
1982-83	Rangers	18	1
1983-84	Rangers	36	2
1984-85	Rangers	31	–
1985-86	Rangers	34	5
1986-87	Rangers	42	7
1987-88	Rangers	44	4
1988-89	Heart of Midlothian	32	4
1989-90	Heart of Midlothian	35	4
1990-91	Heart of Midlothian	34	2
1991-92	Heart of Midlothian	44	2
1992-93	Rangers	34	2
1993-94	Rangers	28	1
1994-95	Rangers	9	–
1994-95	Heart of Midlothian	23	2

SEASON	CLUB	LEAGUE APPEARANCES	GOALS

McQUILKEN, James
Born: Glasgow 03/10/74

SEASON	CLUB	APPEARANCES	GOALS
1992-93	Celtic	1	–
1993-94	Celtic	–	–
1994-95	Celtic	–	–

McSKIMMING, Shaun Peter
Born: Stranraer 29/05/70

SEASON	CLUB	APPEARANCES	GOALS
1986-87	Stranraer	–	–
1987-88	Dundee	–	–
1988-89	Dundee	–	–
1989-90	Dundee	7	–
1990-91	Dundee	16	3
1991-92	Kilmarnock	30	1
1992-93	Kilmarnock	35	3
1993-94	Kilmarnock	40	3
1994-95	Kilmarnock	8	–
1994-95	Motherwell	14	2

McSTAY, Paul Michael Lyons
Born: Hamilton 22/10/64

SEASON	CLUB	APPEARANCES	GOALS
1981-82	Celtic	10	1
1982-83	Celtic	36	6
1983-84	Celtic	34	3
1984-85	Celtic	32	4
1985-86	Celtic	34	8
1986-87	Celtic	43	3
1987-88	Celtic	44	5
1988-89	Celtic	33	5
1989-90	Celtic	35	3
1990-91	Celtic	30	2
1991-92	Celtic	31	7
1992-93	Celtic	43	4
1993-94	Celtic	35	2
1994-95	Celtic	29	1

McWILLIAMS, Derek
Born: Broxburn 16/01/66

SEASON	CLUB	APPEARANCES	GOALS
1981-82	Hibernian	–	–
1982-83	Hibernian	–	–
1984-85	Dundee	16	2
1985-86	Dundee	11	1
1986-87	Dundee	6	–
1986-87	*Stirling Albion*	4	–
1987-88	Dundee	–	–
1987-88	Falkirk	31	4
1988-89	Falkirk	28	11
1989-90	Falkirk	32	16
1990-91	Falkirk	29	10
1991-92	Dunfermline Athletic	24	3
1992-93	Dunfermline Athletic	25	3
1993-94	Dunfermline Athletic	20	3
1994-95	Partick Thistle	29	3

MELDRUM, Colin George
Born: Kilmarnock 26/11/75

SEASON	CLUB	APPEARANCES	GOALS
1993-94	Kilmarnock	–	–
1994-95	Kilmarnock	4	–

MIKHAILITCHENKO, Alexei
Born: Kiev 30/03/63

From Dynamo Kiev, UC Sampdoria SpA

SEASON	CLUB	APPEARANCES	GOALS
1991-92	Rangers	27	10
1992-93	Rangers	29	5
1993-94	Rangers	34	5
1994-95	Rangers	9	2

MILLAR, John
Born: Bellshill 08/12/66

SEASON	CLUB	APPEARANCES	GOALS
1984-85	Chelsea	–	–
1985-86	Chelsea	7	–
1986-87	Chelsea	4	–
1986-87	*Hamilton Academical*	10	–
1986-87	*Northampton Town*	1	–
1987-88	Blackburn Rovers	15	–
1988-89	Blackburn Rovers	38	–
1989-90	Blackburn Rovers	39	1
1990-91	Blackburn Rovers	34	–
1991-92	Heart of Midlothian	41	7

SEASON	CLUB	APPEARANCES	GOALS
1992-93	Heart of Midlothian	24	–
1993-94	Heart of Midlothian	20	4
1994-95	Heart of Midlothian	28	6

MILLEN, Andrew Frank
Born: Glasgow 10/06/65

SEASON	CLUB	APPEARANCES	GOALS
1983-84	St. Johnstone	–	–
1984-85	St. Johnstone	4	–
1985-86	St. Johnstone	36	1
1986-87	St. Johnstone	31	1
1987-88	St. Johnstone	–	–
1987-88	Alloa	36	4
1988-89	Alloa	38	3
1989-90	Alloa	37	2
1990-91	Hamilton Academical	39	–
1991-92	Hamilton Academical	39	1
1992-93	Hamilton Academical	41	3
1993-94	Kilmarnock	44	–
1994-95	Kilmarnock	13	–
1994-95	Hibernian	8	–

MILLER, Charles
Born: Glasgow 18/03/76

SEASON	CLUB	APPEARANCES	GOALS
1992-93	Rangers	–	–
1993-94	Rangers	3	–
1994-95	Rangers	21	3

MILLER, Colin Fyfe
Born: Lanark 04/10/64

SEASON	CLUB	APPEARANCES	GOALS
1985-86	Rangers	1	–
1986-87	Rangers	–	–
1988-89	Hamilton Academical	21	–
1989-90	Hamilton Academical	37	1
1990-91	Hamilton Academical	37	–
1991-92	Hamilton Academical	43	1
1992-93	Hamilton Academical	29	3
1993-94	Hamilton Academical	31	–
1993-94	St. Johnstone	12	–
1994-95	St. Johnstone	12	–
1994-95	Heart of Midlothian	16	1

MILLER, Joseph
Born: Glasgow 08/12/67

SEASON	CLUB	APPEARANCES	GOALS
1984-85	Aberdeen	1	–
1985-86	Aberdeen	18	3
1986-87	Aberdeen	27	6
1987-88	Aberdeen	14	4
1987-88	Celtic	27	3
1988-89	Celtic	22	8
1989-90	Celtic	24	5
1990-91	Celtic	30	8
1991-92	Celtic	26	2
1992-93	Celtic	23	2
1993-94	Aberdeen	27	4
1994-95	Aberdeen	27	–

MILLER, William
Born: Edinburgh 01/11/69

SEASON	CLUB	APPEARANCES	GOALS
1989-90	Hibernian	11	–
1990-91	Hibernian	25	1
1991-92	Hibernian	30	–
1992-93	Hibernian	34	–
1993-94	Hibernian	37	–
1994-95	Hibernian	34	–

MILNE, Callum
Born: Edinburgh 27/08/65

SEASON	CLUB	APPEARANCES	GOALS
1983-84	Hibernian	–	–
1984-85	Hibernian	1	–
1985-86	Hibernian	7	–
1986-87	Hibernian	2	–
1987-88	Hibernian	3	–
1988-89	Hibernian	19	–
1989-90	Hibernian	3	–
1990-91	Hibernian	21	–
1991-92	Hibernian	8	–
1992-93	Hibernian	15	–
1993-94	Hibernian	–	–

SEASON	CLUB	APPEARANCES	GOALS
1993-94	Partick Thistle	31	1
1994-95	Partick Thistle	4	–

MITCHELL, Alistair Robert
Born: Kirkcaldy 03/12/68

SEASON	CLUB	APPEARANCES	GOALS
1988-89	East Fife	18	4
1989-90	East Fife	35	12
1990-91	East Fife	34	7
1991-92	Kilmarnock	42	10
1992-93	Kilmarnock	32	6
1993-94	Kilmarnock	34	5
1994-95	Kilmarnock	35	4

MITCHELL, Graham
Born: Glasgow 02/11/62

SEASON	CLUB	APPEARANCES	GOALS
1980-81	Hamilton Academical	4	–
1981-82	Hamilton Academical	37	–
1982-83	Hamilton Academical	32	1
1983-84	Hamilton Academical	21	1
1984-85	Hamilton Academical	30	–
1985-86	Hamilton Academical	32	6
1986-87	Hamilton Academical	23	1
1986-87	Hibernian	17	1
1987-88	Hibernian	41	1
1988-89	Hibernian	20	–
1989-90	Hibernian	31	–
1990-91	Hibernian	28	–
1991-92	Hibernian	27	1
1992-93	Hibernian	41	–
1993-94	Hibernian	36	1
1994-95	Hibernian	18	–

MONTGOMERIE Samuel Raymond
Born: Irvine 17/04/61

SEASON	CLUB	APPEARANCES	GOALS
1980-81	Newcastle United	–	–
1981-82	Dumbarton	20	5
1982-83	Dumbarton	25	2
1983-84	Dumbarton	39	1
1984-85	Dumbarton	6	–
1985-86	Dumbarton	24	–
1986-87	Dumbarton	35	–
1987-88	Dumbarton	31	–
1988-89	Kilmarnock	31	2
1989-90	Kilmarnock	35	3
1990-91	Kilmarnock	37	–
1991-92	Kilmarnock	30	1
1992-93	Kilmarnock	42	–
1993-94	Kilmarnock	42	–
1994-95	Kilmarnock	12	–

MOORE, Craig Andrew
Born: Canterbury, Australia 12/12/75

SEASON	CLUB	APPEARANCES	GOALS
1993-94	Rangers	1	–
1994-95	Rangers	21	2

MORROW, John
Born: Belfast 20/11/71
From Linfield

SEASON	CLUB	APPEARANCES	GOALS
1988-89	Rangers	–	–
1989-90	Rangers	–	–
1990-91	Rangers	–	–
1991-92	Rangers	3	–
1992-93	Rangers	–	–
1993-94	Rangers	2	–
1994-95	Rangers	–	–

MOWBRAY, Anthony Mark
Born: Saltburn 22/11/63

SEASON	CLUB	APPEARANCES	GOALS
1981-82	Middlesbrough	–	–
1982-83	Middlesbrough	26	–
1983-84	Middlesbrough	35	1
1984-85	Middlesbrough	40	2
1985-86	Middlesbrough	35	4
1986-87	Middlesbrough	46	7
1987-88	Middlesbrough	44	3
1988-89	Middlesbrough	37	3
1989-90	Middlesbrough	28	3
1990-91	Middlesbrough	40	3
1991-92	Middlesbrough	17	–
1991-92	Celtic	15	2

SEASON	CLUB	LEAGUE APPEARANCES	GOALS
1992-93	Celtic	26	2
1993-94	Celtic	22	1
1994-95	Celtic	15	1

MURRAY, Neil
Born: Bellshill 21/02/73

1989-90	Rangers	–	–
1990-91	Rangers	–	–
1991-92	Rangers	–	–
1992-93	Rangers	16	–
1993-94	Rangers	22	–
1994-95	Rangers	20	1

NAPIER, Craig Cameron
Born: East Kilbride 14/11/65

1984-85	Clyde	16	–
1985-86	Clyde	8	–
1986-87	Clyde	42	–
1987-88	Clyde	42	1
1988-89	Clyde	14	–
1988-89	Hamilton Academical	19	1
1989-90	Hamilton Academical	39	6
1990-91	Hamilton Academical	39	6
1991-92	Hamilton Academical	22	2
1992-93	Hamilton Academical	29	1
1993-94	Hamilton Academical	27	2
1993-94	Kilmarnock	15	–
1994-95	Kilmarnock	3	–

NELSON, Craig Robert
Born: Coatbridge 28/05/71

1990-91	Partick Thistle	1	–
1991-92	Partick Thistle	11	–
1992-93	Partick Thistle	27	–
1993-94	Partick Thistle	39	–
1994-95	Partick Thistle	13	–
1994-95	Heart of Midlothian	20	–

NICHOLL, James Michael
Born: Hamilton, Canada 20/12/56

1973-74	Manchester United	–	–
1974-75	Manchester United	1	–
1975-76	Manchester United	20	–
1976-77	Manchester United	30	–
1977-78	Manchester United	37	2
1978-79	Manchester United	21	–
1979-80	Manchester United	42	–
1980-81	Manchester United	36	1
1981-82	Manchester United	1	–
1981-82	Sunderland	3	–
From Toronto Blizzards			
1982-83	Sunderland	29	–
From Toronto Blizzards			
1983-84	Rangers	17	–
1984-85	West Bromwich Albion	27	–
1985-86	West Bromwich Albion	29	–
1986-87	Rangers	42	–
1987-88	Rangers	22	–
1988-89	Rangers	1	–
1989-90	Dunfermline Athletic	17	–
1990-91	Dunfermline Athletic	7	–
1990-91	Raith Rovers	10	–
1991-92	Raith Rovers	32	1
1992-93	Raith Rovers	38	5
1993-94	Raith Rovers	34	1
1994-95	Raith Rovers	13	–

O'CONNOR, Gary
Born: Newtongrange 07/04/74

1991-92	Heart of Midlothian	–	–
1992-93	Heart of Midlothian	–	–
1992-93	Berwick Rangers	13	–
1993-94	Berwick Rangers	26	–
1993-94	Heart of Midlothian	–	–
1994-95	Heart of Midlothian	–	–

O'DONNELL, Philip
Born: Bellshill 25/03/72

1990-91	Motherwell	–	–

SEASON	CLUB	LEAGUE APPEARANCES	GOALS
1991-92	Motherwell	42	4
1992-93	Motherwell	32	4
1993-94	Motherwell	35	7
1994-95	Motherwell	3	–
1994-95	Celtic	27	6

O'NEIL, Brian
Born: Paisley 06/09/72

1991-92	Celtic	28	1
1992-93	Celtic	17	3
1993-94	Celtic	27	2
1994-95	Celtic	26	–

O'NEILL, John Joseph
Born: Glasgow 03/01/74

1991-92	Queen's Park	25	6
1992-93	Queen's Park	27	6
1993-94	Queen's Park	39	18
1994-95	Celtic	1	–

O'NEILL, Michael Andrew Martin
Born: Portadown 05/07/69

1987-88	Newcastle United	21	12
1988-89	Newcastle United	27	3
1989-90	Dundee United	18	5
1990-91	Dundee United	13	–
1991-92	Dundee United	8	4
1992-93	Dundee United	25	2
1993-94	Dundee United	–	–
1993-94	Hibernian	36	3
1994-95	Hibernian	33	10

OLIVER, Neil
Born: Berwick-Upon-Tweed 11/04/67

1985-86	Berwick Rangers	5	–
1986-87	Berwick Rangers	37	–
1987-88	Berwick Rangers	12	–
1988-89	Berwick Rangers	39	–
1989-90	Blackburn Rovers	3	–
1990-91	Blackburn Rovers	3	–
1991-92	Falkirk	35	–
1992-93	Falkirk	25	–
1993-94	Falkirk	33	2
1994-95	Falkirk	27	–

PARKS, Anthony
Born: Hackney 28/01/63

1980-81	Tottenham Hotspur	–	–
1981-82	Tottenham Hotspur	2	–
1982-83	Tottenham Hotspur	1	–
1983-84	Tottenham Hotspur	16	–
1984-85	Tottenham Hotspur	–	–
1985-86	Tottenham Hotspur	2	–
1986-87	Tottenham Hotspur	2	–
1986-87	Oxford United	5	–
1987-88	Tottenham Hotspur	16	–
1987-88	Gillingham	2	–
1988-89	Brentford	33	–
1989-90	Brentford	37	–
1990-91	Brentford	1	–
1990-91	Queens Park Rangers	–	–
1990-91	Fulham	2	–
1991-92	West Ham United	6	–
1992-93	Stoke City	2	–
1992-93	Falkirk	15	–
1993-94	Falkirk	41	–
1994-95	Falkirk	28	–

PATERSON, Jamie
Born: Dumfries 26/04/73

From Halifax Town

1994-95	Falkirk	4	–

PETRIC, Gordan
Born: Belgrade 30/07/69

From Belgrade, FC Partizan Belgrade

1993-94	Dundee United	27	1
1994-95	Dundee United	33	2

PHILLIBEN, John
Born: Stirling 14/03/64

SEASON	CLUB	LEAGUE APPEARANCES	GOALS
1980-81	Stirling Albion	15	–
1981-82	Stirling Albion	37	1
1982-83	Stirling Albion	34	–
1983-84	Stirling Albion	23	–
1983-84	Doncaster Rovers	12	–
1984-85	Doncaster Rovers	36	1
1985-86	Doncaster Rovers	22	–
1985-86	Cambridge United	6	–
1986-87	Doncaster Rovers	1	–
1986-87	Motherwell	37	–
1987-88	Motherwell	35	2
1988-89	Motherwell	19	–
1989-90	Motherwell	24	–
1990-91	Motherwell	11	1
1991-92	Motherwell	32	1
1992-93	Motherwell	31	–
1993-94	Motherwell	28	2
1994-95	Motherwell	31	–

PITTMAN, Stephen Lee
Born: North Carolina 18/07/67

1986-87	East Fife	11	–
1987-88	East Fife	31	2
1988-89	East Fife	25	8
1988-89	Shrewsbury Town	12	–
1989-90	Shrewsbury Town	20	2
1990-91	Shrewsbury Town	–	–
1991-92	Shrewsbury Town	–	–
1992-93	Dundee	20	1
1993-94	Dundee	36	3
1994-95	Dundee	3	1
1994-95	Partick Thistle	27	4

POTTER, Brian
Born: Dunfermline 26/01/77

1993-94	Raith Rovers	1	–
1994-95	Raith Rovers	–	–

RAESIDE, Robert
Born: South Africa 07/07/72

1990-91	Raith Rovers	14	–
1991-92	Raith Rovers	13	–
1992-93	Raith Rovers	10	–
1993-94	Raith Rovers	–	–
1994-95	Raith Rovers	10	–

REID, Brian Robertson
Born: Paisley 15/06/70

1988-89	Morton	2	–
1989-90	Morton	36	1
1990-91	Morton	19	–
1990-91	Rangers	3	–
1991-92	Rangers	–	–
1992-93	Rangers	2	–
1993-94	Rangers	–	–
1993-94	Newcastle United	–	–
1994-95	Rangers	–	–

REID, Christopher Thomas
Born: Edinburgh 04/11/71

1989-90	Hibernian	2	–
1990-91	Hibernian	1	–
1991-92	Hibernian	9	–
1992-93	Hibernian	14	–
1993-94	Hibernian	–	–
1994-95	Hibernian	–	–

REILLY, Mark
Born: Bellshill 30/03/69

1988-89	Motherwell	–	–
1989-90	Motherwell	4	–
1990-91	Motherwell	–	–
1991-92	Kilmarnock	19	–
1992-93	Kilmarnock	19	3
1993-94	Kilmarnock	38	–
1994-95	Kilmarnock	32	–

RENWICK, Michael
Born: Edinburgh 29/02/76

1992-93	Hibernian	–	–

SEASON	CLUB	LEAGUE APPEARANCES	GOALS
1993-94	Hibernian	–	–
1994-95	Hibernian	1	–

RICE, Brian
Born: Bellshill 11/10/63

SEASON	CLUB	LEAGUE APPEARANCES	GOALS
1980-81	Hibernian	1	–
1981-82	Hibernian	1	–
1982-83	Hibernian	22	2
1983-84	Hibernian	25	5
1984-85	Hibernian	35	4
1985-86	Nottingham Forest	19	3
1986-87	Nottingham Forest	3	1
1986-87	*Grimsby Town*	4	–
1987-88	Nottingham Forest	30	2
1988-89	Nottingham Forest	20	1
1988-89	*West Bromwich Albion*	3	–
1989-90	Nottingham Forest	18	2
1990-91	Nottingham Forest	1	–
1990-91	*Stoke City*	18	1
1991-92	Falkirk	16	1
1992-93	Falkirk	17	2
1993-94	Falkirk	37	3
1994-95	Falkirk	26	2

RITCHIE, Innes
Born: Edinburgh 24/08/73

SEASON	CLUB	LEAGUE APPEARANCES	GOALS
1992-93	Motherwell	–	–
1993-94	Motherwell	–	–
1994-95	Motherwell	1	–

ROBERTS, Mark Kingsley
Born: Irvine 29/10/75

SEASON	CLUB	LEAGUE APPEARANCES	GOALS
1991-92	Kilmarnock	1	–
1992-93	Kilmarnock	5	–
1993-94	Kilmarnock	13	2
1994-95	Kilmarnock	4	1

ROBERTSON, David
Born: Aberdeen 17/10/68

SEASON	CLUB	LEAGUE APPEARANCES	GOALS
1986-87	Aberdeen	34	–
1987-88	Aberdeen	23	–
1988-89	Aberdeen	23	–
1989-90	Aberdeen	20	1
1990-91	Aberdeen	35	1
1991-92	Rangers	42	1
1992-93	Rangers	39	3
1993-94	Rangers	32	1
1994-95	Rangers	23	3

ROBERTSON, Hugh Scott
Born: Aberdeen 19/03/75

SEASON	CLUB	LEAGUE APPEARANCES	GOALS
1993-94	Aberdeen	8	–
1994-95	Aberdeen	3	2

ROBERTSON, John Grant
Born: Edinburgh 02/10/64

SEASON	CLUB	LEAGUE APPEARANCES	GOALS
1980-81	Heart of Midlothian	–	–
1981-82	Heart of Midlothian	1	–
1982-83	Heart of Midlothian	23	19
1983-84	Heart of Midlothian	35	15
1984-85	Heart of Midlothian	33	8
1985-86	Heart of Midlothian	35	20
1986-87	Heart of Midlothian	37	16
1987-88	Heart of Midlothian	39	26
1987-88	Newcastle United	–	–
1988-89	Newcastle United	12	–
1988-89	Heart of Midlothian	15	4
1989-90	Heart of Midlothian	32	17
1990-91	Heart of Midlothian	31	12
1991-92	Heart of Midlothian	42	14
1992-93	Heart of Midlothian	42	11
1993-94	Heart of Midlothian	36	8
1994-95	Heart of Midlothian	31	10

ROBERTSON, Lee
Born: Edinburgh 25/08/73

SEASON	CLUB	LEAGUE APPEARANCES	GOALS
1990-91	Rangers	–	–
1991-92	Rangers	1	–

SEASON	CLUB	LEAGUE APPEARANCES	GOALS
1992-93	Rangers	1	–
1993-94	Rangers	–	–
1994-95	Rangers	1	–

RODDIE, Andrew Robert
Born: Glasgow 04/11/71

SEASON	CLUB	LEAGUE APPEARANCES	GOALS
1988-89	Aberdeen	–	–
1989-90	Aberdeen	–	–
1990-91	Aberdeen	–	–
1991-92	Aberdeen	10	2
1992-93	Aberdeen	11	2
1993-94	Aberdeen	6	1
1994-95	Aberdeen	–	–
1994-95	Motherwell	19	–

ROUGIER, Anthony Leo
Born: Trinidad and Tobago 17/07/71

From Trinity Pros

SEASON	CLUB	LEAGUE APPEARANCES	GOALS
1994-95	Raith Rovers	4	–

SCOTT, Colin
Born: Glasgow 19/05/70

SEASON	CLUB	LEAGUE APPEARANCES	GOALS
1987-88	Rangers	–	–
1988-89	Rangers	–	–
1989-90	Rangers	–	–
1989-90	*Brentford*	6	–
1990-91	Rangers	–	–
1990-91	*Airdrieonians*	1	–
1991-92	Rangers	–	–
1992-93	Rangers	–	–
1993-94	Rangers	6	–
1994-95	Rangers	4	–

SHEARER, Duncan
Born: Fort William 28/08/62

SEASON	CLUB	LEAGUE APPEARANCES	GOALS
1983-84	Chelsea	–	–
1984-85	Chelsea	–	–
1985-86	Chelsea	2	1
1985-86	Huddersfield	8	7
1986-87	Huddersfield	42	21
1987-88	Huddersfield	33	10
1988-89	Swindon Town	36	14
1989-90	Swindon Town	42	20
1990-91	Swindon Town	44	22
1991-92	Swindon Town	37	22
1991-92	Blackburn Rovers	6	1
1992-93	Aberdeen	34	22
1993-94	Aberdeen	43	17
1994-95	Aberdeen	23	7

SINCLAIR, David
Born: Dunfermline 06/10/69

SEASON	CLUB	LEAGUE APPEARANCES	GOALS
1989-90	Raith Rovers	–	–
1990-91	Raith Rovers	23	1
1991-92	Raith Rovers	22	1
1992-93	*Portadown*	–	–
1992-93	Raith Rovers	32	–
1993-94	Raith Rovers	36	2
1994-95	Raith Rovers	32	3

SKILLING, Mark James
Born: Irvine 06/10/72

SEASON	CLUB	LEAGUE APPEARANCES	GOALS
1992-93	Kilmarnock	40	4
1993-94	Kilmarnock	23	3
1994-95	Kilmarnock	17	3

SLAVIN, James
Born: Lanark 18/01/75

SEASON	CLUB	LEAGUE APPEARANCES	GOALS
1991-92	Celtic	–	–
1992-93	Celtic	–	–
1993-94	Celtic	–	–
1994-95	Celtic	3	–

SMITH, Barry Martin
Born: Paisley 19/02/74

SEASON	CLUB	LEAGUE APPEARANCES	GOALS
1991-92	Celtic	3	–

SEASON	CLUB	LEAGUE APPEARANCES	GOALS
1992-93	Celtic	6	–
1993-94	Celtic	7	–
1994-95	Celtic	3	–

SMITH, Gary
Born: Glasgow 25/03/71

SEASON	CLUB	LEAGUE APPEARANCES	GOALS
1988-89	Falkirk	3	–
1989-90	Falkirk	36	–
1990-91	Falkirk	31	–
1991-92	Aberdeen	16	1
1992-93	Aberdeen	40	–
1993-94	Aberdeen	21	–
1994-95	Aberdeen	31	–

SMITH, Henry George
Born: Lanark 10/03/56

SEASON	CLUB	LEAGUE APPEARANCES	GOALS
1978-79	Leeds United	–	–
1979-80	Leeds United	–	–
1980-81	Leeds United	–	–
1981-82	Heart of Midlothian	33	–
1982-83	Heart of Midlothian	39	–
1983-84	Heart of Midlothian	36	–
1984-85	Heart of Midlothian	36	–
1985-86	Heart of Midlothian	36	–
1986-87	Heart of Midlothian	43	–
1987-88	Heart of Midlothian	44	–
1988-89	Heart of Midlothian	36	–
1989-90	Heart of Midlothian	36	–
1990-91	Heart of Midlothian	23	–
1991-92	Heart of Midlothian	44	–
1992-93	Heart of Midlothian	25	–
1993-94	Heart of Midlothian	27	–
1994-95	Heart of Midlothian	15	–

SMITH, Thomas William
Born: Glasgow 12/10/73

SEASON	CLUB	LEAGUE APPEARANCES	GOALS
1991-92	Partick Thistle	–	–
1992-93	Partick Thistle	2	–
1993-94	Partick Thistle	8	1
1994-95	Partick Thistle	14	1

SNELDERS, Theodorus G. A.
Born: Westervoort 07/12/63

From FC Twente

SEASON	CLUB	LEAGUE APPEARANCES	GOALS
1988-89	Aberdeen	36	–
1989-90	Aberdeen	23	–
1990-91	Aberdeen	21	–
1991-92	Aberdeen	42	–
1992-93	Aberdeen	41	–
1993-94	Aberdeen	33	–
1994-95	Aberdeen	24	–

STEVEN, Trevor
Born: Berwick Upon Tweed 21/09/63

SEASON	CLUB	LEAGUE APPEARANCES	GOALS
1980-81	Burnley	1	–
1981-82	Burnley	36	3
1982-83	Burnley	39	8
1983-84	Everton	27	1
1984-85	Everton	40	12
1985-86	Everton	41	9
1986-87	Everton	41	14
1987-88	Everton	36	6
1988-89	Everton	29	6
1989-90	Rangers	34	3
1990-91	Rangers	19	2
1991-92	Rangers	2	1
1991-92	Marseille	27	3
1992-93	Rangers	24	5
1993-94	Rangers	32	4
1994-95	Rangers	11	–

STILLIE, Derek
Born: Irvine 03/12/73

SEASON	CLUB	LEAGUE APPEARANCES	GOALS
1990-91	Aberdeen	–	–
1991-92	Aberdeen	–	–
1992-93	Aberdeen	–	–
1993-94	Aberdeen	5	1
1994-95	Aberdeen	–	–

SEASON	CLUB	LEAGUE APPEARANCES	GOALS
TAYLOR, Alexander			
Born: Baillieston 13/06/62			
1980-81	Dundee United	–	–
1981-82	Dundee United	–	–
1982-83	Dundee United	3	–
1983-84	Dundee United	9	1
1984-85	Dundee United	21	5
1986-87	Hamilton Academical	25	1
1987-88	Hamilton Academical	41	4
1988-89	Walsall	13	3
1989-90	Walsall	32	3
1990-91	Walsall	–	–
1990-91	Falkirk	29	2
1991-92	Falkirk	22	1
1992-93	Falkirk	8	1
1992-93	Partick Thistle	8	1
1993-94	Partick Thistle	32	4
1994-95	Partick Thistle	23	2
THOMAS, Kevin Roderick			
Born: Edinburgh 25/04/75			
1992-93	Heart of Midlothian	4	2
1993-94	Heart of Midlothian	12	–
1994-95	Heart of Midlothian	18	5
THOMSON, Scott Munro			
Born: Aberdeen 29/01/72			
1990-91	Brechin City	30	3
1991-92	Brechin City	11	3
1991-92	Aberdeen	–	–
1992-93	Aberdeen	2	–
1993-94	Aberdeen	3	–
1994-95	Aberdeen	10	1
THOMSON, Scott Yuill			
Born: Edinburgh 08/11/66			
1984-85	Dundee United	–	–
1984-85	Dundee United	–	–
1985-86	Dundee United	–	–
1985-86	Raith Rovers	1	–
1986-87	Dundee United	3	–
1987-88	Dundee United	–	–
1988-89	Dundee United	1	–
1989-90	Dundee United	2	–
1990-91	Dundee United	–	–
1990-91	Barnsley	–	–
1991-92	Forfar Athletic	44	–
1992-93	Forfar Athletic	39	–
1993-94	Forfar Athletic	5	–
1993-94	Raith Rovers	34	–
1994-95	Raith Rovers	35	–
THOMSON, William Marshall			
Born: Linwood 10/02/58			
1975-76	Partick Thistle	–	–
1976-77	Partick Thistle	–	–
1977-78	Partick Thistle	–	–
1978-79	St. Mirren	34	–
1979-80	St. Mirren	36	–
1980-81	St. Mirren	36	–
1981-82	St. Mirren	35	–
1982-83	St. Mirren	35	–
1983-84	St. Mirren	30	–
1984-85	Dundee United	11	–
1985-86	Dundee United	28	–
1986-87	Dundee United	42	–
1987-88	Dundee United	36	–
1988-89	Dundee United	36	–
1989-90	Dundee United	7	–
1990-91	Dundee United	5	–
1991-92	Motherwell	43	–
1992-93	Motherwell	9	–
1993-94	Motherwell	–	–
1994-95	Rangers	5	–
TIERNEY, Peter Grant			
Born: Falkirk 11/10/61			
1978-79	Heart of Midlothian	–	–

SEASON	CLUB	LEAGUE APPEARANCES	GOALS
1979-80	Heart of Midlothian	–	–
1980-81	Cowdenbeath	32	1
1981-82	Cowdenbeath	32	2
1982-83	Cowdenbeath	32	2
1983-84	Cowdenbeath	35	1
1984-85	Cowdenbeath	25	3
1984-85	Meadowbank Thistle	8	–
1985-86	Meadowbank Thistle	35	4
1986-87	Meadowbank Thistle	36	4
1987-88	Meadowbank Thistle	36	2
1988-89	Meadowbank Thistle	18	–
1988-89	Dunfermline Athletic	18	1
1989-90	Dunfermline Athletic	33	2
1990-91	Partick Thistle	28	1
1991-92	Partick Thistle	13	1
1992-93	Partick Thistle	16	2
1993-94	Partick Thistle	22	1
1994-95	Partick Thistle	5	–
TORTOLANO, Joseph			
Born: Stirling 06/04/66			
1983-84	West Bromwich Albion	–	–
1984-85	West Bromwich Albion	–	–
1985-86	Hibernian	20	3
1986-87	Hibernian	33	–
1987-88	Hibernian	21	4
1988-89	Hibernian	25	–
1989-90	Hibernian	7	–
1990-91	Hibernian	18	1
1991-92	Hibernian	25	1
1992-93	Hibernian	21	3
1993-94	Hibernian	18	1
1994-95	Hibernian	18	–
TURNER, Thomas Gibson			
Born: Johnstone 11/10/63			
1981-82	Kilmarnock	–	–
1983-84	Greenock Morton	–	–
1984-85	Greenock Morton	13	1
1985-86	Greenock Morton	34	7
1986-87	Greenock Morton	38	4
1987-88	Greenock Morton	29	1
1988-89	Greenock Morton	31	10
1989-90	Greenock Morton	30	6
1990-91	St. Johnstone	27	3
1991-92	St. Johnstone	33	3
1992-93	St. Johnstone	28	1
1993-94	St. Johnstone	40	–
1994-95	St. Johnstone	11	–
1994-95	Partick Thistle	15	2
TWEED, Steven			
Born: Edinburgh 08/08/72			
1991-92	Hibernian	1	–
1992-93	Hibernian	14	–
1993-94	Hibernian	29	3
1994-95	Hibernian	33	3
VAN DER GAAG, Mitchell			
Born: Zutphen 27/10/71			
From PSV Eindhoven			
1994-95	Motherwell	2	–
VAN HOOIJDONK, Pierre			
Born: Steenbergen 29/11/69			
From NAC Breda			
1994-95	Celtic	14	4
VATA, Rudi			
Born: Schroder 13/02/69			
From Dinamo Tirana			
1992-93	Celtic	22	2
1993-94	Celtic	10	1
1994-95	Celtic	7	1
WALKER, Andrew Francis			
Born: Glasgow 06/04/65			
1984-85	Motherwell	11	3
1985-86	Motherwell	22	4
1986-87	Motherwell	43	10

SEASON	CLUB	LEAGUE APPEARANCES	GOALS
1987-88	Celtic	42	16
1988-89	Celtic	22	8
1989-90	Celtic	32	6
1990-91	Celtic	11	–
1991-92	Celtic	1	–
1991-92	Newcastle United	2	–
1991-92	Bolton Wanderers	24	15
1992-93	Bolton Wanderers	32	26
1993-94	Bolton Wanderers	11	3
1994-95	Celtic	26	6
WALKER, Joseph Nicol			
Born: Aberdeen 29/09/62			
1980-81	Leicester City	–	–
1981-82	Leicester City	6	–
1982-83	Motherwell	16	–
1983-84	Motherwell	15	–
1983-84	Rangers	8	–
1984-85	Rangers	14	–
1985-86	Rangers	34	–
1986-87	Rangers	2	–
1986-87	Falkirk	8	–
1987-88	Rangers	5	–
1987-88	Dunfermline Athletic	1	–
1988-89	Rangers	12	–
1989-90	Heart of Midlothian	–	–
1990-91	Heart of Midlothian	13	–
1991-92	Heart of Midlothian	–	–
1991-92	Burnley	6	–
1992-93	Heart of Midlothian	18	–
1993-94	Heart of Midlothian	17	–
1994-95	Heart of Midlothian	2	–
1994-95	Partick Thistle	20	–
WATSON, Gregg			
Born: Glasgow 21/09/70			
1986-87	Aberdeen	–	–
1987-88	Aberdeen	–	–
1988-89	Aberdeen	4	–
1989-90	Aberdeen	4	–
1990-91	Aberdeen	7	–
1991-92	Aberdeen	8	–
1992-93	Aberdeen	–	–
1993-94	Aberdeen	–	–
1993-94	Partick Thistle	37	–
1994-95	Partick Thistle	29	–
WATT, Michael			
Born: Aberdeen 27/11/70			
1989-90	Aberdeen	7	–
1990-91	Aberdeen	10	–
1991-92	Aberdeen	2	–
1992-93	Aberdeen	3	–
1993-94	Aberdeen	4	–
1994-95	Aberdeen	14	–
WEIR, David Gillespie			
Born: Falkirk 10/05/70			
1992-93	Falkirk	30	1
1993-94	Falkirk	37	3
1994-95	Falkirk	32	1
WEIR, Michael Graham			
Born: Edinburgh 16/01/66			
1982-83	Hibernian	–	–
1983-84	Hibernian	–	–
1984-85	Hibernian	12	–
1985-86	Hibernian	7	–
1986-87	Hibernian	24	4
1987-88	Hibernian	5	1
1987-88	Luton Town	8	–
1987-88	Hibernian	13	2
1988-89	Hibernian	7	–
1989-90	Hibernian	18	3
1990-91	Hibernian	20	1
1991-92	Hibernian	31	11
1992-93	Hibernian	33	5
1993-94	Hibernian	–	–
1994-95	Hibernian	19	1

SEASON	CLUB	LEAGUE APPEARANCES	GOALS
WELSH, Steven George			
Born: Glasgow 19/04/68			
1989-90	Cambridge United	–	–
1990-91	Cambridge United	1	–
1991-92	Peterborough United	42	–
1992-93	Peterborough United	45	1
1993-94	Peterborough United	45	1
1994-95	Peterborough United	14	–
1994-95	*Preston North End*	–	–
1994-95	Partick Thistle	20	–
WHITWORTH, Neil			
Born: Wigan 12/04/72			
1989-90	Wigan Athletic	2	–
1990-91	Wigan Athletic	–	–
1990-91	Manchester United	1	–
1991-92	Manchester United	–	–
1991-92	*Preston North End*	6	–
1991-92	*Barnsley*	11	–
1992-93	Manchester United	–	–
1993-94	*Rotherham United*	8	1
1993-94	*Blackpool*	3	–
1994-95	Manchester United	–	–
1994-95	Kilmarnock	30	3
WILLIAMSON Robert			
Born: Glasgow 13/08/61			
1980-81	Clydebank	2	–
1981-82	Clydebank	12	1
1982-83	Clydebank	39	23
1983-84	Clydebank	17	4
1983-84	Rangers	17	6
1984-85	Rangers	1	–
1985-86	Rangers	23	6
1986-87	West Bromwich Albion	31	8
1987-88	West Bromwich Albion	22	3
1988-89	Rotherham United	42	27
1989-90	Rotherham United	42	19
1990-91	Rotherham United	9	3
1990-91	Kilmarnock	23	14
1991-92	Kilmarnock	36	9
1992-93	Kilmarnock	33	6
1993-94	Kilmarnock	38	7
1994-95	Kilmarnock	15	2
WILSON, Barry John			
Born: Kirkcaldy 16/02/72			
1994-95	Ross County	3	1
1994-95	Raith Rovers	26	5
WINNIE, David			
Born: Glasgow 26/10/66			
1983-84	St. Mirren	8	–
1984-85	St. Mirren	30	3
1985-86	St. Mirren	20	1
1986-87	St. Mirren	14	–
1987-88	St. Mirren	26	2
1988-89	St. Mirren	30	–
1989-90	St. Mirren	17	–
1990-91	St. Mirren	1	–
1991-92	Aberdeen	28	1
1992-93	Aberdeen	21	–
1993-94	Aberdeen	6	–
1993-94	*Middlesbrough*	1	–
1994-95	Aberdeen	8	–
WISHART, Fraser			
Born: Johnstone 01/03/65			
1983-84	Motherwell	6	–
1984-85	Motherwell	–	–
1985-86	Motherwell	26	–
1986-87	Motherwell	44	3
1987-88	Motherwell	43	1
1988-89	Motherwell	35	1
1989-90	St. Mirren	20	–
1990-91	St. Mirren	22	–
1991-92	St. Mirren	9	–
1992-93	Falkirk	24	2
1993-94	Rangers	5	–

SEASON	CLUB	LEAGUE APPEARANCES	GOALS
1994-95	Rangers	4	–
1994-95	Heart of Midlothian	8	–
WOODS, Stephen Gerard			
Born: Glasgow 23/02/70			
1989-90	Hibernian	–	–
1990-91	Hibernian	–	–
1991-92	Hibernian	–	–
1991-92	Clydebank	5	–
1992-93	Clydebank	42	–
1993-94	Clydebank	10	–
1993-94	Preston North End	20	–
1994-95	Motherwell	33	–
WOODTHORPE, Colin			
Born: Liverpool 13/01/69			
1986-87	Chester City	30	2
1987-88	Chester City	35	–
1988-89	Chester City	44	3
1989-90	Chester City	46	1
1990-91	Norwich City	1	–
1991-92	Norwich City	15	1
1992-93	Norwich City	7	–
1993-94	Norwich City	20	–
1994-95	Aberdeen	14	–
WRIGHT, George			
Born: South Africa 22/12/69			
1987-88	Heart of Midlothian	–	–
1988-89	Heart of Midlothian	–	–
1989-90	Heart of Midlothian	1	–
1990-91	Heart of Midlothian	17	2
1991-92	Heart of Midlothian	24	1
1992-93	Heart of Midlothian	12	–
1993-94	Heart of Midlothian	12	–
1994-95	Heart of Midlothian	2	–
WRIGHT, Keith			
Born: Edinburgh 17/05/65			
1983-84	Raith Rovers	37	5
1984-85	Raith Rovers	38	22
1985-86	Raith Rovers	39	21
1986-87	Raith Rovers	17	13
1986-87	Dundee	20	10
1987-88	Dundee	42	15
1988-89	Dundee	35	8
1989-90	Dundee	34	11
1990-91	Dundee	36	18
1991-92	Hibernian	40	9
1992-93	Hibernian	42	11
1993-94	Hibernian	42	16
1994-95	Hibernian	19	10
WRIGHT, Paul Hamilton			
Born: East Kilbride 17/08/67			
1983-84	Aberdeen	1	–
1984-85	Aberdeen	–	–
1985-86	Aberdeen	10	2
1986-87	Aberdeen	25	4
1987-88	Aberdeen	9	4
1988-89	Aberdeen	23	6
1989-90	Queens Park Rangers	15	5
1989-90	Hibernian	3	1
1990-91	Hibernian	33	6
1991-92	St. Johnstone	41	18
1992-93	St. Johnstone	42	14
1993-94	St. Johnstone	17	7
1994-95	St. Johnstone	12	1
1994-95	Kilmarnock	7	1
WRIGHT, Stephen			
Born: Bellshill 27/08/71			
1987-88	Aberdeen	–	–
1988-89	Aberdeen	–	–
1989-90	Aberdeen	1	–
1990-91	Aberdeen	17	1
1991-92	Aberdeen	23	–
1992-93	Aberdeen	36	–
1993-94	Aberdeen	36	–
1994-95	Aberdeen	34	1

OFFICIAL LIST OF CLASS 1 REFEREES 1995/96

Graeme R. Alison (Dumfries)

Kevin R. Bisset (Inverness)

Thomas Brown (Edinburgh)

Kenneth W. Clark (Paisley)

Martin A. Clark (Edinburgh)

George T. Clyde (Bearsden)

William N. M. Crombie (Edinburgh)

Hugh Dallas (Bonkle)

Stuart Dougal (Burnside)

Ian S. Elmslie (Aberdeen)

Gerard A. Evans (Bishopbriggs)

John Fleming (Glasgow)

Alan Freeland (Aberdeen)

James A. Herald (Newton Mearns)

Alistair N. Huett (Edinburgh)

James McCluskey (Stewarton)

T. Michael McCurry (Glasgow)

James F. McGilvray (Edinburgh)

Eric Martindale (Newlands)

Garry P. Mitchell (Arbroath)

Leslie W. Mottram (Forth)

Robert Orr (Kilbarchan)

Michael F. Pocock (Aberdeen)

John Rowbotham (Kirkcaldy)

Alexander M. Roy (Aberdeen)

George H. Simpson (Peterhead)

J. Douglas K. Smith (Troon)

Robert T. Tait (East Kilbride)

Ian Taylor (Edinburgh)

Louis B. Thow (Prestwick)

John R. Underhill (Edinburgh)

Andrew W. Waddell (Edinburgh)

John A. Young (Thornliebank)

William S. G. Young (Clarkston)

Dates for your Diary Season 1995/96

TENNENTS SCOTTISH CUP 1995/96

First Round ....9th December, 1995
Second Round ....6th January, 1996
Third Round ....27th January, 1996
Fourth Round ....17th February, 1996
Fifth Round ....9th March, 1996
Semi–Finals..6th April, 1996
Final ....18th May, 1996

EUROPEAN CHAMPIONSHIP QUALIFYING MATCHES

Scotland -v- Greece 16th August, 1995
Scotland -v- Finland 6th September, 1995
Scotland -v- San Marino 15th November, 1995

All matches to be played at The National Stadium, Hampden Park.

FRIENDLY INTERNATIONAL

Sweden -v- Scotland 11th October, 1995

EUROPEAN "UNDER 21" CHAMPIONSHIP 1994/96 (QUALIFYING MATCHES)

Scotland -v- Greece 15th August, 1995
Rugby Park, Kilmarnock

Scotland -v- Finland 6th September, 1995
Broadwood Stadium, Cumbernauld

Scotland -v- San Marino 14th November, 1995
Firhill Park, Glasgow

'B' INTERNATIONAL CHALLENGE MATCH

Sweden -v- Scotland 10th October, 1995

EIGHT NATIONS INTERNATIONAL "UNDER 16" YOUTH TOURNAMENT

Faroe Islands, Iceland, Sweden, Denmark, 1st–7th August, 1995
England, Finland, Norway and Scotland (Ostersund, Sweden)

FOUR NATIONS YOUTH TOURNAMENT FOR "UNDER 17" PLAYERS

Belgium, Denmark, The Netherlands 18th–24th September, 1995
and Scotland (Stirling)

12th EUROPEAN "UNDER 18" YOUTH CHAMPIONSHIP

Mini tournament involving Lithuania, 8th – 14th September, 1995
Estonia and Scotland (Lithuania)

EUROPEAN CLUB COMPETITION DATES

As a result of decisions taken by U.E.F.A.'s Executive Committee in December, 1993, the format of the three club competitions has altered dramatically with the biggest change taking place in the Champion Clubs' Cup where the number of clubs authorised to enter has been reduced. Although each national association will still, in theory, have the opportunity to be represented by its domestic champion in the Champion Clubs' Cup, participation now depends on the results of the club itself over a period of time or on those of its association.

The reviewed format guarantees that the champion clubs ranked in places 1-24 will play in the Champion Clubs' Cup with the champion clubs ranked between 25 and 48 playing in the U.E.F.A. Cup. The final phase of the Champion Clubs' Cup, which has been known as the U.E.F.A. Champions League for the past three seasons, features 16 clubs, with the cup holders and first seven clubs in the list of co-efficients qualifying automatically for the flagship competition. The remaining 16 clubs require to play a qualifying round on a home and away basis and the eight winners will join the clubs that have been seeded 1 - 8 and are divided into four groups of four to be played between September and December, 1995 with the top two clubs in each group thereafter qualifying for the Quarter-Finals. Both the Quarter-Finals and Semi-Final stages of the Champion Clubs' Cup will be played on a home and away basis with the Final being played on a one match basis at a neutral venue still to be decided on Wednesday, 22nd May, 1995.

Accordingly, with the domestic champions ranked between places 25 and 48 playing in the U.E.F.A. Cup, together with a substantial increase in the number of associations now in membership of U.E.F.A., 100 clubs now participate in the U.E.F.A. Cup, necessitating a Preliminary Round to be played. 72 Clubs will participate in this Preliminary Round including the aforementioned domestic champions ranked between places 25 and 48 in the list of co efficients with only the 28 best placed clubs in the list of co-efficients being exempt from this round. The increase in the number of associations now in membership of U.E.F.A. also requires a Preliminary Round to be played in the Cup Winners' Cup and these matches will take place at the same time as the Qualifying matches in the Champion Clubs' Cup and the Preliminary round of the U.E.F.A. Cup.

Another feature of the competition regulations which took place last season and will continue during the course of the 1995 / 96 season is that U.E.F.A. Cup matches will, in principle, be played on Tuesdays, Champion Clubs' Cup matches on Wednesdays, and Cup Winners' Cup matches on Thursdays. Any changes of dates will require the written consent of the two clubs concerned, as well as their respective national associations. The complete list of dates for each of the three competitions is as follows:-

EUROPEAN CHAMPION CLUBS' CUP

Qualifying Matches: Knock-out system in August 1995
First leg matches Wednesday, 9th August, 1995
Second-leg matches Wednesday, 23rd August,1995

Group Matches: Championship system between Sept 1995 and Dec 1995
1st match day: Wednesday, 13th September, 1995
2nd match day: Wednesday, 27th September, 1995
3rd match day: Wednesday, 18th October, 1995
4th match day: Wednesday, 1st November, 1995
5th match day: Wednesday, 22nd November, 1995
6th match day: Wednesday, 6th December, 1995

Quarter-Finals: Knock-out system in March 1996
First-leg matches: Wednesday, 6th March, 1996
Second-leg matches: Wednesday, 20th March, 1996

Semi-Finals: Knock-out system in April 1996
First-leg matches: Wednesday, 3rd April, 1996
Second-leg matches: Wednesday, 17th April, 1996

Final: Wednesday, 22nd May 1996

U.E.F.A. CUP

Preliminary Round:
First-leg matches: Tuesday, 8th August, 1995
Second-leg matches: Tuesday, 22nd August, 1995

First Round:
First-leg matches: Tuesday, 12th September, 1995
Second-leg matches: Tuesday, 26th September, 1995

Second Round:
First-leg matches: Tuesday, 17th October, 1995
Second-leg matches: Tuesday, 31st October, 1995

Third Round:
First-leg matches: Tuesday, 21st November, 1995
Second-leg matches: Tuesday, 5th December, 1995

Quarter-Finals :
First-leg matches: Tuesday, 5th March, 1996
Second-leg matches: Tuesday, 19th March, 1996

Semi-Finals:
First-leg matches: Tuesday, 2nd April, 1996
Second-leg matches: Tuesday, 16th April, 1996

Final:
First-leg match: Wednesday 1st May, 1996
Second-leg match: Wednesday 15th May, 1996

EUROPEAN CUP WINNERS' CUP

Preliminary Round:
First-leg matches: Thursday, 10th August, 1995
Second-leg matches: Thursday, 24th August, 1995

First Round:
First-leg matches: Thursday, 14th September, 1995
Second-leg matches: Thursday, 28th September, 1995

Second Round:
First-leg matches: Thursday, 19th October, 1995
Second-leg matches: Thursday, 2nd November, 1995

Quarter-Finals :
First-leg matches: Thursday, 7th March, 1996
Second-leg matches: Thursday, 21st March, 1996

Semi-Finals:
First-leg matches: Thursday, 4th April, 1996
Second-leg matches: Thursday, 18th April, 1996

Final: Wednesday, 8th May, 1996

EUROPEAN CHAMPIONSHIP – FINAL COMPETITION ENGLAND 1996

Group Matches: 8th , 9th, 10th, 11th, 13th, 14th, 15th, 16th, 18th, & 19th June, 1996
Quarter-Finals: 22nd & 23rd June, 1996
Semi-Finals: 26th June, 1996
Final: 30th June, 1996

Coca-Cola Cup Draw

SEASON 1995/96

1st Round

Ross County	-v-	Arbroath
Brechin City	-v-	East Fife
Queen of the South	-v-	Queen's Park
Clyde	-v-	East Stirlingshire
Berwick Rangers	-v-	Caledonian Thistle
Albion Rovers	-v-	Cowdenbeath
Montrose	-v-	Livingston
Alloa	-v-	Forfar Athletic

Above ties to be played on Saturday, 5th August, 1995

3rd Round

.... -v- ....
.... -v- ....
.... -v- ....
.... -v- ....
.... -v- ....
.... -v- ....
.... -v- ....
.... -v- ....

Ties to be played on Tuesday, 29th
or Wednesday, 30th August, 1995

2nd Round

Aberdeen	-v-	St. Mirren
Clydebank	-v-	Motherwell
Dunfermline Athletic	-v-	Stranraer
Albion Rovers or Cowdenbeath	-v-	Dundee United
Raith Rovers	-v-	Ross County or Arbroath
Queen of the South or Queen's Park	-v-	Falkirk
Kilmarnock	-v-	Dumbarton
Ayr United	-v-	Celtic
St. Johnstone	-v-	Montrose or Livingston
Clyde or East Stirlingshire	-v-	Dundee
Rangers	-v-	Greenock Morton
Berwick Rangers or Caledonian Thistle	-v-	Partick Thistle
Hibernian	-v-	Stenhousemuir
Brechin City or East Fife	-v-	Airdrieonians
Heart of Midlothian	-v-	Alloa or Forfar Athletic
Stirling Albion	-v-	Hamilton Academical

Above ties to be played on Saturday, 19th August, 1995

4th Round

.... -v- ....
.... -v- ....
.... -v- ....
.... -v- ....

Ties to be played on Tuesday, 19th
or Wednesday, 20th September, 1995

Semi–Finals

.... -v- ....
.... -v- ....

Ties to be played on Tuesday, 24th
or Wednesday, 25th October, 1995

COCA–COLA CUP FINAL

.... -v- ....

To be played on Sunday, 26th November, 1995

In the event of a draw after normal time in all rounds, extra time of 30 minutes (i.e. 15 minutes each way) will take place and thereafter, if necessary, Kicks from the Penalty Mark in accordance with the Rules laid down by the International Football Association Board will be taken.

SEASON 1995/96

1st Round

Stirling Albion	-v-	Queen's Park
Albion Rovers	-v-	Ross County
Dumbarton	-v-	Brechin City
Clydebank	-v-	Arbroath
Queen of the South	-v-	Forfar Athletic
Caledonian Thistle	-v-	Alloa
East Fife	-v-	Dundee
Stranraer	-v-	Dundee United
Hamilton Academical	-v-	Airdrieonians
Clyde	-v-	St. Johnstone
East Stirlingshire	-v-	St. Mirren
Ayr United	-v-	Dunfermline Athletic
Livingston	-v-	Greenock Morton
Montrose	-v-	Berwick Rangers

BYES: Stenhousemuir and Cowdenbeath

Above ties to be played on Tuesday, 22nd or Wednesday, 23rd August, 1995

2nd Round

....	-v-	
....	-v-	
....	v-	....
....	-v-	....
....	-v-	....
....	-v-	....
....	-v-	....
....	-v-	

Above ties to be played on Tuesday, 12th or Wednesday, 13th September, 1995

3rd Round

....	-v-	....
....	-v-	....
....	-v-	....
....	-v-	....

Above ties to be played on Tuesday, 26th or Wednesday, 27th September, 1995

Semi-Finals

....	-v-	....
....	-v-	....

Above ties to be played on Tuesday, 3rd or Wednesday, 4th October, 1995

FINAL TIE

....	-v-	....

To be played on Sunday, 5th November, 1995

In the event of a draw after normal time, extra time of 30 minutes (i.e. 15 minutes each way) will take place and thereafter, if necessary, Kicks from the Penalty Mark in accordance with the Rules laid down by the International Football Association Board will be taken.

BREAKDOWN OF HOW ALL THE SPONSORSHIP MONIES WILL BE ALLOCATED DURING SEASON 1995/96

DISTRIBUTION OF BELL'S LEAGUE CHAMPIONSHIP MONIES

Each Premier Division Club will receive	£40,000
Each First Division Club will receive	£17,000
Each Second Division Club will receive	£10,000
Each Third Division Club will receive	£ 8,500

DISTRIBUTION OF COCA-COLA CUP MONIES

8	First Round Losers will each receive	£ 5,000
16	Second Round Losers will each receive	£ 7,000
8	Third Round Losers will each receive	£11,000
4	Fourth Round Losers will each receive	£16,000
2	Semi-Final Losers will each receive	£22,000
	The Runner-Up will receive	£40,000
	The Winner will receive	£60,000

DISTRIBUTION OF CHALLENGE CUP MONIES

14	First Round Losers will each receive	£ 2,125
8	Second Round Losers will each receive	£ 3,200
4	Third Round Losers will each receive	£ 4,400
2	Semi-Final Losers will each receive	£ 5,750
	The Runner-Up will receive	£10,000
	The Winner will receive	£14,000

Saturday, August 12th, 1995

Airdrieonians v Dunfermline Athletic
Clydebank v St. Mirren
Dumbarton v Hamilton Academical
Dundee United v Greenock Morton
St. Johnstone v Dundee

Ayr United v Clyde
Forfar Athletic v East Fife
Queen of the South v Stenhousemuir
Stirling Albion v Montrose
Stranraer v Berwick Rangers

Albion Rovers v Arbroath
Brechin City v East Stirlingshire
Caledonian Thistle v Livingston
Cowdenbeath v Alloa
Ross County v Queen's Park

Saturday, August 26th, 1995

Falkirk v Aberdeen
Heart of Midlothian v Motherwell
Partick Thistle v Hibernian
Raith Rovers v Celtic
Rangers v Kilmarnock

Dundee v Airdrieonians
Dunfermline Athletic v Dundee United
Greenock Morton v Dumbarton
St. Mirren v St. Johnstone

Berwick Rangers v Stirling Albion
Clyde v Forfar Athletic
East Fife v Ayr United
Montrose v Queen of the South
Stenhousemuir v Stranraer

Alloa v Albion Rovers
Arbroath v Livingston
Caledonian Thistle v Brechin City
Queen's Park v Cowdenbeath

Sunday, August 27th, 1995

Hamilton Academical v Clydebank

East Stirlingshire v Ross County

Saturday, September 2nd, 1995

Airdrieonians v St. Mirren
Clydebank v Dundee
Dumbarton v Dunfermline Athletic
Dundee United v Hamilton Academical
St. Johnstone v Greenock Morton

Ayr United v Berwick Rangers
Forfar Athletic v Stenhousemuir
Queen of the South v Clyde
Stirling Albion v East Fife
Stranraer v Montrose

Albion Rovers v Caledonian Thistle
Brechin City v Alloa
Cowdenbeath v East Stirlingshire
Ross County v Arbroath

Tuesday, September 5th, 1995

Livingston v Queen's Park

Saturday, September 9th, 1995

Heart of Midlothian v Falkirk
Kilmarnock v Hibernian
Motherwell v Partick Thistle
Rangers v Raith Rovers

Dumbarton v Airdrieonians
Dundee United v St. Mirren
Dunfermline Athletic v Clydebank
Greenock Morton v Dundee
Hamilton Academical v St. Johnstone

Ayr United v Forfar Athletic
Clyde v Berwick Rangers
East Fife v Montrose
Queen of the South v Stranraer
Stenhousemuir v Stirling Albion

Albion Rovers v Cowdenbeath
Alloa v Arbroath
Brechin City v Ross County
Caledonian Thistle v Queen's Park
East Stirlingshire v Livingston

Sunday, September 10th, 1995

Aberdeen v Celtic

Saturday, September 16th, 1995

Celtic v Motherwell
Falkirk v Rangers
Hibernian v Aberdeen
Partick Thistle v Heart of Midlothian
Raith Rovers v Kilmarnock

Airdrieonians v Greenock Morton
Clydebank v Dundee United
Dundee v Hamilton Academical
St. Johnstone v Dumbarton
St. Mirren v Dunfermline Athletic

Berwick Rangers v Stenhousemuir
Forfar Athletic v Queen of the South
Montrose v Clyde
Stirling Albion v Ayr United
Stranraer v East Fife

Arbroath v Caledonian Thistle
Cowdenbeath v Brechin City
Livingston v Alloa
Queen's Park v East Stirlingshire
Ross County v Albion Rovers

Saturday, September 23rd, 1995

Falkirk v Motherwell
Heart of Midlothian v Celtic
Kilmarnock v Aberdeen
Raith Rovers v Partick Thistle
Rangers v Hibernian

Dumbarton v Dundee
Dundee United v Airdrieonians
Greenock Morton v Dunfermline Athletic
Hamilton Academical v St. Mirren
St. Johnstone v Clydebank

Berwick Rangers v Forfar Athletic
Clyde v Stenhousemuir
East Fife v Queen of the South
Montrose v Ayr United
Stranraer v Stirling Albion

Alloa v Caledonian Thistle
Arbroath v East Stirlingshire
Livingston v Albion Rovers
Queen's Park v Brechin City
Ross County v Cowdenbeath

Saturday, September 30th, 1995

Aberdeen v Raith Rovers
Celtic v Rangers
Motherwell v Kilmarnock
Partick Thistle v Falkirk

Airdrieonians v Hamilton Academical
Clydebank v Dumbarton
Dundee v Dundee United
Dunfermline Athletic v St. Johnstone
St. Mirren v Greenock Morton

Ayr United v Stranraer
Forfar Athletic v Montrose
Queen of the South v Berwick Rangers
Stenhousemuir v East Fife
Stirling Albion v Clyde

Albion Rovers v Queen's Park
Brechin City v Arbroath
Caledonian Thistle v Ross County
Cowdenbeath v Livingston
East Stirlingshire v Alloa

Sunday, October 1st, 1995

Hibernian v Heart of Midlothian

October 3rd, 1995

Rangers v Motherwell

Wednesday, October 4th, 1995

Falkirk v Celtic
Heart of Midlothian v Aberdeen
Partick Thistle v Kilmarnock
Raith Rovers v Hibernian

Saturday, October 7th, 1995

Aberdeen v Rangers
Celtic v Partick Thistle
Hibernian v Falkirk
Kilmarnock v Heart of Midlothian
Motherwell v Raith Rovers

Clydebank v Greenock Morton
Dumbarton v Dundee United
Dundee v St. Mirren
Hamilton Academical v Dunfermline Athletic
St. Johnstone v Airdrieonians

Berwick Rangers v East Fife
Clyde v Stranraer
Forfar Athletic v Stirling Albion
Queen of the South v Ayr United
Stenhousemuir v Montrose

Brechin City v Albion Rovers
Cowdenbeath v Arbroath
East Stirlingshire v Caledonian Thistle
Queen's Park v Alloa
Ross County v Livingston

Saturday, October 14th, 1995

Celtic v Hibernian
Falkirk v Kilmarnock
Heart of Midlothian v Raith Rovers
Motherwell v Aberdeen
Partick Thistle v Rangers

Airdrieonians v Clydebank
Dundee United v St. Johnstone
Dunfermline Athletic v Dundee
Greenock Morton v Hamilton Academical
St. Mirren v Dumbarton

Ayr United v Stenhousemuir
East Fife v Clyde
Montrose v Berwick Rangers
Stirling Albion v Queen of the South
Stranraer v Forfar Athletic

Albion Rovers v East Stirlingshire
Alloa v Ross County
Arbroath v Queen's Park
Caledonian Thistle v Cowdenbeath
Livingston v Brechin City

Saturday, October 21st, 1995

Aberdeen v Partick Thistle
Hibernian v Motherwell
Kilmarnock v Celtic
Raith Rovers v Falkirk
Rangers v Heart of Midlothian

Dundee v Clydebank
Dunfermline Athletic v Dumbarton
Greenock Morton v St. Johnstone
Hamilton Academical v Dundee United
St. Mirren v Airdrieonians

Berwick Rangers v Stranraer
Clyde v Ayr United
East Fife v Forfar Athletic
Montrose v Stirling Albion
Stenhousemuir v Queen of the South

Alloa v Brechin City
Arbroath v Ross County
Caledonian Thistle v Albion Rovers
East Stirlingshire v Cowdenbeath
Queen's Park v Livingston

Saturday, October 28th, 1995

Celtic v Aberdeen
Falkirk v Heart of Midlothian
Hibernian v Kilmarnock
Partick Thistle v Motherwell
Raith Rovers v Rangers

Airdrieonians v Dundee
Clydebank v Hamilton Academical
Dumbarton v Greenock Morton
Dundee United v Dunfermline Athletic
St. Johnstone v St. Mirren

Ayr United v East Fife
Forfar Athletic v Clyde
Queen of the South v Montrose
Stirling Albion v Berwick Rangers
Stranraer v Stenhousemuir

Albion Rovers v Alloa
Brechin City v Caledonian Thistle
Cowdenbeath v Queen's Park
Livingston v Arbroath
Ross County v East Stirlingshire

Saturday, November 4th, 1995

Aberdeen v Hibernian
Heart of Midlothian v Partick Thistle
Kilmarnock v Raith Rovers
Motherwell v Celtic
Rangers v Falkirk

Dumbarton v St. Johnstone
Dundee United v Clydebank
Dunfermline Athletic v St. Mirren
Greenock Morton v Airdrieonians
Hamilton Academical v Dundee

Ayr United v Stirling Albion
Clyde v Montrose
East Fife v Stranraer
Queen of the South v Forfar Athletic
Stenhousemuir v Berwick Rangers

Albion Rovers v Ross County
Alloa v Livingston
Brechin City v Cowdenbeath
Caledonian Thistle v Arbroath
East Stirlingshire v Queen's Park

Tuesday, November 7th, 1995

Motherwell v Heart of Midlothian

Wednesday, November 8th, 1995

Aberdeen v Falkirk
Celtic v Raith Rovers
Hibernian v Partick Thistle
Kilmarnock v Rangers

Saturday, November 11th, 1995

Falkirk v Hibernian
Heart of Midlothian v Kilmarnock
Partick Thistle v Celtic
Raith Rovers v Motherwell
Rangers v Aberdeen

Airdrieonians v Dumbarton
Clydebank v Dunfermline Athletic
Dundee v Greenock Morton
St. Johnstone v Hamilton Academical
St. Mirren v Dundee United

Berwick Rangers v Clyde
Forfar Athletic v Ayr United
Montrose v East Fife
Stirling Albion v Stenhousemuir
Stranraer v Queen of the South

Arbroath v Alloa
Cowdenbeath v Albion Rovers
Livingston v East Stirlingshire
Queen's Park v Caledonian Thistle
Ross County v Brechin City

Saturday, November 18th, 1995

Falkirk v Partick Thistle
Kilmarnock v Motherwell
Raith Rovers v Aberdeen

Dumbarton v Clydebank
Dundee United v Dundee
Greenock Morton v St. Mirren
Hamilton Academical v Airdrieonians
St. Johnstone v Dunfermline Athletic

Berwick Rangers v Queen of the South
Clyde v Stirling Albion
East Fife v Stenhousemuir
Montrose v Forfar Athletic
Stranraer v Ayr United

Alloa v East Stirlingshire
Arbroath v Brechin City
Livingston v Cowdenbeath
Queen's Park v Albion Rovers
Ross County v Caledonian Thistle

Sunday, November 19th, 1995

Heart of Midlothian v Hibernian
Rangers v Celtic

Saturday, November 25th, 1995

Aberdeen v Kilmarnock
Celtic v Heart of Midlothian
Hibernian v Rangers
Motherwell v Falkirk
Partick Thistle v Raith Rovers

Airdrieonians v Dundee United
Clydebank v St. Johnstone
Dundee v Dumbarton
Dunfermline Athletic v Greenock Morton
St. Mirren v Hamilton Academical

Ayr United v Montrose
Forfar Athletic v Berwick Rangers
Queen of the South v East Fife
Stenhousemuir v Clyde
Stirling Albion v Stranraer

Albion Rovers v Livingston
Brechin City v Queen's Park
Caledonian Thistle v Alloa
Cowdenbeath v Ross County
East Stirlingshire v Arbroath

Saturday, December 2nd, 1995

Celtic v Kilmarnock
Falkirk v Raith Rovers
Heart of Midlothian v Rangers
Motherwell v Hibernian
Partick Thistle v Aberdeen

Airdrieonians v St. Johnstone
Dundee United v Dumbarton
Dunfermline Athletic v Hamilton Academical
Greenock Morton v Clydebank
St. Mirren v Dundee

Ayr United v Queen of the South
East Fife v Berwick Rangers
Montrose v Stenhousemuir
Stirling Albion v Forfar Athletic
Stranraer v Clyde

Albion Rovers v Brechin City
Alloa v Queen's Park
Arbroath v Cowdenbeath
Caledonian Thistle v East Stirlingshire
Livingston v Ross County

Saturday, December 9th, 1995

Aberdeen v Motherwell
Hibernian v Celtic
Kilmarnock v Falkirk
Raith Rovers v Heart of Midlothian
Rangers v Partick Thistle

Clydebank v Airdrieonians
Dumbarton v St. Mirren
Dundee v Dunfermline Athletic
Hamilton Academical v Greenock Morton
St. Johnstone v Dundee United

Saturday, December 16th, 1995

Aberdeen v Heart of Midlothian
Celtic v Falkirk
Hibernian v Raith Rovers
Kilmarnock v Partick Thistle

Dundee v St. Johnstone
Dunfermline Athletic v Airdrieonians
Greenock Morton v Dundee United
Hamilton Academical v Dumbarton
St. Mirren v Clydebank

Berwick Rangers v Montrose
Clyde v East Fife
Forfar Athletic v Stranraer
Queen of the South v Stirling Albion
Stenhousemuir v Ayr United

Brechin City v Livingston
Cowdenbeath v Caledonian Thistle
East Stirlingshire v Albion Rovers
Queen's Park v Arbroath
Ross County v Alloa

Tuesday, December 19th, 1995

Motherwell v Rangers

Saturday, December 23rd, 1995

Stirling Albion v Montrose
Albion Rovers v Caledonian Thistle

Tuesday, December 26th, 1995

Falkirk v Aberdeen
Heart of Midlothian v Motherwell
Partick Thistle v Hibernian
Raith Rovers v Celtic
Rangers v Kilmarnock

Airdrieonians v St. Mirren
Clydebank v Dundee
Dumbarton v Dunfermline Athletic
Dundee United v Hamilton Academical
St. Johnstone v Greenock Morton

Ayr United v Clyde
Forfar Athletic v East Fife
Queen of the South v Stenhousemuir
Stranraer v Berwick Rangers

Brechin City v Alloa
Cowdenbeath v East Stirlingshire
Livingston v Queen's Park
Ross County v Arbroath

Saturday, December 30th, 1995

Falkirk v Motherwell
Heart of Midlothian v Celtic
Kilmarnock v Aberdeen
Raith Rovers v Partick Thistle
Rangers v Hibernian
Dumbarton v Dundee

Dundee United v Airdrieonians
Greenock Morton v Dunfermline Athletic
Hamilton Academical v St. Mirren
St. Johnstone v Clydebank

Berwick Rangers v Ayr United
Clyde v Queen of the South
East Fife v Stirling Albion
Montrose v Stranraer
Stenhousemuir v Forfar Athletic

Alloa v Cowdenbeath
Arbroath v Albion Rovers
Brechin City v East Stirlingshire
Livingston v Caledonian Thistle
Queen's Park v Ross County

Monday, January 1st, 1996

Hibernian v Heart of Midlothian
Motherwell v Kilmarnock
Partick Thistle v Falkirk

Airdrieonians v Hamilton Academical
Clydebank v Dumbarton
Dundee v Dundee United
Dunfermline Athletic v St. Johnstone

Ayr United v Stranraer
Forfar Athletic v Montrose
Stenhousemuir v East Fife
Stirling Albion v Clyde

Albion Rovers v Queen's Park
Brechin City v Arbroath
East Stirlingshire v Alloa

Tuesday, January 2nd, 1996

Aberdeen v Raith Rovers
St. Mirren v Greenock Morton
Queen of the South v Berwick Rangers
Caledonian Thistle v Ross County
Cowdenbeath v Livingston

Wednesday, January 3rd, 1996

Celtic v Rangers

Saturday, January 6th, 1996

Celtic v Motherwell
Falkirk v Rangers
Hibernian v Aberdeen
Partick Thistle v Heart of Midlothian
Raith Rovers v Kilmarnock

Airdrieonians v Greenock Morton
Clydebank v Dundee United
Dundee v Hamilton Academical
St. Johnstone v Dumbarton
St. Mirren v Dunfermline Athletic

Saturday, January 13th, 1996

Heart of Midlothian v Falkirk
Kilmarnock v Hibernian
Motherwell v Partick Thistle
Rangers v Raith Rovers

Dumbarton v Airdrieonians
Dundee United v St. Mirren
Dunfermline Athletic v Clydebank
Greenock Morton v Dundee
Hamilton Academical v St. Johnstone

Berwick Rangers v Forfar Athletic
Clyde v Stenhousemuir
East Fife v Queen of the South
Montrose v Ayr United
Stranraer v Stirling Albion

Alloa v Caledonian Thistle
Arbroath v East Stirlingshire
Livingston v Albion Rovers
Queen's Park v Brechin City
Ross County v Cowdenbeath

Sunday, January 14th, 1996

Aberdeen v Celtic

Saturday, January 20th, 1996

Aberdeen v Partick Thistle
Hibernian v Motherwell
Kilmarnock v Celtic
Raith Rovers v Falkirk
Rangers v Heart of Midlothian

Clydebank v Greenock Morton
Dumbarton v Dundee United
Dundee v St. Mirren
Hamilton Academical v Dunfermline Athletic
St. Johnstone v Airdrieonians

Berwick Rangers v East Fife
Clyde v Stranraer
Forfar Athletic v Stirling Albion
Queen of the South v Ayr United
Stenhousemuir v Montrose

Brechin City v Albion Rovers
Cowdenbeath v Arbroath
East Stirlingshire v Caledonian Thistle
Queen's Park v Alloa
Ross County v Livingston

Saturday, February 3rd, 1996

Celtic v Hibernian
Falkirk v Kilmarnock
Heart of Midlothian v Raith Rovers
Motherwell v Aberdeen
Partick Thistle v Rangers

Airdrieonians v Clydebank
Dundee United v St. Johnstone
Dunfermline Athletic v Dundee
Greenock Morton v Hamilton Academical
St. Mirren v Dumbarton

Ayr United v Stenhousemuir
East Fife v Clyde
Montrose v Berwick Rangers
Stirling Albion v Queen of the South
Stranraer v Forfar Athletic

Albion Rovers v East Stirlingshire
Alloa v Ross County
Arbroath v Queen's Park
Caledonian Thistle v Cowdenbeath
Livingston v Brechin City

Saturday, February 10th, 1996

Falkirk v Celtic
Heart of Midlothian v Aberdeen
Partick Thistle v Kilmarnock
Raith Rovers v Hibernian
Rangers v Motherwell

Airdrieonians v Dunfermline Athletic
Clydebank v St. Mirren
Dumbarton v Hamilton Academical
Dundee United v Greenock Morton
St. Johnstone v Dundee

Berwick Rangers v Stenhousemuir
Forfar Athletic v Queen of the South
Montrose v Clyde
Stirling Albion v Ayr United
Stranraer v East Fife

Arbroath v Caledonian Thistle
Cowdenbeath v Brechin City
Livingston v Alloa
Queen's Park v East Stirlingshire
Ross County v Albion Rovers

Saturday, February 17th, 1996

Ayr United v Forfar Athletic
Clyde v Berwick Rangers
East Fife v Montrose
Queen of the South v Stranraer
Stenhousemuir v Stirling Albion

Albion Rovers v Cowdenbeath
Alloa v Arbroath
Brechin City v Ross County
Caledonian Thistle v Queen's Park
East Stirlingshire v Livingston

Saturday, February 24th, 1996

Aberdeen v Rangers
Celtic v Partick Thistle
Hibernian v Falkirk
Kilmarnock v Heart of Midlothian
Motherwell v Raith Rovers

Dundee v Airdrieonians
Dunfermline Athletic v Dundee United
Greenock Morton v Dumbarton
Hamilton Academical v Clydebank
St. Mirren v St. Johnstone

Berwick Rangers v Stirling Albion
Clyde v Forfar Athletic
East Fife v Ayr United
Montrose v Queen of the South
Stenhousemuir v Stranraer

Alloa v Albion Rovers
Arbroath v Livingston
Caledonian Thistle v Brechin City
East Stirlingshire v Ross County
Queen's Park v Cowdenbeath

Saturday, March 2nd, 1996

Aberdeen v Kilmarnock
Celtic v Heart of Midlothian
Hibernian v Rangers
Motherwell v Falkirk
Partick Thistle v Raith Rovers

Airdrieonians v Dundee United
Clydebank v St. Johnstone
Dundee v Dumbarton
Dunfermline Athletic v Greenock Morton
St. Mirren v Hamilton Academical

Ayr United v Berwick Rangers
Forfar Athletic v Stenhousemuir
Queen of the South v Clyde
Stirling Albion v East Fife
Stranraer v Montrose

Albion Rovers v Arbroath
Cowdenbeath v Alloa
East Stirlingshire v Brechin City
Livingston v Caledonian Thistle
Ross County v Queen's Park

Saturday, March 9th, 1996

Ayr United v Montrose
Forfar Athletic v Berwick Rangers
Queen of the South v East Fife
Stenhousemuir v Clyde
Stirling Albion v Stranraer

Albion Rovers v Livingston
Brechin City v Queen's Park
Caledonian Thistle v Alloa
Cowdenbeath v Ross County
East Stirlingshire v Arbroath

Saturday, March 16th, 1996

Falkirk v Partick Thistle
Heart of Midlothian v Hibernian
Kilmarnock v Motherwell
Raith Rovers v Aberdeen

Dumbarton v Clydebank
Dundee United v Dundee
Greenock Morton v St. Mirren
Hamilton Academical v Airdrieonians
St. Johnstone v Dunfermline Athletic